THE EVOLVING AMERICAN PRESIDENCY SERIES

Series Foreword:

The American presidency touche
And the presidency has become,
global political systems. The fra
at such a result. As invented at tl
presidency was to have been a
powers, embedded within a sep;
was the Congress; the presidenc;
that system.

Over time, the presidency has evolved and grown in power, expectations, responsibilities, and authority. Wars, crises, depressions, industrialization, all served to add to the
power of the presidency. And as the United States grew into a world power, presidential
power also grew. As the United States became the world's lea⌐ ⌐rpower, the presidency rose in prominence and power, not only in the ⌐⌐ ut on the world
stage as well.

It is the clash between the presidency ⌐ ⌐s developed
that inspired this series. And it ⌐ ⌐ American
presidency that makes underst⌐ ⌐e American
presidency stands at the vortex ⌐tates and across
the globe.

This Palgrave series recognizes that ⌐ and has been an evolving institution, going from the original constitu ⌐sign as a chief clerk, to today where the
president is the center of the American political constellation. This has caused several
key dilemmas in our political system, not the least of which is that presidents face high
expectations with limited constitutional resources. This causes presidents to find extra-
constitutional means of governing. Thus, presidents must find ways to bridge the
expectations/power gap while operating within the confines of a separation-of-powers
system designed to limit presidential authority. How presidents resolve these challenges
and paradoxes is the central issue in modern governance. It is also the central theme of
this book series.

Michael A. Genovese
Loyola Chair of Leadership
Loyola Marymount University
Palgrave's **The Evolving American Presidency,** Series Editor

The Second Term of George W. Bush
    edited by Robert Maranto, Douglas M. Brattebo, and Tom Lansford
The Presidency and the Challenge of Democracy
    edited by Michael A. Genovese and Lori Cox Han
Religion and the American Presidency
    edited by Mark J. Rozell and Gleaves Whitney

Religion and the American Presidency

Second Edition

Edited by
Mark J. Rozell and Gleaves Whitney

palgrave
macmillan

RELIGION AND THE AMERICAN PRESIDENCY
Copyright © Mark J. Rozell and Gleaves Whitney, 2007, 2012.

All rights reserved.

First published in hardcover in 2007 by
PALGRAVE MACMILLAN® in the
United States - a division of St. Martin's Press LLC,
175 Fifth Avenue, New York, NY 10010.

Where this book is distributed in the UK, Europe, and the rest of the world,
this is by Palgrave Macmillan, a division of Macmillan Publishers Limited,
registered in England, company number 785998, of Houndmills,
Basingstoke, Hampshire RG21 6XS.

Palgrave Macmillan is the global academic imprint of the above companies
and has companies and representatives throughout the world.

Palgrave® and Macmillan® are registered trademarks in the United States,
the United Kingdom, Europe and other countries.

ISBN: 978–0–230–12079–2

The Library of Congress has cataloged the hardcover edition as follows:

Religion and the American presidency / edited by Mark J. Rozell and
    Gleaves Whitney.
        p. cm.—(Evolving American presidency)
        Papers from a conference held at Grand Valley State University in
    Grand Rapids, Mich. in Nov. 2004.
        Includes bibliographical references and index.
        ISBN 978-0-2301-2079-2
        1. Presidents—United States—Religion—Congresses. 2. Presidents—
    United States—Biography—Miscellanea—Congresses. 3. Religion and
    politics—United States—Case studies-Congresses. 4. United States—
    Politics and government—Congresses. 5. United States—Religion—
    Congresses. I. Rozell, Mark J. II. Whitney, Gleaves.

E176.1.R37 2007
322_.1092273—dc22   2006050724

A catalogue record of the book is available from the British Library.

Design by Newgen Imaging Systems (P) Ltd., Chennai, India.

First PALGRAVE MACMILLAN paperback edition: January 2012

10 9 8 7 6 5 4 3 2 1

Printed in the United States of America.
Transferred to Digital Printing in 2011

Contents

Acknowledgments

The first edition of this book (2007) appeared during the second term of the George W. Bush presidency. At the time, there was enormous interest in the intersection of religion and US national policy. Many political observers attributed the rise in interest in the subject uniquely to the faith of President Bush. Through a collection of scholarly papers covering religion and the presidency all the way back to the George Washington administration, we set out to show that religion has been an enduring influence on the decisions and policies of many of the chief executives of the United States.

This new edition continues that theme, with an updated chapter on religion and the Bush presidency as well as two new chapters on the role of religion in the Barack Obama administration. The introduction is written anew to reflect broader themes in the study of religion and the presidency as well the new material in the book.

The origin of this book was a conference sponsored by the Hauenstein Center for Presidential Studies at Grand Valley State University. We acknowledge a number of Grand Rapidians who worked behind the scenes to make the gathering a success. First and foremost, Ralph Hauenstein, the founding benefactor of the center, was enthusiastically supportive from the start. Others at Grand Valley who deserve mention are former president Mark Murray, Vice President Patricia Oldt, Vice President Maribeth Wardrop, Vice President Matt McLogan, Assistant Vice President Mary Eilleen Lyon, photographer Bernadine Carey, and videographer Bill Cuppy. We would also like to thank several of the staff and leadership fellows at the Hauenstein Center: Assistant Director Brian Flanagan along with Kathy Rent, Melissa Ware, Mandi Bird, Patrick Reagan, Mike Kraus, and Megan Smith. Many other staff at Grand Valley, especially in event planning, provided generous assistance. We are ever grateful to Chairman Emeritus Marty Allen and our friends at the Gerald R. Ford Foundation for their ongoing support of our joint programs, plus convivial colleagues at the Gerald R. Ford Presidential Library and Museum, among them, former director Dennis Dallenbach and Associate Director Jim Kratsas and their staff in Grand Rapids and Ann Arbor, Michigan.

Introduction: The Importance of Religion in Understanding the Presidency

Harold F. Bass, Mark J. Rozell, and Gleaves Whitney

Religion is a key, but largely underappreciated factor in the actions of many US presidents. Most of the writings about religion and the presidency focus on the religious beliefs and practices of certain chief executives widely known to have been men of deep faith. There are substantial works, for example, on the role of religion in the lives and administrations of such modern era presidents as Jimmy Carter, George W. Bush, and now Barack Obama. Each of these men expressed his faith commitment as a presidential candidate and as a result attracted support from coreligionists and attention from political observers. Once in the White House, each of them continued to integrate his faith and religious-oriented themes in various decisions and policies.

Leading analyses of many religious presidents have either ignored religion or inaccurately characterized these leaders as nonreligious men who merely used appeals to faith for politically calculated reasons. According to Gary Scott Smith, the contributor of chapter 1 here, "Even though thousands of volumes have been written about America's presidents, we do not know much about the precise nature of their faith or how it affected their performance and policies."[1]

Major biographies of such presidents as Harry S Truman, Dwight Eisenhower, and Ronald Reagan make only a passing reference or none at all to religion in the lives of these leaders who were guided by faith in many of their policies. Much of the leading literature on earlier presidents such as Washington, Jefferson, and Madison repeats common and inaccurate descriptions of the role of religion in their lives.

Neglecting or misunderstanding the religion factor contributes to an incomplete portrayal of presidents and the presidency. There are serious works on the religious beliefs and practices of some of the nation's leading founders and early presidents (chapters 1–3 here), on the faith of Abraham Lincoln (chapter 4), and also on the religious beliefs and practices of modern presidents such as Carter (chapter 8), Reagan (chapter 9), George W. Bush (chapter 11), and Obama (chapters 12–13). There are also a number of highly polemical and better-known works on the importance of faith to certain presidents. During the George W. Bush era in particular there was a near explosion of books and essays on the president's religiosity, with some lavishing praises on him as a man of genuine faith commitment and others characterizing him as a captive of the religious right. Much of what Americans read about religion and the US presidency is agenda driven.

A Wall of Separation?

A part of the widespread discomfort with writing about religion and the presidency is the belief that the US constitutional system supports what Thomas Jefferson called a "wall of separation between church and state." Many have taken Jefferson's famous phrase to advocate the strict separationist view. However, religion scholar Thomas J. Buckley, S.J. (chapter 2) shows that this statement from Jefferson's 1802 letter to the Danbury Baptist Association has often been taken out of context to mean that the third president had advocated a separation that was absolute. Buckley's analysis tells a different story, one in which religion played an important role in many arenas. Jefferson's presidential addresses, private correspondences, and the public papers of his administration reveal that the third president contributed significantly to the development of American religion on the American frontier.

As Buckley reveals, Jefferson directed government funds to support the work of Christian missionary groups to "civilize" and to convert Native American Indians: "With his approval, the federal government encouraged a Presbyterian Minister's work among the Cherokees by appropriating several hundred dollars to found what was designed as a Christian school to teach religion along with other subjects."

Scholars have erroneously placed a number of presidents of the modern era in the nonreligious category. For example, Elizabeth Edwards Spalding (chapter 5) has studied the importance of faith to Harry S Truman's foreign policy and concludes that although widely regarded as one who cared little about religion, Truman, the second Baptist to serve in the White House, was a believer and someone who saw the Cold War as a moral clash against atheistic communism. Spalding reveals that Truman was deeply religious, but that he was often uncomfortable with overt displays of faith, and he was skeptical of those who claimed that their own religion gave them a favored relationship with God.

Truman reached out to religious groups to aid the West in the Cold War. Spalding explains that the president believed that because the battle of the Cold War was a moral as well as strategic one, he needed to enlist the support of different religions. Truman wrote to the president of the Baptist World Alliance: "To succeed in our quest for righteousness we must, in St. Paul's luminous phrase, put on the armor of God."[2]

Many scholars have characterized Dwight D. Eisenhower as perhaps the least religious among the modern presidents. Jack Holl (chapter 6) concludes that the president's biographers have mostly gotten the story wrong. An overriding theme in Eisenhower studies is that although the man had had a strongly religious upbringing, he all but abandoned religious faith after entering West Point. As Holl points out, "No one emphasizes the influence of Eisenhower's deeply ingrained religious beliefs on his public life and work." This finding is almost astonishing given Eisenhower's words and his actions as president. Eisenhower said a mere four years prior to being elected president that "I am the most intensely religious man I know."[3]

A part of the Eisenhower image as nonreligious derives from the rhetoric that he employed that struck many observers as superficial. Frequently quoted was the president-elect's comment in a December 1952 address to the Freedom Foundation: "Our form of government has no sense, unless it is grounded in a deeply felt religious faith, and I don't care what it is."[4] Furthermore, Eisenhower was open about his aversion to organized religion. But Eisenhower was the first president to write his own inaugural prayer; he was baptized in the White House; he approved "one nation, under God" being added to the Pledge of Allegiance and "In God We Trust" to the US currency; and he also appointed a new office of special assistant for religion in his administration.

Like Eisenhower, Ronald Reagan did not attend church services while president, and he also seemed to harbor an aversion to organized religion. Reagan biographers characterized him as indifferent to religion, except to the extent that he could attract the political support of religiously motivated voters who liked his conservative social issue positions. The one scholar to fully examine Reagan's religious faith and commitment has arrived at a completely opposite conclusion.

Paul Kengor (chapter 9) reviewed Reagan's private papers and letters and interviewed many of the people who were closest to the former president. He finds that Reagan was a deeply religious man. The neglect and misunderstanding of Reagan's religiosity, "leaves an unbridgeable gap in our own understanding of Reagan and what made him tick, especially in the great calling of his political life: his Cold War crusade against the Soviet Union." Like Truman, Reagan perceived the battle of the Cold War as not merely a strategic one, but a moral one as well. Reagan avoided church attendance as president largely out of security concerns. He had regularly attended services prior to his presidency, and resumed the practice after he left office. Interest in the role of religion to the presidency took off during the George W. Bush presidency due in large part to his openness about his faith and a perception among many that his policy agenda was driven significantly by his religiosity. Robinson and Wilcox note (chapter 11) that President Bush did not give as much emphasis to the social issues agenda as many critics had expected from him. Indeed, Bush demonstrated more enthusiasm for tax cuts and reforming social security than for pushing against abortion rights and gay rights. The terrorist attacks of September 11, 2001, and the subsequent wars in the Middle East also had a profound effect on Bush's policy emphasis and surely pushed his concerns with social issues to the back of his agenda priorities.

Although it is true that Bush was much less constrained about expressing his faith publicly than many past presidents, he does not stand unique in this regard among America's chief executives. In the modern era, for example, such presidents as Jimmy Carter, Bill Clinton, and Barack Obama—all Democrats—have been at least as open about their faith as Bush, and by some measures perhaps even more so.

In chapter 8, Jeff Walz examines the role of faith to the presidency of Jimmy Carter, who is widely regarded as perhaps the most deeply religious chief executive of the modern era. Yet many conservative evangelicals derided Carter's faith commitment because of their disdain for his policies on such issues as school prayer, abortion, and family issues.

One study shows that Bill Clinton invoked Christ in presidential speeches more often than George W. Bush did.[5] In chapter 10, James Penning examines how Clinton often infused religious values into his rhetoric and public policies. Clinton's conservative evangelical critics questioned the authenticity of his religious-based rhetoric. Penning finds instead that Clinton's religious appeals were a sincere expression of a faith deeply rooted in the former president's childhood experiences.

President Barack Obama's religion and its impact on his policies and perceptions of his administration are the topics of chapters 12 and 13. Like Carter and Clinton before him, many conservative evangelicals question the authenticity of Obama's faith. A significant percentage of conservative evangelicals and some other Americans do not accept the president's Christian identity, and many claim that he actually is a Muslim. Although Obama's Christian faith is not questionable—and even though, as Colin Powell said in 2008, it should not matter in America whether someone is Muslim, Christian, or any other religious identity[6]—the misperception of Obama's religion has political implications, as a sizeable minority of Americans admit in surveys that they are unlikely to vote for a Muslim.

Religion and Presidential Campaigns

One of the challenges in studying the religion-presidency intersection is that all presidents find it useful to connect religious themes to policy goals or to sustain political support. However, it is not always clear whether presidents evoking symbols or using certain rhetoric do so because they believe that they have to, or because it comes naturally to them. In the electoral context, presidential aspirants find it advantageous to evoke religious identity and themes.

Article VI of the Constitution stipulates: "No religious test shall ever be required as a qualification for any office or public trust under the United States." Nevertheless, the presidential selection process has evidenced some norms with regard to religion. The most compelling is the clear expectation that the president be a person of faith. A 2004 poll indicated that almost 60 percent of likely voters surveyed expressed the opinion that it is important that the president believe in God and be deeply religious.[7]

Well into the twentieth century, that faith was presumed to be Protestant Christianity. Governor Al Smith of New York, a Democrat, became the first Roman Catholic to receive serious consideration for a major party's presidential nomination. After falling short in 1920 and 1924, he finally prevailed in 1928; but the fall campaign featured considerable anti-Catholicism, and Smith suffered a decisive general election defeat.

Three decades later, Sen. John F. Kennedy's presidential prospects turned on whether his Catholicism would prove to be an insurmountable obstacle. Kennedy delivered a key speech to an assembly of Protestant ministers in Houston, Texas, in which he assured them that his faith would not compromise his exercise of the powers and duties of the office of president.[8] This commitment to separate his private faith from his public responsibilities resonated well with mid-century American culture and society. In contrast, the contemporary climate embraces the expectation that faith will and should inform public policy positions.

Kennedy won the nomination and the election amid abiding concerns among Protestants. He remains the only Roman Catholic president to date, although the Democrats have subsequently nominated Catholics for vice president (Edmund Muskie, 1968; Sargent Shriver, 1972; Geraldine Ferraro, 1984; Joseph Biden, 2008) and president (John Kerry, 2004). Following Kennedy's election in 1960, the Republican Party nominated William E. Miller, a Roman Catholic, for vice president in 1964.

No person of Jewish faith has received a major party presidential nomination. Sen. Barry Goldwater (AZ), the 1964 Republican nominee, was of Jewish descent on his father's side, but he identified himself as an Episcopalian. Sen. Joseph Lieberman (CT), an Orthodox Jew, received the Democratic vice-presidential nomination in 2000. The effect on public opinion and electoral behavior was negligible.

In 1968, 2008 and 2012, Mormons figured prominently in the Republican presidential nominating contests. Governor George Romney (MI) was a leading contender in 1968 for the nomination that went to Quaker Richard Nixon. Four decades later, Romney's son, Mitt, was a top-tier candidate. The elder Romney's faith was commonly noted, but it did not prove especially controversial in his pursuit of the party nomination. In contrast, his son's religious identity appears much more noteworthy and problematical, reflecting both the rising salience of religion in American politics and significant changes in the nomination process that provide avenues to express religious sensitivities.

Another recent development with regard to the religious backgrounds of presidential aspirants is the presence of former clergy in the nominating contests of the parties: Jesse Jackson in 1984 and 1988 for the Democrats; Pat Robertson in 1988; and Mike Huckabee in 2008 for the Republicans. The emergence of Robertson and Huckabee as credible candidates is related to the rise of evangelical interests in the body politic in general and the Republican Party in particular.

One way in which presidential selection embraces religion is with regard to the efforts by candidates to assemble coalitions of interests. Contests for the presidency have long featured the mobilization of voters based on religious affiliations. Traditionally identifying with the Democratic Party, Catholics and Jews provided stable electoral foundations for Democratic presidential nominees, while mainline Protestants did likewise for the Republicans. These identifications generally coincided with parallel socioeconomic ones, with the Republicans capturing the support of the more established elements of society and the Democrats the more marginal. Similarly, religious identities often correlated with regional and residential ones. For example, Democratic strongholds in the urban Northeast housed substantial numbers of Catholics and Jews. In turn, White Protestants in what used to be called the "Solid South" were part and parcel of the Democratic presidential coalition, based on long-standing regional foundations.

More recent developments have modified these traditional patterns, as parties, candidates, and campaigns have sought to attract support based on issues and ideologies from religiously rooted voters. Democrats have claimed the enthusiastic support of African American Protestants with pro-civil rights commitments. Republicans have appealed to some

Jewish voters by advocating a strong pro-Israel stance. In addition, they have made inroads with some Catholic voters with their prolife position on abortion. Moreover, upward-class mobility has generally made the GOP more attractive to middle-class Catholics.

However, the most important development in recent decades has been the mobilization of evangelicals who were traditionally disengaged from the electoral process. Alternative factors, notably class and region, better explained their political preferences. For example, the traditional inclination of Southern Baptists to vote Democratic reflected a regional norm, reinforced by their lower-middle-class location in Southern society.

The 1970s saw dramatic changes in this pattern due to several factors. One was economic development, which moved evangelicals upward within the middle class. Another was the emergence of issues on the political agenda that enraged and engaged the evangelical community, especially the controversial Supreme Court decisions proscribing prayer in public schools and restricting antiabortion legislation. More generally, cultural changes threatened the traditional values of evangelicals.

The Republicans have benefited from an emerging religiosity gap. Those who frequently attend religious services, regardless of affiliation, are more likely to vote Republican than those who rarely attend. This electoral shift has proven generally significant in the post–New Deal era resurgence in Republican presidential fortunes, particularly in explaining narrow GOP victories in the presidential contests in 2000 and 2004.

Presidential Policy Agendas and Religion

Nineteenth-century presidents rarely advanced ambitious policy agendas. There were some conspicuous exceptions, and religion occasionally loomed large as a foundation for them. Emancipation can be considered as such.

The Progressive Era coincided with and contributed to an expansion of presidential power. In turn, the reform agenda of the Progressive Movement was infused with social-justice concerns advanced by Protestants and Catholics alike. For Protestants, it was the social gospel articulated by Walter Rauschenbusch in *Christianity and the Social Crisis* (1907). For Catholics, Leo XIII's papal encyclical *Rerum Novarum* (1891) heightened sensitivities to the plight of the working class in industrializing society and led to calls for responsive public policies.

Theodore Roosevelt and Woodrow Wilson associated themselves with these causes in their Square Deal and New Freedom agendas. Franklin Roosevelt did so as well with the New Deal. Lyndon Johnson's Great Society, with its commitment to civil rights and the expansion of the welfare state, reflected these emphases as well. Bill Clinton's New Covenant also was an effort to advance these themes. Their efforts to influence the public policy agenda involved mobilization and countermobilization. Successes by one group encouraged others to emulate them. After liberal reforms, the Christian Right emerged around 1980 as a major counterforce in politics. A prolife stance on abortion has been at the forefront of the Christian Right agenda. Freedom of religious expression, against claims that it fosters religious establishment, has been another priority. President Reagan and his Republican successors have rhetorically embraced this agenda. It has certainly figured into their judicial nominations.

On the foreign policy front, in the post–World War II era religious interests and convictions have undergirded several presidential policies. During the Cold War, US presidents led the struggle against "godless" communism on behalf of religious believers. US support for Israel is rooted in the Judeo-Christian heritage. President Carter's commitment to human rights was an expression of his deeply held religious beliefs, as was President George W. Bush's "freedom agenda." Thus, religious interests clearly occupy a seat at the table of presidential politics and policy.

This volume showcases that presidential analysis benefits from examining the religious factor in the lives, electoral campaigns, and policies of our chief executives. Religion is not the prime explanatory factor for most of the decisions of our presidents, but it is often an important one and is deserving of significant attention.

Notes

1. Gary Scott Smith, *Faith and the Presidency* (New York: Oxford University Press, 2005), 6.
2. Elizabeth Edwards Spalding, *The First Cold Warrior: Harry Truman, Containment, and the Remaking of Liberal Internationalism* (Lexington: University Press of Kentucky, 2006), 212–213.
3. Dwight D. Eisenhower comment at press conference at Columbia University, New York, cited in *New York Times*, May 4, 1948, 43.
4. Dwight D. Eisenhower, quoted in *New York Times*, December 23, 1952, 16.
5. Paul Kengor, *God and Ronald Reagan: A Spiritual Life* (New York: Regan Books, 2004).
6. Transcript of Powell endorsement of Obama on "Meet the Press," October 19, 2008. http://www.opednews.com/articles/Transcript-of-Colin-Powell-by- GeoBear-081019-915.html. Accessed by author on July 24, 2011.
7. Adelle M. Banks, "Poll: Americans Want a 'Deeply Religious' Person as President," *Religion News Service*, January 9, 2004.
8. Theodore H White, *The Making of the President, 1960* (New York: Atheneum, 1961), 391–393.

Chapter One

The Faith of
George Washington*

Gary Scott Smith

Even before he died in 1799, a battle began over the nature and significance of George Washington's faith. While more heated at some times than others, this conflict has now been waged for more than 200 years. Among American presidents, only the religious convictions and practices of Abraham Lincoln have been as closely scrutinized as those of Washington. Of all the varied aspects of the Virginian's life, few have caused as much contention as his religious beliefs and habits. Moreover, no other chief executive has had his religious life so distorted by folklore. As Paul Boller, Jr., puts it, Washington's religious outlook has been "thoroughly clouded by myth, legend, misunder standing, and misrepresentation."[1] Many of the hundreds of books, articles, sermons, and essays published about his faith and practices since 1800 have advanced ideological agendas, rather than providing dispassionate analysis. On one side are ministers and primarily Protestant evangelical authors who claim that Washington had a deep, rich, orthodox Christian faith. On the other side are freethinkers and numerous contemporary scholars who argue that Washington was a deist or Unitarian whose faith was not very meaningful to him.

Given Washington's immense contributions to the American republic, demigod status, and importance to American civil religion, this intense debate is not surprising. Many scholars argue that he was indispensable to the success of the patriot cause and the new nation. Risking his reputation, wealth, and life, he led an undermanned and poorly supplied army to an improbable victory over the world's leading economic and military power. He presided over the convention that produced the United States' venerable Constitution. As the country's first president, he established positive precedents for the office and adopted policies that ensured the stability and success of the

*Portions of this essay adapted from FAITH AND THE PRESIDENCY by Gary Scott Smith, (c) 2005 by Oxford University Press. Used with permission of the original publisher.

nascent nation.[2] For nearly a quarter of a century (1775–1799), Washington was the most important person in America, a record unrivaled in the nation's history.[3] He kept his hand on America's political pulse, personified the American Revolution, promoted the ratification of the Constitution, and held the nation together so effectively that some call these years the "Age of Washington."[4] After piloting America safely through the hazardous waters of war, as president he kept it from crashing on the shoals of anarchy, monarchism, or revolution. After his death in 1799, eulogists lavished praise upon his character and accomplishments that is unmatched in American history. Many scholars argue that the nation's first president set a standard that few, if any, of his successors have attained.[5] His sterling character, impressive physique, stately demeanor, and monumental contributions to American independence combined to produce an aura that gave weight to his public statements on all subjects including religion.[6]

This chapter summarizes the debate over Washington's faith and takes a middle position that portrays the first president as a theistic rationalist who believed strongly that God ruled and directed the universe. Although he apparently did not accept several key orthodox Christian doctrines, Washington's belief in God's Providence had a powerful impact on his work as both commander-in-chief and president.

To a certain extent during his life, and even more after his death, Washington was elevated to sainthood. An American civil religion arose that revered the great founder as God's instrument and a larger than life mythological hero.[7] Moreover, Washington helped create this American civil religion and occupies a unique place in its development. In life and death he has been seen as "the deliverer of America," the savior of his people, the American Moses, and even a demigod.[8] In 1778 Henry Muhlenberg, the chief developer of Lutheranism in America, wrote in his journal, "From all appearances" Washington "respects God's Word [and] believes in the atonement through Christ." Therefore, God had "preserved him from harm in the midst of countless perils . . . and graciously held him in his hand as a chosen vessel."[9] Nearly 20 years later, when Washington's second term as president ended, 24 pastors from the Philadelphia area commended his work and proclaimed that "in our special character as ministers of the gospel of Christ, we . . . acknowledge the countenance you have uniformly given to his holy religion."[10] One of these clergymen, Ashbel Green, a pastor of the Second Presbyterian Church in Philadelphia, a chaplain in the House of Representatives during Washington's tenure in office, and later president of the College of New Jersey, declared that he had no doubt about Washington's orthodoxy.[11]

Similarly, in their funeral sermons and other public statements after the general died, many ministers maintained that he was a devout Christian.[12] They repeatedly affirmed that Washington "was not ashamed" of his faith and that he acknowledged and adored "a GREATER SAVIOR whom Infidels and deists" slighted and despised.[13] The Virginian strove to follow Christian moral standards and attributed his accomplishments to God's power. An Episcopal rector described Washington's faith as very "sincere and ardent."[14] Another minister insisted that the general's virtues "were crowned with piety." No one more fully expressed "his sense of the Providence of God" than this "habitually devout" man.[15] Although professing some concerns about the statesman's religious beliefs, Congregationalist Timothy Dwight, president of Yale College, argued that if the general was not actually a Christian, then he was "more like one than any man of the same description, whose life had been hitherto recorded."[16] "At all times" Washington "acknowledged the providence of God, and never was he ashamed of his redeemer," America's first Methodist bishop Francis Asbury confidently declared; "we believe he died, not fearing death." The nation's first Catholic bishop, John Carroll, praised Washington's "Christian piety" and his affirmation that a "superintending providence" prepared, regulated, and governed all human events to accomplish its eternal purposes.[17]

Many of his first biographers such as Episcopal rector Mason Locke "Parson" Weems, Supreme Court Chief Justice John Marshall, Jared Sparks, the editor of the first set of his papers, and novelist Washington Irving insisted that Washington was a faithful Christian.[18] In Marshall's words, while Washington made no "ostentatious professions of religion, he was a sincere believer in the Christian faith, and a truly devout man."[19] In scores of subsequent books and articles authors have praised the Virginian as "a Christian hero and statesman," "the founder of a Christian republic," "Christ's faithful soldier and servant," "the great high priest of the nation," and a "man of abiding faith."[20] These enthusiasts insisted that he regularly attended church services, said grace before all meals, actively participated in church work, filled his public and private statements with religious exhortations, and prayed almost constantly wherever he was—"in his library, in his army tent, at the homes of friends and strangers, and in the woods, thickets, groves and bushes. . . ." If Washington were truly as devout as these effusive testimonies portray him, Boller contends, he would have "had time for little else but the ritual of piety." He demonstrates that most of these claims, which are based on hearsay and legends, are inaccurate.[21]

The most famous fable about Washington's piety pictures him kneeling in prayer in the snow at Valley Forge during the winter of 1777–1778 when the American cause seemed so desperate. According to the story as first told by Weems, the pastor of the Pohick Episcopal Church, which Washington and his family sometimes attended, the general had established his headquarters in the home of Isaac Potts, a Quaker pacifist. "One day, when the prospects, morale, and physical state of the Continental Army were at their lowest," Potts saw Washington on his knees praying in the woods.[22] The Quaker watched the general until he arose and "with a countenance of angelic serenity, retired to headquarters."[23] Although this story is "utterly without foundation in fact," it has been memorialized in poetry, inscribed on a plaque at the base of Washington's statue in New York, commemorated on a 1928 postage stamp, and etched in stained glass in the Washington Memorial Chapel at Valley Forge and a private chapel built in Washington, DC, for the use of members of Congress.[24]

A spate of books published in the first half of the nineteenth century to promote Washington's piety feature stories of him arranging communion services before battles, retreating into the woods during military encampments to pray, and inspiring parishioners in country churches where he worshipped with religious zeal. One popular tale depicts the general attending a communion service at the Presbyterian church in Morristown, New Jersey, during the Revolutionary War. Originated in 1828 by Samuel H. Cox, pastor of Laight Street Presbyterian Church in New York City, it was popularized by Edward G. McGuire in *The Religious Opinions and Character of Washington* (1836).[25] Over the years the story was repeatedly retold and embellished and the location shifted to under an apple tree.[26] During the 1830s, Origen Bacheler and freethinker Robert Dale Owens debated at length on the nature of Washington's religious beliefs and practices in the *Free Enquirer*. Bacheler argued that Washington belonged to a Christian church, considered the Bible God's revelation, regularly attended worship services and read the Scriptures, and "to his dying moment, remained stedfast [*sic*] in his religious views."[27]

Similarly, twentieth-century authors have argued that "abundant evidence" demonstrates that Washington "was a true Christian in every sense that the word implies."[28] They point to the influence of his pious parents, who instructed him in the Anglican catechism, faithfully took him to church, and read him Matthew Hale's *Contemplations*.[29] They emphasize that Washington received much of his early education in Fredericksburg at a school run by the rector of St. George's Church. Arguing that he served diligently as a vestryman, contributed liberally to churches, attended church consistently, had private devotions regularly, followed Christian moral principles devotedly, and relied repeatedly on God's Providence, they conclude that his "every word and act showed clearly" that he was a Christian.[30] Citing the testimony of numerous relatives, friends, and associates of Washington as well as ministers, William Johnstone contended in *How Washington Prayed* (1932) that during his adult life the Virginian faithfully followed his mother's injunction, "Neglect not the duty of secret prayer."[31] Others add that Washington "searched the Scriptures daily" and insist that as a general and president his conduct was "governed by the dictates of Christianity." Washington "made a Christian profession and lived a Christian life." As a soldier, he followed its commands, recommended its virtues, and enforced its duties. He accepted the Bible as the "higher law of nations, inculcated its political and moral principles, . . . and governed as a just man, fearing God." Christianity, therefore, could legitimately claim Washington as a "trophy" of its "transforming power."[32] Echoing this assessment, President Herbert Hoover argued in 1932 that "[t]he great qualities of character by reason of which George Washington towers supreme in our history were products of the Christian virtues inculcated by his deeply religious mother and devoutly practiced by him as a professed churchman."[33] Hoover praised the first president's "devotion to religious faith" and trust in divine inspiration and Providence.[34]

More recently, evangelical authors have contended that Washington and numerous other founders were orthodox Christians.[35] Tim LaHaye, best known for his *Left Behind* books, calls Washington "a godly man" who had "a sterling commitment to God." Convinced that prayers Washington copied as a young man expressed his own lifelong views, LaHaye concludes that Washington "was a devout believer in Jesus Christ" who "accepted Him as His Lord and Savior." Reading these prayers objectively verifies that were "Washington living today, he would freely identify with the Bible-believing branch of evangelical Christianity."[36] Benjamin Hart asserts in *Faith and Freedom* that Washington was "definitely a committed and believing Christian."[37] Verna Hall maintains that the nation's first president was "a Bible-believing scholar."[38] Although it would not be accurate to call Washington an "evangelical," Peter Lillback and Jerry Newcombe declare, he "was an orthodox, Trinity-affirming believer in Jesus Christ," who believed in Christ's atonement for sinners and bodily resurrection.[39]

On the other hand, many have argued that Washington was not a pious, committed, orthodox Christian. While he was president, several individuals either urged him to affirm his faith in Christianity publicly or expressed regret that he had not. Leading Congregationalist clergyman Samuel Langdon spent time with Washington when he was president of Harvard and the general was commanding American troops in Boston. In 1789, Langdon lauded the president because he had focused his eyes on "the great Lord of the Universe, implored his help, acted as his servant," and relied on his aid. He rejoiced that Washington had "taken every opportunity" in his public addresses to acknowledge "the supreme Lord of heaven & earth for the great things he hath done for us." Langdon challenged the president, however, to "let all men know that you are not ashamed to be a disciple of the Lord Jesus Christ, & are seeking the honors of that kingdom which he has prepared for his faithful Servants."[40] Characteristically, the Virginian replied that anyone who could "look on the events of the American Revolution without feeling the warmest gratitude towards the great Author of the Universe whose divine interposition was so frequently manifested in our behalf must be bad indeed." He earnestly prayed that Americans would so conduct themselves that they merited God's continued blessing. He said nothing about Christ either to Langdon or the American people.[41] Shortly after Washington died, Benjamin Tallmadge, who had served as his chief of intelligence during the Revolutionary War, lamented in a letter that the deceased president had never explicitly professed his "faith in, and dependence on the finished Atonement of our glorious Redeemer. . . ."[42]

In his debate with Bacheler in the 1830s, Owen maintained that Washington had not "left behind him one word to warrant the belief that he was other than a sincere deist."[43] Bishop William White, who supervised the three Episcopal parishes in Philadelphia, admitted that he could not recall "any fact which would prove" that Washington believed "in the Christian revelation" except that he constantly attended church.[44] Another Episcopal bishop asserted that Washington paid no attention "to the arguments for Christianity and for the different systems of religion" and "had not formed definite opinions on the subject."[45]

Many contemporary scholars argue that Washington's faith was not very deep or meaningful. Douglas Freeman asserts that Washington did not find any "rock of refuge in religion" and claims that "the warmth of faith" expressed in Washington's Revolutionary War circulars and addresses belonged more to his speechwriters than to him.[46] Dorothy Twohig maintains that his "interest in religion appears to have been perfunctory."[47] Robert F. Jones contends that Washington "lacked a personal religious faith" evident in the fact that he always referred to Providence or other unrevealing terms. His service as a vestryman was another duty expected of Virginia planters, not necessarily a sign of a religious faith."[48] "Washington's practice of Christianity was limited and superficial," Barry Schwartz argues, "because he himself was not a Christian. In the Enlightenment tradition of his day, he was a devout Deist—just as many of the clergymen who knew him suspected."[49] Despite his polite adherence to his ancestral Church of England, James Flexner declares, Washington's "religious convictions merged naturally and completely with his philosophical and political conceptions."[50] John Alden contends that Washington's resignation as a vestryman and his refusal to take communion after the Revolutionary War indicated that he "was no longer a faithful Episcopalian." He suggests that the impact of Unitarianism and deism spawned by the Revolution and his experiences as a Freemason prompted these changes.[51] "Washington was neither religiously fervent nor theologically learned," declares Paul Longmore. His creed centered around one deeply held conviction: "[A]n unseen but beneficent power directed the universe and human affairs." Whenever Washington sensed the call of heaven, he felt compelled to respond.[52] Richard Pierard and Robert Linder aver that Washington was ambivalent toward orthodox Christianity and organized religion in general, attending church sporadically, listening courteously, but participating "little in the life of the local church." He "was notorious for not kneeling to pray in public worship" (in accordance with Episcopal ritual) and never discussed having a personal relationship with Christ.[53]

David Holmes asserts that "with only a few exceptions . . . Washington's speeches, orders, official letters, and other public communications on religion . . . seem clearly to display the outlook of a Deist." They regularly substitute deist terms such as "the Deity," "the Supreme Being," "the Grand Architect," and the "Great Ruler of Events" for "God," "Father," "Lord," and "Savior."[54] Paul Boller contends that to Washington, God "was an impersonal force" and insists that he never "experienced any feeling of personal intimacy or communion" with God. Washington's faith was essentially cerebral and had almost no emotional component.[55] These and other titles Washington used for God such as "Author of all good," "the great arbiter of the universe," "the supreme disposer of all events," "the beneficent Being," "the Sovereign disposer of life and health," "Heaven," and "Providence," all had "a vaguely impersonal, broadly benign, calmly rational flavor."[56]

Determining what Washington actually believed about religious matters is very challenging because he rarely confided his deepest thoughts or emotions on any subject in his diary or in letters to friends.

In 1795 the Virginian wrote to James Anderson that "in politics, as in religion[,] my tenets are few and simple."[57] Presbyterian pastor Samuel Miller asserted that Washington displayed an "unusual, but uniform, and apparently deliberate, reticence on the subject of personal religion."[58] Moreover, as Garry Wills explains, "By inclination and principle, he shied away from demonstrations of piety."[59]

Despite his reluctance to reveal his religious convictions, Washington's statements and actions indicate that he firmly believed that God ruled the world and specially watched over the United States. Judged by the standards of the second half of the eighteenth century, Washington was fairly religious. His support for chaplains and religious services, pattern of church attendance, attitude toward worship, and views of the Bible, prayer, God, Christ, salvation, and life after death all help substantiate this claim. During his military service prior to the Revolution, Washington conducted church services for his troops on Sundays when no chaplains were available. He observed all the fast days the Church of England prescribed for army members.[60] As a commander-in-chief of the Continental Army, he recruited chaplains for his troops, required his soldiers to attend Sunday worship, and held thanksgiving services after victories.

Prior to the Revolution, Washington usually attended church about once a month, but he worshipped more frequently during times of political crisis.[61] During his presidency, perhaps because of the burden of his office or because he wanted to set a positive example, he attended church almost every Sunday. Eleanor Parke "Nelly" Custis, Martha Washington's granddaughter, claimed that Washington worshipped with "reverent respect," and Episcopal Bishop William White insisted that he was "always serious and attentive" in church.[62] While the subject is debated, the best evidence indicates that Washington did not take communion after the Revolutionary War began. Three factors may have deterred him. He may not have felt worthy or in the proper spiritual state to do so, or he may not have believed in the Episcopal understanding of the sacrament, or he may have been reluctant to publicly declare faith in Jesus Christ. His refusal to take communion is one factor that leads some historians to conclude that to him religion was principally a social obligation, not a heartfelt conviction.

While some claim that Washington "read devotedly and prized supremely" the Bible, others counter that he was not an avid reader of Scripture. They point to the inventories of his books at Mount Vernon and contend that his public statements and private letters contain relatively few references to Scriptural passages or to his study of the Bible.[63] Washington did not quote or allude to Scripture in his addresses or urge Americans to read the Bible as much as many later presidents did. Nevertheless, Daniel Dreisbach has shown that Washington frequently cited biblical phrases in his correspondence.[64]

The Virginian professed belief in the power of prayer. Washington wrote to the French King Louis XVI in 1792 that "our constant prayer" was that God would keep America's "dear friend and Ally in his safe and holy keeping," a prayer that was, of course, not granted.[65] He frequently asked religious bodies to pray for him, thanked groups for praying for him, and told individuals he was praying for them.[66] For example, he thanked Methodist bishops in May 1789 for their promise to present prayers "at the Throne of Grace for me" and pledged to pray for them as well.[67] "I shall not cease to supplicate the Divine Author of Life and felicity," he told the Philadelphia clergy in 1797, "that your Labours for the good of Mankind may be crowned with success."[68]

Washington maintained that God was all-powerful, infinitely wise, just, all-good, and inscrutable. Throughout his life, he appealed to "an all-powerful Providence" to protect and guide him and the nation, especially in times of crisis.[69] Writing to his wife in June 1775, after being appointed commander-in-chief of the Continental Army, Washington confessed, "I shall rely . . . confidently on that Providence, which has heretofore preserved and been bountiful to me. . . ."[70] Throughout the War for Independence he asked for and acknowledged God's providential guidance and assistance hundreds of times.[71] In July 1776, the general urged his soldiers to "rely upon the goodness of the Cause, and the aid of the supreme Being, in whose hand Victory is, to animate and encourage us to great and noble Actions."[72] "The hand of Providence has been so conspicuous" in the Revolutionary War, the general asserted in 1778, that anyone who did not thank God and "acknowledge his obligations" to Him was "worse than an infidel that lacks faith, and more than wicked."[73] That Americans had triumphed over a numerically superior and better trained foe in the vales of Brandywine, the fields of Germantown, and the plains of Monmouth was due to God's aid.[74]

Washington saw God's gracious hand in Burgoyne's surrender, the United States' alliance with France, the arrival of the French fleet, the rescue of West Point "from [Benedict] Arnold[']s villainous perfidy," and the victory at Yorktown.[75] After the United States concluded an alliance with France in 1778, for example, he set aside a day to gratefully acknowledge "the divine Goodness" and to celebrate "the important Event which we owe to his benign Interposition."[76] After his forces had defeated Lord Cornwallis and the British at Yorktown in

October 1781, Washington celebrated the "astonishing interpositions of Providence" in an order to his troops.[77] The general prayed in 1782 that "the same providence that has hitherto in so Remarkable a manner Evinced the Justice of our Cause [would] lead us to a speedy and honorable peace."[78] When Congress ratified a preliminary peace treaty the next year, the commander-in-chief ordered his chaplains to hold services to "render thanks to almighty God for all his mercies, particularly for his over ruling the wrath of men to his own glory. . . ."[79] After the war ended, the general routinely gave credit to the "Smiles of Providence," the sacrifices of the American people, the valor of his troops, and the aid of France.[80] He declared, for example, "I attribute all glory to that Supreme Being," who had caused the several forces that contributed to America's triumph to harmonize perfectly together.[81] Washington expressed Americans' "infinite obligations to the Supreme Ruler of the Universe for rescuing our Country from the brink of destruction; I cannot fail at this time to ascribe all the honor of our late successes to the same glorious Being. And if my humble exertions have been in any degree subservient to the execution of the divine purposes, a contemplation of the benediction of Heaven on our righteous Cause, the approbation of my virtuous Countrymen, and the testimony of my own Conscience will be a sufficient reward and augment my felicity beyond anything the world can bestow."[82] "To have been in any degree, an instrument in the hands of Providence, to promote order and union, and erect upon a solid foundation the true principles of Government," he added, "is only to have shared with many others in a labor, the result of which let us hope, will prove through all ages, a sanctuary for Brothers and a lodge for the virtuous."[83] In resigning his commission in December 1783, the commander-in-chief asserted that his lack of assurance in his "abilities to accomplish so arduous a task" had been "superseded by a confidence in the rectitude of our Cause, and the support of the Supreme Power of the Union, and the patronage of Heaven."[84] No people "had more reason to acknowledge a divine interposition in their affairs than those of the United States," the nation's first president declared in 1792.[85] He commended "the interests of our dearest Country to the protection of Almighty God, and those who have the superintendence of them, to his holy keeping."[86] Like many other Protestants, Washington was convinced that the liberty the United States incarnated and sought to export to other nations was the "single greatest political blessing that God had bestowed on humanity in the Christian era."[87]

Washington also rejoiced that God was wise, just, and benevolent. His faith in an "All Wise Creator" who possessed "infinite Wisdom" and "wisely orders the Affairs of Men" helped the Virginian deal with personal and national problems.[88] Almost overwhelmed by "difficulties & perplexities" while camping with his troops at Valley Forge, he wrote to his stepson, "Providence has heretofore saved us in a remarkable manner, and on this we must principally rely."[89] The decrees of Providence, Washington told a friend, were "always just and wise."[90] Because their cause was just, the general contended, Americans had "every reason to hope the divine Providence" would "crown . . . with Success" their efforts to win their independence from Britain.[91] The planter asserted that God was "beneficient," [sic] "the Supreme Author of all Good," and the "supreme Dispenser of every Good."[92] Washington declared that God's ultimate goal was to provide "the greatest degree of happiness to the greatest number of his people."[93] He repeatedly argued that the course of events justified his belief in "the blessings of a benign Providence."[94] That the United States was able against tremendous odds to defeat Britain, establish a stable government, and frame such a promising Constitution convinced Washington that God was working for good in the world and evoked his heartfelt gratitude. That his poorly trained, clothed, fed, and equipped army could defeat the world's premier military seemed nothing short of miraculous to Washington.[95] Their victory was due to God's "reiterated and astonishing" intervention.[96] Reflecting on these developments, he wrote to a friend in August 1788: "I can never trace the concatenation of causes, which led to these events, without acknowledging the mystery and admiring the goodness of Providence. To that superintending Power alone is our retraction from the brink of ruin to be attributed."[97] Because God's decrees are always for the best, Americans must accept them without protest.[98] Since people are "ignorant of the comprehensive schemes [God] Intended," they should simply trust Providence without "perplexing ourselves to seek for that, which is beyond human ken."[99] Writing to the Marquis de Lafayette during the perilous days of the French Revolution, Washington averred, "[T]o the care of that Providence, whose interposition & protection we have so often experienced, do I chearfully [sic] commit you & your Nation."[100] The same year, he told a friend that Americans must remember the "omnipotence of that God who is alone able to protect them."[101] Addressing Congress in 1796, the president once again voiced his "fervent supplications to the Supreme Ruler of the Universe and Sovereign Arbiter of Nations, that his providential care may still be extended to the United States. . . ."[102]

Washington's confidence that God determined the course of events reinforced his sense of duty and helped inspire his prodigious efforts.

He firmly believed that God, not fate or random chance, governed the universe and that God used humans to accomplish His purposes. Washington's faith that God was perfect helped make him more conscious of his own flaws and failures and prompt him usually to be humble about his achievements even when showered with effusive tributes. The Virginian's conviction that he was simply an "instrument of Providence," coupled with his modesty, led him to typically attribute America's successes to God, not himself. "To the Great Ruler of events, not to any exertions of mine," Washington declared in 1795, "is to be ascribed the favourable terminations of our late contest for liberty."[103] Although God was sovereign, Washington maintained, he worked through people. If they wanted to experience "the smiles of Providence," Americans must put forth "Vigorous Exertions."[104] Moreover, his confidence in divine Providence helped fuel his courage, resoluteness, and calmness in the face of adversity and kept him from discouragement and despair when his troops or policies suffered defeat.

While repeatedly stressing God's Providence, Washington rarely referred to Jesus or even Christianity in public or private writings. As John G. West, Jr., puts it, the "evidence on the subject" of what Washington believed about these matters "is partial, contradictory, and in the end, unsatisfactory."[105] That the Virginian said little about Christ in his public addresses is not unusual. In an effort to be as inclusive as possible, other presidents have almost always used general and generic titles for God and avoided mentioning Jesus.[106] It is significant, however, that while often alluding to Providence in letters to friends and associates, Washington seldom mentions Christ or Christianity. Moreover, unlike Thomas Jefferson and Thomas Paine, he never even called Jesus a great ethical teacher.[107]

Washington's beliefs about life after death have been the subject of considerable debate. The Virginian usually expressed a stoic attitude toward death and seemed to be skeptical about seeing loved ones after death. While urging the bereaved to seek consolation in religion, he never assured them that they would spend eternity with God or be reunited with their family members in heaven.[108] He viewed the death of others and himself with resignation, fortitude, and calmness, and as a part of the divine order. People must submit to "the will of the Creator whether it be to prolong, or to shorten the number of our days."[109] His letters contain no "Christian images of judgment, redemption through the sacrifice of Christ, and eternal life for the faithful."[110] On the other hand, Washington rejected the concept of annihilation and did believe in a type of life after death. He referred to going to "the world of Spirits," "the land of Spirits," and "a happier clime." He prayed that "the munificent Rewarder of virtue" would compensate people's good work "here and hereafter."[111] Washington told the masons that he hoped to meet them someday "as brethren in the Eternal Temple of the Supreme Architect."[112] Strikingly, however, his references to immortality are more vague and impersonal than those of John Adams, Benjamin Franklin, Jefferson, and even Paine.[113]

After his last surviving brother died in 1799, Washington wrote a friend, "when I shall be called upon to follow . . . is known only to the giver of life. When the summons comes I shall endeavor to obey it with a good grace."[114] The general strove to deal with the death of relatives and friends according to the eighteenth-century ideal: "[A] controlled style of bereavement—submission to God's authority with no 'affectation of overflowing grief.' " Although he grieved deeply when those close to him died, he did so privately.[115] In letters to the bereaved, Washington emphasized submitting "with patience and resignation to the will of the Creator" "whose decrees are always just and wise."[116]

Throughout his long military career, Washington had "displayed a stoic's contempt for death . . . that awed his contemporaries," and he often put his life at risk (especially during the French and Indian War) by venturing onto the battlefield. Many times he took great risks, and bullets frequently tore though his uniforms or killed his horses, but he suffered no wounds.[117] His final struggle with what he once called "the grim King" would test his fortitude and resolve one last time.[118] Making his rounds at Mount Vernon on December 12, 1799, the planter was stricken with a virulent infection that claimed his life two days later. While on his deathbed, he did not pray, request God's forgiveness, express fear of divine judgment or hope of an afterlife, or call for an Episcopal rector. According to his Personal Secretary Tobias Lear and attending physicians, Washington, after uttering "Tis well," died peacefully and was later buried following Episcopal and Masonic funeral services.[119]

Lear wrote that he hoped to be reunited with Washington in heaven, but he resisted putting such words in the planter's mouth.[120] Others, most notably Parson Weems, did not. In his fabricated account, Washington had everyone leave his room so he could pray alone and his last words were " '*Father of mercies, take me to thyself.*' "[121] While rejecting Weems's version, other nineteenth-century biographers portrayed Washington as emulating Socrates: accepting the inevitable, the general fearlessly prepared to die.[122] The general died in a rational, self-controlled, dignified manner, evinced no pain, and accepted medical treatment only to assuage his wife. Peter Henriques argues that the way Washington lived and died indicates he was more interested in attaining secular than spiritual immortality. In consoling others who lost loved ones and in contemplating his own death, he often stressed the importance of being revered in life, lamented in death, and "remembered with honor in history."[123]

Washington also never clearly expressed his views on the Christian concept of salvation. He apparently thought that conduct, more than belief, made individuals acceptable to God. He told a friend that he constantly strove to walk "a straight line" and endeavored to properly discharge his "duties to his Maker and fellow-men. . . ."[124] Writing to the General Assembly of the Presbyterian Church in May 1789, Washington proclaimed, "[N]o man, who is profligate in his morals, or a bad member of the civil community, can possibly be a true Christian. . . ."[125]

In the final analysis, Washington's faith is better explained by the label "theistic rationalism" than by "Christianity," "Unitarianism," or "deism." This "hybrid belief system" mixes "elements of natural religion, Christianity, and rationalism," with rationalism predominating. To theistic rationalists, these three components are generally in harmony, but reason must be used to resolve any conflict among them. God is unitary and active. Because he intervenes in human affairs, prayer is effectual. Theist rationalists insist that people best serve God by living an upright life and that religion's primary role is to promote morality, which is indispensable to social harmony. They have a higher view of Jesus than deists and assert that revelation complements reason.[126] Because deists have typically been seen as denying God's active presence in the world, the deity of Christ, and the Bible as God's revelation, the concept of theistic rationalism seems preferable to that of Unitarian-deist, "warm deist," or "enlightened deist" to describe Washington and other founders such as Adams, Franklin, Jefferson, James Wilson, and Gouverneur Morris.[127]

Boller concludes that if belonging to a Christian church, fairly regularly attending services, emphasizing the importance of religion for society, and believing that God directed human affairs is enough to be a Christian, then Washington was one. If, on the other hand, to be a Christian, one must publicly affirm the divinity and Resurrection of Christ and his atonement for humanity's sin and participate in the Lord's Supper, then Washington cannot be considered a Christian.[128]

Edwin Gaustad points out that even though the religious views of Washington are difficult to distinguish in broad outline from those of Jefferson, the public reaction to their convictions differed sharply. Unlike Jefferson, Washington was never censured as a "howling atheist" or condemned as an enemy of institutional religion. Americans continually pressed Jefferson as well as Adams and Franklin for more details about their religious principles, but not Washington. The fact that Washington believed in a God who watched over and protected America seemed to be enough for most citizens.[129] While scholars and ordinary Americans will continue to debate the precise nature of Washington's faith, clearly it became deeper as a result of his trying and sometimes traumatic experiences as commander-in-chief of the Continental Army and as the nation's first president. And his faith significantly affected his understanding of life and his duties in both roles. Although he had little interest in theology, as Richard Norton Smith argues, no one who reads his correspondence or the accounts of those who knew him best "can doubt Washington's essential belief" or fail to recognize "his genuine if poorly articulated relationship with his maker."[130] Washington told Rev. William Gordon that no one had "a more perfect Reliance on the alwise, and powerful dispensations of the Supreme Being than I have nor thinks his aid more necessary."[131] The Virginian's words and actions testify to his firm trust in God's wisdom, might, guidance, and help.

Notes

1. Paul F. Boller, Jr., *George Washington and Religion* (Dallas: Southern Methodist University Press, 1963), vii.
2. See Arthur N. Holcombe, "The Role of Washington in the Framing of the Constitution," *Huntington Library Quarterly*, 19 (August 1956): 317–334.
3. Richard Brookhiser, *Founding Father: Rediscovering George Washington* (New York: Free Press, 1996), 162.
4. For example, Fisher Ames, "Eulogy of Washington," February 8, 1800, in *Works of Fisher Ames*, ed. William B. Allen (Indianapolis: Liberty Classics, 1983), 1: 519–538. Although Washington did not publicly endorse ratification, he strongly promoted it in private letters.
5. For example, Richard Brookhiser, "George Washington (1789–97)," in James Taranto, Leo Leonard, and William J. Bennett, eds., *Presidential Leadership: Rating the Best and the Worst in the White House* (New York: Free Press, 2004). The literature on Washington is voluminous. For bibliographical essays, see Don Higginbotham, "The Washington Theme in Recent Historical Literature," *Pennsylvania Magazine of History and Biography*, 114 (1990): 424–437; Albert Furtwangler, "George Washington Fading Away," *American Literary History*, 2 (1990): 319–327; Kenneth R. Bowling, "An Extraordinary Man: A Review Essay on George Washington," *Wisconsin Magazine of History*, 73 (1990): 287–293; and Don Higginbotham, "Introduction: Washington and the

Historians," in *George Washington Reconsidered*, ed. Don Higginbotham (Charlottesville: University Press of Virginia, 2001), 1–12.

6. Richard V. Pierard and Robert D. Linder, *Civil Religion and the Presidency* (Grand Rapids, MI: Zondervan, 1988), 74–75.

7. See Catherine L. Albanese, *Sons of the Fathers: The Civil Religion of the American Revolution* (Philadelphia: Temple University Press, 1976), 143–181.

8. See *Maryland Journal and Baltimore Advertiser*, July 8, 1777, 1; *Pennsylvania Mercury and Universal Advertiser*, July 8, 1785, 1, as cited in Robert P. Hay, "George Washington: American Moses," *American Quarterly* (Winter 1969): 781.

9. Henry Muhlenberg, *The Notebook of a Colonial Clergyman*, trans. and ed. Theodore G. Tappert and John W. Doberstein (Philadelphia Fortress Press, 1975), 195, from his journal entry of May 7, 1778.

10. Philadelphia Protestant Clergy to George Washington, March 3, 1797, in *The Writings of George Washington*, ed. John C. Fitzpatrick, 37 vols. (Washington, DC: GPO, 1931–1942), 35: 416–417 (hereafter *WGW*).

11. Ashbel Green, "Jefferson's Papers," *Christian Advocate*, 8 (1830): 308. Green wrote to rebut Thomas Jefferson's contention that the clergy had composed this address to goad the president into publicly declaring his Christian convictions. For the context of this argument, see Boller, *George Washington and Religion*, 80–86.

12. James Smylie, "The President as Republican Prophet and King: Clerical Reflections on the Death of Washington," *Journal of Church and State*, 18 (Spring 1976): 247.

13. Jonathan Sewall, *An Eulogy on the Late General Washington at the St. John's Church* (Portsmouth, NH: William Treadwell, 1799), 17–18. Cf. Moses Cleaveland, *An Oration, Commemorative of the Life and Death of General George Washington* (Windham, CT: John Byrne, 1800), 14; and Abraham Clarke, *A Discourse Occasioned by the Death of General George Washington* (Providence, RI: n. p., 1800), 8.

14. John Croes, *A Discourse . . . to the Memory of General George Washington* (Philadelphia: John Ormrod, 1800), 25. Cf. Jeremiah Smith, *An Oration upon the Death of General George Washington* (Exeter, NH: Henry Raulet, 1800), 76.

15. John T. Kirkland, *Eulogies and Orations on the Life and Death of George Washington* (1800), 292.

16. Timothy Dwight, *A Discourse . . . on the Character of George Washington . . .* (New Haven, CT: Thomas Green & Son, 1800), 28. See also Jonathan Huse, *A Discourse Occasioned by the Death of . . . Washington* (Wiscasset, ME, 1800), 11; John Carroll, *A Discourse on George Washington* (Baltimore: Warner & Hanna, 1800), 4–5; Thaddeus Mason Harris, *A Discourse . . . after . . . the Death of Washington* (Charlestown, MA: Samuel Etheridge, 1800), 13.

17. Francis Asbury, *Letters and Journals*, Elmer T. Clark, ed., 3 vols. (Nashville: Abingdon Press, 1958), January 4, 1800, 221; Carroll, *A Discourse*, 5, see also 6, 15, 21, and 24.

18. See Mason L. Weems, *The Life of George Washington*, ed. Marcus Cunliffe (Cambridge, MA: Harvard University Press, 1962), 172–186, who emphasizes Washington's faithful church attendance, commitment to prayer, dependence on God's providence, and religious rhetoric. On Weems's efforts to make Washington an exemplary Christian, see François Furstenberg, *In the Name of the Father: Washington's Legacy, Slavery, and the Making of a Nation* (NewYork: Penguin Press, 2006), 123–129. See also Jared Sparks, ed., *The Writings of George Washington*, 12 vols. (Boston, 1837), 12, Appendix, "Religious Opinions and Habits of Washington," 399–411. "If a man who spoke, wrote, and acted as a Christian through a long life . . . and who was never known to say, write, or do anything contrary to his professions . . . is not to be ranked among the believers of Christianity, it would be impossible to establish the point by any train of reasoning." See also Washington Irving, *Life of George Washington*, 8 vols. (New York: G. P. Putnam, 1857), 1: 162, 397; 2: 362–363; 8: 123. Many later biographers agreed that Washington should be considered a Christian. See, e.g., Henry Cabot Lodge, *George Washington*, 2 vols. (Boston, New York: Houghton Mifflin, 1889); Woodrow Wilson, *George Washington* (New York: Harper & Brothers, 1896); William R. Thayer, *George Washington* (Boston: Houghton Mifflin, 1922), 239–240; and Luther A. Weigle, *American Idealism* (New Haven, CT: Yale University Press, 1928), 126, 132–133.

19. John Marshall, *The Life of George Washington* . . . , 5 vols. (New York: C. P. Wayne, 1804–1807), 5: 375.

20. B. F. Morris, *Christian Life and Character of the Civil Institutions of the United States* (Philadelphia: G. W. Childs, 1864), 166, 11; Philip Slaughter, *Christianity the Key to the Character and Career of Washington* . . . (Washington, DC: Judd & Detweiler, 1886), 2; William Meade, *Old Churches, Ministers and Families of Virginia*, 2 vols. (Philadelphia: J. B. Lippincott & Co., 1878), 2: 243; and Norman Vincent Peale, *One Nation under God* (Pawling, NY: Foundation for Christian Living, 1972), 14, quotations are in that order.

21. Boller, *George Washington and Religion*, 3–23, quotations from 5.

22. Pierard and Linder, *Civil Religion and the Presidency*, 71.

23. Weems, *The Life of George Washington*, 181.

24. Boller, *George Washington and Religion*, 10. Potts lived near Valley Forge in the early 1780s, but he was not anywhere near the army encampment during the winter of 1777–1778. The story was first told in print by Parson Weems and was also popularized by Morris, *Christian Life and Character of the Civil Institutions of the United States*, 298. On Potts, see John C. Fitzpatrick, *The Spirit of the Revolution* (Boston: Houghton Mifflin, 1924), 88–89; Rupert Hughes, *George Washington, the Savior of the States, 1777–1781* (New York: W. Morrow & Co., 1930), 270–277; Samuel Eliot Morison, *The Young Man Washington* (Cambridge, MA: Harvard University Press, 1932), 38; and Frank E. Gizzard, Jr., *The Ways of Providence: Religion and George Washington* (Buena Vista, CA: Mariner, 2005), 19–25. See also W. Herbert Burk, *The Washington*

Window in the Washington Memorial Chapel, Valley Forge (Norristown, PA, 1926); and J. Leroy Miller, "Where Washington Prayed: Thousands Now Will Pray," *American Magazine*, 108 (August 1929): 73–74. By 1976 there were at least ten stained-glass versions of the Washington's Valley Forge prayer. See Martin E. Marty, "Legends in Stained Glass," *Christian Century*, 93 (May 5, 1976): 447.

25. Boller labels this work "the longest, most ambitious, and most influential of all the books ever published" about Washington's religion (*George Washington and Religion*, 18).

26. Boller, *George Washington and Religion*, 11–14. This story has not been verified and contradicts Washington's known attitude toward communion. The Cox story is included in David Hosack, *Memoir of DeWitt Clinton* (New York: J. Seymour, 1829), 183–184. See also Edward McGuire, *The Religious Opinions and Character of Washington* (New York: Harper, 1836), 412–414; "Washington at the Communion Table in Morristown, New Jersey," *Presbyterian Magazine*, 1 (December 1851): 569; and "Washington at Morristown during the Winter of 1779–80," *Harper's*, 18 (February 1859): 295. A large painting of the event was hung in the Presbyterian hospital in Philadelphia and a sundial was placed in the orchard to mark the spot where the service allegedly occurred.

27. Origen Bacheler, *Discussion on the Existence of God and the Authenticity of the Bible, between Origen Bacheler and Robert Dale Owen*, 2 vols. (London: J. Watson, 1840), 2: 122. Bacheler cited the testimonies of Parson Weems; George Bancroft (*History of the United States, from the Discovery of the American Continent*, 10 vols. (Boston: Little, Brown, 1861–1875); and David Ramsay, *The Life of George Washington: Commander in Chief of the Armies of the United States . . .* (London: Longman, Hurst, Rees, & Orme, 1807) and on Washington's piety, character, and dependence on God (120–121). See also 98–99, 123, 161–163.

28. Albert R. Beatty, "Was Washington Religious?" *National Republic*, 20 (February 1933): 3.

29. See Matthew Hale, *Contemplations* (London: D. Brown, 1711).

30. Beatty, "Was Washington Religious?" 4–5, 28 and Part II, March 1933, 18–19, 29, quotation from 29; and Arthur B. Kinsolving, "The Religion of George Washington," *Historical Magazine of the Protestant Episcopal Church*, 18 (September 1949): 326–332. See also Frederick Conrad, "Washington: Christianity and the Moulding Power of His Character," *Lutheran Quarterly*, 26 (1896): 89–115; John C. Fitzpatrick, *Washington as a Religious Man*, pamphlet no. 5 of the series Honor to George Washington, ed. Albert Bushnell Hart (Washington, DC: George Washington Bicentennial Commission, 1931); Francis Landon Humphreys, *George Washington, the Churchman* (Palm Beach, FL: n.p., 1932); John S. Littell, *Washington, Christian* (Keene, NH: Hampshire Art Press, 1913); "Washington as a Christian," *Presbyterian*, 102 (September 15, 1932): 4; and Vernon B. Hampton, *Religious Background of the White House* (Boston: Christopher Publishing House, 1932), 330–337.

31. William J. Johnstone, *How Washington Prayed* (New York: Abingdon Press, 1932), 9. Johnstone includes 14 pages of prayers that Washington wrote in a book at about age 20. Scholars do not know if he composed them or copied them from another source, but given their style and substance, it is very unlikely that he composed them. See also W. Herbert Burk, *Washington's Prayers* (Norristown, PA: n.p., 1907), 87–95. While presenting numerous unverified stories about Washington praying, Johnstone also features the testimony of soldiers such as General Robert Porterfield, ministers including Ashbel Green, Washington's granddaughter Nelly Custis, and Washington's nephew and private secretary Robert Lewis who all said they saw him praying on several or many occasions. They and others also testified that he attended church regularly, worshipped very reverently, and took communion frequently before the Revolution. Among the sources upon which Johnstone relied are Paul Leicester Ford, *The True George Washington* (Philadelphia: J. B. Lippincott & Co., 1903); Eliphalet Nott Potter, *Washington: A Model in His Library and Life* (New York: E. & J. B. Young & Co., 1895); Meade, *Old Churches, Ministers and Families of Virginia*; Caroline M. Kirkland, *Memoirs of Washington* (New York: D. Appleton & Co., 1857); *The Presbyterian Magazine*, February 1851; and George Washington Parke Custis, *Recollections and Private Memoirs of Washington . . .* , ed. Benson J. Lossing (New York: Derby & Jackson, 1860).

32. Conrad, "Washington: Christianity and the Moulding Power of His Character," 99, 100–104, 106, 112, first two quotations from 99, last three from 112.

33. Herbert Hoover, "Message on Luther Day, Aug. 13, 1932," in *The Public Papers of Presidents of the United States: Herbert Hoover, 1932–33* (Washington: GPO, 1977), 379.

34. Herbert Hoover, "Address to a Joint Session of Congress Opening the Celebration of the Bicentennial of the Birth of George Washington," February 22, 1932, in *The Public Papers of Presidents of the United States*, 71.

35. See Peter Marshall and David Manuel, *The Light and the Glory* (Old Tappan, NJ: Revell, 1977), 284–288, 322–324, 326, 332, 342–343, 348–349 (this book rehashes earlier accounts); David Martin, *The Myth of Separation* (Aledo, TX: WallBuilder Press, 1991); Marshall Foster, *The American Covenant* (Thousand Oaks, CA: Mayflower Institute, 1992); Gary DeMar, *America's Christian History: The Untold Story* (Atlanta: American Vision Publishers, 1993); William Federer, comp., *America's God and Country: Encyclopedia of Quotations* (St. Louis, MO: Amerisearch, 1999); and various sermons and works of Pat Robertson and Jerry Falwell.

36. Tim LaHaye, *Faith of Our Founding Fathers* (Brentwood, TN: Wolgemunt and Hyatt, 1987), 103, 110, 113, quotations in that order.

37. Benjamin Hart, *Faith and Freedom: The Christian Roots of American Liberty* (San Bernardino, CA: Here's Life Publishers, 1988), 273–274.

See also 228–234, 275–278, 291–295, 335. Hart also emphasizes Washington's "private prayer book" (274). Many authors record another example of the kind of prayer Washington allegedly prayed from June 1779, which concludes "Grant the petition of Thy servant, for the sake of Him whom Thou hast called Thy beloved son; nevertheless, not my will, but Thine be done." See McGuire, *The Religious Opinions and Character of Washington*, 162–167; Johnstone, *George Washington—The Christian*, 126–127; and Federer, comp., *America's God and Country*, 644.

38. Verna Hall, *George Washington: The Character and Influence of One Man, A Compilation*, ed. Dorothy Dimmick (San Francisco: Foundation for American Christian Education, 2000), 153. This volume includes excerpts from the books of David Ramsay, John Marshall, Washington Irving, Philip Slaughter, Edward McGuire (all mentioned above), Washington's own writings, and Aaron Bancroft's *The Life of George Washington, Commander in Chief of the American Army* (London: Printed for J. Stockdale, 1808), vol. 2.

39. Peter Lillback with Jerry Newcombe, *George Washington's Sacred Fire* (Bryn Mawr, PA: Providence Forum Press, 2006), 27. They add that Washington was a "devout Anglican," which meant "he believed in the basics of orthodox Trinitarian faith" (30). To refute "modern skeptics" who "have read into Washington their own unbelief," they emphasize his "exemplary prayer life," his extensive knowledge of Scripture, his work as an Anglican vestryman, and his repeated calls for public and private piety (30–34, quotations from 34, 30). See especially 59, 81, 133, 155, 190, 205–206, 232, 254–255, 263–269, 276–281, 285, 300–303, 307–308, 311–320, 333, 343–349, 375, 395–401, 447–448, 551–552, 572, 583, 587, 591–603, 612–615, 625–626. Similarly, Michael and Jana Novak contend in *Washington's God: Religion, Liberty, and the Father of Our Country* (New York: Basic Books, 2006) that "Washington cannot be said to be a deist. He was a serious Christian, perceived to be so by many close to him." They add that "Washington easily met the standards for being considered an Anglican in good standing"—"baptism, acceptance of the Apostles' and Nicene Creeds . . . and some regular attendance at church" (212). The Novaks stress that Washington served as a godfather for eight children, was almost universally perceived "to be at least a friend to Christianity and to some significant degree a good Christian," faithfully attended vestry meetings and "often took the lead in projects to improve the church or its functioning," insisted that all his soldiers participate regularly and sincerely in communal prayer, and swore his oath of office as president on the Bible when he was not required to do so (216–218, 220, quotations from 217). They acknowledge that the major objections to Washington being a Christian "have a grain of truth in them": he never took communion after the Revolutionary War began; he stood rather than knelt during prayers; "he refused to declare his specific beliefs" publicly; he rarely mentioned Jesus in public or private correspondence or the Christian names for God; "his death seemed more Stoic than Christian"; and "his

view of Providence was Greek or Roman, as if it were a synonym of fate" (219). Nevertheless, they offer rebuttals to them (220–227). Mary V. Thompson's "In the Hands a Good Providence," a manuscript in the Library of Mount Vernon, offers a similar perspective on Washington's faith.

40. Samuel Langdon to George Washington, July 8, 1789, in *Papers of George Washington* (hereafter *PGW*), ed. Dorothy Twohig, 11 vols., Presidential Series (hereafter Pres. Ser.) (Charlottesville: University Press of Virginia, 1987–2000), 3: 149–151, first three quotations from 150, fourth one from 151. The sermon was probably *The Republic of the Israelites as an Example to the American States* . . . (Exeter, NH: Lamson & Ranlet, 1788), which was in Washington's library. Few, if any, dared to lament publicly what some did privately: he was never "explicit in his profession of *faith in, and dependence on* the finished Atonement of our glorious Redeemer." Benjamin Tallmadge to Manasseh Cutler, as quoted in Charles Swain Hall, *Benjamin Tallmadge, Revolutionary Soldier and American Businessman* (New York: Columbia University Press, 1943), 167.

41. George Washington to Samuel Langdon, September 28, 1789, in *PGW*, Pres. Ser., 4: 104.

42. Quoted in Charles Swain Hall, *Benjamin Tallmadge*, 161. Cf. Samuel Miller, *Life of Samuel Miller*, 2 vols. (Philadelphia: Claxton, Remsen & Haffelfinger, 1869), 1: 123.

43. Bacheler, *Discussion on the Existence of God and the Authenticity of the Bible*, 2: 140. Owen emphasized Washington's refusal to take communion and to ask for spiritual aid on his deathbed (112–113, 197).

44. Bishop William White to B. C. C. Parker, December 21, 1832, in Bird Wilson, *Memoir of Life of the Right Reverend William White* (Philadelphia: J. Kay, Jun. & Brother, 1839), 193.

45. "After-Dinner Anecdotes of James Madison, Excerpts from Jared Sparks' Journal for 1829–31," *Virginia Magazine of History and Biography*, 60 (April 1952): 263.

46. Douglas Freeman, *George Washington: A Biography*, 7 vols. (New York: Scribner, 1952), 2: 387–388, 397; 5: 443, 493–494, quotation from 2: 397. He argues that several of Washington's staff writers were devout Christians who often added religious phrases to the public statements they drafted for him while he was commander-in-chief.

47. Dorothy Twohig, "The Making of George Washington," in *George Washington and the Virginia Backcountry*, ed. Warren R. Hofstra (Madison, WS: Madison House, 1998), 19.

48. Robert F. Jones, *George Washington: Ordinary Man, Extraordinary Leader* (New York: Fordham University Press, 2002), 27, 99, quotations from 27. Cf. Willard Sterne Randall, *George Washington: A Life* (New York: Henry Holt, 1997), 256.

49. Barry Schwartz, *George Washington: The Making of an American Symbol* (New York: Free Press, 1987), 175. Cf. James T. Flexner, *Washington: The Indispensable Man* (Boston: Little, Brown, 1974), 216.

50. James T. Flexner, *George Washington*, 4 vols. (Boston: Little, Brown, 1965–1972), 2: 543. Believing that Providence "was a virtuous force" that promoted human welfare, he was convinced that fighting the American Revolution was a form of worship to God who would protect, guide, and reward his servants.

51. John R. Alden, *George Washington: A Biography* (Baton Rouge: Louisiana State University Press, 1984), 217.

52. Paul K. Longmore, *The Invention of George Washington* (Berkeley: University of California Press, 1988), 169.

53. Pierard and Linder, *Civil Religion and the Presidency*, 74.

54. David L. Holmes, *The Religion of the Founding Fathers* (Charlottesville, VA: Ash Lawn-Highland, 2003), 84. Cf. Boller, *George Washington and Religion*, 94, who also notes he used stock Deist phrases including Supreme Ruler, Great Creator, Director of Human Events, Higher Cause, and Governor of the Universe.

55. Boller, *George Washington and Religion*, 108–109, quotation from 108.

56. Edwin Gaustad, *Faith of Our Fathers: Religion and the New Nation* (San Francisco: Harper & Row, 1987), 77. Randall argues that Washington's involvement with the Free Masons influenced his use of these terms (*George Washington: A Life*, 67).

57. George Washington to James Anderson, December 24, 1795, in *WGW*, 34: 407.

58. Samuel Miller, *Life of Samuel Miller*, 1: 123. While he was commander-in-chief and president, many ministers sent Washington their sermons that had been printed as pamphlets. The general thanked them for dedicating sermons to him and complimenting his public service, but he very rarely commented on the substance of their sermons, and when he did, he provided few clues about what his views of Christian doctrines are (Boller, *George Washington and Religion*, 77). As examples, Boller points to George Washington to William White, May 30, 1799, in *WGW*, 37: 216–217; George Washington to Nathaniel Whitaker, December 20, 1777, in *WGW*, 10: 175; George Washington to Uzal Ogden, August 5, 1779, in *WGW*, 16: 51; George Washington to Israel Evans, March 13, 1778, in *WGW*, 11:78; and George Washington to Jedidiah Morse, February 28, 1799, in *WGW*, 37: 140. Boller found only two letters where Washington actually commented on the substance of sermons, and in both cases he simply affirmed their doctrine as sound. Upon leaving the presidency, Washington thanked the Episcopal rectors of Philadelphia for their "liberal and interesting discourses." George Washington to the United Episcopal Churches of Christ Church and St. Peters, March 2, 1797, in *WGW*, 35: 410–411.

59. Garry Wills, *Cincinnatus: George Washington and the Enlightenment* (Garden City, NY: Doubleday & Co., 1984), 23.

60. Holmes, *The Religion of the Founding Fathers*, 79.

61. Boller, *George Washington and Religion*, 29; ibid., 79–80; Longmore, *The Invention of George Washington*, 130–131, 138; and John C. Fitzpatrick, *George Washington Himself* (Indianapolis: Bobbs-Merrill

Co., 1933), 130. He attended much more regularly during the Stamp Act controversy of 1765 and in 1774 when American relations with Britain were very strained.

62. Eleanor Parke Custis to Jared Sparks, February 26, 1833, in Sparks, ed., *The Writings of George Washington*, 12: 406; William White to B. C. C. Parker, November 28, 1832, in Bird Wilson, *Memoir of Life of the Right Reverend William White*, 189. On Nelly's faith, see David Riblett, *Nelly Custis, Child of Mount Vernon* (Mount Vernon, VA; Mount Vernon Ladies' Association, 1993), 23 and passim.

63. Boller, *George Washington and Religion*, 40; Longmore, *The Invention of George Washington*, 217; Morison, *The Young Man Washington*, 37; and "How the Bible Made America," *Newsweek*, 27 (December 1982): 47. The list of Washington's books compiled at Mount Vernon in 1783 contains no Bible. The 1799 inventory of Washington's estate lists three Bibles, but one is in Latin and the other two were probably gifts. In addition, his library contained few popular religious works. See Appleton P. C. Griffin, comp., *A Catalogue of the Washington Collection in the Boston Athenaeum* (Boston, 1897), 497–503. The quotation is from Potter, *Washington*, 181. Cf. McGuire, *The Religious Opinions and Character of Washington*, 404.

64. See Daniel L. Dreisbach, "The 'Vine and Fig Tree' in George Washington's Letters: Reflections on a Biblical Motif in the Literature of the American Founding Era," paper presented at the Tyndale Society 2004 Conference, Virginia Beach, Virginia, September 25, 2004. Dreisbach found nearly 50 references in Washington's letters and addresses to the phrase "vine and fig tree" as presented in Micah 4:4. Washington cites the biblical language of converting "swords into plowshares" in at least four letters. He also refers several times to "war and rumors of war" (George Washington to Catherine Macaulay Graham, July 19, 1791, in *WGW*, 31: 317; George Washington to Marquis de la Luzerne, April 29, 1790, in *WGW*, 31: 40). He refers to Mathew 13:25 ff. in a May 31, 1776 letter to John Augustine Washington (*WGW*, 5: 93) and to Psalms 121:4 in a March 31, 1779 letter to James Warren (*WGW*, 14: 313). Washington's 1785 letter to Lafayette contains numerous biblical references, including the argument that Americans must settle the West to fulfill "the first and great commandment, *Increase and Multiply*." George Washington to Lafayette, July 25, 1785, in *WGW*, 28: 206–207, quotation from 206. Washington apparently had in mind the first commandment before humanity fell rather than the first commandment taught by Jesus. Dreisbach called my attention to the Longmore, Morison, and *Newsweek* references in the previous endnote and to most of the Washington letters cited in this endnote in his essay and a January 18, 2005 e-mail.

65. George Washington to Louis XVI, March 14, 1792, in *PGW*, Pres. Ser., 10: 108. Cf. George Washington to Louis XVI, October 9, 1789, *PGW*, Pres. Ser., 4: 152–153.

66. For example, George Washington, "To the United Brethren of Wachovia, North Carolina," June 1, 1791, in *PGW*, Pres. Ser., 8: 226; George Washington to William Gordon, July 19, 1791, in *PGW*, Pres. Ser., 8: 356–357; George Washington to Hannah Washington, May 20, 1792, in *PGW*, Pres. Ser., 10: 403; and George Washington to Marquis De Lafayette, June 13, 1793, in *WGW*, 32: 501.

67. George Washington, "To the Bishops of the Methodist Episcopal Church," in *PGW*, Pres. Ser., 26. See also George Washington, "To the General Assembly of the Presbyterian Church in the United States of America," May 1789, in *PGW*, Pres. Ser., 2: 420–421; George Washington, "To the Ministers and Elders of the German Reformed Congregations in the United States," June 1789, in *Washington's Letter Books*, 29: 30; George Washington, "To the . . . Protestant Episcopal Church," in *Washington's Letter Books*, 29: 42; and George Washington, "To the Congregationalist Ministers of the City of New Haven," October 1789, in *Washington's Letter Books*, 29: 56.

68. George Washington, "To the Clergy of Different Denominations Residing in and near the City of Philadelphia," in *Washington's Letter Books*, 31: 282. Cf. George Washington, "To the General Assembly of the PCUSA," in 2: 420; George Washington, "To the Bishops of the Methodist Episcopal Church," in *PGW*, Pres. Ser., 2: 411.

69. George Washington, "To the Massachusetts Legislature," March 28, 1776, in *WGW*, 4: 441–442; George Washington to Martha Custis, July 20, 1758, in *WGW*, 2: 242; George Washington to Israel Putnam, March 26, 1776, in *WGW*, 4: 444; George Washington to Thomas Ruston, August 31, 1788, in *WGW*, 30: 79. See also Robert P. Hay, "Providence and the American Past," *Indiana Magazine of History*, 65 (1969): 79–101.

70. George Washington to Martha Washington, June 18, 1775, in *WGW*, 3: 294. Cf. George Washington to Landon Carter, May 30, 1778, in *WGW*, 11: 492; and George Washington to Joseph Reed, January 14, 1776, in *WGW*, 4: 243.

71. For example, George Washington to Landon Carter, March 25, 1776, in *WGW*, 4: 433–434; and George Washington to John Augustine Washington, March 31, 1776, in *WGW*, 4: 447–448.

72. General Orders, July 2, 1776, in *PGW*, 13 vols., Revolutionary War Series (hereafter Rev. War Ser.) (Charlottesville: University Press of Virginia, 1985–), 5: 180. Cf. George Washington, "Answer to an Address from the Massachusetts Legislature, March 28, 1776": Washington praised "the interposition of that Providence, which has manifestly appeared in our behalf through the whole of this important struggle. . . . May that being, who is powerful to save, and in whose hands is the fate of nations, look down with an eye of tender pity and compassion upon the whole of the United Colonies." Because "Liberty, Honor, and Safety are all at stake," he argued in August 1776, "Providence will smile upon our Efforts, and establish us once more, the inhabitants of a free and happy country."

George Washington, "To the Officers and Soldiers of the Pennsylvania Associators," August 8, 1776, in *WGW*, 5: 398.

73. George Washington to General Thomas Nelson, August 20, 1778, in *WGW*, 12: 343.

74. Marshall, "Eulogy on Washington," 290.

75. General Orders, October 18, 1777, in *WGW*, 9: 391 ("General Burgoyne, and his whole Army, surrendered themselves prisoners of war. Let every face brighten, and every heart expand with grateful Joy and praise to the supreme disposer of all events, who has granted us this signal success"); General Orders, May 5, 1778, in *WGW*, 11: 354; George Washington to Thomas Nelson, Jr., August 20, 1778, in *WGW*, 12: 343; Washington to John Laurens, October 13, 1780, in *WGW*, 20: 173 (quotation); General Orders, October 20, 1781, in *WGW*, 23: 247; and George Washington to John A. Washington, October 18, 1777, in *WGW*, 9: 397.

76. General Orders, May 5, 1778, in *WGW*, 11: 354.

77. General Orders, October 20, 1781, in *WGW*, 23: 247.

78. George Washington, "To the Ministers, Elders and Deacons of the Reformed Protestant Dutch Church of the Town of Schenectady," June 30, 1782, in *WGW*, 24: 391.

79. General Orders, April 18, 1783, in *WGW*, 26: 334–335.

80. Boller, *George Washington and Religion*, 58.

81. George Washington, "To the Inhabitants of Princeton and Neighborhood Together with the President and Faculty of the College," August 25, 1783, in *WGW*, 27: 116. Cf. George Washington, "To the Synod of the Dutch Reformed Church in North America," October 1789, in *WGW*, 26: 334: "I fear, Gentlemen, your goodness has led you to form too exalted an opinion of my virtues and merits. . . . the glory should be ascribed to the manifest interposition of an over-ruling Providence." *PGW*, Pres. Ser., 4: 263–264.

82. George Washington, "To the Minister Elders, Deacons & Members of the Reformed German Congregation in the City of New York," November 29, 1783, in *Religious References in the Writings, Addresses, and Military Orders of George Washington* (Washington, DC: G. W. Bicentennial Commission, 1932), 5. Cf. George Washington, "To Elizabeth, New Jersey, Magistrates, and Citizens," August 21, 1783. In his General Orders of April 18, 1783, Washington declared, "The Chaplains with the several Brigades will render thanks to almighty God for all his mercies, particularly for his over ruling the wrath of man to his own glory, and causing the rage of war to cease amongst the nations. . . ." Cf. George Washington, "To the Learned Professions of Philadelphia," December 13, 1783: Americans must give "whatever glory may result from our successful struggle to a higher and more efficient Cause." In his address, "To the Mayor Recorder Aldermen and Common Council of the City of Annapolis," December 22, 1783, the general insisted, "I owe it to that supreme being who guides the hearts of

all, who has so signally interposed his aid in every Stage of the Contest and who had graciously been pleased to bestow on me the greatest of Earthly Rewards. . . ."

83. George Washington to the Pennsylvania Grand Lodge Masons, December 27, 1796, George Washington Papers at the Library of Congress, 1741–1799: Series 4, General Correspondence, 1697–1799.

84. George Washington, "Address to Congress on Resigning His Commission," December 23, 1783, in *WGW*, 27: 284.

85. George Washington to John Armstrong, March 11, 1792, in *PGW*, Pres. Ser., 10: 86.

86. George Washington, "Address to Congress on Resigning His Commission," December 23, 1783, in *WGW*, 27: 284.

87. Mark Y. Hanley, *Beyond a Christian Commonwealth: The Protestant Quarrel with the America Republic, 1830–1860* (Chapel Hill: University of North Carolina Press, 1994), 19.

88. George Washington to Dr. James Anderson, July 25, 1798, in *WGW*, 36: 365; George Washington to Thomas Nelson, August 3, 1788, in *WGW*, 30: 34; and George Washington to Jonathan Trumbull, July 18, 1775, in *WGW*, 3: 344, quotations are in that order. See also George Washington to Rev. Bryan Fairfax, March 1, 1778, in *WGW*, 11: 3: "The determinations of Providence are all ways wise; often inscrutable, and though its decrees appear to bear hard upon us at times [it] is nevertheless meant for gracious purposes. . . ." Cf. George Washington to William Pearce, March 25, 1794, in *WGW*, 33: 375.

89. George Washington to John Parke Custis, January 22, 1777, in *PGW*, Rev. War Ser., 8: 123.

90. George Washington to Rev. Bryan Fairfax, March 6, 1793, in *WGW*, 32: 376.

91. George Washington, "To the Magistrates and Military Officers of Schenectady," June 30, 1782, in *WGW*, 24: 390.

92. George Washington, "To the Mayor, Corporation, and Citizens of Alexandria," April 16, 1789, in *WGW*, 30: 287; General Orders, May 2, 1778, in *WGW*, 11: 343; and George Washington to Major General Philip Schuyler, January 27, 1776, in *WGW*, 4: 281, quotations are in that order.

93. George Washington to Jonathan Trumbull, September 6, 1778, in *WGW*, 12: 406. Washington assured Lafayette that "peace and tranquility" would reign in France "under the sanction of a respectable government founded on the broad basis of liberality and the rights of man—It must be so—the great Ruler of events will not permit the happiness of many millions to be destroyed." George Washington to Lafayette, September 10, 1791, in *PGW*, Pres. Ser., 8: 516.

94. George Washington to John Smith, William McGuire, Charles Thurston, Robert White, Jr., and Hugh Holmes, November 28, 1796, in *WGW*, 35: 294.

95. George Washington to Samuel Holden Parsons, April 23, 1777, in *WGW*, 7: 456; and George Washington, "Farewell Orders to the Armies of the United States," November 2, 1783, in *WGW*, 27: 223.

96. George Washington, "To the Ministers, Elders and Deacons of the Reformed Protestant Dutch Church of the Town of Schenectady," June 30, 1782, in *WGW*, 24: 391.

97. George Washington to Annis Boudinot Stockton, August 31, 1788, in *WGW*, 30: 76. Cf. George Washington to Rev. William Gordon, July 8, 1783, in *WGW*, 27: 50; George Washington to Philip Schuyler, May 9, 1789, in *WGW*, 30: 317; George Washington to William Tudor, August 18, 1788, in *Papers of George Washington*, ed. W. W. Abbot and Dorothy Twohig, 6 vols., Confederation Series (hereafter Conf. Ser.) (Charlottesville: University Press of Virginia, 1992–1997), 6: 465–466.

98. George Washington to Jonathan Boucher, August 15, 1798, in *WGW*, 36: 414; George Washington to James McHenry, July 31, 1778, in *WGW*, 30: 30.

99. George Washington to John Robinson, September 1, 1758, in *Papers of George Washington*, ed. W. W. Abbot, 9 vols., Colonial Series (hereafter Col. Ser.) (Charlottesville: University Press of Virginia, 1983–1984), 5: 432–433; and George Washington to David Humphreys, March 23, 1793, in *WGW*, 32: 398, quotations in that order.

100. George Washington to Lafayette, June 10, 1792, in *PGW*, Pres. Ser., 10: 447.

101. George Washington to John Armstrong, March 11, 1792, in *PGW*, Pres. Ser., 10: 86.

102. George Washington, "Eighth Annual Address to Congress," December 7, 1796, in *WGW*, 35: 320.

103. George Washington to Jonathan Williams, March 2, 1795, in *WGW*, 34: 130.

104. George Washington to Jonathan Trumbull, August 18, 1776, in *WGW*, 5: 453. Cf. George Washington, "To the Officers and Soldiers of the Pennsylvania Associators"; George Washington to Samuel Holden Parsons, April 23, 1777, in *WGW*, 7: 456; George Washington to Thomas Nelson, November 8, 1777, in *WGW*, 10: 28; and George Washington, "To the Trustees of the Public School of Germantown," November 6, 1793, in *WGW*, 33: 149.

105. John G. West, Jr., "George Washington and the Religious Impulse," in *Patriot Sage: George Washington and the American Political Tradition*, ed. Greg L. Gregg II and Matthew Spalding (Wilmington, DE: ISI Books, 1999), 271.

106. It should be noted, however, that in his thanksgiving proclamations, John Adams used expressions such as "Redeemer of the World," "the grace of His Holy Spirit," and "The Great Mediator and Redeemer." See his proclamations of days of "solemn humiliation, fasting, and prayer," March 23, 1798 and March 6, 1799 in James D. Richardson, comp., *A Compilation of the Messages of and Papers of the Presidents, 1789–1897*, 10 vols. (New York: Bureau of National Literature and Art, 1901–1906 [1896–1899]), 1: 269–270, 284–286. Boller, *George Washington and Religion*, 64, called my attention to this point.

107. Boller, *George Washington and Religion*, 74–75. While the statesmen of his generation mentioned God and Providence in their letters much more than Jesus, some of them like Benjamin Rush did refer to the "Son of God" and the "Saviour of the World." See L. H. Butterfield, ed., *Letters of Benjamin Rush*, 2 vols. (Princeton, NJ: Princeton University Press, 1951), 1: 7, 10–11, 419. Boller (*George Washington and Religion*, 75) called my attention to this point. For Washington's references to Christ, see George Washington, General Orders, July 9, 1776, in *WGW*, 5: 245; General Orders, May 2, 1778, in *WGW*, 11: 343; "Speech to the Delaware Chiefs," May 12, 1779, in *WGW*, 15: 55; and "Circular to the States," June 8, 1783, in *WGW*, 26: 496.

108. For example, George Washington to David Humphreys, October 10, 1787, in *PGW*, Conf. Ser., 5: 365–366; and George Washington to Mary Butler, January 6, 1792, in *PGW*, Pres. Ser., 9: 386.

109. George Washington to George Augustine Washington, January 27, 1793, in *WGW*, 32: 315–316.

110. Peter R. Henriques, "The Final Struggle between George Washington and the Grim King: Washington's Attitude toward Death and an After Life," in Higginbotham, ed., *George Washington Reconsidered*, 259–262, quotation from 262.

111. George Washington, "To the Presbyterian Minister of Massachusetts and New Hampshire," November 2, 1789, in *PGW*, Pres. Ser., 4: 274.

112. George Washington, "To the Grand Lodge of Pennsylvania," January 3, 1792, in *PGW*, Pres. Ser., 9: 371.

113. Adams declared, "Let us then wish for Immortality at all hazards and trust the Ruler with his Skies." Lester Cappon, ed., *The Adams-Jefferson Letters*, 2 vols. (Chapel Hill: University of North Carolina Press, 1959), 2: 486. Franklin told Ezra Stiles he believed that the "soul of man is immortal, and will be treated with Justice in another Life respecting its Conduct in this." Jefferson expected after dying "to ascend in essence to an ecstatic meeting with the friends we have loved and lost." Paine declared, "I hope for happiness beyond this life." See Albert Henry Smyth, ed., *The Writings of Benjamin Franklin*, 10 vols. (New York: Macmillan, 1907), 10: 84; Albert Ellery Bergh, ed., *The Writings of Thomas Jefferson*, 20 vols. (Washington, DC: Thomas Jefferson Memorial Association of the United States, 1904–1905), 17: v; and Daniel Edwin Wheeler, ed., *Life and Writings of Thomas Paine*, 10 vols. (New York: V. Parke, 1908), 6: 2. Martha Washington expected to be reunited with her husband in heaven. See Martha Washington to Jonathan Trumbull, January 15, 1800, in *Worthy Partner: The Papers of Martha Washington*, ed. Joseph E. Fields (Westport, CT: Greenwood Press, 1994), 339.

114. George Washington to Burgess Ball, September 22, 1799, in *WGW*, 37: 372.

115. Henriques, "The Final Struggle," 257, 259. The quotation is from Daniel Blake Smith, *Inside the Great House: Planter Family Life in*

Eighteenth-Century Chesapeake Society (Ithaca, NY: Cornell University Press, 1980), 265.

116. George Washington to George Augustine Washington, January 27, 1793, in *WGW*, 32: 315–316; George Washington to Bryan Fairfax, March 6, 1793, in *WGW*, 32: 376, quotations in that order.
117. Flexner, *Washington: The Indispensable Man*, 26, 36.
118. George Washington to Richard Washington, October 20, 1761, in *PGW*, Col. Ser., 7: 80.
119. See David L. Holmes, ed., *A Nation Mourns: Bishop James Madison's Memorial Eulogy on the Death of George Washington* (Mount Vernon, VA: Mount Vernon's Ladies' Association, 1999).
120. Tobias Lear, "Journal Account," Mount Vernon Ladies' Association. Lear's original journal and "diary" account are available at http//www.virginia.edu/gwpapers/exhibits/mourning/leatr.html. For a discussion of the accuracy of his account, see Henriques, "The Final Struggle," 266.
121. Weems, *The Life of George Washington*, 168. Cf. Ramsay, *The Life of George Washington: Commander in Chief of the Armies of the United States . . .* , 319; and Jared Sparks, *Life of Washington* (Boston: Ferdinand Andrews, 1839), 525.
122. Albanese, *Sons of the Fathers*, 180. For example, Thomas Condie, *Biographical Memoirs of Gen. George Washington, First President of the United States . . .* (Lexington, KY: Downing & Phillips, 1815), 265–266; and Caroline M. Kirkland, *Memoirs of Washington*, 457.
123. Schwartz, *George Washington: The Making of an American Symbol*, 184–185; Henriques, "The Final Struggle," 263 (quotation). See also Douglass Adair, *Fame and the Founding Fathers: Essays*, ed. Trevor Colbourn (Indianapolis: Liberty Fund, 1998); George Washington to Lafayette, May 28, 1788 and David Humphreys to George Washington, July 17, 1785, in *PGW*, Conf. Ser., 6: 297–298 and 3: 131; George Washington to James Tilghman, June 5, 1786, in *PGW*, Conf. Ser., 4: 96; and George Washington to Sarah Cary Fairfax, September 25, 1758, *PGW*, Col. Ser., 6: 42.
124. George Washington to Bryan Lord Fairfax, January 20, 1799, in *WGW*, 37: 94–95.
125. George Washington, "To the General Assembly of the PCUSA," 2: 420.
126. Gregg Frazer, "The Political Theology of the American Founding," paper presented at the Symposium on Religion and Politics, Calvin College, May 1, 2004, 1–2, quotation from 1.
127. See Kerry S. Walters, *The American Deists* (Lawrence: University Press of Kansas, 1992), 26–33, 41; E. Graham Waring, ed., *Deism and Natural Religion: A Source Book* (New York: Frederick Ungar, 1967), x; Peter Gay, comp., *Deism: An Anthology* (Princeton, NJ: D. Van Nostrand Co., 1968), 11, 42, 167–168, 176; and Kerry S. Walters, *Elihu Palmer's "Principles of Nature"* (Wolfeboro, NH: Longwood Academic, 1990), 35, 114–115, 231–232.

128. Boller, *George Washington and Religion*, 89–91. As noted above, however, Washington undoubtedly publicly affirmed these cardinal Christian tenets by reciting the Apostles' and Nicene creeds in Anglican/Episcopal church services.
129. Gaustad, *Faith of Our Fathers*, 77–78.
130. Richard Norton Smith, *Patriarch: George Washington and the New American Nation* (New York: Houghton Mifflin, 1993), 148.
131. George Washington to William Gordon, May 13, 1776, in *PGW*, Rev. War Ser., 4: 286.

Chapter Two

Thomas Jefferson and the Myth of Separation

Thomas E. Buckley, S.J.

People interested in a popular or even academic discussion of religion and the presidency might consider Thomas Jefferson an easy subject. Everyone knows what he thought. In American public life, separation of church and state is a consecrated phase normally associated with the third president. Its modern usage dates from the *Everson* decision that extended the Establishment Clause of the First Amendment to all the states. In that 1947 case, the U.S. Supreme Court split 5–4 in upholding a New Jersey law that reimbursed parents for the cost of transporting their children to parochial schools.[1] Writing for the majority, Justice Hugo Black presented a strict separationist interpretation of the Establishment Clause, but argued that the law was acceptable on the grounds of what would later be called the "child benefit theory." The dissenting justices saw the New Jersey practice as an unconstitutional support for religion. What united the Court, however, was a common interpretation of the historical background of the Establishment Clause; and both sides relied principally upon selected writings of Thomas Jefferson and James Madison and a history of the post-Revolutionary struggle for religious freedom in Virginia, which preceded the First Amendment by several years.[2]

According to Black's perspective in *Everson*, religious liberty advanced steadily toward the strict separation of religion from government with Virginia providing "able leadership for the movement" toward the First Amendment. Virginians were convinced that freedom of religion "could be achieved best" when the state had no authority "to tax, to support, or otherwise to assist any or all religions, or to interfere with the beliefs of any religious individual or group."[3] The state endorsed this policy, Black asserted, by rejecting a proposal for a general assessment for religion after Madison wrote his famous "Memorial and Remonstrance" opposing such a tax, and then by enacting Jefferson's statute for religious freedom in 1786. Forbidding any sort of compulsion in matters of religion, this law offered the most iron clad guarantee of religious liberty in the new United States and became the principal antecedent of the First Amendment a few years later. Black also emphasized Jefferson's letter in 1802 to a group of Baptists in Danbury, Connecticut, in which the president opined that the Establishment Clause was intended to erect "a wall of separation between church and state."

Thus *Everson* endorsed the view that the First Amendment furnished "the same protection against governmental intrusion on religious liberty as the Virginia statute" and embraced Jefferson's "wall of separation" as the authoritative interpretation of the prohibition of an establishment of religion. "The First Amendment has erected a wall between church and state," Black concluded. "That wall must be kept high and impregnable." Writing for the minority, Justice Wiley Rutledge thought that the Court's majority had not made the wall high enough, but he embraced Black's historical approach. "No provision of the Constitution," he wrote, "is more closely tied to or given content by its generating history than the religion clauses of the First Amendment."[4] An elaborate and, in some details, more accurate account of the Virginia struggles over religious freedom forms the centerpiece of his argument against the New Jersey law.

Thus the Supreme Court stamped its judicial imprimatur upon a particular interpretation of America's past. According to this judicial perspective, Jefferson believed in a church-state separation that was absolute, total, and complete. The Court canonized the phrase he used in his letter to the Danbury Baptists as the ruling interpretation of the First Amendment's Establishment Clause, and popular thought and much scholarly opinion in courtroom and classroom embraced strict separation as the received doctrine on church-state relations.

Yet, in recent years, historians and political scientists have steadily chipped away at this construal of Jefferson's understanding of the place of religion in the Republic.[5] Supreme Court justices also began to take another look. In a 1984 case involving a Christmas display in a public park, Chief Justice Warren Burger found Jefferson's "wall of separation" metaphor to be "useful" but not entirely "accurate" in describing the church-state relationship.[6] The next year in a vigorous dissent from a school prayer decision, Justice William Rehnquist, who would soon succeed Burger, pushed historical revisionism even further when he insisted, "It is impossible to base sound constitutional doctrine upon a mistaken understanding of constitutional history. . . . The 'wall of separation between church and state' is a metaphor based on bad history, a metaphor which has proved useless as a guide to judging.

It should be frankly and explicitly abandoned."[7] Most recently, Philip Hamburger, in a study entitled *Separation of Church and State*, has pointed out that Jefferson's "wall" metaphor only came into play in the second half of the nineteenth century.[8] What did Jefferson mean? What did he intend? To understand this extraordinarily complex man and how he understood the relationship between religion and the republic, we need to turn to the period when he personally was most responsible for leading that republic: his presidency.

This chapter examines the place of religion in his presidency in terms of two distinct aspects. First, his religiously oriented rhetoric—his public speeches, writing, and behavior during his presidency. In this respect, Jefferson's famous letter to the Danbury Baptist Association is but a single item among many to be considered. Whether intentional or not, Jefferson can be held more responsible for developing an American civil religion than any of his contemporaries. Second is his presidential policies and directives that lent direct government support to religion. Most notable was his use of religious missions for the purpose of "civilizing" the Native American population. Here too his contribution has important modern ramifications. He helped to establish a precedent for what today is called the faith-based initiative.

The Campaign of 1800

To discuss these elements adequately, we need the larger context provided by the bitter election campaign of 1800 that proceeded Jefferson's first term in office. That election, the first to elevate religion to a major issue nationally, focused on moral values and particularly on Jefferson's fitness to be president.[9] In the process, it afforded the intensely sensitive Virginian with the most painful and embarrassing moments of his political career. For the rest of his life Jefferson profoundly resented the extraordinary efforts that certain ministers in the New England and Mid-Atlantic States had made to prevent his election. These Federalist supporters of John Adams seized upon Jefferson's published work, especially his *Statute of Religious Freedom* and his *Notes on the State of Virginia* to denounce him as an infidel determined to destroy the religious pillars of society. Their abusive treatment of him in pulpit and press during the summer and fall preceding the canvass of 1800 determined the place religion would occupy in his presidency.

From at least 1776 the Virginian had been an outspoken proponent of religious freedom, though often enough what he proposed as liberty of conscience, conservative opponents had labeled as license. Shortly after independence was declared, the new commonwealth of Virginia had appointed Jefferson to a committee to prepare a complete revision of the colonial laws. In that capacity, he had composed a statute "for establishing religious freedom." In place of "the church established by law" his proposed law would establish religious freedom. When first presented to the state legislature in 1779, the lawmakers postponed this radical measure. But in January 1786 after an extraordinarily heated petition campaign across the state, the General Assembly approved Jefferson's proposal. Following an extraordinary preamble, which proclaimed that conscience rights were sacred and inviolable, the enacting clause offered the most sweeping guarantee of complete religious liberty made by any state at that time.[10] But when its author became a candidate for president, his political enemies assailed this measure as the first step in a program to abolish "the Christian religion."[11] Federalist Congressman William Loughton Smith of South Carolina anticipated many of their arguments in a 1796 pamphlet entitled *The Pretensions of Thomas Jefferson to the Presidency Examined*.[12] In 1800 the clergy waded into the fray. In a lengthy pamphlet serialized in various Federalist newspapers, William Linn, the pastor of Philadelphia's First Presbyterian Church, argued that Jefferson wanted "a government where the people have *no religious opinions and forms of worship*" (emphasis is in the original). His election would "destroy religion, introduce immorality, and loosen all the bonds of society."[13] In a Sunday sermon at nearby Christ Church, Episcopal minister James Abercrombie invited other ministers "to aid me in support of our great and common cause." It would be a tragedy if "a Christian community" like the United States, should "*voluntarily . . .* place at their head, as their *ruler* and *guide*, an acknowledged *unbeliever*, . . . an *enemy* to their faith."[14]

Abercromie did not simply refer to the Statute. Instead, Jefferson's remarks on religion in his *Notes on Virginia*, the only book he ever wrote, came back to haunt him. Composed while he was United States minister to France, after he had written the religious liberty statute but before the legislature approved it, his impassioned plea for its passage included the memorable lines: "It does me no injury for my neighbour to say there are twenty gods, or no god. It neither picks my pocket nor breaks my leg."[15] For such apparent indifference toward religion, critics called him an atheist and an "infidel" whose public policy would destroy "all *religion, order, and civil government*."[16] From their perspective, his years in France and his association with Voltaire and D'Alembert had fatally contaminated the Virginian.

He had not been inside a church for fourteen years, claimed Boston's *Columbiad Centinel*. What had complete religious freedom and the end of public support for religion done to the Old Dominion? The newspaper pointed to the result: "cock-fighting, horse-racing, gaming, debauchery, and profanity."[17] Almost gleefully, the author of this series cited Bishop James Madison's fulminations against "immorality and vice" as evidence of the depths to which Jefferson's statute had dragged the state.[18]

Jefferson's friends and political allies fought back, of course. DeWitt Clinton and Samuel Knox each published a point-by-point rebuttal.[19] One Republican writer referred to the clergy as "political pimps" who were "shamefully influencing elections."[20] And his good friend Benjamin Rush penned a consoling letter to Jefferson in early October agreeing with his desire "to keep religion and government independent of each other." "Were it possible," Rush added, "for St. Paul to rise from his grave at the present juncture, he would say to the Clergy who are now so active in settling the political affairs of the world, 'Cease from your political labors your kingdom is not of *this* world.' "[21] But the charge of "atheism," leveled against him by Samuel Chase, an Associate Justice of the Supreme Court and rabid Federalist, stung the notoriously thin-skinned Jefferson.[22] The sage of Monticello never quite got over that election.

Jefferson's Presidential Rhetoric

He would have his revenge on Chase and the New England clergy, but during his years in office he would also do everything possible to prove his critics wrong. Lacing his speeches and public writings with religious rhetoric, the new president strove to conciliate a nation seriously divided by the election. He sought common ground. His inaugural address made religious pluralism in the United States the paradigm for political pluralism. Just as Americans had "banished . . . religious intolerance" so also they must eliminate "a political intolerance as despotic, as wicked, and capable of as bitter and bloody persecutions." In his statute, Jefferson had defined religion as "opinion" which could not be coerced without violating a person's natural rights. Now in his address he referred to the recent political campaign as a "contest of opinion." And he pointed out that "every difference of opinion is not a difference of principle. We are called by different names brethren of the same principle. We are all Republicans, we are all Federalists." Divergent theologies, church polities, and religious perspectives were essentially unimportant. The United States possessed "a benign religion, professed, indeed, and practiced in various forms, yet all of them inculcating honesty, truth, temperance, gratitude, and the love of man; acknowledging and adoring an overruling Providence, which by all its dispensations proves that it delights in the happiness of man here and his greater happiness hereafter." Denominational differences, whether religious or political were essentially unimportant. The new president ended with an appeal to "that Infinite power which rules the destinies of the universe [to] lead our councils to what is best, and given them a favorable issue for your peace and prosperity."[23] That address turned the tide. As Benjamin Rush reported to an English friend, Jefferson had decisively refuted the allegation that he was "unfriendly to religion."[24]

Religious language worked in the public forum, and the third president returned to it repeatedly as an instrument to bind the nation together. Though his enemies continued to characterize his *Notes on Virginia* as "an instrument of infidelity," Jefferson's religious rhetoric effectively blunted their attack.[25] Was he simply being disingenuous? Consider his previous work. A belief in a providential God who is personally concerned for his creation permeates the documents he crafted for the colonies in revolt. "The god who gave us life, gave us liberty at the same time," he wrote in his *Summary View of the Rights of British America* two years before the Revolution. Both his draft for the Declaration of the Causes and Necessity for Taking up Arms and, more importantly, his Declaration of Independence affirms a faith in a Creator who personally guides and judges his creation.[26] These public statements find reinforcement in a section of his *Notes on Virginia* his clerical critics chose to ignore. Speaking of the evil of slavery, Jefferson commented, "And can the liberties of a nation be thought secure when we have removed their only firm basis, a conviction in the minds of the people that these liberties are of the gift of God? That they are not to be violated but with His wrath? Indeed I tremble for my country when I reflect that God is just." Jefferson took God seriously.[27]

Moreover, Jefferson's views on church and state were far more complex than some historians and judges have recognized. He was, after all, the author of the bill punishing "Sabbath breakers" as well as three other measures pertaining to church and religion, which had all been drafted at the same time as his religious freedom proposal. These included laws to guarantee the property of the Episcopal Church in Virginia, to appoint "Days of Public Fasting and Thanksgiving," and to annul marriages "prohibited by the Levitical law." As legal historian Daniel Dreisbach has cogently argued, taken together these measures substantially refine the Jeffersonian model of church-state relations. In particular, the measures to protect Sabbath observance and provide days of state-sponsored prayer show Jefferson endorsing limited government activity in support of religion.[28]

Those who would paint Jefferson as a strict separationist most often cite his Danbury letter. Early in 1802 Jefferson drafted his famous "wall of separation" letter to the Danbury Baptist Association in Connecticut. Though ostensibly a private document, he knew it would be quickly published in the press. The Baptists had written to congratulate him on his election and applaud his opposition to "the alliance between Church, and State, under the authority of the Constitution." Such an alliance was precisely what they objected to in Connecticut. Jefferson responded, as he explained to his Attorney General Levi Lincoln of Massachusetts with one eye cocked on New England's Federalist clergy, who had fought his election and still enjoyed a system of state tax support. He knew his Danbury letter would offend them, but he told Lincoln, "[T]he advocate of religious freedom is to expect neither peace nor forgiveness from them."[29] On New Year's Day, he had written to his son-in-law John Wayles Eppes that he hoped to win back "all the New England states . . . to their antiant [*sic*] principles, always excepting the real Monarchists and the Priests, who never can lose sight of the natural alliance between the crown & mitre."[30]

Jefferson had originally planned to use the Danbury letter to state his reason for not following the example of George Washington and John Adams in issuing proclamations of prayer and fasting. He postponed that explanation, however, until his second inaugural address.[31] His position on the president's proper responsibilities was integrally related to his conviction that the federal government's powers were strictly limited. Writing to Samuel Miller, a Presbyterian minister at Princeton, the president explained his reasoning more fully in 1808. What was forbidden to the "general government" he wrote, "must rest with the states." His predecessors had assumed that what was appropriate for the chief magistrate in a state was suitable for the president of the United States as well. Jefferson read the Constitution more strictly. It gave him only "civil powers," and he had "no authority to direct the religious exercises of his constituents."[32] He recognized the nation's dependence upon God and invited his fellow citizens to prayer. He did not command it.

Nor did Jefferson erase religion from public discourse. Far from it. While expressing a hope that as president he could "strengthen . . . religious freedom," Jefferson asserted that he did not desire a "government without religion." That change, he confided to a political ally, was a "lie" fostered by his enemies.[33] His annual messages to Congress repeatedly encouraged the belief the a providential God was watching over the country, keeping it out of European wars and blessing it with prosperity.[34] In his second inaugural address he returned again to a biblical event to describe the nation's relationship with God. "I shall need, too," he said,

> the favor of that Being in whose hands we are, who led our fathers, as Israel of old, from their native land; and planted them in a country flowing with all the necessaries and comforts of life: who has covered our infancy with his providence and our riper years with his wisdom and power, and to whose goodness I ask you to join in supplication with me."[35]

He had drawn upon the same biblical typology almost 30 years earlier in his proposal for the seal of the United States. As John Adams had explained to his wife in 1776, Jefferson wanted to place on one side of the seal "the Children of Israel in the Wilderness, led by a Cloud by day, and a Pillar of Fire by night."[36] He thought in terms designed to set the American experiment apart in the minds and hearts of his fellow citizens. In his rhetoric, the Exodus event in and through which God had formed his chosen people prefigured the formation of the American nation. The implications were obvious. Americans knew their Bible history. George Washington and John Adams in their inaugural addresses had invoked God's Providence, but neither of them identified America as a new type of Israel, or Americans as a people specially chosen. In this respect, Jefferson played a definitive role in the formulation of an American civil religion. What he personally believed or thought is beside the point. He understood the necessity of binding a disparate nation together. As the country's chief executive in Washington, he further developed ideas and themes present in his previous careers in Williamsburg, Richmond, and Philadelphia. Taken together his religious perspective, as publicly expressed, recognized God's providential design at work in the history of the United States, committed the new nation to religious freedom, and fostered a sense that the country had been specially chosen by God.

Public Policy

While Jefferson spoke publicly about the benefits of religion to his fellow citizens, he also gave them an example. As James Hutson has pointed out, the sage of Monticello was the master of symbolic gestures. During his presidency, he regularly attended church services in the chamber of the House of Representatives. Though he had first joined the Episcopal congregation in the District of Colombia, the Capital was not only more convenient, it was also a more public venue in which to appear and the services led by a variety of ministers were nondenominational in character. By his regular presence at public worship, Jefferson made it clear that his "wall of separation" did not keep him out of church.

Nor did it inhibit the president from facilitating the free exercise of religion for people in the District of Columbia. While the legislative branch provided the religious setting, the executive branch supplied the Marine Band for the instrumental music to accompany the singing. Moreover, Jefferson also permitted particular religious groups such as the Baptists, Presbyterians, and Episcopalians to worship in government buildings. Individual congregations held communion services in the Treasury building and the offices of the War Department. As Hutson concludes, "on Sundays in Washington during Thomas Jefferson's presidency, the state became the church."[37]

Moreover, his administration openly fostered Christianity among the Native Americans. In a message to the chiefs of various Indians tribes, Jefferson urged them to accept "the will of the Great Spirit to which we must all submit."[38] Those who look for historic justification for the faith-based initiative can—for better or worse—look back to Jefferson's record. He openly supported what had been the policy of his Federalist predecessors, Washington and Adams, in helping to fund Christian missionaries, Protestant and Catholic, in their efforts to convert (and thereby civilize) the Native American population. Despite Secretary of State Madison's concern that the president might be violating "the exemption of Religion from civil power," Jefferson endorsed a treaty with the Kaskaskia Indians that provided $300 to build a church and $100 annually for 7 years to maintain a Catholic priest "to perform . . . the duties of his office" as well as serve as school teacher. With his approval, the federal government encouraged a Presbyterian minister's work among the Cherokees by appropriating several hundred dollars to found what was designed as a Christian school to teach religion along with other subjects.[39]

Religious freedom, much more than separation, was Jefferson's guiding principle. In this respect, his "wall of separation" remarks to the Danbury Baptist Association were out of character with the official face that he maintained as president not only toward religion but also toward the churches. The phrase can only be understood in light of its larger context: the bitter residue left by the politicization of Federalist clergy during the campaign of 1800 and his belief that religion should be free from the coercion of state taxation employed in Connecticut and Massachusetts. Elevating the "wall of separation" metaphor into a definite statement of Jeffersonian belief about the relationship between church and state served the purpose of others after him much more than it reflected his settled opinion. Indeed, it created a myth about Jefferson's views of the relationship between religion and government that too many Americans have uncritically accepted.

Notes

1. *Everson v. Board of Education of the Township of Ewing*, 330 U.S. 3 (1947). Before *Everson*, the Establishment Clause only applied to the federal government, but in 1947 the Supreme Court used the Fourteenth Amendment to nationalize the Establishment. Clause as it had done for the Free Exercise Clause in 1940.
2. In taking this path, the Court broke no new ground. In an 1878 case involving polygamy among the Mormons in Utah Territory, Chief Justice Morrison Waite had emphasized Virginia's experience and Madison's and Jefferson's views as normative for interpreting the First Amendment (*Reynolds v. United States*, 98 U.S. 164 [1878]).
3. *Everson*, 330 U.S. at 11. For the context of the Everson case, Black's personal background, and his role in the decision, see Philip Hamburger, *Separation of Church and State* (Cambridge, MA, 2002), 422–434, 454–478.
4. *Everson*, 330 U.S. at 13, 18, and 33.
5. Among the multiple studies that have contributed to this development, see especially Daniel L. Dreisbach, *Thomas Jefferson and the Wall of Separation between Church and State* (New York, 2002).
6. *Lynch v. Donnelly*, 465 U.S. 668 (1984) at 1359.
7. *Wallace v. Jaffree*, 472 U.S. 38 (1985) at 107. For an evaluation of the significance of Rehnquist's opinions, see Derek Davis, *Original Intent: Chief Justice Rehnquist and the Course of American Church/State Relations* (Buffalo, NY, 1991).
8. Hamburger, *Separation of Church and State*, 259–260.
9. Studies of this campaign include Charles F. O'Brien, "The Religious Issue in the Election of 1800," *Essex Institute Historical Collections*, 107 (1971): 82–93; and Constance Bartlett Schulz, "Of Bigotry in Politics and Religion: Jefferson's Religion, the Federalist Press, and the Syllabus," *Virginia Magazine of History and Biography*, 91 (1983): 73–91.
10. Thomas E. Buckley, S.J., *Church and State in Revolutionary Virginia, 1776–1787* (Charlottesville, VA, 1977).
11. "Caius," in the *Federal Gazette and Baltimore Daily Advertiser*, August 4, 1800. The next step, according to "Caius" (*Federal Gazette and*

Baltimore Daily Advertiser, August 12, 1800) was the 1799 Virginia law revoking previous assemblies' guarantees of the Protestant Episcopal Church's right to its property.

12. William Loughton Smith, *The pretensions of Thomas Jefferson to the presidency examined: And the charges against John Adams refuted: Addressed to the citizens of America in general, and particularly to the electors of the president* (United States, 1796), 36–40.

13. "Serious Considerations on the Election of a President," *The Connecticut Courant* [Hartford], September 8, 1800.

14. Emphasis is in the original. *Gazette of the United States and Daily Advertiser* [Philadelphia], August 30, 1800.

15. Thomas Jefferson, *Notes on the State of Virginia*, ed. William Peden (Chapel Hill, NC, 1955), 159.

16. Emphasis is in the original. "The Jeffersoniad, No. *III*," *Columbiad Centinel* [Boston], July 5, 1800.

17. "The Jeffersoniad, No. *IV*," *Columbiad Centinel* [Boston], July 9, 1800.

18. "The Jeffersoniad, No. *XI*," *Columbiad Centinel* [Boston], August 20, 1800. Bishop Madison of Virginia was a cousin of the other James Madison and a good friend of Jefferson's.

19. [DeWitt Clinton], *A vindication of Thomas Jefferson; against the charges contained in a pamphlet entitled, "Serious considerations etc"* (New York, 1800); and [Samuel Knox], *A vindication of the religion of Mr. Jefferson . . . By a friend to real religion* (Baltimore, 1800).

20. *American Mercury* [Hartford], October 2, 1800.

21. Emphasis is in the original. Benjamin Rush to Thomas Jefferson, October 6, 1800, Thomas Jefferson Papers, series 1, reel 22 (microfilm), Library of Congress, Washington, DC.

22. Thomas Jefferson to James Monroe, May 26, 1800, abstract of a letter, transcript, Thomas Jefferson Papers, series 3, reel 4 (microfilm), University of Virginia, Charlottesville, Virginia. As president in 1804 Jefferson encouraged Chase's impeachment, which failed in the Senate.

23. Noble E. Cunningham, Jr., *The Inaugural Addresses of President Thomas Jefferson, 1801 and 1805* (Columbia, MO, 2001), 4, 5, 6.

24. Benjamin Rush to Granville Sharp, March 31, 1801, in John A. Woods, ed., "The Correspondence of Benjamin Rush and Granville Sharp 1773–1809," *Journal of American Studies*, 1 (1967): 34.

25. C[lement] C[larke] Moore, *Observations upon certain passages in Mr. Jefferson's Notes on Virginia, which appear to have a tendency to subvert religion, and establish a false philosophy* (New York, 1804), 29.

26. Julian P. Boyd, ed., *The Papers of Thomas Jefferson* (Princeton, NJ, 1960–), 1: 135. For an elaboration of this theme, see Thomas E. Buckley, S.J., "The Political Theology of Thomas Jefferson," in *The Virginia Statute for Religious Freedom: Its Evolution and Consequences in American History*, ed. Merrill D. Peterson and Robert C. Vaughan (Cambridge and New York, 1988), 75–109.

27. Jefferson, *Notes on the State of Virginia*, 163.

28. Boyd, ed., *Jefferson's Papers*, 2: 553–558; Daniel L. Dreisbach, "A New Perspective on Jefferson's Views on Church-State Relations: The Virginia Statute for Establishing Religious Freedom in its Legislative Context," *American Journal of Legal History*, 35 (1991): 172–202.

29. Paul Leicester Ford, ed., *The Works of Thomas Jefferson* (New York, 1904–1905), 8: 129. See also Daniel L. Dreisbach, " 'Sowing Useful Truths and Principles': The Danbury Baptists, Thomas Jefferson, and the 'Wall of Separation,' " *Journal of Church and State*, 39 (1997): 455–501.

30. Thomas Jefferson to J[ohn] W[ayles] Eppes, January 1, 1802, Thomas Jefferson Papers, series 3, reel 5 (microfilm), University of Virginia, Charlottesville, Virginia.

31. Cunningham, *Inaugural Addresses of President Thomas Jefferson*, 77.

32. Ford, ed., *Works of Jefferson*, 9: 175, 176.

33. Thomas Jefferson to John Bacon, April 30, 1802; and Jefferson to DeWitt Clinton, May 27, 1807, in Ford, ed., *Works of Jefferson*, 8: 229; 9: 63.

34. Thomas Jefferson, "First Annual Message," December 8, 1801; "Second Annual Message," December 15, 1802; "Third Annual Message," October 17, 1803; "Fifth Annual Message," December 8, 1805; and "Eight Annual Message," November 8, 1808, in *A Compilation of the Messages and Papers of the Presidents* (New York, 1897), 1: 314, 330, 349, 371, 444.

35. Cunningham, *Inaugural Addresses of President Thomas Jefferson*, 79.

36. John Adams to Abigail Adams, August 14, 1776, in *Adams Family Correspondence*, ed. L. H. Butterfield (Cambridge, MA, 1963), 2: 96.

37. James H. Hutson, *Religion and the Founding of the American Republic* (Washington, DC: Library of Congress, 1998), 84–96, quote on 91. Hutson notes that Jefferson contributed liberally to the construction of at least ten churches and chapels of various denominations in the District of Columbia, Georgetown, and Alexandria (*Religion and the Founding of the American Republic*, 85, 94–96).

38. Thomas Jefferson to Chiefs of Indian Tribes, April 11, 1806, transcript, Thomas Jefferson Papers, series 3, reel 4 (microfilm), University of Virginia, Charlottesville, Virginia.

39. [Madison to Jefferson], in Message to Congress of 17 October 1803, Thomas Jefferson Papers, series 1, reel 29 (microfilm), Library of Congress; U.S. Government, *A Compilation of All the Treaties between the United States Government and the Indian Tribes Now in Force as Laws* (Washington, DC, 1873), 425; and Dorothy C. Bass, "Gideon Blackburn's Mission to the Cherokees: Christianization and Civilization," *Journal of Presbyterian History* (1974): 203–226. For very different perspectives on Jefferson, the missionaries, and the Indians, see William G. McLoughlin, *Cherokees and Missionaries, 1789–1839* (New Haven: Yale University Press, 1984); and Anthony F. C. Wallace, *Jefferson and the Indians: The Tragic Fate of the First Americans* (Cambridge, MA, 1999).

Chapter Three

Religion in the Life, Thought, and Presidency of James Madison

Vincent Phillip Muñoz

Was James Madison a Christian? Was his political thought grounded upon traditional religious faith? Did he seek—to borrow a phrase from Thomas Jefferson—to erect "a wall of separation" between church and state? This chapter addresses these questions though a close examination of some of Madison's writings and presidential actions. It begins with a discussion of the role of religion in Madison's life and thought. It then proceeds to examine Madison's view of the proper role of religion in American public life.

Religion in Madison's Life and Thought

Madison's Religious Beliefs

The nature of James Madison's religious beliefs has long confounded scholars. Some find his writings to reflect God-fearing Christianity. His major nineteenth-century biographer William C. Rives, for example, claims that on "Christian doctrinal points" Madison is a model of "orthodoxy and persuasion."[1] More recently, Garrett Ward Sheldon has written that Madison "operated from a Christian perspective and commitment."[2] The prolific author Michael Novak asserts that "there can be no doubt that his [Madison's] world view is no other than Christian. . . . [W]hile it does not affirm everything that ortho-dox Christian faith affirms, Madison's vision is sufficiently impreg-nated with Christian faith to be not only unconvincing, but *unintelligible* without it."[3]

Other scholars disagree. Irving Brant, Madison's major twentieth-century biographer, concludes that Madison adopted "a quiet unorthodoxy differing more in manner than in matter from the housetop-shouted heretical deism of Jefferson."[4] John West, Jr., finds it decisive that "Madison in his later years expressed very little personal interest in religion."[5] "Given Madison's adult indifference to religion," West continues, "he, more than any other major Founder, was the forerunner of the modern secularist."[6]

Some scholars try to split the difference. According to Lance Banning, Madison's "mature [religious] opinions are a matter for conjecture."[7] Madison biographer Ralph Ketcham suggests, "It seems clear he [Madison] neither embraced fervently nor rejected utterly the Christian base of his education. He accepted its tenets generally and formed his outlook on life within its world view."[8]

The disagreement over Madison's personal faith results, in part, from the fact that after 1776 Madison wrote almost nothing about his religious convictions—in the words of William Lee Miller, "he kept his mouth shut" about his religious beliefs.[9] All we know for certain are basic facts pertaining to Madison's religious life. His father was a vestryman in the established Anglican Church; his mother was a devout Anglican. Madison's parents had him baptized in the Church of England. He received much of his primary education from his paternal grandmother, who was remembered as a pious Christian woman and an intellectual.[10] At age 12, Madison was sent to a boarding school run by the Scottish minister Rev. Donald Robertson. After four years, he returned home and continued his education under Rev. Thomas Martin, who was also a Scotsman. Madison then attended Princeton College, passing examinations in English, Latin, Greek, and New Testament Bible. At Princeton, where according to Mark Noll "religious considerations were always central to the working out of republican theory,"[11] Madison was mentored by Rev. Dr. John Witherspoon, an archetypical Scots Presbyterian Calvinist.[12] After finishing his college requirements in two years, Madison completed six months of graduate studies, which included work in Hebrew and theology. He and Dolly were married by an Episcopal priest in an Episcopalian ceremony. Madison preferred Episcopalian services his entire life, yet he never entered full communion or identified himself as an Episcopalian.[13] According to Librarian of Congress James Hutson, Madison was not conscientious about attending church services while away from home serving in Congress in the 1780s and 1790s, but as president, he followed Jefferson's practice of worshipping at a local congregation and in the hall at the House of Representatives.[14] At the end of his life, Madison was buried according to the Book of Common Prayer.[15]

Speculation about Madison's faith—and it is important to emphasize that all we can do is speculate—necessarily must center on the few revealing personal statements Madison made. His youthful correspondence with his good friend and Princeton classmate William Bradford suggests that the young Madison believed in an afterlife and was favorably disposed toward religious faith. "Yet however nice and cautious we may be in detecting the follies of mankind and frame our Oeconomy [*sic*] according to the precepts of Wisdom and Religion," Madison wrote in late 1772,

> I fancy there will commonly remain with us some latent expectation of obtaining more than ordinary Happiness and prosperity till we feel the convincing argument of actual disappointment. Tho [*sic*] I will not determine whether we shall be much the worse for it if we do not allow it to intercept our views towards a future State, because strong desires and great Hopes instigate us to arduous enterprises fortitude and perseverance. Nevertheless a watchful eye must be kept on ourselves lest while we are building ideal monuments of Renown and Bliss here we neglect to have our names enrolled in the annals of Heaven.[16]

Upon learning that his friend had chosen not to enter religious ministry, Madison composed the following seemingly faithful response:

> I cannot however suppress this much of my advice on that head that you would always keep the Ministry obliquely in View whatever your profession be. This will lead you to cultivate an acquaintance occasionally with the most sublime of all Sciences and will qualify you for a change of public character if you should hereafter desire it. I have sometimes thought there could be no stronger testimony in favor of Religion or against temporal Enjoyments even the most rational and manly than for men who occupy the most honorable and gainful departments and are rising in reputation and wealth, publicly to declare their unsatisfactoriness by becoming fervent Advocates in the cause of Christ, & I wish you may give in your Evidence in this way. Such instances have seldom occurred, therefore they would be more striking and would be instead of a "Cloud of Witnesses."[17]

Such statements disappear from Madison's writings after 1776. Whether he maintained his belief in an afterlife beyond his youth he does not say (although, as we shall discuss below, the argument of his famous "Memorial and Remonstrance" written in 1785 depends on it).

Brief passages from private letters written toward the end of Madison's life seem to reveal a more detached, philosophical disposition that appears to neither affirm nor deny the existence of God or an afterlife. Of these letters, perhaps the most revealing is Madison's response to Frederick Beasley, dated November 20, 1825. Beasley, a professor of moral philosophy at the University of Pennsylvania, had written to Madison requesting his opinion on a pamphlet titled *Vindication of the Argument a prior in Proof of the Being and Attributes of God, from the Objection of D^r. Waterland.* Madison's response included the following:

> DEAR SIR I have duly rec^d the copy of your little tract on the proofs of the Being & Attributes of God. To do full justice to it, would require not only a more critical attention than I have been able to bestow on it, but a resort to the celebrated work of Dr. Clarke, which I read fifty years ago only, and to that of D^r. Waterland also which I never read. . . .
>
> The finiteness of the human understanding betrays itself on all subjects, but more especially when it contemplates such as involves infinity. What may safely be said seems to be, that the infinity of time & space forces itself on our conception, a limitation of either being inconceivable; that the mind prefers at once the idea of a self-existing cause to that of an infinite series of cause & effect, which augments, instead of avoiding the difficulty; and that it finds more facility in assenting to the self-existence of an invisible cause possessing infinite power, wisdom & goodness, than to the self-existence of the universe, visibly destitute of those attributes, and which may be the effect of them. In this comparative facility of conception & belief, all philosophical Reasoning on the subject must terminate.[18]

Madison posits that philosophical reasoning can deduce two possible alternatives to explain the cause of existence: an invisible self-caused cause that itself is the cause of all that exists or, alternatively, the infinite self-existence of the universe. The mind, he says, "prefers at once" the former. It "finds more facility" in assenting to belief in an invisible cause possessing "infinite power, wisdom, and goodness" than it does to the self-existence of the universe without such attributes.

But why? Why, we might ask, does *the mind* prefer the self-existing cause possessing infinite power, wisdom, and goodness? It is not difficult to understand why we might emotionally or spiritually embrace the conclusion most compatible with a creator god, but as a matter of strict philosophical reasoning, does Madison suggest that the self-existing cause is more intellectually sound than belief in an infinite series of cause and effect?

Madison says the possibility of an infinite series of cause and effect "augments, instead of avoid[s] the difficulty." Perhaps Madison means to suggest that belief in the eternal existence of the universe with an infinite series of cause and effect fails to offer a satisfactory resolution to the question of how existence itself came into being since our finite minds struggle to contemplate infinity. If this is correct, then it is the finiteness of our minds that leads it to prefer belief in an invisible self-caused cause over the eternal existence of the world—that is, Madison does not claim that reason itself sides with belief in an invisible cause possessing infinite power, wisdom, and goodness over belief in the eternal existence of the world. This conclusion would seem to be confirmed by Madison's statement that "in this comparative facility of conception & belief, all philosophical Reasoning must terminate." Madison suggests that philosophical reasoning alone cannot arbitrate between the possibility of the eternity of the world and the existence of a self-caused cause. In short, Madison's position seems to be that reason suggests the possibility of but does not confirm the existence of a creator god, possessing infinite power, wisdom, and goodness.

Strikingly, we do not find in Madison's writings an explicit appeal to Scripture. We have copies of the notes Madison took from his study of the Bible as a young man, but as far as I can tell, Madison never cites Scripture to resolve questions pertaining to the existence or nature of God.[19] In *Federalist* 37, moreover, Madison seems to question the certainty with which man can apprehend the meaning of divine revelation:

> When the Almighty himself condescends to address mankind in their own language, his meaning, luminous as it may be, is rendered dim and doubtful by the cloudy medium through which it is communicated.[20]

On theological matters, Madison was first and foremost a rationalist. The starting point (and perhaps the end point) of his reflections seems to have been unaided philosophical reasoning—not so much reason aided by faith but human reason simply. In the aforementioned response to Beasley, Madison also states,

> But whatever effect may be produced on some minds by the more abstract train of ideas which you so strongly support, it will probably always be found that the course of reasoning from the effect to the cause, "from Nature to Nature's God," Will be the more universal & more persuasive application.[21]

Madison seems to reveal the type of reasoning that he himself found most persuasive—"from Nature to Nature's God."

Did Madison's philosophical speculations, then, ultimately lead him to embrace religious faith? The evidence from Madison's personal writings does not lead to a definitive conclusion. Madison's natural theology suggests that he was not an atheist—he never intimates that reason disproves God's existence—yet it also does not definitively confirm a firm belief in the precepts of Christianity or in any sectarian religious faith.

Madison's Theology of Religious Freedom

Regardless of his personal views, Madison embraced theological assumptions in his public arguments. The "Memorial and Remonstrance," his most developed articulation and defense of the right to religious liberty, assumes a fundamental theological starting point.[22]

The "Memorial" begins with the premise " 'that Religion or the duty which we owe to our Creator and the Manner of discharging it, can be directed only by reason and conviction, not by force or violence,' " language Madison borrowed from Article 16 of the Virginia Declaration of Rights.[23] It then continues: "The Religion then of every man must be left to the conviction and conscience of every man; and it is the right of every man to exercise it as these may dictate." Madison does not defend this particular understanding of religious obligation. He does not explain why religion can be directed only by reason and conviction. He takes these theological premises as given.

The Memorial's argument that a "Creator" exists and that He is attentive to our interior beliefs (our "conviction and conscience"). It assumes, moreover, that men owe this providential deity a particular sort of "homage": our religious duties must be "directed by reason and conviction" in accordance with our "conviction and conscience." The God presumed by the "Memorial and Remonstrance" favors only free and voluntary worship that reflects the individual's interior conviction; He does not recognize religious duties discharged on account of force or violence. The "Memorial" does not specify the particular forms of worship God requires (if such forms exist), but it does claim that whatever they may be, the individual himself must believe that they are acceptable to God. If God requires specific rituals or actions, they must be performed with sincere belief to be salutary. In the "Memorial's" theology, faith is primary; an individual conceivably could achieve salvation with faith alone, but he could not with acts absent faith.[24]

The "Memorial's" focus on the individual conscience necessarily implies that salvation is granted to individuals as such. The argument assumes that God does not save nations, communities, or territories, and that He does not reward particular peoples or traditions as such. Memorial's god must grant salvation to individuals as such because it posits that the sincerity of an individual's beliefs is essential in the economy of salvation. Madison's God, moreover, does not allow one individual to meet the religious obligations of another. Proselytizing can only take the form of persuasion. Insofar as law fails to speak to interior conviction, the coercive force of law cannot lead men to salvation. Lawgivers, accordingly, are all but impotent in such matters. Because "it is the duty of every man to render to the Creator such homage, and only such, as he believes to be acceptable to him," citizens cannot have a duty to render homage deemed appropriate by those who possess political power. Scripture might say, "Let every person be subject to the government authorities; for there is no authority except from God, and those authorities that exist have been instituted by God,"[25] but according to the "Memorial," political rulers possess no special authority to determine religious obligations.

The "Memorial" in fact denies that God establishes specific political authorities or that He enforces religious obligations through them. Political authorities "are but the creatures and vicegerents" of society at large (Article 2). If men abuse their natural freedom and fail to meet their religious duties, "it is an offence against God, not against man" (Article 2). Our failure to perform our religious obligations cannot offend the authority of other men because no man has been given authority by God to enforce religious obligations.

Given this theology, one might easily agree with Lance Banning that "the 'Memorial' was obviously written from a Christian point of view."[26] Precision demands, however, that all we say with certainty is that Madison's argument for religious freedom adopts a theology compatible with many forms of Protestant Christianity. This reservation accounts for the possibility that Madison may have believed his argument was grounded upon natural theology alone. We must also consider that Madison wrote the "Memorial" in the midst of a fierce battle over Patrick Henry's proposed general religious establishment bill. His first (though certainly not his only) intention was to persuade a late eighteenth-century Protestant audience. Although the political context is not decisive in itself, it should not surprise us that Madison employed arguments that appealed to his immediate audience.[27]

Madison's View of the Role of Religion in American Public Life

Madison's Criticism of Government Support of Religion

Given his lack of revealing statements and the nature of his theology, Madison's personal religious beliefs are bound to remain elusive. That is not the case regarding his views on the role of religion in American public life. Madison articulates a clearly developed position on the proper relationship between church and state.

The dominant scholarly opinion, especially among those concerned with First Amendment religious jurisprudence, is that Madison championed Thomas Jefferson's "wall of separation." This interpretation was planted in the public mind by the Supreme Court in its first modern-day Establishment Clause case, *Everson v. Board of Education* (1947). After invoking Madison and Jefferson as the individuals most responsible for the existence and meaning of the First Amendment, the *Everson* Court stated:

> The "establishment of religion" clause of the First Amendment means at least this: Neither a state nor the Federal Government can set up a church. Neither can pass laws which aid one religion, aid all religions, or prefer one religion over another. . . . No tax in any amount, large or small, can be levied to support any religious activities or institutions, whatever they may be called, or whatever from they may adopt to teach or practice religion. . . . In the words of Jefferson, the clause against establishment of religion by law was intended to erect "a wall of separation between Church and State."[28]

In his *Everson* opinion, Justice Rutledge claimed, "Madison opposed every form and degree of official relation between religion and civil authority,"[29] an interpretation that received authoritative support four years later by Irving Brant, Madison's distinguished biographer. According to Brant, freedom of religion was for Madison "the fundamental item upon which all other forms of civil liberty depended," and the fundamental requirement for religious freedom "was the total separation between government and religion."[30] Today the strict separationist interpretation of Madison is championed by Supreme Court Justice David Souter.[31]

I have attempted to demonstrate elsewhere that strict separationism misinterprets Madison's thought.[32] Madison did write that the taxpayer-funded legislative chaplain instituted by the First Congress was a "palpable violation" of constitutional principles and that religious proclamations by the president were "shoots from the same root." Madison even went so far as to identify a prohibition on taxpayer-funded chaplains for navy crewmen insulated at sea as "the consequence of a right principle."[33] But Madison thought these matters violated constitutional principles because they required the state to take cognizance of religion as such. He objected to the government legislating on religious matters as such, not—as strict separationists think—to government policies that aid religion. Strict separationists overlook the fact that Madison also opposed government policies that penalized individuals on account of religion. Madison, for example, criticized Jefferson's proposed constitution for Virginia because it excluded religious ministers from the state legislature:

> EXCLUSIONS. Does not the exclusion of Ministers of the Gospel as such violate a fundamental principle of liberty by punishing a religious profession with the privation of a civil right? does it [not] violate another article of the plan itself which exempts religion from the cognizance of Civil power? does it not violate justice by at once taking away a right and prohibiting compensation for it? does it not in fine violate impartiality by shutting the door against the Ministers of Religion and leaving it open for those of every other?[34]

Madison sought to prevent the government from either privileging or penalizing religion as such. Strict separationists capture only half of Madison because they mistake a consequence of his principle for the principle itself, thus distorting his true position. Madison did not favor the exclusion of religion from the public square.

To some extent, the strict separationist misinterpretation is understandable. More forcefully than any other American founder, Madison broke from the classical republican teaching that the state ought to nurture and support religion because religion is good for republican government. Madison can be contrasted with individuals like George Washington, who offered one of the clearest expressions of the traditional approach in his Farewell Address. "Of all the disposition and habits which lead to political prosperity," Washington wrote,

> Religion and morality are indispensable supports. In vain would that man claim the tribute of Patriotism, who should labor to subvert these great pillars of human happiness, these firmest props of the duties of Man and citizens. The mere Politician, equally with the pious man ought to respect and to cherish them. A volume could not trace all their connections with private and public felicity.[35]

Because he thought religion was indispensable in nurturing the moral qualities necessary for republican citizenship, Washington thought that the government ought to endorse and promote religion.[36]

Madison rejected this classical republican teaching. He did not deny that virtue was an important aid to republican government or that religion helped to nourish virtue. Madison himself wrote in a private letter that

> the belief in a God All Powerful wise & good, is so essential to the moral order of the World & to the happiness of man, that arguments which enforce it cannot be drawn from too many sources nor adapted with too much solicitude to the different characters & capacities to be impressed with it.[37]

But Madison vehemently disagreed that religion required the support of government. He articulated his position most forcefully in Article 6 of his "Memorial and Remonstrance":

> Because the establishment proposed by the Bill[38] is not requisite for the support of the Christian Religion. To say that it is, is a contradiction to the Christian Religion itself; for every page of it disavows a dependence on the powers of this world: it is a contradiction to fact; for it is known that this Religion both existed and flourished, not only without the support of human laws, but in spite of every opposition from them; and not only during the period of miraculous aid, but long after it had been left to its own evidence, and the ordinary care of Providence: Nay it is a contradiction in terms; for a religion not invented by human policy, must have pre-existed and been supported, before it was established by human policy. It is moreover to weaken in those who profess this Religion a pious confidence in its innate excellence, and the patronage of its Author; and to foster in those who still reject it, a suspicion that its friends are too conscious of its fallacies, to trust it to its own merits.[39]

After he left the presidency, Madison made this same point repeatedly in his private correspondence. In an 1819 letter to Robert Walsh touting the increase of religious instruction since the American Revolution, Madison wrote:

> It was the Universal opinion of the Century preceding the last, that Civil Gov^t. could not stand without the prop of a Religious establishment, & that the X^n. religion itself would perish if not supported by a legal provision for its clergy. The experience of Virginia conspicuously corroborates the disproof of both opinions. The Civil Gov^t., tho' bereft of every thing like an associated hierarchy possesses the requisite

stability, and performs its functions with complete success; Whilst the number, the industry, and the morality of the Priesthood, & the devotion of the people, have been manifestly increased by the total separation of the Church from the State.[40]

In response to receiving a sermon sent by New York clergyman F. L. Schaeffer, Madison stated,

The experience of the United States is a happy disproof of the error so long rooted in the unenlightened minds of well-meaning Christians, as well as in the corrupt hearts of persecuting usurpers, that without legal incorporation of religious and civil polity, neither could be supported. A mutual independence is found most friendly to practical religion, to social harmony, and to political prosperity.[41]

Madison sounded the same theme the following year in a letter to Edward Livingston:

We are teaching the world a great truth that Governments do better without kings and nobles than with them. The merit will be doubled by the other lesson: that Religion flourishes in greater purity without, than with the aid of government.[42]

Madison's position that religion does not need the support of government—nay, that it will better flourish without the support of government—reflects two prior suppositions. He believed that religion contained within itself the prerequisites for its own perpetuation. "[T]here are causes in the human breast, which ensure the perpetuity of religion without the aid of the law," Madison wrote to Edward Everett.[43] In a letter to Rev. Jasper Adams written at the end of his life, Madison similarly stated,

There appears to be in the nature of man what insures his belief in an invisible cause of his present existence, and anticipation of his future existence. Hence the propensities & susceptibilities in that case of religion which with a few doubtful or individual exceptions have prevailed throughout the world.[44]

Madison did not elaborate or explain what these "causes in the human breast" are. Given his comments cited above about "the finiteness of the human understanding" and its inability to resolve questions pertaining to the beginning of the world, Madison may have thought man's inability to grasp the beginning of existence placed "in the nature of man" a propensity to turn to religion, a propensity supported by the hope for life after death. Whatever the causes, Madison thought men were naturally disposed to seek a power beyond themselves, and thus naturally inclined toward religious belief. This fact, he claimed, comported with the history of early Christianity itself, which demonstrated that government does not need to support religion for religion to flourish.

Madison also argued against government support of religion because he believed that such support tended to corrupt religion and to encourage religious persecution. He identified two types of corruption in particular. First, dependence on government corrupted religious clergy by freeing them from accountability to the laity. "Experience witnesseth [*sic*]," Madison wrote in Article 7 of the "Memorial and Remonstrance,"

> that ecclesiastical establishments, instead of maintaining the purity and efficacy of Religion, have had a contrary operation. During almost fifteen centuries, has the legal establishment of Christianity been on trial. What have been its fruits? More or less in all places, pride and indolence in the Clergy; ignorance and servility in the laity; in both superstition, bigotry and persecution. Enquire of the Teachers of Christianity for the ages in which it appeared in its greatest lustre; those of every sect, point to the ages prior to its incorporation with Civil policy. Propose a restoration of this primitive state in which its Teachers depended on the voluntary rewards of their flocks; many of them predict its downfall. On which side ought their testimony to have greatest weight, when it is for or against their interest?[45]

Madison suggests that when clergy are dependent on the voluntary contributions of church members for their income, they must serve the laity. Excessively prideful and indolent ministers will likely be unpopular and, hence, unsupported. Without state support, moreover, the laity themselves are less likely to be passive, because they must actively choose to contribute to those who minister to them. Government support of clergy thus lessens responsibility in both the clergy and the laity, causing the spiritual harm to both.

Madison thought that state support corrupted religion, secondly, by introducing incentives to religious persecution. Because funded religions depend on the state for their livelihood, their clergy, Madison wrote to Bradford,

> will naturally employ all their art and interest to depress their rising adversaries; for such they must consider dissenters who rob them of the good will of he people, and may, in time, endanger their livings and security.[46]

Without state funding, religious ministers would face competition from clergy of other sects for voluntary contributions—with religious pluralism, some form of competition was inevitable. But Madison thought state involvement encouraged a harmful type of competition. Instead of directly appealing to the laity to secure voluntary contributions, clergy funded by the state would be more likely to attempt to protect their position through nonmarket means, such as state regulation or even legal constraints on minority sects. Connection with and dependence on the state encouraged government-supported religions to use the power of the state to curb religious dissent. State funding of religion thus inevitably introduced the "diabolical, hell-conceived principle of persecution."[47]

Religion and Madison's Presidencies

Madison most significantly shaped church-state relations as a legislator in Virginia where he led the battle to pass Jefferson's "Virginia Statute for Religious Freedom" and as a U.S. congressman when he drafted and shepherded the passage of the First Amendment. His presidencies, accordingly, are usually not the object of focus for scholars concerned with his understanding of the role of religion in American public life. Yet we can learn something about the rigidity and the difficulty of maintaining his principle of noncognizance by turning to his presidential period.

In February 1811, Madison vetoed a bill passed by Congress that incorporated the Protestant Episcopal Church of Alexandria, D.C.[48] In addition to recognizing the church as a corporate body, the bill specified rules for electing and removing the church's ministers. This, Madison said, would make the church a religious establishment by law, because it would subject sundry rules and proceedings pertaining purely to the church's internal organization to enforcement by the state. Madison also objected to Section 8 of the bill, which stated, "That it shall and may be lawful for the said vestry to make such provisions for the support of the poor of the said church as shall by them be thought proper." This provision, Madison claimed, "would be a precedent for giving to religious Societies as such, a legal agency in carrying into effect a public and civil duty."[49] The most important words of Madison's sentence are "as such." Madison feared that the bill's language suggested that the church possessed legal sanction to help the poor because it was a church. Madison objected to giving "religious societies as such" a legal agency in carrying into effect public duties, because a government noncognizant of religion cannot grant privileges to religious groups on account of their religious character.

Madison's veto reflects a strict application of his noncognizance principle; he was less doctrinaire, however, when asked to proclaim official days for prayer, fasting, and thanksgiving. Madison issued four such presidential proclamations, despite believing they were constitutionally suspect.

After his second term, Madison backtracked, offering a fivefold objection to religious proclamations by the president.[50] He claimed, first, that government ought not to interpose in those matters in which it lacks authority to pass laws. "An *advisory* Govt [*sic*]," he said, "is a contradiction in terms." Since the national government could not pass a law mandating citizens pray and fast, Madison decided that it ought not recommend such measures. Second, members of the government "can in no sense be regarded as possessing an advisory trust from their Constituents in their religious capacities." Madison grants that in his private capacity the president might recommend that citizens pray; but, if so, his recommendation ought to reflect its true character. Third, presidential proclamations "imply and certainly nourish the erroneous idea of a *national* religion." Fourth, the proclamations have a tendency to narrow the recommendation to the standard of the predominant sect. Fifth, and finally, Madison warns that such proclamations too easily can be used (or appear to be used) for partisan gain, which is "to the scandal of religion, as well as to the increase of party animosities."[51]

Given these concerns, which Madison intimates he possessed while president, how could he issue four religious proclamations and so clearly violate his own philosophical and constitutional principle? In his postpresidential critique of the presidential religious proclamations, Madison never admits that he did compromise his principle. Instead, he explains that at the time it was known that he was "disinclined" to issue official religious proclamations. Congress, nonetheless, passed joint resolutions requesting them, and Madison says, "[I]t was thought not proper to refuse a compliance altogether."[52]

But Madison could have refused. President Jefferson declined to issue official religious proclamations during his presidency because he believed they violated the First Amendment. A precedent had been established; a refusal by Madison would not have broken new ground. Madison must have concluded that the political price of not issuing the proclamations was too high. No doubt his calculations were influenced by the trials of the War of 1812, during which the proclamations were issued, but this does not seem to justify a clear violation of principle.

In his own defense, Madison notes that he employed a form and language in his proclamations that were

> meant to deaden as much as possible any claim of political right to enjoin religious observances by resting these expressly on the voluntary compliance of individuals, and even by limiting the recommendation to such as wished simultaneous as well as voluntary performance of a religious act on the occasion.[53]

A perusal of the text of the proclamations reveals Madison's carefulness in writing them and his hesitancy in issuing them. He begins all four recommendations by explicitly noting that Congress has called for them. All four proclamations make clear that they are advisory only, each using a form of the word "recommend" before suggesting the possibility of prayer. In his second proclamation, Madison recommends vows and adorations only "to all those who should be piously disposed." He states, furthermore,

> If the public homage of a people can ever be worthy the favorable regard of the Holy and Omniscient Being to whom it is addressed, it must be that in which those who join in it are guided only by their free choice, by the impulse of their hearts and the dictates of their consciences.

The proclamations, moreover, were not sectarian. None contain any references to Jesus Christ, but rather they encourage public homage to "the Sovereign of the Universe and Benefactor of Mankind" (first proclamation), "Great Parent and Sovereign of the Universe" (second proclamation), "Almighty God" and "Beneficent Parent of the Human Race" (third proclamation), and "Almighty God" and "Great Disposer of Events" (fourth proclamation).[54]

Despite his efforts to emphasize their advisory character, Madison's proclamations directly contradict his standard of religious "noncognizance." During his presidency, Madison was unable to maintain a strict adherence to his principled understanding of religious liberty.

Conclusion

James Madison would disagree with those today who call for state recognition of religion or state support for religion as such. As a legislator and president, James Madison sought (not always successfully) to privatize religion. He acknowledged that religion can play an important role in public life insofar as it supports personal virtue, but, unlike George Washington, Madison did not believe that the government ought to support religion as such. Religion, he concluded, ought not to receive special privileges or considerations. Madison's fundamental prudential assumption, which was not shared by more classical republicans like Washington, was that religion did not need governmental support and that such support inevitably proved to be detrimental to religion and religious freedom.

Madison would also disagree agree with today's strict separationists and those who champion "the wall of separation" interpretation of the Establishment Clause. Madison interpreted the right to religious freedom to prevent the state from adopting policies that unfavorably target or disfavor religion as such.

The extent to which these political teachings flowed from Madison's personal religious convictions is impossible to say, as the tenets of his personal creed are elusive. We can say that his argument for the right to religious freedom is built upon a political theology of religious individualism consistent with many forms of Protestant Christianity.

Regardless of its origin, James Madison offers a thoughtful and comprehensive political philosophy of church-state relations. Whether he offers a politically wise approach we must decide for ourselves. Whatever verdict we render, our deliberations surely will be profited by attention to Madison's thought and practice regarding the role of religion in American public life.

Notes

1. Cited in James Hutson, "James Madison and the Social Utility of Religion: Risks vs. Rewards," paper presented as part of the symposium James Madison: Philosopher and Practitioner of Liberal Democracy at The Library of Congress, Washington, DC, March 16, 2001, http://www.loc. gov/loc/madison/hutson-paper.html, 2. Rives summarizes his interpretation of Madison's religious studies as follows:

   What was the result in his [Madison's] mind of these profound and laborious inquiries [into Scripture and theology], prosecuted with all the freshness and energy of his intellectual powers, appears very significantly, although incidentally in a letter written by him two years later [in 1774] to his young Pennsylvanian friend [William Bradford]. Speaking of the celebrated Tracts of Dean Tucker on the dispute between England and her American colonies, which he had just then read with much satisfaction at the practical solution of the controversy recommended by that author, in a voluntary separation of the two countries, Mr. Madison adds:—"At the same time, his ingenious and plausible defence [*sic*] of parliamentary authority carries in it such defects and misrepresentations as confirm me in political authority, after the same manner as the specious arguments of infidels have established the faith of inquiring Christians."

William C. Rives, *History of the Life and Times of James Madison*, 3 vols. (New York: Books for Libraries Press, 1859–1868; repr. 1970), 1: 35–36. Rives seems to assume that Madison identifies himself as the "inquiring Christian" whose faith has been established. Such an inference may be possible, but is not necessary from the text itself. It is not clear that Madison means to suggest that his faith had been established by reading "the specious arguments of infidels."

2. Garrett Ward Sheldon, "Religion and Politics in the Thought of James Madison," in *The Founders on God and Government*, ed. Daniel L. Dreisbach, Mark D. Hall, and Jeffry H. Morrison (Lanham, MD: Rowman & Littlefield, 2004), 84.

3. Emphasis is in the original; Michael Novak, *On Two Wings: Humble Faith and Common Sense at the American Founding*, expanded ed. (San Francisco: Encounter Books, 2003), 139.

4. Irving Brant, *James Madison* (New York: Bobbs-Merrill Company, 1941), 1: 277.

5. John West, Jr., *The Politics of Revelation and Reason: Religion and Civic Life in the New Nation* (Lawrence: University Press of Kansas, 1996), 67.

6. Ibid., 68.

7. Lance Banning, *The Sacred Fire of Liberty: James Madison and Founding of the Federal Republic* (Ithaca, NY: Cornell University Press, 1995), 80.

8. Ralph Ketcham, *James Madison: A Biography* (Charlottesville: University Press of Virginia, 1990), 46–47.

9. William Lee Miller, *The Business of May Next: James Madison and the Founding* (Charlottesville: University Press of Virginia, 1992), 106.

10. Sheldon, "Religion and Politics in the Thought of James Madison," 86.

11. Mark Noll, *Princeton and the Republic* (Princeton, NJ: Princeton University Press, 1989), 8–9.

12. Sheldon and Mary-Elaine Swanson emphasize Madison's education as decisive in shaping what they believe to be his Calvinist idea of man and politics. According to Sheldon, Madison adopted a "distinctively Calvinist" view of human nature (91). Swanson claims that while at Princeton Madison "imbibed Witherspoon's Calvinistic view of [depraved] human nature" (126). The significant weakness in both of these authors' accounts is they ascribe to Madison ideas and concepts that he himself does not use. Sheldon, for example, repeatedly claims that *Federalist* 10 reflects Madison's appreciation of "sinful humanity (101)."

13. Banning, *The Sacred Fire of Liberty*, 80.

14. Hutson, "James Madison and the Social Utility of Religion," 4.

15. Miller, *The Business of May Next*, 106.

16. James Madison to William Bradford, November 9, 1772, in *James Madison on Religious Liberty*, ed. Robert S. Alley (Buffalo: Prometheus Books, 1985), 44.
17. James Madison to William Bradford, September 25, 1773, in Alley, ed., *James Madison on Religious Liberty*, 45–46.
18. James Madison to Frederick Beasley, November 20, 1825, in *Writings of James Madison*, ed. Gaillard Hunt, 9 vols. (New York: G. P. Putnam's Sons, 1910), 9: 230–231.
19. Ralph Ketcham reports, "Four large pages of closely written notes in Madison's hand on The Gospel of St. John, The Acts of the Apostles, and the Proverbs of Solomon have been dated 1772 by Irving Brant." See Ketcham, "James Madison and Religion," 181–182. Ketcham's citation to Brant, however, is missing and therefore cannot be easily verified. For Brant's discussion of Madison's notes on Scripture see Brant, *James Madison*, 1: 118–119. For Rives's discussion of the same material see Rives, *History of the Life and Times of James Madison*, 1: 33–34.
20. Publius (Madison), *Federalist 37*. Alexander Hamilton, James Madison, and John Jay, *The Federalist Papers*, ed. Clinton Rossiter, intro. Charles Kesler (New York: Mentor, 1999), 101. But in Federalist10, Madison himself never uses the term "sinful." Madison's political thought may be compatible with a Calvinist view of man's sinfulness, but this does not make Madison's thought necessarily Calvinist. See Sheldon, "Religion and Politics in the Thought of James Madison"; and Mary-Elaine Swanson, "James Madison and the Presbyterian Idea of Man and Government," in *Religion and Political Culture in Jefferson's Virginia*, ed. Garrett Ward Sheldon and Daniel L. Dreisbach (Lanham, MD: Rowman & Littlefield, 2000), 197.
21. James Madison to Frederick Beasley, November 20, 1825, in Hunt, ed., *Writings of James Madison*, 9: 230. Three days later in a letter to Charles Caldwell Madison wrote,
    I concur with you at once in rejecting the idea maintained by some diviners of more zeal than discretion that there is no road from nature up to Nature's God, and that all the knowledge of his existence and attributes which preceded the written revelation of them, was derived from oral tradition. James Madison to Doctor C. Caldwell, November 23, 1825, in *Letters and Other Writings of James Madison*, 4 vols. (New York: R. Worthington, 1884), 3: 505.
22. It lies beyond the scope of this chapter to present a thorough interpretation of the argument of the "Memorial and Remonstrance". Elsewhere I have argued that Madison's principle of religious liberty in the "Memorial" is most accurately understood as a principle of religious "noncognizance." See Vincent Phillip Muñoz, "James Madison's Principle of Religious Liberty," *American Political Science Review*, 97 (February 2003): 17–32.
23. For Madison's contribution to the drafting of Article 16 of the Virginia Declaration of Rights see Daniel L. Dreisbach, "George Mason's Pursuit

of Religious Liberty in Revolutionary Virginia," *The Virginia Magazine of History and Biography*, 108 (2000): 5–44.

24. I disagree with Thomas Lindsay who, in interpreting the "Memorial and Remonstrance," claims, "Madison's project for religious liberty is theoretically grounded in the denial of human capacity to know the nature of and existence of the commands of—and thus the duties toward—revelation's God." See Thomas Lindsay, "James Madison on Religion and Politics: Rhetoric and Reality," *American Political Science Review*, 85 (4) (December 1991): 1326.

25. Romans 13: 1 (*New Revised Standard Version*).

26. Banning, *The Sacred Fire of Liberty*, 436, n. 68. Gary Rosen makes a similar point, referring to "the obvious Protestant subtext" of the "Memorial." Rosen then draws out the following theological implications: "Religious truth becomes a particular sort of experience rather than a doctrine. In this view, sincerity takes the place of right-thinking and—acting." Gary Rosen, *American Compact: James Madison and the Problem of Founding* (Lawrence: University Press of Kansas, 1999), 23.

27. With regards to this point, Lance Banning states,

> Admittedly, this [the Christian point of view of the "Memorial" may have been a tactical consideration, but it was not a *necessary* tactic in this situation. I am convinced that Madison consistently adopted tactics that did not dissemble his private views, that there was a very little of the propagandist in his makeup. The Memorial is thus my major reason for concluding that his thinking still had room for the authority of revelation at least as late as 1785.

Banning's emphasis; *Sacred Fire of Liberty*, 436, n. 68. Thomas Lindsay, on the contrary, argues that Madison's theology in the "Memorial" was merely rhetorical and disconnected to his private views. See Lindsay, "James Madison on Religion and Politics," 1321.

28. *Everson v. Board of Education*, 330 U.S. 1, 15–16 (1947).

29. Ibid. at 1, 39, 41. It should be noted that Justice Rutledge dissented in *Everson*. His interpretation of Madison, however, was shared by Justice Black, who wrote the Court's majority opinion.

30. Irving Brant, "Madison: On the Separation of Church and State," *William and Mary Quarterly*, series 3, vol. 8 (January 1951): 3.

31. See Justice Souter's concurring opinions in *Lee v. Weisman*, 505 U.S. 577, 615 (1992) and *Rosenberger v. University of Virginia*, 515 U.S. 819 (1995). The strict sepationist interpretation of Madison has been challenged by justices Rehnquist and Thomas. See Rehnquist's dissenting opinion in *Wallace v. Jaffree*, 472 U.S. 38 (1985) and Thomas's concurring opinion in *Rosenberger*. For further discussion of the use of Madison in Establishment Clause jurisprudence and scholarship see Muñoz, "James Madison's Principle of Religious Liberty," 17–19.

32. See Muñoz, "James Madison's Principle of Religious Liberty"; and "Religion and the American Founding," *Intercollegiate Review*, 38(2) (Spring/Summer 2003): 33–43.

33. Brant, "Madison: On the Separation of Church and State," 21–24; Elizabeth Fleet, "Madison's 'Detached Memoranda,' " *William and Mary Quarterly*, series 3, vol. 3 (October 1946): 558–562.
34. James Madison, "Remarks on Mr. Jefferson's Draught of a Constitution," sent to John Brown, ca. October 15, 1788, in Hunt, ed., *Writings of James Madison*, 5: 284–294. Madison's reference "to another article of the plan" refers to next three paragraphs below the provision excluding clergymen from public office. That text states, "The general assembly shall not have power to infringe this constitution, to abridge the civil rights of any person on account of his religious belief, to restrain him from professing and supporting that belief." The relevant passages of Jefferson's draft of a constitution can be found in *The Writings of Thomas Jefferson*, ed. Andrew A. Lipscomb, 20 vols. (Washington, DC: Thomas Jefferson Memorial Association, 1904), 2: 286–287.
35. George Washington, "Farewell Address," September 19, 1796, in *The Writings of Washington*, ed. John C. Fitzpatrick, 38 vols. (Washington, DC: United States Government Printing Office, 1931–1944), 35: 229. Washington's Farewell Address was not a speech but a long letter addressed "To the PEOPLE of the United States," first published in *American Daily Advisor*, Philadelphia's largest newspaper. For a discussion of the drafting and publication of the Farewell Address, see Matthew Spalding and Patrick J. Garrity, *A Sacred Union of Citizens: George Washington's Farewell Address and the American Character*, introduction by Daniel J. Boorstin (Lanham, MD: Rowman & Littlefield, 1996), 45–61; and Felix Gilbert, *To The Farewell Address: Ideas of Early American Foreign Policy* (Princeton: Princeton University Press, 1961), chapter V.
36. For an elaboration of George Washington's position, see Vincent Phillip Muñoz, "George Washington on Religious Liberty," *The Review of Politics*, 65 (Winter 2003): 11–33. The Washingtonian classical republican position was adopted most clearly in the Massachusetts Constitution of 1780, Pt. 1, Article 3:

> As the happiness of a people and the good order and preservation of civil government, essentially depend upon piety, religion and morality, and as these cannot be generally diffused through a community, but by the institution of the public worship of GOD, and of public instructions in piety, religion and morality: Therefore, to promote their happiness and to secure the good order and preservation of their government, the people of this commonwealth have a right to invest their legislature with power to authorize and require, and the legislature shall, from time to time, authorize and require, the several towns, parishes, precincts, and other bodies-politic, or religious societies, to make suitable provision, at their own expense, for the institution of the public worship of GOD, and for the support and maintenance of public protestant teachers of piety, religion and morality, in all cases where such provisions shall not be made voluntarily.

37. James Madison to Fredrick Beasly, November 20, 1825, in Hunt, ed., *Writings of James Madison*, 9: 230.
38. Madison wrote the "Memorial and Remonstrance" to oppose Patrick Henry's pending bill erecting a general Protestant religious establishment in Virginia. Henry's bill was a property tax, in which each property owner was to specify the Christian denomination to which he wished his tax directed. If a taxpayer failed or refused to specify a Christian society, his tax would go to the public treasury "to be disposed of under the direction of the General Assembly, for the encouragement of seminaries of learning . . . and to no other use or purpose whatsoever." The taxes received by the various denominations were to be "appropriated to a provision for a Minister or Teacher of the Gospel, or the providing of places of divine worship, and to none other use whatsoever." The purpose of the bill was to keep the Christian ministry, particularly Episcopalian clergy, active and solvent. In effect, it would have granted a direct subsidy to Christian clergymen.
39. Even as a young man, Madison expressed doubts regarding whether religion needed the support of government. In 1773, he posed the following questions to his good friend William Bradford:
    > Here allow me to propose the following Queries. Is an Ecclesiastical Establishment absolutely necessary to support civil society in a supreme Government? and [*sic*] how far is it hurtful to a dependent State? I do not ask for an immediate answer but mention them as worth attending to in the course of your reading and consulting experienced Lawyers and Politicians upon. When you have satisfied yourself in these points I should listen with pleasure to the Result of your researches.

    James Madison to William Bradford, December 1, 1773, in Alley, ed., *James Madison on Religious Liberty*, 46–47.
40. James Madison to Robert Walsh, March 2, 1819, in Alley, ed., *James Madison on Religious Liberty*, 81.
41. James Madison to F. L. Schaeffer, December 3, 1821, in Alley, ed., *James Madison on Religious Liberty*, 82.
42. James Madison to Edward Livingston, July 10, 1822, in Hunt, ed., *Writings of James Madison*, 9: 102–103. See also James Madison's letter to Edward Everett, March 19, 1823, in Hunt, ed., *Writings of James Madison*, 9:127.
43. James Madison to Edward Everett, March 19, 1823, in Hunt, ed., *Writings of James Madison*, 9: 126–127.
44. James Madison to Jasper Adams, Spring 1833, in Alley, ed., *James Madison on Religious Liberty*, 87.
45. Madison's reproachful view of the established Anglican clergy in colonial Virginia may have decisively shaped his thinking on ecclesiastical establishments. As early as 1774 he wrote to his good friend William Bradford,
    > If the Church of England had been the established and general religion in all the northern colonies as it has been among us here [in Virginia],

and uninterrupted tranquility had prevailed throughout the continent, it is clear to me that slavery and subjection might and would have been gradually insinuated among us.

James Madison to William Bradford, January 24, 1774, in *The Mind of the Founder: Sources of the Political Thought of James Madison*, ed. and intro. Marvin Meyers, rev. ed. (Hanover: University Press of New England, 1981), 2.

46. James Madison to William Bradford, January 24, 1774, in Meyers, ed., *The Mind of the Founder*, 3.

47. Ibid.

48. The following description of Madison's presidential vetoes is taken from Muñoz, "James Madison's Principle of Religious Liberty," 27–28.

49. Veto Message to the House of Representatives, February 21, 1811, in *The Papers of James Madison*, Congressional Series (17 vols.), Secretary of State Series (7 vols.), and the Presidential Series (5 vols.), ed. Stagg, Cross, and Perdue (Charlottesville: University of Virginia Press, 1984–), 3:176. Congress passed the bill on February 8, 1811. Following Madison's veto, the House of Representatives debated the constitutionality of the bill and the means of reconsidering it before voting against its passage on February 23, 1811. See *Annals of Congress*, 11th Congress, 3rd Session, 129, 453, 828, 983–985, 995–998.

50. The exact date of Madison's comments is unknown, but they are thought to have been written between 1817 and 1832. See Fleet, "Madison's 'Detached Memoranda,' " 534–536.

51. All emphasis belongs to Madison; ibid., 560–161.

52. Ibid.

53. Ibid.

54. Madison's four proclamations requesting days of prayer and thanksgiving can be found in James D. Richardson, *A Compilation of the Messages and Papers of the Presidents: 1789–1897* (Washington, DC: Government Printing Office, 1896), 1: 513, 532–533, 558, 560–561.

Chapter Four

Lincoln's Political Religion and Religious Politics: Or, What Lincoln Teaches Us about the Proper Connection between Religion and Politics

Lucas E. Morel

Much of the debate over Lincoln and religion centers on his faith (or lack thereof), with scholars and laymen alike arguing for or against Lincoln's Christianity in a way that has virtually eclipsed what Lincoln would have seen as a more important issue: How should religion inform politics, especially in a self-governing regime? What can we learn about Lincoln's political appeal to, and use of, religion that teaches us its proper role in Republican government?

First, as a successful republic requires a moral or self-controlled people, Lincoln believed that religion could help moderate the excesses of passion and self-interest in the community. As a means of achieving this social order, Lincoln promoted "support of the Constitution" and "reverence for the laws" to become what he called "the *political religion* of the nation."[1] Lincoln believed that the perpetuation of the free government established by the American Revolution depended on this almost sacred law-abidingness,[2] and he called on both politician and preacher to promote this "political religion."

Second, while the political uses of religion seem to predominate in Lincoln's politics, he never forgot that religion existed for a higher purpose than supporting government. Lincoln, in other words, did not confuse the political utility of religion with religion's true aim: to connect people to God, not to their government. This is why he accommodated the religious expression of the American citizenry through various public acts. For example, in 1862 he issued an order for a Sabbath observance "by the officers and men in the military and naval service"[3]; in 1861, he recommended that Congress appoint and pay for hospital chaplains. He also protected the religious free-dom of Southerners from Union generals, who in some instances had undertaken to govern churches in the South. Between 1861 and 1864, Lincoln issued ten executive proclamations of local and national days of fasting, thanksgiving, and prayer. Regardless of Lincoln's own religious beliefs, as a politician he spoke and acted so as to preserve the legitimate sphere of action for both government and religion.

Third, Lincoln noted, however, that religion was not all sweetness and light for America. He also concerned himself with the detrimental effect that religious extremists could have on free government, as exhibited by some moral reform movements that promoted temperance and abolition. Some of these reform societies tended to approach their causes with a self-righteousness that allowed little room for discussion and hence posed a threat to the deliberative processes of self-government.[4] In them he sensed a religious character that could lead to excesses adverse to constitutional government: namely, theocratic absolutism, which would undermine a regime based on public deliberation as opposed to a theological litmus test. This is seen most clearly in his 1842 speech to the Springfield Washington Temperance Society. Lincoln's genius was displayed in his preaching and practice of a political religion and religious politics that preserved the respective domains of both government and religion.

As early as 1838, at the Young Men's Lyceum of Springfield, Lincoln addressed a problem the United States faced as its Revolutionary War veterans passed this earth, leaving no living memory to help perpetuate the grand American experiment in self-government. Vigilante justice was on the rise in the United States. Lincoln saw this as a major weakening of the republic, and believed only a "political religion" of reverence for the laws and the Constitution could prevent mob rule and the resultant anarchy from giving rise to a "towering genius" who sought to gratify his thirst for fame "at the expense of emancipating slaves, or enslaving freemen."[5] In the address, Lincoln proclaims,

> Let reverence for the laws, be breathed by every American mother, to the lisping babe, that prattles on her lap—let it be taught in schools, in seminaries, and in colleges;—let it be written in Primmers, spelling books, and in Almanacs;—let it be preached from the pulpit, proclaimed in legislative halls, and enforced in courts of justice. And, in short, let it become the *political religion* of the nation; and let the old and the young, the rich and the poor, the grave and the gay, of all sexes and tongues, and colors and conditions, sacrifice unceasingly upon its altars.[6]

His religious examples—"reverence," "seminaries," "preached from the pulpit," and "sacrifice unceasingly upon its altars"—and religious tone rouse the listener to the seriousness of his cause, a seriousness evoked earlier by calls to one's patriotism and ancestry and now complemented by the aura of religion. Religion, here, serves the republic as the handmaiden of government in the latter's effort to ensure obedience to its laws—an obedience conducive of not only civil but also religious liberty.[7]

Curiously, Lincoln omits the executive branch when he lists the key individuals and institutions that should preach what he calls "political religion." By calling strict obedience to the laws a political "religion," Lincoln emphasizes the importance of spreading this message in the same manner that a preacher spreads the word of God. Perhaps the executive department is present under the guise of "the pulpit," implying that a religious aspect must be donned by the chief administrator of government—the executive, one uniquely situated among the branches of government to speak with one voice. As the chief law enforcer of the community, and thus one called to promote law-abidingness, the executive must adopt the mode of a preacher to enlist the community as fellow believers. If a republic needs a "political" religion to survive, as Lincoln makes clear, its executive must become its "political" preacher—which is precisely what Lincoln is doing in this speech.

Aside from "political religion" and, more generally, the political utility of religion, Lincoln's political practice also points to political respect for religion. This may have been driven, in part, from his own growing appreciation of religion in his own life. For example, in the summer of 1864, Lincoln invited his longtime friend Joshua F. Speed to spend the night at his retreat at Soldiers' Home, just three miles north of the White House. Speed wrote of his stay at Soldiers' Home years later, and it gives perhaps the clearest indication of Lincoln's religious faith late in life:

> As I entered the room, near night, he was sitting near a window intently reading his Bible. Approaching him I said, "I am glad to see you so profitably engaged." "Yes" said he, "I am profitably engaged." "Well," said I, "If you have recovered from your skepticism, I am sorry to say that I have not." Looking me earnestly in the face, and placing his hand on my shoulder, he said, "You are wrong Speed, take all of this book upon reason that you can, and the balance on faith, and you will live and die a happier and better man."[8]

Speed notes that Lincoln had come a long way from his early days of religious "skepticism."[9] This famous recollection of Lincoln's dearest friend reveals an appreciation of religion that transcends its mere usefulness to the government. For Lincoln, religion qua religion had a purpose far beyond that of simply supporting the government: it existed to fulfill a divine purpose between an individual and God and ought not to be viewed solely in light of its political utility. Because religion's reason for being stands independent of political necessity, Lincoln made sure to enlist its services to the regime without subverting its own reason for being. He saw to it that government, while he was at the helm, accommodated religion as the citizenry saw to its higher end.

This understanding of religion's ambivalent support of the state has only recently been revived in scholarly circles.[10] For example, historian Mark Y. Hanley argues that "Protestant spiritual discourse, anchored by religious jeremiads and regular sermons, . . . placed faith's temporal benefits on a fulcrum that gave weighted advantage to a transcendent spirituality beyond the Commonwealth." In other words, while some religious leaders saw a close affinity of purpose between Christianity and the American republic, others presented "faith's capacity to improve society as a subordinate aim" to its highest priority: pointing men and women toward "a spiritual destiny beyond the commonwealth."[11]

A telling example of Lincoln's respect for revealed religion, especially as a principal influence on society, is his 1846 "Handbill Replying to Charges of Infidelity." In his run for Congress in 1846, Lincoln campaigned against the well-known Methodist circuit rider Peter Cartwright. Friends told Lincoln that Cartwright "was whispering the charge of infidelity" against him,[12] suggesting that Lincoln held unorthodox views about religion. Lincoln, therefore, responded with a handbill explaining his understanding of the controversy.

As the July 31, 1846 handbill contains the most direct expression of Lincoln's view of religion and public life, at least to that point in his life, we quote it in its entirety:

> *To the Voters of the Seventh Congressional District.*
>
> FELLOW CITIZENS:
>
> A charge having got into circulation in some of the neighborhoods of this District, in substance that I am an open scoffer at Christianity, I have by the advice of some friends concluded to notice the subject in this form. That I am not a member of any Christian Church, is true; but I have never denied the truth of the Scriptures; and I have never spoken with intentional disrespect of religion in general, or of any denomination of Christians in particular. It is true that in early life I was inclined to believe in what I understand is called the "Doctrine of Necessity"— that is, that the human mind is impelled to action, or held in rest by some power, over which the mind itself has no control; and I have

sometimes (with one, two or three, but never publicly) tried to maintain this opinion in argument. The habit of arguing thus however, I have, entirely left off for more than five years. And I add here, I have always understood this same opinion to be held by several of the Christian denominations. The foregoing, is the whole truth, briefly stated, in relation to myself, upon this subject.

I do not think I could myself, be brought to support a man for office, whom I knew to be an open enemy of, and scoffer at, religion. Leaving the higher matter of eternal consequences, between him and his Maker, I still do not think any man has the right thus to insult the feelings, and injure the morals, of the community in which he may live. If, then, I was guilty of such conduct, I should blame no man who could condemn me for it; but I do blame those, whoever they may be, who falsely put such a charge in circulation against me.[13]

Lincoln admits that he is not a member of any Christian church. As a state legislator, Lincoln did not attend church services regularly. Soon after he moved to Springfield, the new state capital, he wrote to Mary Owens, "I've never been to church yet, nor probably shall not be soon. I stay away because I am conscious I should not know how to behave myself."[14] In the midst of the Civil War he would confess, "I have often wished that I was a more devout man than I am."[15] His closest friend, Joshua F. Speed, also recalled Lincoln's personal struggle of faith during his early years in Springfield: "When I knew him, in early life, he was a skeptic." Speed added, however, that Lincoln "was very cautious never to give expression to any thought or sentiment that would grate harshly upon a Christian's ear."[16] The exoneration implicit in his handbill—"I have never denied the truth of the Scriptures"—lies with his belief that infidelity or lack of faith lies primarily in one's view of the Holy Scriptures and not with membership at a particular church congregation.

Most important, Lincoln wishes to address the political relevance of a candidate's religious beliefs and practice. He adds that he never spoke "with intentional disrespect" of religion or any particular denomination. His concern not to show disrespect toward the faith of others can be seen in his draft of a speech comparing Thomas Jefferson and Zachary Taylor (the Whig presidential candidate in 1848) on the presidential veto power: "They are more alike than the accounts of the crucifixion, as given by any two of the evangelists—more alike, or at least as much alike, as any two accounts of the inscription, written and erected by Pilate at that time."[17] In his only term as congressman, Lincoln omitted the biblical reference in his final draft. He knew enough not to stir up controversy over apparent inconsistencies in the Bible.

Some have been troubled by Lincoln's reticence in the 1846 handbill to profess anything specific about his religious beliefs.[18] To be sure, Lincoln had little time for religious doctrines and sectarian institutions derived from the Holy Scriptures by fallible human minds and was careful not to misrepresent himself religiously on the stump.[19] But this view places too great an emphasis on Lincoln's "political expediency," for he only intended to clarify his rumored "infidelity." Lincoln felt no obligation to share personal religious views that he believed bore little or no relevance to the campaign at hand. He therefore shows that his avoidance of sins of commission is the only relevant political consideration, not any sins of omission. The latter may have "eternal consequences" to be worked out "between him and his Maker," but this bears no import to political affairs. Lincoln chose to explain his understanding of religion and civil society to help his constituents know the legitimate expectations they should have regarding a candidate's public attitude toward religion.

This is why Lincoln does not state explicitly what he thinks about the Bible or any particular Christian doctrine. Like George Washington, James Madison, and other American founders, Lincoln did not think the public profession of one's religious convictions contributed much for the community to consider when deciding on a candidate for office or when discussing the merits of a specific public policy. An undue emphasis on one's religious beliefs, moreover, could easily lead to factious politics, with no easy means of resolving disagreements. Here religion in the public square could give rise to factious majorities ruling according to their numerical might, as opposed to principled right, and therefore threaten the perpetuation of American self-government. In short, elections should not be turned into a forum for resolving religious quarrels.

In the handbill, Lincoln volunteers an account of his belief "in early life" in the doctrine of necessity, which seems to deny the free will of man. However, he emphasizes that five years had passed since he last made these arguments, they were never made in public, and they were understood by him to be shared by several Christian denominations. A case in point would be his own parents' church in Kentucky, Little Mount Separate Baptist Church. They were part of the "Separate" Baptist movement, otherwise known as primitive or "hardshell" Baptists for their strict predestination doctrines.[20] In short, Lincoln's belief in the doctrine of necessity was a private matter not intended for the public ear and one that did not threaten Christian orthodoxy because none existed on the subject. He offers this personal information in the event that it might have been the source of the rumor of his religious infidelity. In the second paragraph, Lincoln shares his understanding of how the rumor might trouble the consciences of some of his constituents—hence, the reason for no longer debating his said belief even privately "with one, two or three." As already noted, Lincoln stated his uncertainty in supporting a political candidate whom he knew to be "an open enemy of, and scoffer at, religion." Lincoln defends the community's "feelings" connected with religion; they should be immune from public "insult." While the private insult of a neighbor's religion is hardly intended by Lincoln, his emphasis on the feelings of "the community" leaves room for *discussing* the truth of a particular religion with one's neighbor without the malice and recklessness accompanying the intentional slight of a fellow citizen's convictions. Religion deals with a man's conscience and hence should be handled with care—especially if that man is a neighbor and fellow citizen.

During his first run for Congress in 1842, Lincoln showed respect for a community's religious sensibilities—despite personally experiencing "the strangest church influence" against him—in a letter written to a delegate to the Seventh Congressional District convention after the campaign was over:

> Baker is a Campbellite, and therefore as I suppose, with few exceptions got all that church. My wife has some relatives in the Presbyterian and some in the Episcopal Churches, and therefore, wherever it would tell, I was set down as either the one or the other, whilst it was every where contended that no ch[r]istian ought to go for me, because I belonged to no church, was suspected of being a deist, and had talked about fighting a duel. With all these things Baker, of course had nothing to do. *Nor do I complain of them. As to his own church going for him, I think that was right enough*, and as to the influences I have spoken of in the other, though they were very strong, it would be grossly untrue and unjust to charge that they acted upon them in a body or even very nearly so. I only mean that those influences levied a tax of a considerable per cent. upon my strength throughout the religious community.[21]

In the eyes of churchgoers, his dueling episode with James Shields the previous year,[22] lack of church membership, and suspected deism crippled his campaign to be nominated as the Whig candidate of Sangamon County. Lincoln confesses that he found his campaign hampered by public doubts over his religious inclinations; yet, he does not begrudge his opponent (and close friend) for drawing the support of his own community church. Here, Lincoln grants not only the likelihood but the propriety of winning the support of those most

acquainted with you. For example, in his first run for the Illinois State
House, the 23-year-old Lincoln received 277 out of 300 votes from his
hometown precinct—the political equivalent of a congregation.[23] Even
though it turned out to be a losing bid, Lincoln's first campaign for
public office demonstrated the power of proximity or affection for
what is near and dear, which he extends to one's church.

He also guards the "morals" fostered by the religious sentiments of
the community from public "injury." To disregard the consequences of
undermining a community's religious beliefs is to place too sanguine a
confidence in the principles and practices of what one would substitute in their place. As George Washington expressed this in his
Farewell Address:

> Of all the dispositions and habits which lead to political prosperity,
> Religion and morality are indispensable supports. In vain would that
> man claim the tribute of Patriotism, who should labour to subvert these
> great Pillars of human happiness, these firmest props of the duties of
> Men and citizens. The mere Politician, equally with the pious man
> ought to respect and cherish them.[24]

Lincoln leaves "the higher matter of eternal consequences" to the
offending party "and his Maker," and preserves religious freedom, on
the one hand, and promotes social responsibility, on the other. George
Washington set the example:

> The liberty enjoyed by the people of these states of worshipping
> Almighty God agreeably to their consciences, is not only among the
> choicest of their *blessings*, but also of their *rights*. While men perform
> their social duties faithfully, they do all that society or the state can with
> propriety demand or expect; and remain responsible only to their
> Maker for their religion, or modes of faith, which they may prefer or
> profess.[25]

As president, Lincoln explicitly acknowledged the nation's debt to the
Almighty through proclamations of days of religious observance. Lincoln
called for national days of thanksgiving, fasting, and prayer 11 times. In
his last public address, following Lee's surrender at Appomattox, Lincoln
states, "In the midst of this [celebration], however, He, from Whom all
blessings flow, must not be forgotten. A call for a national thanksgiving
is being prepared, and will be duly promulgated."[26] These proclamations, as well as other speeches involving religion in the public sphere,
show the mutual benefit that Lincoln believed religion and government
could have on each other.

An early example of Lincoln's attempt to show the limits of religious expression in the public square is found in his 1842 Temperance Address, a speech ostensibly about moderation or temperance with regards to alcohol but at its core focused on tempering or moderating excess in political discussion. Ironically, this speech about speech judiciously employs religious imagery to subtly point out how excessive religious expression in public debate can subvert the political trust, humility, and compromise that greases the wheels of Republican government.[27]

Lincoln's reference to the early temperance reformers as "Old School" champions alludes to a recent division among American Christians over the severity of original sin. In 1838 the Presbyterian Church suffered a schism, presaged by heresy trials earlier that decade, that produced an "Old School" and a "New School" bloc.[28] C. Bruce Staiger writes that as the Presbyterian Church sought to minister to the western settlements under its 1801 "Plan of Union," the incorporation of Congregationalists in their endeavor brought in "the liberalizing Pelagian and Arminian ideas of Unitarianism." The result was "a bitter theological quarrel between the strictly orthodox Calvinists of the Old School and the New School group which embraced the 'radical' New Divinity representative of the Congregational influence."[29] The debate centered around the doctrine of original sin, that men are born into the sin of Adam with only a few foreordained for salvation and the rest destined for damnation.[30] Opposed to the strict Calvinism of old guard Presbyterians, the New School held that man possessed free will. Charles Finney, the New School revivalist par excellence, described a man's conversion as an act of his will: " '[I]f the sinner ever has a new heart, he must . . . make it himself.' " Moreover, " 'All sin consists in selfishness; and all holiness or virtue, in disinterested benevolence.' "[31] Here lies the connection between the Second Great Awakening and the social reform movements that would sweep across America from the late 1820s through the 1830s.[32] A few examples of Lincoln's subtle employment of religious imagery should illustrate the threat he saw in religious movements becoming political causes.

Lincoln alludes to both the predestination and temperance controversies in his discussion of "persuasion," where he uses a more fitting and hopeful means of convincing a person of one's opinion: "On the contrary, assume to dictate to his judgment, or to command his action, or to mark him as one to be shunned and despised, and he will retreat within himself, close all the avenues to his head and his heart; and though your cause be naked truth itself, transformed to the heaviest lance, harder than steel, and sharper than steel can be made, and tho' you throw it with more than Herculean force and precision, you shall be no more able to pierce him, than to penetrate the hardshell of a tortoise with a rye straw." Not only does "hardshell" connote the Old School understanding of original sin and predestination, held by so-called hardshell or primitive Baptists and the like,[33] but "rye straw" also alludes to the distilling cereal of rye whiskey, the frontiersman drink of choice. By alluding to the "hard doctrines" of Old School, hardshell Calvinists along with frontier rye whiskey, he juxtaposes religious and drinking imagery as a not so subtle critique of Old School rhetoric. To penetrate a "hardshell" with a "rye" straw was a roundabout way of saying that it would be as difficult to force a tee-totaling (Old School) Calvinist to drink as it would be to persuade someone to give up drinking by condemning them. Given the Old School Presbyterian connotation to "Old School" temperance reform, Lincoln's use of the phrase could not have been missed by his audience—seated as they were in the Second Presbyterian Church of Springfield. He could not have picked a more coincidental (and controversial) pairing of religious doctrine and social reform.

Of course, the greatest example of Lincoln's religious politics comes in his Second Inaugural Address. Beginning his second term as president, Lincoln delivers a four-paragraph reflection on American theodicy—the problem of evil, specifically, slavery, in God's Providence. Where the original draft of the Gettysburg Address contains no direct reference to God, the Second Inaugural Address places God's purposes in the American Civil War front and center.[34] Lincoln interprets how the war had progressed under both human and divine intention and action, and where the Almighty may yet direct its consummation. Significantly, the address shows the extent to which Lincoln sees the reason and religion of men fall short in averting a civil war. In a telling demonstration of Republican statesmanship under the Providence of God, Lincoln ironically uses both reason and religion to deliver the lesson.[35]

Foremost in his mind was uniting a divided nation. Only a common understanding of the war—its cause and meaning for the fractured country—could ensure a lasting peace. At the height of his rhetorical powers, Lincoln showed how both the war and emancipation came to the country despite the initial intentions of either side of the conflict. Another power must be at work, and Lincoln returned the country to that other, higher power in hopes that a common, national humility before the Almighty would help Americans both North and South to fix what they had broken. How else could Lincoln expect there to be "malice toward none" and "charity for all"? Only by the grace of God could all Americans experience and live out that "new birth of freedom" he called for at Gettysburg.[36]

After a brief opening paragraph that explains why there's no need for "an extended address," like that at his first inauguration, Lincoln devotes the remaining three paragraphs to an explanation of the Civil War—how it began, and what must follow its conclusion.[37]

In the second paragraph, Lincoln states that at his first inauguration, no one North or South, Unionist or Secessionist, wanted a "civil war." Thus, neither North nor South was initially culpable for a war that would cost so much in blood and treasure. But something proved more important than avoiding war. For Lincoln as president, "*saving the Union*" initially without war—through the words of his First Inaugural Address—was the goal, but eventually he would "*accept war rather than let it perish.*" For "insurgent agents," as Lincoln put it (and not "the South" or "Southern legislatures"), to "*destroy*" the Union without war through words of their own—"negotiation"—was the initial priority, but they soon would "*make* war rather than let the nation survive.*"

Implicit in shifting the focus from war—i.e., its avoidance—to the Union—i.e., its preservation—is an invitation to consider the significance of the Union. Why is it so important that it is worth defending by force, if words fail? What would be lost in its dissolution, or what would be gained by preserving it? Why is the *United* States so important? But despite separating the combatants into saviors and destroyers, the second paragraph closes with a statement of the war's arrival and not a judgment of its earthly cause by linking the start of the war with the guilty party. This was not the time to foster sectional animosities. Lincoln's demonstration in the second paragraph of the failure of reason to avert the war will now be followed by a demonstration in the third paragraph of the failure of religion to do the same.

The third paragraph, the key paragraph of the speech, begins with his first reference to slaves—*the* issue that needs explaining as the Civil War nears its conclusion. He now says that slavery "somehow" was "the cause of the war," with insurgents seeking to bolster slavery's hold on the United States "even by war." The federal government only sought to "restrict" its extension. Somehow, the Union and slavery (and freedom by implication) are connected in some moral sense. Emancipation was a surprise to both sides—one more "fundamental and astounding." In short, the war brought about a momentous change in the American regime, but one that neither side intended. If unintended, then the Radical Republicans and Northerners, in general, could afford to tone down their pride at being "victorious in the strife."

So, neither side intended the war or the abolition of slavery, but both cataclysms took place anyway. What else needs to be explored? The ways of Providence in American history. Here Lincoln's "God talk" begins in earnest.

Lincoln observes that both sides "read the same Bible, and pray to the same God." Implication? No war should have been started, since both sides should have viewed the cause of the conflict in the same way—God's way. No such luck! Lincoln notes that despite their common faith in God, "each invokes His aid against the other."

Lincoln now pauses to comment on the audacity of invoking God's help to enslave others: "It may seem strange that any men should dare to ask a just God's assistance in wringing their bread from the sweat of other men's faces; but let us judge not that we be not judged." While the loaded language (i.e., "dare," "just God's," "wringing," and "sweat") indicates where Lincoln stands regarding the justice of slavery, he asks the nation not to "judge" those who would dare ask God for help in enslaving others. In the context of the verse he quotes (Matthew 7:1), the judgment feared is divine. Lincoln seeks to avoid a further reckoning on top of that which may already be working itself out as punishment for the offense of slavery. Lincoln concludes that the "Almighty has His own purposes" because the prayers of neither have been answered fully. This conclusion becomes the premise upon which Lincoln bases his theological supposition about the meaning of the war and slavery's passing from the American stage.

Lincoln now connects the Civil War and slavery theologically by citing Matthew 18:7: "Woe unto the world because of offences! for it must needs be that offences come; but woe to that man by whom the offence cometh!" This verse expresses one of the fundamental paradoxes of Christianity: free will and the sovereignty of God (or, human, moral agency and hence responsibility coupled with original sin or man's fall from grace). Lincoln suggests that although slavery appears to be an offense allowed "in the providence of God," the human beings who introduced and maintained it in America are still morally culpable.

Lincoln cannot tell this story of the nation at war with itself without bringing God into the fray. The American people need a common understanding of the war—its ultimate and efficient causes—in order to move forward as a unified country. For the eminent termination of the war to produce the "lasting peace" he mentions in the fourth paragraph, for the war between Americans really to be over, they must all have the same memory of it—the same history of it. And to Lincoln's mind, the ending of the war must be a "just" one to produce this peace that endures. Most important, a common view of the justice of the war requires a godly perspective. By his own earlier reasoning, Lincoln has his work cut out for him, for despite the nation's common Bible and God, the American people did not have a common, biblical view of slavery. Its justice or injustice was the source of disagreement among Americans that led to the Civil War.

Lincoln tries to produce a common view of the war by withholding judgment upon the South alone for the evil of slavery. He supposes that slavery was an offense that came due to both Southern and Northern citizens, and one that God "now wills to remove" through "this terrible war," which afflicts Americans both North and South.

But why should Americans, especially those on the Confederate side, believe this rendering of history? Why should Southern Secessionists and former slaveholders now believe that slavery was wrong and thus view the war as a "scourge" of the Almighty? Because it offers the best explanation for what Americans experienced with regards to the war and slavery. How else to explain what Lincoln showed was inexplicable in the second paragraph and early in the third paragraph? How else to account for a war no one wanted and an emancipation no one expected? Moreover, if God visited a war upon the United States as punishment for the offense of slavery, and slavery disappears by virtue of that war, no American North or South can blame the other for the calamity *and* escape blame himself. Put simply, common guilt means common punishment—and if accepted as such, a common future is possible under God. The third paragraph offers a collective punishment for collective guilt in order to set up the collective healing process and peace of the concluding paragraph of Lincoln's speech.

The last paragraph begins with the most famous line of the address: "With malice toward none; with charity for all . . ." Because of the losses suffered by Americans due to the Civil War, Lincoln suggests an end to the blame game insofar as it divides Americans into hostile camps. Crudely stated, what Americans broke as a nation, they must now fix as a nation—with God's help. He exhorts them to "finish the work" they are in, which means conclude the war with a Union victory, and to heal the wounds of citizen against citizen by caring for the soldier and his family. He then states that "to do all which may achieve and cherish a just, and a lasting peace," Americans must be firm "in the right, as God gives [them] . . . to see the right." Here Lincoln calls on the nation to do what the war could not do: build a common life from the ruins of a divided country. Only as Americans rely upon God and His enlightenment, as He allows them "to see the right," does Lincoln believe the battle for Union on the field of war can be won off the field and in the hearts of every American. The temptation to malice will be great; the temptation to withhold charity, including forgiveness, will be great as well.

But how can Lincoln encourage Americans to act "with firmness in the right"? Both sides had read the same Bible and prayed to the same God, but drew opposite conclusions that led to a devastating Civil War. What has Lincoln done in his speech to bolster their confidence that they can not only "see the right," but also come to a common understanding of it despite their previous differences of opinion? If Americans have learned anything from the war and slavery's abolition, it's their inability to produce good on their own. Lincoln hopes to foster a Republican humility and moderation, borne of a renewed reliance upon God, that can reconstruct a bitterly divided nation.

And so Lincoln starts them with what can be clearly understood from their common Bible and prayers to God: "With malice toward none, with charity for all."[38] On their own, Americans would be tempted to harbor malice in their hearts toward their perceived erring brethren, and find little incentive to act with goodwill and love toward them. Only by the grace of God will they be able to experience "a new birth of freedom" as a self-governing people free of the taint of slavery. With one-eighth of the population now newly freed men, and still greatly concentrated in the South, the task of national reconstruction is made all the more difficult.

In addition, if the war is seen as a divine scourge and not an earthly one, then one's hatred of the enemy must dissipate or else be directed toward the heavens. But "the believers in a Living God" could not permit themselves this option, for they worship a God whose judgments they believe to be "true and righteous altogether" (Psalms 19:9). This includes the malice Northerners would wish to express against Southerners, and vice versa, as well as that by former slaves toward their former masters. Charity, not malice, must mark their actions toward each other—North versus South, former slave versus former master, white versus black. Unfortunately, peace between North and South was purchased primarily for whites and at the cost of scapegoating blacks following the failure of Reconstruction.

Having gone through the speech as a whole, we can now see why Lincoln had to hide or diminish the culpability of the South for the Civil War: "a just, and a lasting peace, among ourselves"—in short, a restoration of the Union—depended on blame being shared by all

Americans. But Lincoln could not ignore the issue entirely, for he also sought to unite the country as one where slaves would be free from their bondage. In other words, as he declared at Gettysburg, he intended the American people, North and South, to experience "a new birth of freedom." This meant that Southern Secessionists would not be held solely responsible for causing the war; but it also required that they change their mind about the meaning of America. The Union was now to be what Lincoln always understood it to be in principle—a union devoted to protecting the equal rights of all her citizens. It was a bargain of sorts, which Lincoln explained with a rhetoric both political and theological far exceeding any of his public career.

Following his second inaugural, Lincoln wrote of his address:

> I expect the latter to wear as well as—perhaps better than—any thing I have produced; but I believe it is not immediately popular. Men are not flattered by being shown that there has been a difference of purpose between the Almighty and them. To deny it, however, in this case, is to deny that there is a God governing the world. It is a truth which I thought needed to be told; and as whatever of humiliation there is in it, falls most directly on myself, I thought others might afford for me to tell it.[39]

Through reason and religion, Lincoln shows how reason and religion failed to avert the American Civil War in order to induce the humility that will be needed for the work ahead. What failed to prevent war among Americans must now succeed in order to unite them.

For me, to examine Abraham Lincoln's view of religion's role in Republican politics is to learn about American self-government: namely, to learn about the abiding tension between our commitment to the equal rights of humanity and our obligation to secure those rights by the consent of the governed. Understanding the relevance of religion and, especially, Christianity, to Lincoln's politics helps us better understand his defense of the American constitutional union as an expression of his faith in God's purposes for himself and his country. As Lincoln put it before the New Jersey Senate en route to his first inauguration:

> I am exceedingly anxious that this Union, the Constitution, and the liberties of the people shall be perpetuated in accordance with the original idea for which that struggle was made, and I shall be most happy indeed if I shall be an humble instrument in the hands of the Almighty, and of this, his almost chosen people, for perpetuating the object of that great struggle.[40]

Notes

1. "Address before the Young Men's Lyceum of Springfield, Illinois (27 January 1838)," in *The Collected Works of Abraham Lincoln*, ed. Roy P. Basler, 9 vols. (New Brunswick: Rutgers University Press, 1953–1955), 1: 112. Hereafter cited as *Collected Works*; all emphases in original except where otherwise noted.

2. For an interpretation of Lincoln's religious development as it influenced his politics that emphasizes his early devotion to "republican ideals" instead of "God or scripture," see Nicholas Parrillo, "Lincoln's Calvinist Transformation," *Civil War History*, 46 (3) (September 2000): 227–253.

3. "Order for Sabbath Observance (15 November 1862)," in *Collected Works*, 5: 497.

4. Cf. John G. West, Jr., *The Politics of Revelation and Reason: Religion and Civic Life in the New Nation* (Lawrence: University Press of Kansas, 1996). West shows that some evangelical reform movements—in particular, those addressing the Sunday mails and the Cherokee removal controversies—made their social and political appeals not merely on religious grounds but on the basis of human reason:
   > Because government authority would be kept separate from ecclesiastical authority, churches now could be trusted to create—and defend—civic morality. Stripped of any pretensions that might have made them dangerous to republicanism, churches were free to reform society according to the moral law held in common by both revelation and reason. *The Politics of Revelation and Reason*, 210.

   Robert N. Bellah observes that the more moderate wing of abolitionism, led by Theodore Dwight Weld, sought reform by calling for greater enforcement of the U.S. Constitution:
   > Weld and his associates developed a constitutional argument that even as early as 1835 described the treatment in the North of free Negroes and abolitionists as "denials of rights to the equal protection of the laws, the safeguards of due process, and the privileges and immunities of citizens." . . . Unlike Garrison the group around Weld believed that emancipation was implicit in the Constitution and that what that document needed was not burning [as Garrison did] but clarification and enforcement. *The Broken Covenant*, 52.

5. "Address before the Young Men's Lyceum of Springfield, Illinois (27 January 1838)," in *Collected Works*, 1: 114.

6. Ibid., 1: 112.

7. An exhortation to law-abidingness can be found in the Bible in 1 Timothy 2: 1–4, among other places, which gives Christians the hope that their obedience to the government will produce both peace for them and salvation for others:
   > I exhort therefore, that, first of all, supplications, prayers, intercessions, and giving of thanks, be made for all men; For kings, and for all that are

in authority; that we may lead a quiet and peaceable life in all godliness and honesty. For this is good and acceptable in the sight of God our Saviour; Who will have all men to be saved, and to come unto the knowledge of the truth.

8. Joshua F. Speed, *Reminiscences of Abraham Lincoln and Notes of a Visit to California* (Louisville, KY: John P. Morton & Company, 1884), 32–33. Don E. Fehrenbacher and Virginia Fehrenbacher, in their compilation of recollected Lincoln utterances, rank this story a "C" on a scale of "A" to "E" for reliability. ("A" denotes a Lincoln quotation recorded by the auditor within days of hearing it, and "E" denotes a quotation that "is probably not authentic.") "C" is a quotation "recorded noncontemporaneously." In Speed's case, his published account of his encounter came 20 years after the fact. Don E. Fehrenbacher and Virginia Fehrenbacher, *Recollected Words of Abraham Lincoln* (Stanford: Stanford University Press, 1996), 414, lii–liii. According to Mary Todd Lincoln, Lincoln "read the bible a good deal about 1864." See "Mary Todd Lincoln (William Herndon (hereafter referred to as WHH) interview [September 1866])," in *Herndon's Informants: Letters, Interviews, and Statements about Abraham Lincoln*, ed. Douglas L. Wilson and Rodney O. Davis (Urbana: University of Illinois Press, 1998), 360. Wayne C. Temple records that Joshua F. Speed joined Trinity Methodist Church late in life in Wayne C. Temple, *Abraham Lincoln: From Skeptic to Prophet* (Mahomet, IL: Mayhaven Publishing, 1995), 295, n. 123. See also infra, n. 15.

9. In an 1866 letter to William Herndon, Speed commented on Lincoln's faith: "I think that when I first knew Mr L he was skeptical as to the great truths of the Christian Religion. I think that after he was elected President, he sought to become a believer—and to make the Bible a preceptor to his faith and a guide for his conduct." "Joshua F. Speed to WHH (12 January 1866)," in Wilson and Davis, eds., *Herndon's Informants*, 156.

10. For a similar interpretation offered earlier this century, see Christopher Dawson, *Religion and the Modern State* (London: Sheed & Ward, 1935), chapter 6, "Religion and Politics," and chapter 7, "The Religious Solution," 102–128.

11. Mark Y. Hanley, *Beyond a Christian Commonwealth: The Protestant Quarrel with the American Republic, 1830–1860* (Chapel Hill: University of North Carolina Press, 1994), 158, 31. See also Christoph Schönborn, "The Hope of Heaven, the Hope of Earth," *First Things* (52) (April 1995): 32–38; and George Weigel, "The Church's Political Hopes for the World; or, Diognetus Revisited," in *The Two Cities of God: The Church's Responsibility for the Earthly City*, ed. Carl E. Braaten and Robert W. Jenson (Grand Rapids, MI: Wm. B. Eerdmans Publishing Company, 1997), 59–77.

12. "To Allen N. Ford (11 August 1846)," in *Collected Works*, 1: 383.

13. "Handbill Replying to Charges of Infidelity (31 July 1846)," in *Collected Works*, 1: 382.

14. "To Mary S. Owens (7 May 1837)," in *Collected Works*, 1: 78.

15. "Remarks to Baltimore Presbyterian Synod: Two Versions [No. 1] (24 October 1863)," in *Collected Works*, 6: 535. The context for his remark, though, paints a less skeptical picture of Lincoln's faith. In the immediately preceding sentence, Lincoln states that as president he "was early brought to a living reflection that nothing in my power whatever, in others to rely upon, would succeed without the direct assistance of the Almighty, but all must fail." The sentence that follows Lincoln's wish that he was "more devout" actually affirms his piety: "Nevertheless, amid the greatest difficulties of my administration, when I could not see any other resort, I would place my whole reliance in God, knowing that all would go well, and that he would decide for the right." *Collected Works*, 6: 535, 536. Among the earliest extant writings of Lincoln's is a hand-written copybook of arithmetic, a page of which includes the following rhyme: "Abraham Lincoln/his hand and pen/he will be good but/god knows When." "Copybook Verses [1824–1826]," in *Collected Works*, 1: 1. Cf. the assessment by Francis B. Carpenter, a portrait painter who lived at the White House for six months in 1864 as he painted a reenactment of Lincoln's first reading of the Emancipation Proclamation: "In the ordinary acceptation of the term, I would scarcely have called Mr. Lincoln a *religious* man,—and yet I believe him to have been a sincere *Christian*." Emphasis is in the original; Francis B. Carpenter, *The Inner Life of Abraham Lincoln* (Lincoln: University of Nebraska Press, 1995; originally published in 1866 as *Six Months at the White House with Abraham Lincoln* by Hurd and Houghton, NY), 185–186. Biographer Ward Hill Lamon, a member of Lincoln's inner circle as president, turns Carpenter's view on its head semantically, while expressing the same sentiment: "He was not a Christian in the orthodox sense of the term, yet he was as conscientiously religious as any man." *Recollections of Abraham Lincoln, 1847–1865*, ed. Dorothy Lamon Teillard (Lincoln: University of Nebraska Press, 1994; originally published by A. C. McClurg & Co., 1895, 2nd ed., expanded in 1911, Washington, DC), 334. This echoes Mary Todd's statement to William H. Herndon: "[H]e was a religious man always, as I think," but "he was not a technical Christian." "Mary Todd Lincoln (WHH interview [September 1866])," in *Herndon's Informants*, 360.

16. Speed, *Reminiscences of Abraham Lincoln*, 32. Cf. Douglas L. Wilson, *Honor's Voice: The Transformation of Abraham Lincoln* (New York: Alfred A. Knopf, 1998), 309–312, which argues of Lincoln: "Disguising his religious views, or construing them in a more favorable light, became necessary for an ambitious and rising man who needed the good opinion of the public to succeed" (312).

17. "Speech in U.S. House of Representatives on the Presidential Question (27 July 1848)," in *Collected Works*, 1: 503.

18. Hans J. Morgenthau, "The Mind of Abraham Lincoln: A Study in Detachment and Practicality," in *Essays on Lincoln's Faith and Politics*,

ed. Kenneth W. Thompson (Lanham, MD: University Press of America, 1983), 8.

19. The passage cited most often on this subject comes from a eulogy Congressman Henry C. Deming delivered before the General Assembly of Connecticut in 1865: "He [Lincoln] said, he had never united himself to any church, because he found difficulty in giving his assent, without mental reservations, to the long complicated statements of Christian doctrine which characterize their Articles of Belief and Confessions of Faith." William J. Wolf, *The Religion of Abraham Lincoln* (New York: Seabury Press, 1963; originally published under the title *The Almost Chosen People: A Study of the Religion of Abraham Lincoln* by Doubleday & Company, 1959), 74. The Fehrenbachers rank Deming's recollection a "C" (on a scale of "A" to "E") for reliability. *Recollected Words of Abraham Lincoln*, 137.

20. Allen C. Guelzo, "Abraham Lincoln and the Doctrine of Necessity," *Journal of the Abraham Lincoln Association*, 18 (Winter 1997): 66–67; Temple, *Abraham Lincoln*, 6.

21. Emphasis added; "To Martin S. Morris (26 March 1843)," in *Collected Works*, 1: 320.

22. "To James Shields (17 September 1842)" 1: 299–300; and "Memorandum of Duel Instructions to Elias H. Merryman [19 September 1842]," in *Collected Works*, 1: 300–302. For a brief history of Christian antagonism toward dueling in early America, see *Church and State in the United States: Historical Development and Contemporary Problems of Religious Freedom under the Constitution*, ed. Anson Phelps Stokes, 3 vols. (New York: Harper & Brothers, 1950), 2: 5–12.

23. "Communication to the People of Sangamo County (9 March 1832)," in *Collected Works*, 1: 5, n. 1. He ran eighth out of 13 candidates for 4 seats in the lower house of the Illinois General Assembly. Nevertheless, his New Salem returns were all the more impressive given that he only recently moved to the area six months prior to announcing his candidacy for Illinois State Representative. In addition, he interrupted the campaign for three months to lead a local militia brigade in the Black Hawk War, being elected captain by his men. Two years later, he would run second in a field of 13 candidates for 4 Sangamon County seats, and poll first (out of 17 candidates) in his next two reelection bids.

24. "Farewell Address (19 September 1796)," in *George Washington: A Collection*, ed. W. B. Allen (Indianapolis: Liberty Fund, 1988), 521. Lincoln would make explicit reference to Washington's Farewell Address in his famous Cooper Institute Address; however, the context was not religion but rather sectionalism due to the slavery controversy. "Address at Cooper Institute, New York City (27 February 1860)," in *Collected Works*, 3: 536–537.

25. "To the Annual Meeting of Quakers (September 1789)," in Allen, ed., *George Washington*, 533.

26. "Last Public Address (11 April 1865)," in *Collected Works*, 8: 399–400.

27. For a close interpretation of Lincoln's Temperance Address, see Lucas E. Morel, *Lincoln's Sacred Effort: Defining Religion's Role in American Self-Government* (Lanham, MD: Lexington Books, 2000), chapter 4, "The Political Vices of Religion."

28. For an examination of this split as it related to the political tensions of the times (slavery, in particular), see C. Bruce Staiger, "Abolitionism and the Presbyterian Schism of 1837–1838," *The Mississippi Valley Historical Review*, 36 (December 1949): 391–414. See also Mitchell Snay, *Gospel of Disunion: Religion and Separatism in the Antebellum South* (Chapel Hill: University of North Carolina Press, 1997; originally published by Cambridge University Press, NY, 1993), chapter 4, "Harbingers of Disunion: The Denominational Schisms," 113–150; *Dictionary of Christianity in America*, Daniel G. Reid with Robert D. Linder, ed. Bruce L. Shelley, and Harry S. Stout (Downers Grove, IL: InterVarsity Press, 1990), s.v. "New School Presbyterians," 819–820; and *Encyclopedia of the American Religious Experience: Studies of Traditions and Movements*, ed. Charles H. Lippy and Peter W. Williams, 3 vols. (New York: Charles Scribner's Sons, 1988), s.v. "Presbyterianism," by Louis Weeks, 1: 502–503. The Methodists and Baptists would split in 1843 and 1845, respectively, over the issue of slavery. See Edwin S. Gaustad, ed., *A Documentary History of Religion in America: To the Civil War* (Grand Rapids, MI: Wm. B. Eerdmans Publishing Company, 1982), 491–497.

29. Staiger, "Abolitionism and the Presbyterian Schism of 1837–1838," 393.

30. For a brief history of this doctrinal development within the Presbyterian Church, see Gilbert Hobbs Barnes, *The Antislavery Impulse, 1830–1844* (New York: D. Appleton-Century Company, 1933), 3–12. See also Clifton E.Olmstead, *History of Religion in the United States* (Englewood Cliffs, NJ: Prentice-Hall, 1960), 311–314 and 189–190 for discussion of the preceding generation's dispute over the doctrine of original sin and the free will of man.

31. Cited in Barnes, *The Antislavery Impulse*, 11.

32. Barnes lists several of the early aims of "the Great Eight" societies that would take shape under the leadership of the Great Revivalists like Charles Grandison Finney and protégé Theodore Dwight Weld: promoting home and foreign missions, distributing Bibles and tracts, funding Sunday schools, promoting temperance, and converting sailors. He notes, "[T]he benevolent empire was dominated by 'New-School' Presbyterians, liberals of the Great Revival." Barnes, *The Antislavery Impulse*, 17, 18. See also Staiger, "Abolitionism and the Presbyterian Schism," 397: "Although Finney devoted himself almost exclusively to revivalism, his doctrines lent themselves to a great interest in social reform. Theodore Dwight Weld, a convert of Finney's, shaped this interest into another revival, one in which slaveholding was identical with sin." Weld would go on to become the great temperance speaker of frontier America, as well as write *Slavery as It Is*, an 1839 book from which Harriet Beecher Stowe mined details for her 1852 literary bombshell, *Uncle Tom's Cabin*.

See Joan D. Hedrick, *Harriet Beecher Stowe: A Life* (New York: Oxford University Press, 1994), 230.

33. For derivation of the "hard shell" label and its theological import, see "Baptist Churches in U.S.A." and "Primitive Baptists" descriptions in the *Dictionary of Christianity in America*, 110–111 and 940, respectively, and "Primitive Baptist" in Frank S. Mead, ed., *Handbook of Denominations in the United States*, rev. Samuel S. Hill, 9th ed. (Nashville: Abingdon Press, 1985), 51–52.

34. Lincoln probably added the phrase "under God" on the platform as he listened to Edward Everett's oration. Lincoln's famous last line reads as follows: "[T]hat this nation, under God, shall have a new birth of freedom—and that government of the people, by the people, for the people, shall not perish from the earth." "Address Delivered at the Dedication of the Cemetery at Gettysburg (19 November 1863)," in *Collected Works*, 7: 23 and 7: 20, n. 19. Cf. Garry Wills, *Lincoln at Gettysburg: The Words That Remade America* (New York: Simon & Schuster, 1992), 194, 198, and 261: "[T]hat the nation shall, under God, have a new birth of freedom, and that the government of the people, by the people, and for the people, shall not perish from the earth."

35. See Morel, *Lincoln's Sacred Effort*, chapter 5, "The Political Limits of Reason and Revelation."

36. But as David W. Blight argues in *Race and Reunion: The Civil War in American Memory* (Cambridge, MA: Belknap Press of Harvard University Press, 2001), national unity would soon come at the expense of black Americans.

37. All citations from Lincoln's Second Inaugural Address are from "Second Inaugural Address (4 March 1865)," in *Collected Works*, 8: 332–333.

38. Cf. Andrew Jackson, "Second Inaugural Address (4 March 1833)," in *A Compilation of the Messages and Papers of the Presidents: 1787–1897*, ed. James D. Richardson, 20 vols. (Washington, DC: Government Printing Office, 1896), 3: 3: "To do justice to all and to submit to wrong from none has been during my Administration its governing maxim . . ."

39. "To Thurlow Weed (15 March 1865)," in *Collected Works*, 8: 356.

40. "Address to the New Jersey Senate at Trenton, New Jersey (21 February 1861)," in *Collected Works*, 5: 236.

Chapter Five

"We Must Put on the Armor of God": Harry Truman and the Cold War

Elizabeth Edwards Spalding

Harry Truman was the second Baptist—Warren G. Harding was the first—to be president of the United States. In the mid-1940s and early 1950s, America was a country of believers and churchgoers, but mainline Protestant subtleties—more than biblical sermons—resonated in the halls of the State Department as well as in higher education. Intellectuals found direct appeals to religious faith to be ignorant, coarse, and even detrimental to political progress: They criticized the president for lack of tact and sophistication, viewing the growing conflict with the Soviet Union in Manichean terms, and refusing to negotiate with the Kremlin. It is interesting to note that if we substitute Methodist for Baptist, and the war on terrorism for the cold war, we can see some parallels between the twenty-first century and Truman's time in office. For a deeper understanding of the modern era overall and some insights into today's connections between religion and politics in the White House, let us take another look at Harry Truman. Not only will we see the influence of faith and religion on one man's worldview and his politics, but we will also see how faith and religion can be central to understanding the main global conflict of the twentieth century.

Truman was both a believer and a practical man. Strongly opinionated and ecumenical at the same time, he aimed to build an international coalition to fight world communism. We are accustomed to thinking of this coalition in political terms: of the Truman Doctrine, the Marshall Plan, NATO, and the other policies and alliances defending the West. But Truman also included the world's main religious denominations in his coalition against communism. In key respects, he held that religious groups and institutions were more primary than political or strategic alliances to winning the cold war, since the clash was fundamentally between the atheism of communist totalitarianism and the theism of the rest of the world. Granting that different language was used and different texts were read, Truman argued that all believers agreed with the sense of the Ten Commandments and the Sermon on the Mount.

Along the way, and perhaps not entirely intentionally, Truman developed special relationships with the Roman Catholic Church and the Jewish people. There were domestic political considerations, to be sure, since American Catholics—numbering 24 million in 1946 and 30 million by 1953—were the largest national minority and reliable urban Democratic Party voters, while American Jews at almost 5 million were dependably for the Democratic Party and gaining in political, economic, and cultural influence throughout Truman's presidency. But beyond domestic concerns, Truman believed that both Jews and Catholics deserved political as well as religious recognition and that these two religious groups were important to world politics. The newly formed Jewish state of Israel, most important to Truman, fulfilled a biblical mandate for God's chosen people and, almost as important to Truman, embodied the seeds of democracy and freedom in the Middle East, a significant region in the cold war and in world history. For the universal Catholic Church, Pope Pius XII was the preeminent anticommunist spokesman and agreed with the president about the fundamental meaning of the East-West conflict. At home, Francis J. Spellman's first published article after being elevated to cardinal by Pius XII in 1946 was entitled "Communism is Unamerican," in which the most influential leader among the American bishops vowed "no conspiracy of silence" on the subject; meanwhile, popular radio orator and future bishop Fulton Sheen was actively anticommunist in his lectures and books, such as his 1948 *Communism and the Conscience of the West* and *Philosophy of Religion.*[1] The Catholic Church proved to be an indispensable anticommunist ally, and arguably the common cold war goals—and successes—of the Vatican and the Reagan administration in the 1980s were built on the cornerstone laid by Truman.[2]

Truman, Faith, and Religion

Scholars have generally ignored Harry Truman's faith and its influence on his politics, or they have characterized his religion as crude and simplistic. Even his best, recent biographers have given faith a restricted role in Truman's thought and action. Neither Robert Ferrell nor David McCullough discusses Truman's religion at length. Ferrell describes Truman's Baptist faith as part of a rural upbringing and credits Truman with considerable open-mindedness toward other creeds.[3] McCullough makes a reference to Truman's emphasis on acting out rather than talking about religion.[4] Similarly, Alonzo Hamby states that Truman left the formal practices of religion to his wife. He is the only major biographer who speaks of a "larger religious sense" in Truman, but it is nonetheless limited. Although Hamby refers to Truman's reliance on the Bible and prayer for guidance, he considers Truman's Baptist religion only an aspect of traditional Midwestern values and his selection of that denomination in keeping with his democratic attitude. Hamby does a good job of dissecting Truman's liberalism; ultimately, he believes Truman's religion was part of, and subordinate to, his politics.[5] Since biographers who know their subject well think that religion was incidental to Truman, the conclusion seems to be that matters of faith are not central to understanding the man.

Yet religion was important to Truman and his worldview. Upon inspection, what emerges is a man of deep, if simple, faith, who depended only a little on formal religion but prayed daily.[6] And Truman did not change when he became president. He carried his faith into his statecraft, arguing that an ethical code was necessary to politics properly understood. Reflected in private writings, public speeches, and other official documents, his religious convictions also informed his cold war statesmanship.[7]

Truman chose the Baptist religion in part for the reasons given by Hamby: he was comfortable with the democratic bearing of Baptists. Yet Truman did not select his religion because of his politics. In fact, his politics seemed to have derived from his faith perhaps more than from his parents. He joined the Baptist church at the age of 18 and was baptized soon after in 1903. Although his family background was mostly Baptist, he chose that denomination deliberately, after exposure to Presbyterian Sunday school as a child, interaction with members of the main Christian and Mormon churches, and many readings of the Bible. He believed that his Baptist sect gave "the common man the shortest and most direct approach to God."[8] Around the same time, his interest in politics was just emerging, even though his father was a partisan Democrat, and he did not seem to develop strong ties to the party until his participation in Missouri state politics in the 1920s.[9] Even then, as he appealed to independent Democrats, he at times sided with Republicans who supported the Pendergast political machine.[10]

Truman biographers are partially correct about Truman's outlook on religion. He did not have much use for that religion which he considered a sensationalized kind. In the early months of their formal courtship, he wrote to his future wife Bess in a February 1911 letter: "I am by religion like everything else. I think there is more in acting than in talking." McCullough quotes only these lines from the letter, but the context of the two sentences is critical. Truman was describing to Bess a revival meeting that he had heard about, where the antics of those present (especially the jumping, dancing woman who had a lizard on her dress rather than "religion" in her heart) amused him; he was also unimpressed by the preacher, who had "exhorted and ranted and done everything else they usually do when they try to get something started as they call it." He went on to tell Bess that although religion had its place at regular assemblies and on Sunday, the preacher's meeting was "mostly excitement and when the excitement wears off people are as they always were."[11] This last observation underscores the consistent view of human nature held by Truman. He maintained that mankind could be good and achieve good, particularly when helped by government, but that individuals made their choices primarily because of their character rather than their religion. In his opinion, character was created by a moral code (of which Christianity embodied the best) that was revealed in action.

Truman's ideas about religion remained constant to the end of his life. When they were courting, he told Bess that he eschewed hypocrites; in his postpresidential years in the 1950s and 1960s, he wrote that all his family "disliked a hypocrite." He used the same story once told by his grandfather to make his point in 1911 to Bess and in the late 1950s and 1960s to a broad American audience.[12] He was, in short, leery of showiness in religion, in and of itself and because it could be hypocritical. Echoing what he wrote Bess in 1911, Truman noted privately in the 1940s, "I've always believed that religion is something to live by and not to talk about." After speculating that God was not interested in pomp and circumstance, he added, "Religious stuffed shirts are just as bad or worse than political ones in my opinion."[13] His religious views, on this point, informed and correlated with his political outlook: in both cases, excessive form could lead to or hide hypocrisy and might result in a sensationalism that masked man's nature and purpose. In his twenties and in his sixties, he insisted that people know right from wrong and practice what they preached.[14]

Harry Truman was also ecumenical and remained so over the course of his life. While fighting in World War I and commanding the predominantly Catholic Battery D, he wrote to Bess in 1918 that "all churches, even the Roman Catholic can do a man a lot of good. I had a Presbyterian bringing up, a Baptist education, and Episcopal leanings, so I reckon I ought to get to heaven somehow, don't you think so?"[15] Writing in 1936 to his wife, he summarized his distinction of faith from religion: "It was a pleasure to hear of Margaret going to the Baptist Sunday school. She ought to go to one every Sunday—I mean a Sunday school. If a child is instilled with good morals and taught the value of the precepts laid down in Exodus 20 and Matthew 5, 6, and 7, there is not much to worry about in after years. It makes no difference what brand is on the Sunday school."[16] In longhand notes from 1952, Truman reflected both his ecumenism as well as his religious personalism: "If Jesus Christ were to return he'd be on the side of the persecuted all around the world. . . . He'd no more recognize his teachings in St. Peter's or Canterbury Cathedrals than he would in Riverside or Trinity Churches in New York or the First Baptist or Foundry Methodist Churches in Washington. . . . He taught that every man is the creation of a merciful God, that men are sinners and that he had come into the world to teach sinners how to approach His Father—and the way was not through Caiaphas the High Priest or Augustus the roman Emperor. The way is direct and straight. Any man can tell the Almighty and Most Merciful God his troubles and directly ask for guidance. *He will get it.*"[17]

To Truman, all Christians, even every revealed religion, could agree on the meaning as well as the value of the biblical precepts of the Ten Commandments and the Sermon on the Mount. In his later years, he recounted what his grandfather had told him: that all Christians "wanted to arrive at the same place but they had to fight about it to see who had the inside track with the Almighty." His grandfather concluded that "none of them had any special 'in' with God Almighty because He would make His own decision about who had been good or bad on this planet." Truman adopted this opinion and its attendant ecumenism from a man "who belonged to no church, but he supported many of them."[18] Shortly after becoming president, he wrote in his longhand notes, "A lot of the world's troubles have been caused by the interpretation of the Gospels and the controversies between sects and creeds. It is all so silly and comes of the prima donna complex again." God, he wrote, never played favorites.[19]

Faith, Freedom, and the Cold War

In order to fight the cold war, President Truman oversaw a revolution in American foreign policy. Characterized by policies and institutions such as the Truman Doctrine, the Marshall Plan, NATO, and the Berlin airlift, the strategy of containment redefined liberal internationalism and involved the United States in the world as never before.

Despite such programs, however, the Communists made gains in atomic weapons, propaganda, Europe, and China in the late 1940s. In 1950, NSC 68—primarily and theoretically—and Korea—secondarily and practically—confirmed for Truman what he already believed: In the end, the cold war would be won or lost on moral grounds. But he could not turn to the United Nations for moral authority, since the Soviets had subverted the international organization's original intent. Instead, the president endeavored to take the moral high ground in the East-West conflict by developing a two-pronged political strategy involving the mass media and the world's major religions that also coupled the governmental and private sectors.

In this project, Truman focused first on the dissemination of public information. On April 20, 1950—within two to three weeks of reading NSC 68, perhaps the most important U.S. government document of the cold war—he launched what he called the Campaign of Truth. Central to the undertaking was an expansion of the Voice of America beyond what the president had requested in preceding years. As he explained to the American Society of Newspaper Editors, the cold war "is a struggle, above all else, for the minds of men." Truman went on to argue that the propaganda used by the "forces of imperialistic communism" could be overcome by the "plain, simple, unvarnished truth." On the home front, he urged the press to enlist in the campaign by informing the American people "well and completely." "If you misinform them," he said, "their decisions will be bad; our country will suffer and the world will suffer." On a global scale, an enlarged VOA would join with the private efforts of international businessmen, labor unions, newspapers and magazines, radio, motion pictures, and others in communicating information in simple form to people of varied backgrounds and cultures. Truman emphasized that the truth must reach people around the world or "we will lose the battle for men's minds by pure default."[20] Assistant Secretary of State for Public Affairs Edward Barrett, who came up with the actual "Campaign of Truth" phrase, testified before an executive session of the Senate Foreign Relations Committee in July 1950 that it derived from the "inevitable conclusion" of NSC 68 "that the world situation was deteriorating and deteriorating rapidly. On the basis of that the president, on the advice of numerous people, reached the conclusion that we needed to step up [overseas propaganda] activities."[21] William Benton, a Democratic senator from Connecticut who had once held Barrett's position, sponsored a Senate resolution for "a Marshall Plan in the field of ideas," in recognition "that the central issue of our time is intellectual and spiritual, and that the heart of the present conflict is a struggle for the minds and loyalties of mankind."[22] After the Korean War began, Truman submitted an appropriation request in July for $89 million to implement the campaign; after the House of Representatives reduced the amount by over $20 million, he pressed in August for his original allocation.[23]

Truman saw the dangers of what came to be known technically as disinformation and misinformation. He had seen the inroads made by Soviet propaganda in western Europe, particularly in 1947 through 1949, and believed that American will and policies had defeated the USSR's efforts to sway elections and upset the Marshall Plan. The Voice of America, Radio Free Europe, and, in the following year, Radio Liberation (soon Radio Liberty) became part of the institutional fabric of containment.[24] The president thought that he had learned correctly from recent history, and he went on to the next step of his strategy in the partnership between the public and private sectors: the moral suasion and power of faith. As leader of the strongest power of the free world, he aimed to harness and coordinate the world's religions in an effort to stop the Communists and what he viewed as their elemental godlessness.

In 1946 and 1947, Truman attempted this component of containment with mixed results. On the day after Churchill's Fulton Address in March 1946, he urged Protestants, Roman Catholics, and Jews to spur a "moral and spiritual awakening" in the aftermath of World War II and deploy the full power of freedom in meeting the threats of "new conflicts, new terror, and new destruction."[25] In May 1946, he reappointed Myron Taylor as his personal representative to Pius XII, this time with the added rank of ambassador, marking what would have been the Vatican's first full diplomatic recognition by the United States. He reasoned that the Roman Catholic Church was his strongest religious ally in the moral battle against international communism, but numerous objections, particularly from Protestants, led the president to retract the proposal. Nevertheless, Truman sent Taylor on special missions to the pontiff for the next several years and in 1947 involved him in embarking on a global endeavor. As he wrote to Bess, "Had Myron Taylor in too. Looks as if he and I may get the morals of the world on our side. We are talking to the Archbishop of Canterbury, the bishop at the head of the Lutheran Church, the Metropolitan of the Greek Church at Istanbul, and the pope. I may send him to see the top Buddhist and the Grand Lama of Tibet. If I can mobilize the people who believe in a moral world against the Bolshevik materialists, who believe as Henry Wallace does—'that the end justifies the means'—we can win this fight." He then added, "Treaties, agreements, or a moral code mean nothing to Communists. So we've got to organize the people who do believe in honor and the Golden Rule to win the world back to peace and Christianity."[26] The Catholic Church expressed interest, but other faiths rejected the idea and, perhaps, the implied ecumenism. Although his efforts came to naught, Truman maintained that a world crusade of religions against communism would be unbeatable over time and continued to argue that recognition of the Vatican was past due, in and of itself and as part of a cold war strategy.

Truman resurrected the idea of a global religious campaign in 1951. At minimum, he hoped that the major religions would agree to an international conference; at maximum, he looked for the defeat of communism through a concerted religious effort, which would place before the peoples of the world the superiority and strength of what he called truth and freedom. The president laid the groundwork to renew his proposal during the course of 1950, especially after reading NSC 68 in April. Joining politics and faith, he set forth his argument for the union of strength and freedom as the precursor to genuine peace in May 1950 at Gonzaga University in Washington: "In the face of aggressive tyranny, the economic, political, and military strength of free men is a necessity. But we are not increasing our strength just for strength's sake. We must be strong if we are to expand freedom. We must be strong if free men are to be able to satisfy their moral obligations. It is the moral and religious beliefs of mankind which alone give our strength meaning and purpose."[27] Truman considered the speech a significant address at a critical time to an important audience; because he believed that Catholic participation was crucial to an international campaign against communism, he deliberately chose to speak at a Catholic school.[28] Myron Taylor had resigned as of January 18, 1950, and Truman wanted to replace him with an ambassador. With this speech, the president hoped to further both goals.

Truman led up to his conclusion at Gonzaga University by describing how a good society existed when men followed "the will of the Lord" based on the fundamental belief "that all men are equal before God." From this understanding flowed the securing of individual rights and equal opportunity for all citizens. Just as this belief in equality had enabled America to build a great nation of liberty, Truman added, so too could it serve as the foundation of world peace. The president held that equality before God, recognized in good government, would undergird a brotherhood of man—much in the sense that Pius XII sketched in their Christmas 1949 exchange of messages— around the world.[29] Truman believed that peace would follow, not from world government but from the understanding of equality, morality and religion, strength, and freedom. "The greatest obstacle to peace," he said, "is a modern tyranny led by a small group who have abandoned their faith in God. These tyrants have forsaken ethical and moral beliefs. They believe that only force makes right. They are aggressively seeking to expand the area of their domination." But he did not claim that ridding the world of tyranny would bring eternal peace. As a Christian, he saw both the "barriers of ignorance and poverty" and the "barriers of tyranny"; as a Christian statesman, however, he concentrated his attention on the worst offender.[30]

Shortly after the Korean War began, Truman expounded on his belief that a revival of religion and a rededication of the United States to the "unchanging truths" of the Christian religion was needed to defeat communism. He contrasted America's freedom of religion to the suppression of freedom and a concomitant denial of human rights by communism behind the "impenetrable iron curtain." To the president of the Baptist World Alliance in his home state of Missouri, Truman forthrightly disclosed these views in July 1950: "To succeed in our quest for righteousness we must, in St. Paul's luminous phrase, put on the armor of God." At the time, various religious leaders and journals of the Truman era—notably, the *Christian Century*—consistently criticized what they viewed as the president's simplistic religious exhortations on complex issues.[31] But Truman believed, as he explained in the letter, that problems—including the threat from international communism—could be best solved if free men were to use their intelligence, courage, and faith and to seek solutions in the spirit of the Sermon on the Mount.[32] He invoked a consistent theme of his life and presidency: that all, especially but not only Christians, could understand, accept, and act upon the message of Jesus' Beatitudes and golden rule. And by emphasizing the spirit of the Sermon on the Mount, he left open the possibility that many could join in the fight against communism.

In preparing the American people and the world for what was, essentially, a religious Campaign of Truth in 1951, President Truman closed 1950 with an accent on the theme of comprehensive strength. He placed the fighting in Korea in the context of "the struggle between freedom and communist slavery" in order to remind his audience that, in respect to defense, "we need the combined resources and the common determination of the free world to meet the military threat of communism." While not playing down the military aspect of the cold war, the president focused again on the moral and spiritual dangers from communism: "Communism attacks our main basic values, our belief in God, our belief in the dignity of man and the value of human life, our belief in justice and freedom. It attacks the institutions that are based on these values. It attacks our churches, our guarantees of civil liberty, our courts, our democratic form of government. Communism claims that all these things are merely tools of self-interest and greed—that they are weapons used by one class to oppress another."[33]

It is unclear if Truman had a specific date in mind for the announcement of a new international religious campaign against communism in 1951, but he worked toward that end during the early part of the year. In February 1951, Truman used the dedication of a chapel commemorating four chaplains (Protestant, Catholic, and Jewish) who gave their lives on a torpedoed, sinking ship during World War II so that four other men could survive, to stress that the unity of the United States, as with these four men, was also unity under God. "It is a unity in freedom," he remarked, "for the service of God is perfect freedom." Truman repeated his stated 1950 goal for peace through freedom and brotherhood—quoting the famous passage from St. John: "Greater love hath no man than this, that a man lay down his life for his friends." Using the story of heroism at hand, he argued that the United States could not lead the forces of freedom from behind. He compared the chaplains' sacrifice with that of those who fought in the American Revolution, and contrasted both with the summer soldiers and sunshine patriots rebuked by Thomas Paine. While drawing an additional parallel to the Americans dying in Korea "to save us from the terrible slaughter and destruction which another world war would surely bring," the president upheld the American model of religious diversity and political unity as an example to the world.[34]

In April 1951, between the third anniversary of the Marshall Plan's enactment and the second anniversary of the signing of the North Atlantic Treaty, Truman developed further his argument that faith was integral to any meaningful shift—let alone victory—in the cold war. Speaking at the New York Avenue Presbyterian Church in Washington, DC, he reiterated that the American republic was founded on the same principles of the moral law taught by the great religions. He contended that faith should set moral standards for domestic as well as international conduct and that "[w]e should judge our achievements, as a nation, in the scales of right and wrong." Quick to emphasize that freedom was the most important principle of American civilization, he distinguished freedom—based upon moral principles—from an unmoored freedom, which degenerated rapidly into selfishness and license in individuals and anarchy in society. The president then returned to familiar themes of preceding years: he tied the application of moral standards to American efforts in the world and the buildup of the country's defenses; stressed that international communism was opposed to the tenets, including the right to worship God, which Americans lived by and cherished; and concluded that religious faith gave the United States the ability to answer the false beliefs of communism.[35] This cumulative argument was, for Truman, the basis for the American understanding of the East-West conflict. He saw the United States as the primary free power of the world and believed that that was a sufficient justification for world leadership. Yet he thought that the obligation to lead stemmed from America's moral underpinnings.

To the Washington Pilgrimage of American Churchman in September 1951, Truman made explicit the renewed call for a religious Campaign of Truth. By this point, he believed that he had done all he could to encourage the cooperation of the world's major religions in such a movement. It was time not only to present his case definitively to the public but also to entreat, perhaps shame, his prospective crusaders. Reminding his listeners of the difficulties faced by the people of Israel, he urged American believers to live up to their religious and political heritage, since, like the chosen people, they were held to higher standards and would be judged harshly if they failed in their responsibilities. All but calling his fellow Christians hypocritical, he drew extensively on Jesus' condemnation of those "who were superficially and publicly good" yet refused to act upon their words. Truman then suggested the link between America's future and that of the world: "Today, our problem is not just to preserve our religious heritage in our own lives and our own country. Our problem is a greater one. It is to preserve a world civilization in which man's belief in God can survive. Only in such a world can our own Nation follow its basic traditions, and realize the promise of a better life for all our citizens." The president argued that the "whole human enterprise is in danger" from communist expansion, which employed the "weapons of deceit and subversion as well as military might." The enemy at the root of either totalitarian expansionism or nuclear devastation in war was communism, which, in attempting to master life, might eradicate mere life. Truman hoped that all men of goodwill would realize that acknowledging God as "the ruler of us all" and asking Him for the strength and wisdom to carry out His will would be the first step in preserving civilization throughout the world.[36]

Once again, the president called for a religious campaign—now an international crusade—against communism. He requested that all men who believed in God set aside their differences during the current crisis in human affairs and come together "in a common affirmation of faith." Truman insisted, as he often had in the past, that all creeds could agree on the teachings of the Ten Commandments and the Sermon on the Mount. And he expected that Christians, at least, would support the affirmation, testifying "to the strength of our common faith and our confidence in its ultimate victory over the forces of Satan that oppose it." He regretted that "the great religious leaders of the world" were not joined yet in such a declaration of faith, but he was especially distressed that the main Christian churches would not agree to a statement "of their faith that Christ is their Master and Redeemer and the source of their strength against the hosts of irreligion and danger in the world."[37] The president ended his forthright remarks with a prayer to unite the churches and the free world.

Despite the resistance to a common affirmation of faith, Truman held to his conviction that spiritual strength would be most effective in an organized movement and must inform and augment political strength. Less than a month after calling for the international religious crusade, he turned again to the Roman Catholic Church. Secretary of State Dean Acheson hoped that he had convinced the president to delay indefinitely an appointment of a U.S. ambassador to the Vatican. In Acheson's view, recognizing the Vatican would start a religious controversy when the need for national unity against the USSR was great.[38] Truman, however, still wanted official recognition, for political, diplomatic, and strategic reasons, which he thought he had explained well over the space of several years. After Myron Taylor retired due to health reasons, Truman nominated General Mark Clark as ambassador in October 1951, stressing that the Vatican was "vigorously engaged in the struggle against communism" and that "[d]irect diplomatic relations will assist in coordinating the effort to combat the Communist menace."[39] The president's nomination met with fierce objections from Protestants generally and from U.S. senators, especially Southern Democrats. Substantial amounts of White House mail ran six-and-a-half to one against sending an ambassador to the Vatican.[40] Although Truman remained committed to the nomination, Clark asked to have his name withdrawn from consideration in January 1952. With no support and no nominee, the president reluctantly abandoned recognition of the Vatican and, effectively, the religious Campaign of Truth.

It frustrated Truman that some of the world's main religions rejected his reasoning that faith was the most powerful weapon in the cold war. And he was irked that Protestant denominations would not grant the Catholic Church a unique religious and political role in combating communism. Shortly after Clark's withdrawal as nominee, the president described privately his conversation with the head bishop of the Episcopal Church, who was objecting to formal and full U.S.-Holy See relations. Truman replied that his concern was not protocol but "to organize the moral forces against the the [*sic*] immoral forces. I told him that Stalin and his crowd had no intellectual honesty and no moral code, that they had broken 30 or 40 treaties they'd made with us and the free world and that all I wanted to do was to organize Exodus XX, Matthew V, VI, & VII to save morals in the world." Apparently, the bishop disparaged the Catholic Church as another version of totalitarianism and a menace to free religion. "What a travesty," wrote Truman. "If a Baptist can see what's toward—why not a high hat Church of England Bishop?"[41] In the president's containment strategy, the Catholic Church was always the fulcrum of a global religious movement for faith and freedom and against communism, but it was also always the main impediment in Protestant eyes.[42]

The "great purpose" of the United States, according to Truman, was to defend "the spiritual values—the moral code—against the vast forces of evil that seek to destroy them."[43] While admittedly a broad agenda, the president had fleshed out how to achieve such a purpose through containment, now including the widespread, accurate dissemination of information, and the previously untapped reserves of religious faith. Truman sought to combine moral and religious, political, military, economic, and rhetorical means in a grand strategy. In order to face the extraordinary circumstances of the East-West conflict, he started with what many others refused to acknowledge: that the cold war began and ended with a clash of moral and political worldviews manifested in opposing regime types. Harry Truman supplied what was missing from the narrow, negative version of containment that was preferred by his realist critics; in so doing, he created and implemented a different strategy entirely.

Faith, Freedom, and Palestine

What we now call human rights, the president placed in the context of his political and, even, theological understanding of world events. Truman, often depicted as unsentimental, felt keenly the displacement, enslavement, and death of various peoples by tyranny, whether Nazi or communist. From the early postwar period into 1948 when the problem was at its worst, he frequently commented in private meetings about the starvation of people throughout Europe and sometimes saw the Soviets aggravating the grim food situation. And he deplored the displacement of hundreds of thousands of Europeans in the wake of World War II and communism's spread. Truman was more successful in promoting larger immigration numbers to the United States, especially of Jews and Asians, later in his presidency; nevertheless, he tried to liberalize immigration in 1945 through 1947 (in the face of much congressional hostility), particularly as a way of addressing the problem of displaced persons (DPs). He wanted the same for those DPs who sought to stay in their native countries or, when that was not possible, make homes in new countries. Apart from its stated intentions, the president hoped that the Marshall Plan directly and indirectly would ameliorate a postwar problem that he viewed as a calamity.

In this regard, a homeland for the Jews, who made up 20 percent of the displaced persons, was vital to Truman. Much has been speculated—ranging from domestic politics to preemption of Soviet influence in the Middle East—about his motivations for promoting a Jewish homeland and, in May 1948, recognizing the new state of Israel. To be sure, the president aimed to prevent a Kremlin foothold in the region, as evidenced by the Truman Doctrine. And it was hoped that the new Jewish state would introduce democracy to the Middle East. But beyond primary cold war strategic concerns and secondary domestic interests, Truman had long been sympathetic to the plight of the Jewish people. His study of history and the Bible informed his opinions of the Jews and the region of the Middle East, while his lifelong friendship with businessman Eddie Jacobson—which, apart from their army service in World War I and owning a store together from 1919 to 1922, included many poker games with other Jewish friends—and his working relationships with advisers Max Lowenthal, David Niles, and others during his senatorial and presidential years, reinforced his religious tolerance.[44] In the 1930s, he handled many requests to facilitate Jewish emigration from Germany. In April 1943, Senator Truman openly recognized that the Nazis sought to slaughter the Jews, which was another reason to support a Jewish homeland: "Today—not tomorrow—we must do all that is humanly possible to provide a haven and place of safety for all those who can be grasped from the hands of the Nazi butchers. Free lands must be opened to them."[45]

As president, Truman endorsed the Balfour Declaration of 1917, in which the British had promised support to the Jews for a national homeland in Palestine; building on this foundation, Truman first backed partition of Palestine and then, on May 14, 1948, had the United States confer de facto recognition upon the state of Israel, within minutes of its declaration of independence. Within a week of

Israel's first elections in late January 1949 to establish its government and having been informed officially of the results, the United States extended de jure recognition.[46] Before, during, and after these developments, Truman advocated a home, as well as general, liberalized international immigration, for the Jews, and did so in the face of significant opposition from the Arab world. In October 1946, for example, he sent a polite but firm message to the king of Saudi Arabia, in which he restated his belief that at least 100,000 Jewish survivors of the Holocaust should receive immediate entry to Palestine.[47] Although the Holocaust had caused the displacement as well as deaths of millions of Jews, Truman identified a legitimate Jewish right to Palestine that preceded the horrors of World War II and the Balfour Declaration. He would cite, among other biblical passages, 1 Deuteronomy 8 as his evidence—"Behold, I have given up the land before you; go in and take possession of the land which the Lord hath sworn unto your fathers, to Abraham, to Isaac, and to Jacob"—and believed that historical, moral, and religious rights met in their defense of a Jewish homeland.[48]

Truman persevered in spite of resistance from most of the State Department, the secretary of defense, and other top advisers in his administration. With respect to the State Department, Truman had thought that Marshall would "set them right but he has had too much to do and the 3rd & 4th levels over there are the same striped pants conspirators." He blamed them in March 1948 for having "balled up the Palestine situation" by promoting trusteeship rather than partition for Palestine.[49] In this context, the president came the closest he ever did to criticizing Marshall. On the same day that he expressed his frustration with lower-level State Department personnel, he also wrote, "I spend the day trying to right what has happened. No luck. Marshall makes a statement. Doesn't help me a mite."[50] No help was forthcoming. Two days before the president's recognition of the state of Israel in May 1948, the secretary of state intensified his objections to Truman in a tense Oval Office meeting. Marshall went as far as to say that, if he voted in the next election, he would vote against the president if Truman recognized the Jewish state.[51] Special Counsel Clark Clifford was the only key adviser who consistently advocated the president's position on Palestine. Truman relied on him to manage the opposition from Marshall, Forrestal, and others, so that he could concentrate on the larger international picture. Between them, Clifford and Undersecretary of State Robert Lovett (who sided with Marshall) placated the secretary of state, and Truman conferred recognition of the state of Israel without causing a public breach with Marshall.

Domestically, Truman refused to take sides with not only pro-Arab and other leery State Department professionals but also with Zionist interest groups; and he withstood the Arabs, British, and Zionists abroad. He believed that Jews deserved equality, not preferential treatment, in setting up their state and government.[52] In February 1948, he explained his disappointment with the fighting among the parties involved to his friend, Jacobson: "The Jews are so emotional, and the Arabs are so difficult to talk with that it is almost impossible to get anything done. The British, of course, have been exceedingly noncooperative in arriving at a conclusion. The Zionists, of course, have expected a big stick approach on our part, and naturally have been disappointed when we can't do that."[53] Although he voiced doubt at the time about the possibility of a desirable outcome, he vowed to continue his support for the partition of Palestine and a homeland for the Jews. In doing so, he acted independently, avoided the extremes, and steadily pursued what he saw as his moral commitment to the Jewish people.

Faith, Freedom, and Peace

From the first day of his presidency, Truman invoked the Almighty and believed that America had been called to a responsibility, which had been dodged after World War I, to foster peace in the world. He often explained that this duty now extended from U.S. participation in the United Nations to combating the onslaught of worldwide communism. In numerous speeches, he said that God meant for the United States to be a beacon of liberty and to hold out the same right for others. But only in the context of freedom, he believed, could man exercise the free will necessary to the formation of peace and happiness. As he concluded in his 1949 inaugural address, "But I say to all men, what we have achieved in liberty, we will surpass in greater liberty. Steadfast in our faith in the Almighty, we will advance toward a world where man's freedom is secure. To that end we will devote our strength, our resources, and our firmness of resolve. With God's help, the future of mankind will be assured in a world of justice, harmony, and peace."[54] The problem was that the free world faced a foe that denied that "human freedom is born of the belief that man is created equal in the image of God and therefore capable of governing himself."[55] The framework of freedom in which peace could be established, as well as the tenuousness of the extant peace in the free world, must be protected.

In a postpresidential collection of reflections and articles, *Mr. Citizen*, Truman spelled out the political theory of peace that stemmed from his faith. Writing to Bess and then as president, he had touched on the same themes, but, as an elder statesman, he had the public opportunity to speak at greater length about them. In one week, he addressed 1,200 students at a Baptist college, spoke to 6,500 young people at the annual Catholic Youth Conference, and dedicated a plaque at the Jewish Chapel at the University of Missouri. Excerpting from his subsequent remarks to a Methodist congregation in Dallas, Truman "preached"—his word—about the moral code that the Bible conferred.

When he was young, Truman began, he preferred the Bible "as it should be" in the King James form rather than the Revised Version. When sworn in as president, however, he selected the Vulgate or Latin translation of the Bible. "And as you know," he wrote, "I had them turn to the twentieth chapter of Exodus."[56] This chapter in the second book of the Old Testament provided the cornerstone to Truman's thought. For Truman, "the fundamental basis of all government" was found in the Bible, starting with the laws given to Moses on Mount Sinai. Moses, he noted, was familiar with the Babylonian lawgiver, Hammurabi, who established the first code for government; in Moses, Truman perceived revelation and reason joining to assure a peace of justice and harmony. He then added the sixth chapter of Deuteronomy, the fourth book of the Pentateuch.[57] The primary purpose of man, he pointed out, was revealed there: "[A]nd thou shalt love the Lord thy God with all thine heart, and with all thy soul, and with all thy might." Throughout his career in political and private service, Truman pointed out that Deuteronomy's fifth chapter was a reiteration of the Decalogue leading, significantly, to the statement of the great commandment in the sixth chapter.

Truman then turned to the prophets to illustrate his understanding of peace. Concentrating on Isaiah, Micah, and Joel, he argued that, major and minor prophets alike, "[t]hey were all trying to get the people to understand that they were on this earth for a purpose, and that in order to accomplish that purpose they must follow a code of morals." Of Isaiah, the great prophet who presaged the Gospel of St. Matthew, Truman cited where Isaiah explained that God would judge among the nations and rebuke many people, and they would beat their swords into plowshares and spears into pruning hooks. But then he quoted the prophet Joel, who seems to make the opposite point. Truman noted that in Joel 3:10, the prophet proclaimed, "Beat your ploughshares into swords and your pruning hooks into spears.

Let the weak say: I am strong." Truman maintained that the passages were not contradictory: "Which one do you want? It depends on what the condition is." Joel, Truman explained, was trying to teach the people that they had to protect their regime if they "expected ever to have a free government."[58] Different circumstances demanded different actions, and the prudent leader—Isaiah, Joel, or even Harry Truman—must determine whether the time demands plowshares or swords.

If the Decalogue laid the cornerstone of peace, the prophets contributed to the structure of the building, and the Sermon on the Mount completed the edifice. Maintaining that they can never be read too much, Truman turned to chapters five through seven of St. Matthew. In presidential speeches and press conferences, he often referred to living by the golden rule of doing unto others as you would have them do unto yourself found in Matthew 7 and embracing all of Matthew 5–7 for its guidance in life. In one of his earliest foreign policy speeches as president, Truman argued that the golden rule should direct international affairs.[59] As he wrote in 1952, "Confusius [*sic*], Buddah [*sic*], Moses, our own Jesus Christ, Mohomet [*sic*], all preached—'Do as you'd be done by.' Treat others as you'd be treated. So did all the other great teachers and philosophers."[60] Now, in his comments to the Methodists, he emphasized the fifth chapter of St. Matthew and the Beatitudes and quoted: "Blessed are the peacemakers, for they shall be called the children of God." Here, he believed, was the universal wish of all people of goodwill: "That is exactly what we all want to be. We want to be peacemakers. Not just individually, but *internationally*."[61] Truman thought that he was called to advance God's peace, particularly around the world in his presidential foreign policy. "I am here this morning to try to get you to understand that I believe what these things say," he concluded, "and I try to act like it."[62] To Jews, he emphasized that the unabridged law was in the Ten Commandments and the Hebrew Bible; to Christians, he accented that Christ as Messiah fulfilled the law of the Old Testament. To all of goodwill, he offered a high common ground touched by the transcendent.

In the end, the peace Truman desired was the peace of the Bible. Not that he expected this peace to come easily or any time soon; only God could effect the peace that Truman longed for. In the meantime, for the individual, it meant constant humility and the seeking of grace. And for nations it required a dedication to justice and the rule of law, based on a moral code and standards of right and wrong. These things, through education and habituation, shaped men and citizens by forming their character. Over the course of history, Truman's readings had convinced him, human nature had not changed much.

Man still had "to be guided in the proper direction under a moral code, and then there must be some machinery to make him live within that moral code. A man cannot have character unless he lives within a fundamental system of morals that creates character."[63]

The cold war both modified and moderated Truman's optimism about the possibilities of global peace. On the one hand, he rejected the idealism of those who ignored reality—he may have preferred plowshares, but he knew that now was a time to turn those plowshares into swords and not the other way around. Truman also rejected, on the other hand, that narrow realism, which failed to recognize the moral challenge of communism. The cold war, for all of its complications, was for Truman a battle between "the world of morals" and the "world of no morals," and only the combined strength of the West—military, political, economic, and moral—could defeat the immorality of communism and bring international peace.[64] The East-West conflict made the peace he envisioned all the more distant, and perhaps unattainable. It also made Truman think hard about what could be achieved, and what had to be done to achieve it. Freedom, justice, and order emerged in his writings and speeches as the principles that created the circumstances under which a real and durable peace might be possible. And of those principles, Truman reasoned that freedom had to take root first—and had to be defended first. Peace was the fruit of liberty, he concluded, not its precondition.

The lesson of peace—that it is sometimes necessary to learn and make war—was difficult for Truman and a generation of Americans who had fought one war to make the world safe for democracy and another, recently, to rid it of Nazism. They had hoped, and many had believed, that World War II had accomplished what World War I had failed to achieve. Instead, they found themselves in a different kind of war, which was even more terrifying and more threatening to liberal democracy and the cause of free government. In this circumstance, with fortitude and prudence, Harry Truman reminded his time of the centrality and universality of human freedom and, like the prophet Joel, that peace requires not only freedom but also the strength and willpower to defend it.

Notes

1. James Hennesey, S. J., *American Catholics: A History of the Roman Catholic Community in the United States* (New York: Oxford University Press, 1981), 289–290. Organizations such as the Knights of Columbus and the Catholic War Veterans were also strongly anticommunist.

2. Including that full diplomatic relations between the United States and the Holy See did not occur until 1984 during the Reagan administration.
3. Robert H. Ferrell, *Harry S. Truman: A Life* (Columbia, MO: University of Missouri Press, 1994), 49, 134.
4. David McCullough, *Truman* (New York: Simon & Schuster, 1992), 83.
5. Alonzo L. Hamby, *Man of the People: A Life of Harry S. Truman* (New York: Oxford University Press, 1995), 21, 474.
6. For the text of Truman's daily prayer, which he said from his high school days until his death, see *Memorial Services in the Congress of the United States and Tributes in Eulogy of Harry S Truman, Late a President of the United States*, 93rd Congress, 1st Session, House Document No. 93–131, compiled under the direction of the Joint Committee on Printing (Washington, DC: United States Government Printing Office, 1973), 8. This prayer is also reproduced in William Hillman, ed., *Mr. President: The First Publication from the Personal Diaries, Private Letters, Papers and Revealing Interviews of Harry S. Truman* (New York: Farrar, Straus and Young, 1952), before the foreword.
7. George Elsey, who worked with Truman on many presidential speeches, recalled that Truman believed in the spiritual and moral statements he had made in his speeches and that "[m]any of these phrases and sentences were added by him in longhand very near the final draft of a speech." See Oral History Interview with George M. Elsey, Washington, DC, February 10 and 17, 1964; March 9, 1965; July 10 and 17, 1969; and July 7 and 10, 1970 by Charles T. Morrissey and Jerry N. Hess, Harry S. Truman Library (hereafter HSTL), May 1974.
8. Autobiographical sketch, biographical file, box 298, president's secretary's files (hereafter PSF), Harry S. Truman Papers (hereafter HSTP), HSTL. From the context, it appears that Truman wrote this sketch some time after January 20, 1945.
9. Ferrell, *Harry S. Truman*, 49; and Margaret Truman, ed., *Where the Buck Stops: The Personal and Private Writings of Harry S. Truman* (New York: Warner Books, 1989), 341–343. In 1906, Truman upheld his civic duties of citizenship by serving as a Democratic Party election clerk in Jackson County, Missouri.
10. Tom Pendergast, with whom Truman worked most closely, was Catholic.
11. Truman to Bess, February 7, 1911, in *Dear Bess: The Letters from Harry to Bess Truman, 1910–1959*, ed. Robert H. Ferrell (New York: W. W. Norton & Company, 1983), 22–23.
12. Harry S Truman, *Mr. Citizen* (New York: Popular Library, 1961), 95. Truman credited this to his grandfather: "When a man spends Saturday night and Sunday doing too much howling and praying, you had better go home and lock your smoke house."
13. Autobiographical sketch, biographical file, box 298, PSF, HSTP, HSTL.
14. This sentiment was one he learned from both his grandfathers. See Truman, *Mr. Citizen*, 95.
15. Truman to Bess, July 31, 1918, in Ferrell, ed., *Dear Bess*, 268.

16. Truman to Bess, June 22, 1936, in Ferrell, ed., *Dear Bess*, 388.
17. Truman, June 1, 1952, in *Off the Record: The Private Papers of Harry S. Truman*, ed. Robert H. Ferrell (New York: Harper & Row, 1980), 251–252.
18. Truman, *Mr. Citizen*, 95.
19. Truman, June 1, 1945, longhand notes file, 1945–1952, box 333, PSF, HSTP, HSTL. Truman maintained that God picked no "priorities," in the context of writing that Jews were not picked out for special privilege by God. See also Ralph E. Weber, ed., *Talking with Harry: Candid Conversations with President Harry S. Truman* (Wilmington, DE: Scholarly Resources, 2001), 289; speaking of religious divisions, Truman said, "There isn't any sense in it at all, because when you get right down to brass tacks, they all believe in honor and the welfare of the individual, and some time or other, we'll come to the conclusion where we can sit down side by side and let the other fellow do as he pleases."
20. Truman, "Address on Foreign Policy at a Luncheon of the American Society of Newspaper Editors," April 20, 1950, in *Public Papers of the Presidents of the United States: Harry S. Truman, 1945–53*, 8 vols. (Washington, DC: Government Printing Office, 1961–1966), (1950), 6: 260–264 (hereafter *Public Papers*). The expansion of VOA involved not only additional and improved information and educational services but also new technology to overcome Soviet jamming of the broadcasts.
21. Edward W. Barrett testimony, "Voice of America," July 27, 1950, U.S. Senate Committee on Foreign Relations, Subcommittee on Public Affairs, executive session, SFRC selected documents, box 10, HSTL, cited in Walter L. Hixson, *Parting the Curtain: Propaganda, Culture, and the Cold War, 1945–1961* (New York: St. Martin's Griffin, 1998), 14.
22. Quoted in Hixson, *Parting the Curtain*, 15.
23. See, e.g., "Letter to Senator Flanders on the Appropriation for the Campaign of Truth," August 30, 1950, in *Public Papers* (1950), 602–603. Walter Hixson points out that Truman aide Mark Etheridge recalled that Dean Acheson was not enthusiastic about the overseas program: "He didn't think information ought to be mixed with policy." Hixson, *Parting the Curtain*, 241, n. 49.
24. The American Committee for Freedom for the Peoples of the USSR was started in 1951, and its broadcast station became known as Radio Liberty. For more on VOA during this period, see David F. Krugler, *The Voice of America and the Domestic Propaganda Battles, 1945–1953* (Columbia: University of Missouri Press, 2000); and for more on Radio Free Europe and Radio Liberty (herafter RFE/RL), see Arch Puddington, *Broadcasting Freedom: The Cold War Triumph of Radio Free Europe and Radio Liberty* (Lexington: University Press of Kentucky, 2000).
25. "Address in Columbus at a Conference of the Federal Council of Churches," March 6, 1946, in *Public Papers* (1946), 141–144. The main thrust of this speech concerns rebuilding America in the aftermath of World War II as well as the new challenge of atomic energy. Secondarily, Truman seems to be referring to the threat from communism.

26. Truman to Bess, October 2, 1947, in Ferrell, ed., *Dear Bess*, 551–552. Particularly in 1946 and 1947, Truman met constant objections from Protestants, including from leaders of his own Baptist faith, about Taylor's ongoing mission in Rome.

27. "Address in Spokane at Gonzaga University," May 11, 1950, in *Public Papers* (1950), 374–377.

28. For the connection between the Catholic Church and larger anticommunist efforts and this particular speech, see File on Foreign Relations—Mission to Vatican, box 65, Papers of George M. Elsey, HSTL. Elsey was active in helping Truman with the Gonzaga University speech.

29. "Exchange of Messages with Pope Pius XII," December 23, 1949, in *Public Papers* (1949), 587–588.

30. "Address in Spokane at Gonzaga University," May 11, 1950, in *Public Papers* (1950), 374–377.

31. See Merlin Gustafson, "Harry Truman as a Man of Faith," *The Christian Century*, 90 (January 17, 1973): 75–77 on this point. In the 1970s, Gustafson wrote this and another article on Truman's religion; in each, he misread Truman as a Calvinist determinist.

32. Truman to Rev. Johnson, President of the Baptist World Alliance, July 15, 1950, file 220, 1949–1953, box 823, HSTP, HSTL.

33. "Address Before the Midcentury White House Conference on Children and Youth," December 5, 1950, in *Public Papers* (1950), 733–737.

34. "Address in Philadelphia at the Dedication of the Chapel of the Four Chaplains," February 3, 1951, in *Public Papers* (1951), 139–141.

35. "Address at the Cornerstone Laying at the New York Avenue Presbyterian Church," April 3, 1951, in *Public Papers* (1951), 210–213.

36. "Address to the Washington Pilgrimage of American Churchmen," September 28, 1951, *Public Papers* (1951), 547–550.

37. Ibid.

38. Dean Acheson, *Present at the Creation: My Years in the State Department* (New York: W. W. Norton & Company, 1969), 574–575. As Acheson recalled, "At one of our meetings early in October the President observed that I was an even greater practitioner of the delaying tactic than Fabius Maximus Cunctator himself and that, if left to me, no appropriate time would come."

39. Footnote explanation in "The President's News Conference of October 25, 1951," in *Public Papers* (1951), 601.

40. Donald R. McCoy, *The Presidency of Harry S. Truman* (Lawrence: University Press of Kansas, 1984), 277. Clark himself was a Protestant, as was Myron Taylor.

41. February 26, 1952, longhand notes (Harry S Truman), longhand personal memos, 1952, folder 1, PSF, HSTP, HSTL.

42. As Truman recalled in 1959, "I wanted the moral forces of the world to make a common front against the unmoral forces, and we got pretty well along with it. It made quite an impression on a great many of the countries and the leaders of the religious sects in various countries. The people who

were most violently opposed to it were the Protestants right here in the United States." See Weber, ed., *Talking with Harry*, 290.

43. "Address at the Cornerstone Laying at the New York Avenue Presbyterian Church," April 3, 1951, in *Public Papers* (1951), 210–213.

44. In this regard (and also with respect to blacks), Truman was atypical of much of his generation and much of his elders' generation of Midwesterners. Although he abided by Bess's mother's wishes until her death about who should and should not enter her house, he socialized and worked with people of all religions and races. In addition to having Jewish and Catholic staff members over the years, Truman appointed four Catholic cabinet members during his presidency. A Catholic and longtime adviser to Truman—including appointments of secretary throughout the administration—Matthew J. Connelly, e.g., said that Truman had no religious bigotry. See Oral History Interview with Matthew J. Connelly, New York, NY, November 28 and November 30, 1967 and August 21, 1968 by Jerry N. Hess, HSTL, May 1969.

45. Quote is from Truman's speech to United Rally, Chicago, April 14, 1943, cited in Hamby, *Man of the People*, 269 (where Hamby also describes the rest of Truman's commitment during his senatorial years).

46. When Truman approved the papers for de jure recognition of Israel and Transjordan, he asked for 24 hours notice, if possible, of the date and hour proposed for recognition because he was anxious to have a close friend of his from Kansas City with him when he made the announcement. This friend seems to have been Jewish and was perhaps Jacobson. See Acheson meeting with Truman, January 27, 1949, memoranda of conversations, January–July 1949, box 64, papers of Dean Acheson, HSTL.

47. "Message to the King of Saudi Arabia Concerning Palestine," October 28, 1946, in *Public Papers* (1948), 467–469.

48. See Clark Clifford, *Counsel to the President: A Memoir* (New York: Anchor Books, Doubleday, 1992), 8.

49. Truman to Mary Jane Truman, March 21, 1948; and Truman to Mrs. John A. Truman and Sister Mary Jane Truman, January 25, 1946–November 7, 1948, postpresidential memoirs, box 47, HSTP, HSTL.

50. Truman, longhand, March 21, 1948, reprinted in Ferrell, ed., *Off the Record*, 127.

51. Clifford, *Counsel to the President*, 13–14. For the rest of Clifford's retelling of Truman's commitment to Palestine and to the founding of Israel as well as the infighting at home and disputes abroad, see pages 4–15 and 18–25.

52. Truman expressed this opinion as early as June 1945. He was against sectarianism and division and did not believe that God picked favorites among "race, creed or color." See Truman, June 1, 1945, longhand notes file, 1945–1952, box 333, PSF, HSTP, HSTL.

53. Truman to Eddie Jacobson, February 27, 1948, Truman Digital Archive, Project Whistlestop, available from http://www.whistlestop.org/study_collections/israel/large/folder3/isc22–1.htm, accessed January 20, 2002.

54. "Inaugural Address," January 20, 1949, in *Public Papers* (1949), 112–116.
55. "Address at the Unveiling of a Memorial Carillon in Arlington National Cemetery," December 21, 1949, in *Public Papers* (1949), 582–583. The connection between what Truman said here and his consistent request for additional funding for VOA and, eventually, RFE/RL seems strong.
56. Truman, *Mr. Citizen*, 101. As Truman described his earliest exposure to the Bible: "My mother, married in 1881 to my father, had a great big gold-back Bible with the first part of the Revised Version. One column represented the Bible as it should be, the other side was the Revised Version. And I got a chance to read them both. If I wanted to find out anything in either Testament, I didn't read the Revised Version. I read the translation that was made under King James of Great Britain. That was the greatest thing he ever did in his life, and the reason for that, in my opinion, is the fact that that, along with Shakespeare, established the English language as we know it." As Truman said of his inauguration, "I was presented with a Vulgate and a copy of the Gutenberg Bible, and I was sworn in on that Latin Book." As was common of those of his generation, Truman had studied Latin in school. He seemed to be quite proficient, for he did extra drilling with Bess as a schoolboy since poor vision prevented him from joining in neighborhood sports. During his presidency, he corrected Chief Justice Fred Vinson's Latin. For this last point, see Ferrell, *Harry S. Truman*, 19.
57. Truman, *Mr. Citizen*, 102.
58. Ibid., 103.
59. Truman, "Address on Foreign Policy at the Navy Day Celebration in New York City," October 27, 1945, in *Public Papers* (1945), 431–438. Truman often invoked the golden rule in speeches and press conferences.
60. Harry S Truman, longhand notes, longhand personal memos, 1952, folder 1, box 333, PSF, HSTP, HSTL.
61. Truman, *Mr. Citizen*, 104. "Do you know where the Good Neighbor Policy of the United State originated?" Truman continued. "It originated in the tenth chapter of St. Luke. If you will read this tenth chapter of Luke, you will find out exactly what a good neighbor means. It means treat your neighbor as you yourself would like to be treated. . . . Luke gives us the best definition of it, and you don't have to go anywhere else to find it." See Truman, *Mr. Citizen*, 105.
62. Ibid., 105.
63. Ibid., 98.
64. Harry S Truman, longhand notes, longhand personal memos, 1952, folder 1, box 333, PSF, HSTP, HSTL. Truman singled out Marx, Lenin, Trotsky, and Stalin as those who "upset morals and intellectual honesty."

Chapter Six

Dwight D. Eisenhower: Civil Religion and the Cold War

Jack M. Holl

When I shared with my graduate students that I thought Dwight D. Eisenhower was the most religious president in the twentieth century, they hooted back in unison, "Jimmy Carter, Jimmy Carter." Soon thereafter, I read Philip Yancey's accounts of Billy Graham's ministry to Lyndon Johnson in the 1960s and of Yancey's own religious conversations in the White House with Bill Clinton.[1] I have been chastened by the reminder that American presidents have, in their own way, embodied a variety of religious experiences. I also have had to remind myself that we cannot reliably know the outward signs of inward grace even among American presidents.

Even so, Dwight D. Eisenhower would have ranked himself high among presidents of deep religious faith. In 1948, more than four years before becoming president of the United States, Eisenhower stated, "I am the most intensely religious man I know."[2] This extraordinary statement was not made by a zealous teenage catechumen, but by a mature 58-year-old adult who was president of Columbia University. What could Eisenhower have meant by his 1948 proclamation? He was not naive about religious sentiment, nor unacquainted with intensely religious believers. As a hero of World War II, he had met international religious leaders; he knew of the religious faith of subordinates such as his friend George Patton; he testified to the deep religious faith of his parents, especially his mother; he was the grandson of the River Brethren minister who had led his flock from Pennsylvania to Kansas in the nineteenth century; and in Abilene he grew up in the house of his uncle, another River Brethren minister and itinerant missionary. In other words, Eisenhower was well acquainted with religious fervor—and yet he characterized himself as "the most intensely religious man" that he knew.

Eisenhower's breathtaking religious self-assessment does not play large in traditional Eisenhower biography. Every biographer acknowledges the importance of religion in Eisenhower's upbringing, but after Eisenhower left home for West Point religion disappears as a major theme in his biography and no one emphasizes the influence of Eisenhower's deeply ingrained religious beliefs on his public life and work. Yet, if Eisenhower authentically perceived himself as a profoundly religious person, one would expect to encounter his religious values shaping the Eisenhower administration's domestic and foreign policy. And it did—except that Midwestern habits of privacy and an intensively held conviction that religion was a personal matter often masked Eisenhower's most deeply held sentiments. Nevertheless, the outward signs of his religious faith were often dramatically evident.

Eisenhower is the only American president to write his own Inaugural Prayer; he is the only president known to have been baptized in the White House; he was the first president to appoint a special assistant for religion—pastor Frederic Fox—who faithfully presided over White House prayer breakfasts; he approved adding "In God We Trust" to the U.S. currency and "one nation, under God" to the Pledge of Allegiance; and it was the president, not his speech writers, who most frequently inserted religious references and themes into his public speeches.

Soon after his election as president of the United States, in December 1952 Eisenhower addressed the Freedom Foundation: "Our form of government has no sense," he stated, "unless it is grounded in a deeply felt religious faith, and I don't care what it is."[3] Not surprising, while Republican politicians, clergyman, and laity praised Eisenhower's piety and fervent spirituality, Democrats and liberal commentators grumped that Eisenhower's religious beliefs were "bland" and "shallow." Ernest W. Lefever, for example, defined Eisenhower as a personification of American popular piety and superficial religiosity. Quoting William Lee Miller, Lefever conceded that "President Eisenhower, like many Americans, [was] a fervent believer in a very vague religion." The president was, in a word, "moral without being unpleasant."[4] More caustically, radio commentator Elmer Davis observed how "unbecoming" it had been for the president to declare July 4, 1953, as a day of prayer and penance, and then go fishing in the morning, play golf in the afternoon, and play bridge with cronies into the night. Perhaps most "damning" for Lefever was the praise Eisenhower received from both evangelist Billy Graham who celebrated Eisenhower as the nation's spiritual leader, and the President of Republic Steel who proclaimed that Eisenhower was "the only man since Christ who [could] bring peace to the world."[5]

To the president's disadvantage, Lefever compared Eisenhower's religious beliefs to those of Adlai Stevenson. Stevenson, the Democratic Party's presidential candidate against Eisenhower in 1952 and 1956, was a Unitarian (as was his mother) who joined the Presbyterian church (his father's) just prior to the 1956 election. The fact that Stevenson maintained membership in both congregations escaped political comment. According to Lefever, membership in the mainline Presbyterian church was about all that Stevenson and Eisenhower had in common religiously. Stevenson's religious heritage was "more intellectual and sophisticated" than Eisenhower's. Educated at Princeton and Harvard, Stevenson reportedly admired the "breadth, perception and social morality" of Reinhold Niebuhr. To his credit, Lefever did not claim that Stevenson converted to Niebuhr's worldview by reading *The Nature and Destiny of Man* or other works by the theologian:

> Rather, like George F. Kennan and other men in public life, he has found in Niebuhr an eloquent and convincing spokesman for an understanding of man and history which grew out of his own experience in practical politics. Niebuhr has often been able to articulate, clarify and enrich ideas which these men held only vague and tentatively.[6]

Although Niebuhr had not directly influenced Stevenson's religious thought, Lefever argued that Niebuhr provided an accurate lens through which to examine Stevenson's religious beliefs. If Eisenhower's religion was "simple, vague, fervent and crusading," Stevenson's beliefs as illuminated by Niebuhr were both "more complex and more specific." Like Niebuhr, Stevenson pondered the paradox and irony of American history. While Stevenson acknowledged the sovereignty and transcendence of God, he also stressed the limits of human wisdom and power. Stevenson's God prompted examination of human finiteness and self-interest. The pervasiveness of evil in the world precluded quick or morally unambiguous solutions to social problems. Lefever inferred that "Stevenson's Niebuhrian view of man and history [was] coupled with an equally Niebuhrian sense of responsibility for justice and peace."[7]

Predictably, in Lefever's uneven comparison of Stevenson's Niebuhr with Eisenhower's Eisenhower, the supposed simplicity and naivety of the president's religious faith was accentuated. Rather than understood as textured and subtle, Eisenhower's thought was parodied as the antithesis of Stevenson's sensitive and ironic understanding of the human existential condition. At the White House, Special Assistant Frederic Fox was infuriated by *The Christian Century*'s partisan mixture of politics and religion at the president's expense.[8] In retrospect, the 1950s political dynamic to which Fox objected was more understandable than the scholarly willingness to attribute more substance to Stevenson's religious views than was warranted. It never occurred to Lefever to explore Eisenhower's River Brethren heritage, the Russellite influences of his youth, or his West Point education that were, in their own way, both spiritual and intellectual, but did not employ a religious vocabulary that Lefever understood or took seriously.

Another person who did not trust Eisenhower's religious sincerity was CBS commentator Eric Sevareid. For Sevareid, Eisenhower's religious concerns were too political, too secular, and too opportunistic to be taken seriously. (Sevareid did not believe that Kennedy and Nixon were deeply religious men, either).[9] Political scientist Merlin Gustafson identified the perceptual problem of the liberal press and intelligentsia when it came to evaluating the religious beliefs of active politicians. While conservatives believed they understood Eisenhower's religious vocabulary, liberals suspected that the president had been "newly thrust into a situation in which there was a need to appear religious. He did not leave on [liberals] the impression that he had thought very much about theology or the social implications of the Scirptures."[10] But then, liberals had rarely seriously explored the religious culture of the American heartland.

In 1955, before Robert Bellah had recovered Rousseau's "civil religion" vocabulary, Ernest W. Lefever described what he called the "Protestant non-political approach to politics." According to Lefever (a disciple of Reinhold Niebuhr), the Protestant nonpolitical approach to politics tends to be utopian (especially in international politics), individualistic and moralistic, harmonistic, and mugwumpian. Lefever's analysis neatly fit Eisenhower in every category. Until his nomination for president in 1952, Eisenhower had been conspicuously nonpolitical as well as nonreligious—so much so that the Democrats actually considered nominating him for president in 1948.[11]

Eisenhower's nonpolitical ideology shared the same theological and nontheological roots of other nonpolitical Protestants. First, there was a major strain of secular humanism that could be traced to the eighteenth-century Enlightenment philosophers, especially John Locke and Thomas Jefferson. This tradition, described in Carl Becker's *The Heavenly City of the Eighteenth Century Philosophers*, emphasized liberty, equality, brotherhood, reason, education, civic responsibility and goodwill—the building blocks of Eisenhower's social philosophy learned at Abilene high school and West Point.[12] A second strain contributing to nonpolitical Protestantism contained the strong influence of nineteenth-century pietism that blessed "private virtues such as thrift, honesty, purity, sobriety and hard work"—all Midwestern small town values associated with Eisenhower's boyhood and religious upbringing.

Lefever observed that in the 1950s many liberal Protestants still yearned for the Heavenly City of the eighteenth-century philosophers, but their faith in the perfectability of man had been shattered by the Great Depression, World War II, and the cold war. Conservatives, like Eisenhower who had been deeply influenced by pietism, on the other hand, clung to the old American civil faith in reason, progress, and basic human goodness.[13]

During his presidency, Dwight Eisenhower became a major exegete of America's civil religion. One should not confuse the constitutional requirement for separating church and state for the national habit of conflating religion and politics. While the U. S. Constitution prohibits the establishment of a national church, it has not prevented Americans from adopting a public or civil religion. As early as 1831, Alexis de Tocqueville observed that "religion in America takes no direct part in the government of society, but it must be regarded as the first of their political institutions." Among Jacksonian Americans, a man who was not a Christian, de Tocqueville noted, offered "so social guarantee."[14] Not a great deal had changed in this regard by the 1950s. Although the American civil religion supported no official ministerium, the public faith itself firmly linked national mission and destiny with the belief that as "One Nation, under God" the United States enjoyed an especially ordained history. The civil religion that Eisenhower shared with countless Americans was defined by Robert Bellah as the "American Democratic Faith" encompassed in the "American Way of Life" based on a widespread consensus on the transcendent power of the "American Destiny and Dream" founded on a common belief in a Supreme Being.[15]

Richard Pierard and Robert Linder believe that the foundation of Eisenhower's civil religion rested on three suppositions well established by the time he graduated from West Point: the dignity of individuals was warranted by God; American democracy was established on that faith; and each generation was called to fight its own crusade to defend freedom against godless forces.[16] In 1947, Eisenhower offered confession of his personal faith to the Daughters of the American Revolution:

Insistence upon individual freedom springs from unshakable conviction in the dignity of man, a belief—a religious belief—that through the possession of a soul he is endowed with certain rights that are his not by the sufferance of others, but by reason of his very existence.[17]

Five years later at the dedication of the Eisenhower Museum in Abilene, Eisenhower rededicated himself to the civil faith of the Founding Fathers:

> Faith in a Provident God whose hand supported and guided them; faith in themselves as the children of God, endowed with purposes beyond the mere struggle for survival; faith in their country and its principles that proclaimed man's right to freedom and justice, rights derived from his divine origin. Today, the nation they built stands as the world's mightiest temporal power, with its position still rooted in faith and in spiritual values.[18]

Following his inauguration, Eisenhower met with the leaders of the National Council of Churches where he compared his soldier's duty with a pastor's religious calling. This descendent of pacifist River Brethren preachers acknowledged that his military profession might seem the antithesis of the religious vocation of the assembled clergy. But even before he became president, Eisenhower believed "with very great vehemence" that military duty called him to an identical purpose of the ordained clergy. Both soldier and pastor were dedicated to the preservation of free government, which meant affirming the equality and dignity of man and, therefore, "the glory of God."[19]

Eisenhower stated his civil faith simply. The U.S. government was "merely a translation in the political field" of America's deeply felt civil religion. Among the sacred texts of the American civil religion, he explained to the National Council of Churches, were the Magna Carta, the American Declaration of Independence, and the French Declaration of the Rights of Man. Together, these historic documents had established the principle that government recognized the equality and dignity of man. But this premise, Eisenhower stated repeatedly and consistently, would be completely meaningless without the belief in a Supreme Being, "in front of whom we are all equal."[20] On its face, Eisenhower's personal religion harmonized smoothly with the public faith of the Founding Fathers. In this regard, Lefever correctly identified the intellectual and theological basis for Eisenhower's civil religion.

Prayer was the central religious act of Eisenhower's civil religion. In contrast to formal liturgies, sacramental systems, worship customs, and conflicting doctrines, in Eisenhower's view prayer united all who believed in a Supreme Being. Although so-called nonsectarian prayers might not satisfy doctrinaire believers, when couched in the rhetoric of civil religion such prayers could both galvanize political will and mask ideological differences. It was prayer, Eisenhower believed, that most distinctly differentiated the communist system from the American way of life. It was religion, rather than government, economics, or strategic interests, that distinguished Americans from communists. "More precisely than in any other way, prayer places freedom and communism in opposition, one to the other," Eisenhower remarked at the 1953 lighting of the national Christmas tree. Communism could find no purpose in prayer, Eisenhower observed, because Marxist materialism and statism denied the existence of God, the foundation of America's belief in the dignity of man. The United States, on the other hand, drew hope and strength from prayer, Eisenhower believed. "As religious faith is the foundation of free government, so is prayer an indispensable part of that faith."[21]

Although prayer was central both to Eisenhower's personal faith and to his civil religion, he did not believe that God eternally meddled in history or acted as a transcendent "fixer-upper." As a youth, Eisenhower had suffered a knee injury that led to blood poisoning, delirium and a coma. Doctors concluded that his leg should be amputated, but with the help of his brother Edgar, Dwight insisted that his leg be spared even at the risk of death. Later grateful that his life and limb had been saved somewhat miraculously, Eisenhower nevertheless pooh-poohed stories that his family had prayed on their knees night and day for his recovery. They were not faith healers, and he quashed rumors that the Jehovah's Witnesses beliefs of their parents might have rejected medicine in favor of prayer. For the Eisenhower family prayers were daily requests for God's strength and blessing, not petitions for divine intervention in human affairs.[22]

His father's death in 1942, not the war, rekindled Eisenhower's traditional religious concerns. Trapped in Washington, DC, in March 1942 when David died, Eisenhower could not return home to bury his father or comfort his mother. He felt terrible because the war allowed no time "to indulge even the deepest and most sacred emotions." Eisenhower stole 30 minutes to meditate and pray in private, first thinking of his father and then about his mother.[23] This prayerful interlude was his first acknowledged religious activity since leaving West Point.

World War II intensified Eisenhower's prayful religiosity. In a rare public display of public religion, Eisenhower held a "little service" for his staff watching the Allied Forces depart Malta for their invasion of Sicily in July 1943. Scanning the scene from a high hilltop, Eisenhower suddenly snapped to attention, reverently saluted the armada below him, and then bowed his head in silent prayer.

Afterward, he confided to an aid,

> There comes a time when you have done all that you can possibly do,
> when you have used your brains, training, and your technical skill,
> when the die is cast, and events are in the hands of God—and there you
> have to leave them.[24]

Significantly, this comment echoed advice his mother had given him as
a boy, "Do the best you can, and leave the rest to God."[25]

Similarly, prior to the D-Day invasion of Normandy in June 1944,
Eisenhower asked for "the blessing of Almighty God upon this great
and noble undertaking."[26] Faced with uncertain weather that could
spell disaster for the invasion forces, Eisenhower knew that the decision
to launch Operation OVERLORD was his alone. At this defining
moment, he did not pray for God's intervention with the weather or
even for assured victory on the French beaches. In the early morning
of June 5 with the rain still falling, Eisenhower was assured by his
weather officer that the storm would abate enabling the invasion to
proceed. "Okay, we'll go," Eisenhower said simply. Afterward, as
Geoffrey Perret has reported, "On D-Day, he could only smoke and
worry, hope and pray."[27] But pray about what? Eisenhower's prayers
at this time were private prayers for wisdom, strength, and resolution.
Subsequent mythology that Ike spent hours on his knees in prayer
before the Normandy invasion congers similar images of Washington
at Valley Forge. Instead, in a sentiment reflecting his River Brethren
heritage, Eisenhower wrote about the hours before D-Day:

> If there were nothing else in my life to prove the existence of an almighty
> and merciful God, the events of the next twenty-four hours did it. This
> is what I found out about religion. It gives you courage to make the
> decisions you must make in a crisis, and then the confidence to leave the
> result to higher power. Only by trust in one's self and trust in God can a
> man carrying responsibility find repose.[28]

During Christmas in 1953, Eisenhower remembered Washington at
Valley Forge. During that "bitter and critical winter" when the
Patriot's cause was near defeat, Washington's best reserve was "sincere
and earnest prayer" from which he and the Continental troops
received "new hope and new strength of purpose" in the cause of
freedom. According to Eisenhower's credo, God responded to personal
and community prayers petitioning that He help, teach, strengthen
and receive our thanks. Again, God helped not as a divine Manager of
human affairs, but rather as a transcendent Reminder of America's

common heritage bequeathed by the founders of America who had cherished Divinely ordained freedom. More than help, prayer provided personal and collective instruction and renewal. Prayer fostered wisdom and humility, courage and integrity, perspective and patience. Prayer should teach Americans "to shun the counsel of defeat and of despair, of self-pride and self-deceit." While prayer taught trust, hope, and self-dependence, more importantly, prayer taught "the security of faith."[29]

These religious sentiments were not simply the president's pious meanderings. Eisenhower had given deep thought to the meaning and function of prayer and had concluded that prayer was the central religious act of his personal faith and civil religion. He once confided to his White House Secretary, Ann Whitman, that he did not conceive of "God as any being," but as a source of "affection" otherwise absent from his life. Eisenhower's "craving for affection" was not for love provided by family or church. It was the same affection, the assurance that he was a child of God, sought by David and Ida. Although he "abhorred the trappings of the church as much as anyone" and believed that religion was a crutch for many, Eisenhower had no patience for atheists whom he characterized as persons who did not think. Democracy was founded on the religious presumption that all men are created equal. "I know that I am better than lots of men," Eisenhower confessed to Ann Whitman, but democracy worked because in the sight of God all persons were equal. Eisenhower's reliance on God's assurance of the equality and dignity of man was the transcendent Affection that lay at the core of Eisenhower's Faith.[30]

Given his aversion to organized religion, prayer provided Eisenhower the spiritual equivalent of the Word and Sacrament offered by the mainline sacramental liturgical churches. His had an individualistic, robust faith, less focused on public worship of the Almighty or on securing God's blessing for the United States; his faith was more centered on seeking community understanding of America's historic mission "under God." Eisenhower's religious concerns could not be bounded within the context of denominational or sectarian faith. His God was never as personal as that of evangelicals, nor as distant as that the rationalists. Like his mother Ida, Eisenhower possessed strong universalist inclinations, as his famous London Guildhall address revealed.[31] Whether he celebrated American national unity, extolled the commonality of the English-speaking peoples, or promoted his vision for a "United States of Europe," Eisenhower's elastic civil religion included all who shared his belief in God who helped mankind to walk in dignity, "without fear" and "beyond the yoke of tyranny." First and foremost then, this man from Abilene, who craved

God's affection, prayed to strengthen universal human brotherhood. As he stated in his Inaugural Address and repeated at Christmas, he prayed for the strength of conviction that "whatever America hopes to bring to pass in the world must first come to pass in the heart of America." Even imperfect prayer was a civic necessity, Eisenhower stated, because regardless of national shortcomings, prayer bound all Americans together in their efforts to reach out toward the Infinite.[32]

Eisenhower's Inaugural Prayer, the first written by a president, faithfully reflected his civil religion. His "little private prayer," as befitting public prayer, was universalist in tone and content. Predictably, he prayed for God's help, teaching, and strength; Eisenhower prayed for the power of discernment so that his administration might govern in the interests of all the people, "regardless of station, race, or calling."[33] And his authority? Eisenhower believed that the American Revolution marked a great turning point in history when, "to establish a government for free men and a Declaration and Constitution to make it last," the founders had professed that "[w]e hold that all men are endowed by their Creator" with certain rights. This one sentence confirmed that American government was imbedded in a "deeply-felt religious faith." To think otherwise, Eisenhower believed, made no sense.[34]

As William Pickett has shown, Eisenhower's decision to run for president in 1952 was complex. Political mythology aside, a reluctant Eisenhower was not simply drafted by Republicans eager to place the hero/general on their ticket. Taking nothing away from the political nature of his decision to run for president, Eisenhower also experienced a religious-like transformation in this "call to duty." Perhaps, as critics have suggested, this was Eisenhower's self-serving way of transcending sordid politics that he so much detested. But Eisenhower also responded to a deeply felt sense of duty to America. As commanding general of the Allied Forces in World War II and as supreme commander of the NATO, Eisenhower had dedicated the better part of his life to securing world peace. He ran for president in 1952 to save the United States, and the world, from falling into a nuclear abyss.[35]

Eisenhower's conversion and baptism on February 1, 1953, has largely gone unnoticed by his biographers and was only obliquely mentioned by Eisenhower himself in his White House memoir *Mandate for Change*.[36] Eisenhower and Mamie (who was Presbyterian) began attending the National Presbyterian Church before the 1952 election and had participated in a prayer service there on Inauguration Day. Supporters, including Clare Booth Luce, had encouraged the candidate to join a church before the 1952 presidential election, but Eisenhower angrily refused to commit such a blatantly political act.

While Luce believed that Eisenhower's candidacy was weakened without church membership, Eisenhower responded that his religion was a matter strictly between himself and God. This denominational independence, of course, was in line with Eisenhower's upbringing and evidently persisted to the eve of his baptism.[37]

Why then did Eisenhower present himself for baptism in the Presbyterian Church shortly after his inauguration in 1953? While not for votes, no doubt Eisenhower's decision was a political act. Neither Eisenhower nor his pastor Edward L. R. Elson ever explained the president's motives. But Luce, Eisenhower's brother Milton, and evangelist Billy Graham all reported similarly: Eisenhower believed his duty as president required membership and regular attendance at church to set a religious example and moral tone for the nation. Granting, then, a significant political incentive to his religious conversion and baptism, were there more traditionally religious concerns also motivating Eisenhower?

Paul Tillich, writing concurrently, defined religion as the object of our "ultimate concern," usually centering on issues concerning being and nonbeing or death.[38] Discern someone's "ultimate concern," Tillich argues, and you discover their religion:

> The concern about our work often succeeds in becoming our god, as does the concern about another human being, or about pleasure. The concern about science has succeeded in becoming the god of a whole era in history, the concern about money has become an even more important god, and the concern about the nation the most important god of all.[39]

Eisenhower was not obsessed with the atomic bomb when he became president in 1953, but the former general had observed more than his share of human carnage on World War II battlefields, the Nazi death camps, and the Korean Peninsula. Almost alone among U.S. military leaders, during World War II he had opposed the atomic bombing of Hiroshima. "It was not necessary to hit them with that awful thing," he later reflected. On a postwar low-level flight between Berlin and Moscow, Eisenhower was appalled that he saw no undamaged buildings and few living things from the Polish border to the Russian capital. Conditions in Germany differed in scale but not in kind with those in the Soviet Union. Millions were dead or missing. Millions more were homeless. Cities were in ashes and industry reduced to rubble. In the aftermath of unimaginable destruction and incomprehensible inhumanity Eisenhower experienced intensified stirring of religious revival.[40]

Eisenhower's moral revulsion over the atomic bomb never lessened, but rather became a major force shaping his worldview, politics, and civil religion. Following his meeting with Secretary of War Henry Stimson at Potsdam in 1945 where he first learned about the successful Trinity test, Eisenhower became depressed not only because he did not believe the atomic bomb was needed to defeat Japan, but also because he did not believe the United States should be morally responsible for using a weapon of mass destruction needlessly to save American lives. He had hoped for postwar friendship with the Soviet Union, but the atomic bomb blasted any chance for peace. "I had hoped the bomb wouldn't figure in this war," he lamented. But the world had changed. "Now I don't know," Eisenhower worried, "People are frightened and disturbed all over. Everyone feels insecure again."[41] Contrasting Eisenhower with other American leaders, Gar Alperovitz later marveled at Eisenhower's moral instincts. "Why is it that some men were able to preserve their hold on ethical standards? And some were not?"[42]

Had Alperovitz known of Eisenhower's religious youth, he may have understood the origins of Eisenhower's moral compass. Eisenhower had pondered fiery Armageddon as a child and had rejected his father's apocalyptic religion. While the prospects of nuclear holocaust were depressing, Eisenhower was an incurable optimist. He possessed a religious-like faith that the worst circumstances could be turned toward good. In this regard, he saw divine possibility even in the most demonic events. Whether it was the unspeakable horrors of World War II or the terrible portent of the atomic bomb, Eisenhower not only believed, but virtually willed, that these events would work toward the ultimate benefit of mankind. Stephen Ambrose has described Eisenhower as a Wilsonian idealist— that is, like Woodrow Wilson before him, he believed in the power of goodwill and personal diplomacy to overcome cultural, economic, and ideological differences to achieve peace, prosperity, and progress.[43] As presidential leaders of America's civil religion, Wilson and Eisenhower had much in common, not least of which was their utopian international vision based on traditional Protestant nonpolitical values.[44]

Death, including his own mortality, was not far from Eisenhower's mind after World War II. While fashioning his administration's nuclear policy, for example, on October 19, 1953, he made an unrelated trip to dedicate the Falcon Dam on the lower Rio Grande. In extraordinary off-the-cuff remarks to school children gathered just off the dam, he gave a little homily on international friendship. Civilization as we know it, he warned the children, will have a meager future unless diplomacy replaced war. Then, characteristically upbeat but curiously morbid, he encouraged the children to look forward to the next 60 years of "a future brighter than any civilization has known." For himself, Eisenhower thought he would be lucky to live 15 more years. He missed predicting his own death by 1 year.[45]

In October 1953, Eisenhower graphically described the deadly horrors of nuclear warfare to the United Church Women. Although America had escaped the physical ravage of World War II, the United States' former security had disappeared with the threat of nuclear attack by intercontinental bombers. America had few choices. The choice that spells terror and death is symbolized by a mushroom cloud floating upward from the release of the mightiest natural power yet uncovered by those who search the physical universe. The energy that it typifies is, at this stage of human knowledge, the unharnessed blast. In its wake we see only sudden and mass destruction, erasure of cities, the possible doom of every nation and society.[46]

But Eisenhower would not abandon hope that the "titanic force" of nuclear energy could be directed to the useful service of mankind.

When Soviet Premier Joseph Stalin died in March 1953, Eisenhower believed the United States stood at a turning point in history, a time of unique danger and opportunity. His father had predicted such moments of judgment. Eisenhower was neither a millenarian nor a manichean, but his religious worldview was informed by dialectical struggle between divine and demonic forces in history, an understanding not dissimilar to that of his father or contemporary theologian Paul Tillich. Typically, Eisenhower had described his struggles against the dark forces of history in the rhetoric of crusades, which was his way of highlighting the epic nature of history. But Eisenhower was not unaware of the complexities of history. His universalist beliefs regarded the Russians as "children of the same God who is the Father of all peoples everywhere." And, despite his transformation into a cold war president, Eisenhower believed, as he had in 1945, that the Russian people genuinely longed for peace and friendship. In the spring of 1953 he saw a "chance for peace."[47] It is mystifying how scholars can read Eisenhower's "A Chance for Peace" speech presented to the American Society for Newspaper Editors, April 16, 1953, and still conclude that he was bland, vague, uninformed, and disinterested. The president's estimate of "A Chance for Peace" presented a manifestly political agenda while latently revealing Eisenhower's religious transformation.

David Eisenhower had believed in three ages, or dispensations, in history, the last of which would be preceded by a fiery holocaust that foretold the second return of Christ. Eisenhower's vision of the "middle-way" in human affairs, in contrast, rejected belief in an apocalyptic end to history. Eisenhower preferred to seek salvation within nature and human history and entertained no capitulation to evil or death in this world. Theologian Paul Tillich offered a more pacific version of this historical trinity in his Protestant interpretation of history in which ages of autonomy and heteronomy, dialectically interacting, were superceded by a theonomous age that is "directed toward" the divine principle in history revealed by the Kairos—the turning point in history that revealed the meaning and destiny of history.[48]

For Dwight Eisenhower, the spring of 1953 was just such a time of Kairos when the world was summoned to choose between peril and hope. "A Chance for Peace" described the Kairos literally:

> This is one of those times in the affairs of nations when the gravest choices must be made, if there is to be a turning toward a just and lasting peace. It is a moment that calls upon the governments of the world to speak their intentions with simplicity and honesty. It calls upon them to answer the question that stirs the hearts of all sane men: *is there no other way the world may live?*[49]

What could the world hope for if there were no turning on this dreadful road, Eisenhower asked rhetorically? The worst was nuclear war. And the best that could be hoped for was a life of perpetual fear and tension; wealth and labor dissipated in an endless arms race; and governments discredited by the failure to achieve prosperity and happiness for mankind.

The costs of the cold war were staggering and debilitating. "Every gun that is made, every warship launched, every rocket fired signifies, in the final sense, a theft from those who hunger and are not fed, those who are cold and are not clothed."[50] And, according to Eisenhower, the costs were not paid in cash alone. The cold war consumed the daily work of laborers, the creativity of scientists, the future of children. In social priorities, a bomber cost 30 schools, 2 electric power plants, 2 hospitals, or 50 miles of highway. A single destroyer would buy 8,000 new homes for a small Kansas town. Paraphrasing the 1908 presidential nominee of the Democratic Party William Jennings Bryan Eisenhower solemnly observed, "Under the cloud of threatening war, it is humanity hanging from a cross of iron."[51]

As pessimistic as Eisenhower's remarks may have seemed, the exegetical president proceeded to outline his personal agenda for extricating the United States from the cold war. Despite the increasing intensity of the nuclear arms race, Eisenhower continued to hope for an international rapprochement with the Soviet Union. He recalled that brief moment of joyous victory in the spring of 1945 when Americans and Russians had been comrades in arms seeking to rebuild a world at peace as a fitting tribute to the millions who had died to defeat tyranny. In the aftermath of Hiroshima and Nagasaki, the United States and the Soviet Union had taken different paths, each seeking in its own way to buy security through international alliances and nuclear arms. The results were ironic and tragic. Enormous invest-ment in weapons of mass destruction had lessened everyone's security. But Eisenhower rejected despair. Although some of his prerequisites for peace included standard cold war demands for a free Germany and free eastern Europe that would not move the Soviet leaders, he also offered to explore more modest, incremental steps toward arms control and disarmament. Even these suggestions, including international control of atomic energy for peaceful purposes, were neither new nor original with Eisenhower. But they did represent confidence-building initiatives certain to lessen cold war animosity if adopted.[52]

"A Chance for Peace" was one of Eisenhower's finest speeches. It was not free of raw cold war propaganda in its obligatory denunciation of Soviet oppression. Eisenhower hated Stalin's heteronomy as intensely as he had hated Hitler's tyranny. But in contrast to the Nazis with whom no compromise had been possible, Eisenhower hoped that the new Communist Party leaders in the Kremlin might be amenable to making small steps toward peace. Eisenhower was not naive about the difficulty of the new path to be taken. Trust, confidence, and goodwill would be difficult to establish with the Soviets in the cold war atmosphere. If his arms control proposals were modest, it was because Eisenhower knew full well that the "details of disarmament programs were necessarily crit-ical and complex . . . and no nation possessed a perfect, immutable for-mula. But," he concluded, "the formula mattered less than the faith."[53]

Nightmares of nuclear Armageddon haunted Eisenhower. In his role as president/pastor, he wanted both to educate and assure the American people, while offering hope and leadership to the world. He might not be able to dismiss his ultimate concerns about nuclear death, but he could draw on his faith that God intended for humans to employ the atom for peaceful purposes. "A Chance for Peace" was a public prayer offering a "middle-way" in public policy while reminding Americans of their historical destiny, instructing the public in the realities of nuclear arms race, and strengthening the world in its resolve to seek new, and risky, paths to peace. Characteristically, he tried to seize an historical opportunity in 1953 rather than drift passively/negatively with the cold war tide. "A Chance for Peace" outlined an agenda for nuclear arms control and disarmament from which Eisenhower and his administration would not deviate. At the United Nations in December 1953, at the Geneva conferences in 1955 and 1958, and during seemingly endless and fruitless negotiations to limit atomospheric nuclear testing, Eisenhower never lost sight of the historical objective envisioned in "A Change for Peace."[54] Biographer Geoffrey Perret believes the speech was "the most trenchant criticism ever made of the Cold War."[55] Unfortunately, Eisenhower lost heart after the U-2 incident and the collapse of the Paris Peace talks just when a test ban agreement seemed within reach. Ironically, it would be John F. Kennedy, representing a new generation, who reaped the historical and moral credit for the landmark 1963 Limited Test Ban Treaty, often cited as the most important achievement of Kennedy's brief Presidency.

Liberals bitterly criticized Eisenhower for not using the president's "bully pulpit" to denounce McCarthyism or promote civil rights. Instead, Dwight D. Eisenhower dedicated himself politically, morally, and religiously to securing international peace during the cold war.[56] May I compare Eisenhower's Tillich to Stevenson's Niebuhr? An exegetical president, Eisenhower wrestled with the tension between the divine and demonic associated with managing a horrific, but potentially beneficial, nuclear technology. Eisenhower's vision was not prophetic; he preached no nuclear Jeremiads, not even in his farewell "Military-Industrial Complex" speech. His role was exegetical—defining, explaining, and encouraging. As we have seen, this intensely religious president interpreted the West's nuclear dilemma with the context of American civil religion and applied the precepts of the civil religion in pursuit of nuclear peace in the depths of the cold war.

Notes

A version of this paper, "Dwight D. Eisenhower: Exegetical President in the Nuclear Age," was given at a conference on "Freedom, Race and Bondage" in honor of David Brion Davis, Yale University, New Haven, Connecticut, May 9, 2002.

1. Philip Yancey, *What's So Amazing About Grace?* (Grand Rapids, MI: Zondervan, 1997), 225–236, 264.
2. Press conference at Columbia University, *Times* [New York], May 4, 1948, 43, as cited in Richard V. Pierard and Robert D. Linder, *Civil Religion and the Presidency* (Grand Rapids, MI: Academic Books, 1988), 185.

3. *Times* [New York], December 23, 1952, 16, as cited in Pierard and Linder, *Civil Religion and the Presidency*, 184.
4. Ernest W. Lefever, "The Candidates' Religious Views," *The Christian Century*, September 1956, 1072.
5. Ibid.
6. Ibid., 1073.
7. Ibid., 1074.
8. Frederick Fox, White House special assistant to Harold Frey, editor of *The Christian Century*, November 2, 1956 (not sent), papers of Frederick Fox, White House special assistant, to Harold Frey, editor of the *Christian Century*, November 2, 1956 (not sent). Records of Frederick Fox, Box 25, November 1956, Dwight D. Eisenhower Presidential Library, Abilene, Kansas.
9. Eric Sevareid, *This is Eric Sevareid* (New York: McGraw-Hill, 1964), 117.
10. Merlin Gustafson, "The Religion of a President," *The Christian Century*, April 1969, 610.
11. William Pickett, *Eisenhower Decides to Run: Presidential Politics and Cold War Strategy* (Chicago: Ivan R. Doe, 2000), 17.
12. Carl Becker, *The Heavenly City of the Eighteenth Century Philosophers* (New Haven, CN: Yale University Press, 1932).
13. Ernest W. Lefever, "The Protestant Nonpolitical Approach to Politics," *The Christian Scholar*, 38 (2) (June 1955): 90–98.
14. George Wilson Pierson, *Tocqueville in America* (Garden City, NY: Doubleday Anchor, 1959), 321–322.
15. Robert M. Bellah, "Civil Religion in America," *Daedalus*, 96 (Winter 1967): 1–21.
16. Pierard and Linder, *Civil Religion and the Presidency*, 195–197.
17. Eisenhower, as quoted in ibid., 195; *Times* [New York], May 20, 1947, 22.
18. Eisenhower as quoted in Pierard and Linder, *Civil Religion and the Presidency*, 195–196; *Times* [New York], June 5, 1952, 16.
19. Eisenhower, Remarks at a Luncheon of the General Board of the National Council of Churches," November 18, 1953 in *Public Papers of the Presidents, Dwight D. Eisenhower*, U.S. Government Printing Office, 1960 (hereafter cited as PPP/DDE 1953).
20. Ibid.
21. Eisenhower, "Remarks Upon Lighting the National Community Christmas Tree," December 24, 1953, in PPP/DDE 1953, 858–859.
22. Stephen E. Ambrose, *Eisenhower: Soldier and President* (New York, Simon and Schuster, 1990), 21.
23. Eisenhower, *At Ease: Stories I Tell to Friends*, Military Classics Series (Blue Ridge Summit, PA: TAB Books), 304–305.
24. Pierard and Linder, *Civil Religion and the Presidency*, 193.
25. Gustafson, "The Religion of a President," 611.
26. As quoted in Ambrose, *Eisenhower: Soldier and President*, s135.
27. Geoffrey Perret, *Eisenhower* (New York: Random House, 1999), 286.
28. As quoted in Pierard and Linder, *Civil Religion and the Presidency*, 193.

29. Eisenhower, "Remarks Upon Lighting the National Community Christmas Tree," December 24, 1953, in PPP/DDE 1953, 859.

30. Ann C. Whitman to E. S. Whitman, n.d., personal papers of Ann C. Whitman, box 1, correspondence, Whitman, E. S., Eisenhower Presidential Library.

31. Eisenhower, "Guildhall Address," June 12, 1945, as noted in Eisenhower, *At Ease*, 298–300, 388–390.

32. Eisenhower, "Inaugural Address," January 20, 1953, 7; "Remarks upon Lighting the National Community Christmas Tree," December 24, 1953, 859; and "Remarks at the Dedicatory Prayer Breakfast of the International Christian Leadership," February 5, 1953, 8; all in PPP/DDE 1953

33. Eisenhower, "Inaugural Address," January 20, 1953, 1, in PPP/DDE 1953.

34. Eisenhower, "Remarks at the Dedicatory Prayer Breakfast of the International Christian Leadership," February 5, 1953, in PPP/DDE 1953, 7–8. For an extended modern exploration of this theme see Robert Lowry Clinton, *God & Man in the Law* (Lawrence, KS: University Press of Kansas, 1997).

35. Pickett, "A Question of Duty," in *Eisenhower Decides to Run*, 210–215.

36. Dwight D. Eisenhower, *Mandate for Change: The White House Years, 1953–1956* (Garden City, NY: Doubleday, 1963), 100.

37. Keith Bates, "Edward L. R. Elson: 'Spiritual Helper' to Dwight D. Eisenhower," graduate seminar on the Eisenhower Era, Kansas State University, May 11, 2001, unpublished, 2–5. See also interview with Clare Booth Luce by John Luter, January 11, 1968, Columbia Oral History Project, Eisenhower Presidential Library.

38. Paul Tillich, *Systematic Theology* (Chicago: University of Chicago Press, 1951), I: 11–14.

39. Paul Tillich, *The New Being* (New York: Charles Scribner's Sons, 1955), 158.

40. Eisenhower, *Crusade in Europe*, 443 (New York: Doubleday, 1948); John S. D. Eisenhower, *Strictly Personal* (Garden City, NY: Doubleday, 1974), 97; and Gar Alperovitz, *Atomic Diplomacy: Hiroshima and Potsdam, the Use of the Atomic Bomb and American Confrontation with Soviet Power* (New York: Penguin, 1985), 60.

41. Peter Lyon, *Eisenhower: Portrait of a Hero* (Boston: Little, Brown, 1974), 356–357, as quoted in Edgar Snow, *Journey to the Beginning* (New York: Random House, 1958), 360–361.

42. Alperovitz, *Atomic Diplomacy*, 60.

43. Ambrose, *Eisenhower: Soldier and President*, 426–427.

44. See also Pierard and Linder, "Woodrow Wilson and the Moralization of America's Special Mission," in *Civil Religion and the Presidency*, 136–160.

45. Eisenhower, "Remarks Following the Dedication of Falcon Dam," October 19, 1953, in PPP/DDE 1953, 696–697.

46. Eisenhower, "Address at the Sixth National Assembly of the United Church Women, Atlantic City, New Jersey," October 6, 1953, in PPP/DDE 1953, 636.

47. Eisenhower, *Mandate for Change*, 144.

48. Paul Tillich, *The Protestant Era* (Chicago: University of Chicago Press, 1948), 43–44.
49. Italics in the original; DDE, "The Chance for Peace," speech delivered before the American Society of Newspaper Editors, April 16, 1953, in *Public Papers of the Presidents*, DDE 1953, 179–188.
50. Ibid.
51. Ibid.
52. Ibid.
53. Eisenhower, *Mandate for Change*, 146.
54. For an extended discussion of Eisenhower nuclear policy see, Richard G. Hewlett and Jack M. Holl, *Atoms for Peace and War, 1953–1961: Eisenhower and the Atomic Energy Commission* (Berkeley: University of California Press, 1989).
55. Perret, *Eisenhower*, 454; see also Ambrose, *Eisenhower: Soldier and President*, 324–326.
56. James David Barber, "Eisenhower as a 'Passive-Negative' President," in *The Eisenhower Presidency and the 1950s*, ed. Michael S. Mayer, Problems in American Civilization Series (Boston: Houghton Mifflin, 1998), 3–16; Erwin C. Hargrove, *The President as Leader: Appealing to the Better Angels of our Nature* (Lawrence, KS: University Press of Kansas, 1998), 61–64; and Fred L. Greenstein, *The Hidden-Hand Presidency: Eisenhower as Leader* (New York: Basic Books, 1982).

Chapter Seven

Secular Icon or Catholic Hero?: Religion and the Presidency of John F. Kennedy

Thomas J. Carty

My grandfather James B. Murphy sponsored John F. Kennedy's admission into the second and third degrees of the Knights of Columbus, a Catholic fraternal organization. As a Catholic who attended daily mass, Mr. Murphy seemed proud that Kennedy's victory against anti-Catholic prejudice proved that his grandson might achieve the nation's highest office. He kept a picture of himself with Kennedy in his office. Steven J. Danenberg, the headmaster of the Williams School, a private (independent) day school that I attended in the 1980s, also held Kennedy in high esteem, but for a completely different reason. As an agnostic and a humanist, Mr. Danenberg had two heroes, Captain James T. Kirk (of the television program *Star Trek*) and John Kennedy, who symbolized for him a secular faith in science and progress. Having spent two years in Venezuela as a Peace Corps volunteer, he viewed Kennedy's call to public service as an inspiration for educators ambitious to inspire critical thought and intellectual curiosity in young people.

The appeal of a single politician to two people with such contrasting worldviews is exceptional, and Kennedy's unique ability to balance secular and religious ideas explains his position of high esteem among these distinct constituencies. After World War II, these groups clashed in what we might today call "culture wars" in the fields of education and foreign policy. Kennedy became president of the United States during a period of clashing interpretations about America's mission, especially regarding the constitutional dictum of separation of church and state. This chapter shows how President Kennedy struggled to fashion an image as a secular icon to some Americans and a Catholic hero to others.

Kennedy's attempt to balance these clashing cultures has continuing significance because this unique challenge helps explain why, nearly

50 years later, no other Catholic has been elected president. Kennedy continues to enjoy great popularity among U.S. citizens. In 1996, more respondents to a *New York Times*/CBS News public opinion survey chose Kennedy over all other former presidents as the best leader.[1] Americans again rated Kennedy as the nation's greatest president in a 2000 Gallup poll.[2] Kennedy would seem to have proven to U.S. voters that a Catholic can perform as president at the highest level. Why would American political parties fail to nominate another Catholic prior to 2004?

Senator John F. Kerry's (D-MA) defeat in the 2004 presidential election reminds us of how difficult it is for a Catholic to reconcile secular and religious values. More Catholics (even in Kerry's home state) chose incumbent President George W. Bush than Kerry. Many Democrats credited Kerry's loss to the party's militant secularism and opposition to Catholic positions on abortion and embryonic stem cell research.[3] This political reality elevates the significance of Kennedy's success at embracing secularism without alienating Catholics.

Secular Icon?

John Kennedy became a secular icon to many Americans by demonstrating independence from institutional religion. Educated at nonsectarian schools, such as Choate boarding school in Wallingford, Connecticut, and Harvard University, Kennedy neither learned nor appreciated the intricacies of Catholic liturgy and theology. As a politician, Kennedy presented an image as an ironic rather than a devotional Catholic. When challenged about a Catholic's ability to demonstrate absolute loyalty to the U.S. government as a Massachusetts congressman in 1947, Kennedy strongly denied that religious belief determined his public decisions: "We have an old saying in Boston that we get our religion from Rome and our politics at home."[4]

This declaration of political faith seems genuine in light of statements by those who lived and worked with Kennedy. Speechwriter Richard Goodwin called his boss "the most secular of men," and claimed that "his values derived not from his catechism, but from the mainstream of Western thought, Christian and pagan."[5] Kennedy did not want to be known as "a very religious man," wrote his closest clerical ally, Boston Archbishop Richard Cardinal Cushing.[6] According to journalist Arthur Krock, Kennedy's wife offered a more severe assessment of his faith. As opponents of a Catholic president challenged her husband's political ambitions in 1960, Jacqueline Kennedy protested, "I think it is unfair for Jack to be opposed because he is a Catholic. After all, he's such a poor Catholic. Now if it were [his brother] Bobby: he never misses mass and prays all the time."[7]

Competing for the Democratic Party presidential nomination in 1960, Kennedy tried hard to dispel fears that he would use the executive office to pay special favors to the Roman Catholic Church. Many non-Catholic Americans believed that a Catholic president could not separate issues of church and state. Even prior to announcing his presidential bid, therefore, Kennedy disavowed support for federal aid to Catholic schools. In a 1959 interview with *Look* magazine, Kennedy declared that such assistance would violate the Constitution's prohibition against an establishment of religion. Kennedy also reaffirmed his opposition to the appointment of an ambassador to the Holy See, which the Catholic hierarchy had anxiously pursued for years. (Two years earlier, he had joked that he would appoint Methodist Bishop G. Bromley Oxnam, one of the more vociferous opponents of an official emissary to the Holy See, to this post.) In Kennedy's words, "[W]hatever one's religion in private life may be, for the officeholder, nothing takes precedence over his oath to uphold the Constitution in all its parts—including the First Amendment and the strict separation of church and state."[8] Many Catholic publications expressed frustration, and even outrage, about Kennedy's statements, including a succinct rebuke by the *Indiana Catholic and Record*: "Young Senator Kennedy had better watch his language."[9]

Even after Kennedy won the presidency, many observers doubted the Catholic character of this politician. According to John Cogley, editor of the Catholic lay publication *Commonweal*, Kennedy expressed frustration about religious questions in a letter that stated, "It's hard for a Harvard man to answer questions in theology. . . . I imagine my answers will cause heartburn at Fordham and B.C. [Boston College]."[10] Kennedy continued to deny that his obligations to the Catholic Church would compromise his political independence. When Kennedy won the election, newspaperman Murray Kempton called him the nation's "first anti-clerical President."[11] Catholic Congressman Eugene McCarthy (D-MN), who pursued the presidency eight years later, declared, "If I'm elected, I'll be the first Catholic president."[12] More recently, author Charles Morris argued that Kennedy's election symbolized the end of a distinct Catholic culture in America.[13]

More than 40 years later, Catholic scholars continue to lament Kennedy's secular statements. In a 2004 book, *Anti-Catholicism in America: The Last Acceptable Prejudice*, Fordham University professor

Mark Massa, S. J., argued that Kennedy's ambitious attempts to demonstrate freedom from religious pressure ensured a "privatization of religious belief." By disavowing so completely Catholicism's role in his public life, Kennedy "helped to categorize Catholic politicians as . . . hypocritical opportunists—professing a very public faith while denying the obvious social implications of that faith for public/political policy."[14] In the words of Catholic priest Richard J. Neuhaus, this divorce between religion and politics had created a "naked public square" that tolerated only secular views.[15]

Catholic Hero?

Prior to the 1960 campaign, however, Kennedy had earned a heroic reputation with American Catholics. As the representative of Massachusetts' heavily Catholic Eighth District from 1947 to 1953, he supported federal funding of textbooks, medical care, and food for nonpublic schools.[16] Along with most other Catholics, Kennedy cheered the 1947 Supreme Court decision, *Everson v. Board of Education*, which allowed public funding of transportation to Catholic schools. New York Archbishop Francis Cardinal Spellman, the most outspoken proponent of government aid, described denial of such assistance to children in private schools as discriminatory.[17] When former first lady Eleanor Roosevelt argued that church-state separation prevented such aid to nonpublic schools, Spellman declared this position "unfit for an American mother."[18]

Kennedy did not disappoint his fellow Catholics when Congress considered an education bill in 1950. Kennedy's successful efforts to secure federal funds for busing and health services won high praise from Boston's Catholic archdiocese paper, *The Pilot*, which credited him with "courageous representation of his constituency" by defending the right of children at Catholic schools.[19] The editors presented this Catholic politician as outnumbered and vulnerable in the hostile territory of Washington, DC: "Standing out as a white knight in the crepuscular haze, we are very proud to note, is our own Congressman John F. Kennedy." The enthusiasm of the Catholic press for Kennedy's efforts appeared even more bubbling in the *Sign*: "Boston's boyish congressman was in the thick of the adroit intra-committee maneuvering over the boiling hot aid to education issue." Calling Kennedy a "Galahad in the House," the editors lauded his ability to block two bills that excluded federal aid to Catholic schools.[20]

Kennedy's foreign policy positions also aligned closely with the Catholic hierarchy and his large Catholic constituency. As communists sought power in southern and western Europe, and Soviet Allies in eastern Europe tortured and even killed Catholic clerics in the late 1940s, Spellman and other American clerics portrayed the communist threat as the pivotal political crisis for the United States. Kennedy adopted the policies and rhetoric of a militant Cold Warrior. Traditionally Catholic nations, such as Italy and Poland, appeared especially important to Kennedy. In 1947, Kennedy supported more than $200 million in foreign aid to protect Italy from "the onslaught of the communist minority." Although both parties opposed communism in theory, Kennedy showed no fear of criticizing the highest officials in his own party for insufficient vigilance against communist regimes. When the United States welcomed 18,000 displaced Polish soldiers, Kennedy justified this action as compensation for "the betrayal of their native country" by former Democratic President Franklin D. Roosevelt.[21] To challenge the party's leadership may have seemed risky, but Kennedy earned the respect of many Polish Catholics in his district, state, and nation.

Kennedy's open challenge to party leaders on the communism issue provided political benefits at home. Kennedy blamed incumbent Democratic President Harry S Truman's administration publicly for the communist seizure of power in China in 1949, as well as U.S. inability to stop the advance of communist North Korea into South Korea during the summer of 1950. Kennedy voted for requiring the internment of communists in a national emergency, the McCarran Act (named after Patrick A. McCarran, a Catholic and Democratic senator from Nevada), which Truman vetoed in 1950. Calling President Roosevelt's former State Department official Alger Hiss a "traitor," Kennedy praised Catholic Senator Joseph R. McCarthy (R-WI), who accused several liberals and Democrats of communist sympathies, as a "great American patriot." These maverick positions would later cause Kennedy some political grief at the national level, but Massachusetts Catholics rallied behind this uncompromising attitude toward communism. In the state's 1952 contest for senator, Kennedy detached the vast majority of the Catholic vote from incumbent Republican Henry Cabot Lodge. Six years earlier, Lodge secured as much as two-thirds of Catholics against an incumbent Catholic senator, David I. Walsh. Lodge's Catholic support against Kennedy fell below 40 percent, a drop of more than 25 percentage points.[22] For Catholics, Kennedy symbolized a success story of a Catholic politician who had risen to the highest levels of the U.S. political system without compromising his core principles.

As a Catholic who challenged the Protestant monopoly on the White House eight years later, Kennedy had a golden opportunity to reaffirm his image as a Catholic hero. Historians should not underestimate the anti-Catholicism that Kennedy confronted. As popular author James A. Michener observed after the election, "If, thirty years from now, all of this can be explained away in clever articles which prove that religion played no significant role in the 1960 election, it seems to me that the writers of that age will have to blind themselves to what actually happened."[23] My own book *A Catholic in the White House?*, documented the critical significance of Kennedy's Catholicism in this campaign.

Scholars have labeled anti-Catholicism the nation's oldest prejudice. Suspicion of papal designs on the United States appeared even prior to the nation's inception. England's rivalry with Catholic governments in France and Spain intensified in competition to colonize the Western Hemisphere. Many settlers of English North America, especially in Puritan Massachusetts, hanged effigies of the pope to commemorate a failed Irish plot to bomb Parliament. Although the small Catholic population assimilated without major incident in the nation's early decades, nativist anti-Catholicism revived in the 1830s. One prominent proponent of this fear was Samuel F. B. Morse, inventor of the telegraph. He posited Catholic corruption of American youth through parochial schools with the ultimate goal of conquering the United States for the Holy See. Sensationalist literature also exploited this sentiment. A woman who called herself Maria Monk alleged that, in nearby Canada, Catholic priests impregnated nuns and murdered the children born of these illicit liaisons. Even Harriett Beecher Stowe's *Uncle Tom's Cabin*, a classic nineteenth-century novel still read in many high schools today, posits a conspiracy between the Roman Catholic hierarchy and the South's "slavocracy."[24]

In the political sphere, anti-Catholicism peaked during the 1928 presidential campaign, when New York Governor Alfred E. Smith encountered the vestiges of the most absurd nativism. The Ku Klux Klan and other anti-Catholic propagandists warned the pope would move to the White House if Smith won. Some pamphleteers claimed that the Holland Tunnel, which opened for vehicular traffic between New Jersey and Manhattan in late 1927, extended beneath the Atlantic Ocean to facilitate the pope's secret arrival upon Smith's election.[25] After Smith's overwhelming defeat, a rumor circulated that he immediately sent a one-word telegram to the pope—"UNPACK."[26] These anecdotes, however outrageous, bitterly reminded Catholics of the glass ceiling that blocked this group from the nation's highest office.

The Catholic memory of victimization by religious prejudice allowed Kennedy to manage the 1960 campaign's "religious issue" as a means of securing Catholic support. Four years earlier, Kennedy's aide Theodore Sorensen argued that a Catholic vice presidential candidate, such as Kennedy, could help the Democrats secure victory in 14 states with large Catholic populations. In the winner-take-all system, the Democratic ticket would secure the electoral votes of these states. The large population of these states had determined that they carried a substantial number of electoral votes. A Catholic candidate, Sorensen claimed, could therefore ensure Democratic victory in the Electoral College.[27]

Four years later, the Kennedy campaign successfully targeted these "Catholic states" as the party's presidential nominee. In Detroit, Michigan, for example, the pro-Democrat United Auto Workers distributed a pamphlet that juxtaposed an image of the Statue of Liberty with a Klansman. Entitled "Liberty or Bigotry? Which Do You Choose?" the pamphlet portrayed support for Kennedy as necessary to preserve freedom from religious hatred. In heavily Catholic and Jewish New York City, former president Truman raised the campaign's "Catholic issue" (at the encouragement of the Democratic National Committee) in order to ensure these groups' support for Kennedy. This strategy of portraying Kennedy as a Catholic knight resisting religious prejudice paid dividends on Election Day. Nearly 80 percent of Catholics voted for Kennedy in 1960.[28] While several political scientists argued Kennedy lost more votes nationwide than he gained due to religion, a Massachusetts Institute of Technology computer analysis determined that Kennedy's religion resulted in a net gain of 22 electoral votes.[29] Catholic voters in Illinois, Pennsylvania, and New York had made a significant impact in the Electoral College.

As the nation's first Catholic president, Kennedy symbolized success and respectability for American Catholics. University of Notre Dame historian Jay P. Dolan has argued that "[Kennedy's] popularity enabled Catholics to stand a little taller."[30] More recently, historian Robert Dallek credited Kennedy's Catholicism with his continued recognition as one of the nation's most popular presidents: "Public attachment to Kennedy . . . rests on the conviction that his election reduced religious and ethnic tests for the presidency."[31] Journalist Thomas Maier echoed this sentiment by describing the Kennedy clan as "the ultimate Irish Catholic family" in a subtitle to his 2004 book, *The Kennedys: America's Emerald Kings.*[32]

The Kennedy Presidency

The verdict about Kennedy's lasting legacy as either secular icon or Catholic hero must rest on his presidency. With the responsibilities of national office, Kennedy would face his greatest challenge to please both secular and Catholic Americans. In Kennedy's less than three years as president, secularists and Catholics clashed openly on domestic cultural issues, especially in the sphere of education, and international struggles with the officially atheist communist world.

This potential divide appeared even prior to inauguration day. Protestants and Other Americans United for Separation of Church and State (POAU), an organization dedicated to limiting Catholic power in public policy, issued a public warning about Catholic pressure on Kennedy. POAU's December 1960 newsletter *Church and State* published a cartoon entitled "The President's Appointment List." The sketch portrayed Catholic priests and nuns waiting outside the president-elect's office to lobby for government aid to Catholic schools, censorship of books and movies, a ban on birth control, and other Catholic causes.[33] While this image clearly discouraged Kennedy from partiality toward Catholic institutions, the title also carried another level of meaning. Would Kennedy appoint a disproportionate number of Catholics to Cabinet posts? With this cartoon, POAU challenged Kennedy to maintain the promises of strict secularism that he had made during the campaign.

Kennedy's nomination process demonstrated the incoming administration's intent on projecting a secular image. Kennedy consciously appointed men (nearly all were male) who became known as the "whiz kids," "action intellectuals," and ultimately "the best and the brightest" because they derived from the highest levels of corporate and academic America.[34] A Catholic Cabinet nominee was considered a liability rather than an asset. The irony was rich. Kennedy's brother-in-law, Sargent Shriver, who was very active in Catholic organizations such as the Catholic Interracial Council, headed the transition team assigned to construct the Cabinet. While considering Robert McNamara, the newly appointed chief executive officer of Ford motor company, as secretary of defense, Shriver was favorably impressed. McNamara, a Republican, supported the American Civil Liberties Union and had read *The Phenomenon of Man*, a theological work by Jesuit scholar Teilhard de Chardin. Yet Kennedy halted the process abruptly at the last minute to ask if McNamara was Catholic. As Shriver's assistant Harris Wofford recounted, "There musn't be too many in the cabinet, the first Catholic President said." After searching a few minutes, Shriver and Wofford informed Kennedy that McNamara was not Catholic, and the nomination was announced.[35]

Rather than disappoint his secular supporters, Kennedy proved willing as president to defy Catholic pressure on issues of church and state. Prior to abortion's appearance as an issue of national salience in the 1970s, education proved the most controversial divide between Catholic and secular advocacy groups. Kennedy's campaign promise to defend an absolute separation of church and state placed the Catholic president in direct confrontation with his church's authorities. One of the first pieces of proposed legislation that he faced as president challenged him to maintain or reject that pledge.

When congressmen proposed a bill to provide federal funds to public schools in early 1961, Kennedy quietly resisted attempts to extend this aid to Catholic schools by Spellman and other Catholic officials. Without this provision, Spellman argued, the legislation would discriminate against families who chose a "God-centered education" for their children.[36] Running for president in February 1960, Kennedy had opposed an amendment, introduced by Senator Wayne Morse (D-OR), to include low-interest loans for private schools in an education bill. Kennedy's vote pointedly distinguished him from the Senate's other 11 Catholics, each of whom supported this provision, which would have extended federal aid to Catholic schools.[37] When the U.S. Catholic bishops, speaking with one voice as the National Catholic Welfare Conference (NCWC), argued for the inclusion of these loans in a 1961 education bill, Sorensen advised Kennedy, "My personal conviction is that the first Catholic president cannot now reverse his vote on the Morse amendment in 1960, when he was a candidate, to support the first parochial aid bill."[38] Fearful of offending Catholic voters, Sorensen secretly brokered a compromise with the NCWC by proposing to include loans for nonpublic schools seeking to build science, mathematics, foreign language, physical fitness, and lunch facilities. Yet Kennedy maintained a position of plausible deniability, as Sorensen ensured the president in a private memorandum, "There was to be no mention or indication that the Administration had played any role or taken any position on the amendment or course of strategy."[39] This provision for parochial schools failed to gain congressional support without Kennedy's strong endorsement. Other Catholic politicians endorsed a bill that would aid public schools only. But Catholic Congressman James Delaney (D-NY), who echoed Spellman's argument that such a law would unfairly penalize Catholic families, refused to vote for legislation that excluded Catholic schools. Delaney's vote, along with Republicans who opposed permanent federal aid to teachers' salaries as an inappropriate expansion of the national government's authority, defeated the bill by a margin of eight to seven in the House Rules Committee.[40]

Refusing to moderate his secular views, Kennedy appeared quite comfortable with the tension that this decision created between government and religious institutions. In the nation's Capitol, Kennedy frequently belittled his rift with Catholic and other religious authorities through humor. Speaking in 1961 at the Gridiron Club, a social organization for members of the print media, Kennedy quipped that he had "talked to the Chief Justice about the education bill. He said it was constitutional—it hasn't got a prayer."[41] Recalling the joke that Al Smith had telegraphed a one-word note to the pope—"UNPACK!"— after his 1928 defeat, Kennedy said, "After my stand on the school bill, I received a one-word wire from the pope myself. It said, 'PACK!' "[42]

Despite this levity, Catholic authorities expressed grave disappointment with Kennedy's secularism on church-state issues. Many bishops had remained silent during the presidential campaign because they understood that Kennedy needed to demonstrate freedom from Catholic pressure in order to win the election. These prelates nonetheless believed that Kennedy would not reject his church's appeals as completely as his campaign speeches implied. In December 1961, the Jesuit magazine *America* recalled that poet Robert Frost had discouraged Kennedy from repudiating his Catholic roots. In a poem offered to the president at the inaugural, Frost counseled Kennedy to be "more Irish than Harvard." One year later, *America* lamented that Kennedy's first year failed to follow this prescription. Writing at the close of college football season, the magazine's editors printed a headline, "Harvard 6; Irish 6."[43] To many Catholics, the metaphor of a tie game between Harvard and Notre Dame symbolized the competitive political contest between a secular culture—which marginalized religion—and Catholic traditions.

Catholic fear of creeping secularism and Kennedy's inaction against this trend surfaced again with the Supreme Court decision banning prayer in public schools. More than half of Americans opposed the Court's ban on school prayer, and a less secular president might have supported a constitutional amendment to challenge this decision. Yet Kennedy defended the consequences of this ruling by endorsing the privatization of religion. In a press conference, Kennedy challenged religious people to improve their personal spiritual lives rather than to demand the right to worship in public places: "We have in this case a very easy remedy and that is to pray ourselves. And I think that it would be a welcome reminder to every American family that we can pray a good deal more at home, we can attend our churches with a good deal more fidelity, and we can make the true meaning of prayer much more important in the lives of all our children."[44]

Kennedy's secularism on education issues contributed to the origins of a Christian Right in U.S. politics. Conservative Catholics and Protestants both placed a high priority on preserving America's religious culture. In response to the Supreme Court's ban on prayer in public schools, Cardinal Spellman charged judges with trying to "strip America of all her religious tradition." Revivalist Billy Graham described the decision as "another step toward secularism." The Catholic president may not have risked many votes by offending Graham, who privately encouraged Republican nominee Richard M. Nixon and President Dwight D. Eisenhower to exploit anti-Catholicism against Kennedy in the 1960 campaign.[45] Yet some Catholics believed that Eisenhower had defended religious institutions better than Kennedy. In contrast to the nation's secular slant in the 1960s, the U.S. government added "Under God" to the Pledge of Allegiance and "In God We Trust" to the coinage during Eisenhower's administration.[46]

Kennedy's international programs also reflected secular rather than religious goals. Kennedy initiated the Peace Corps and the Alliance for Progress based on social science notions that secular, democratic, and capitalist systems would tarnish the luster of communism. The Kennedy administration adopted U.S. aid to noncommunist nations as a means of promoting the development of democratic governments and capitalist economies. Under the rubric of modernization theory, a school of thought popular at Harvard, Kennedy's advisers asserted that political and economic freedom, not religious tradition, would best prevent revolutions sponsored by the Soviet Union for strategic advantage. In Latin America, modernization advocates believed that Catholic Spain's corporate model of governance stifled rather than encouraged the creativity of a liberal political economy and society.[47]

Even when confronting the Soviet Union in communist Cuba, Kennedy repudiated the militant anticommunism characteristic of the Roman Catholic hierarchy and the Protestant Right. Although some liberals had believed that Kennedy would succumb to Catholic pressure and wage a "holy war" against communism, these fears proved unjustified.[48] Kennedy authorized the CIA-sponsored Bay of Pigs invasion of communist Fidel Castro's Cuba by expatriate Cubans, but he consistently refused to allow any direct participation of U.S. troops in the operation. Anxious to avoid any appearance of appeasing communism,

Kennedy reluctantly approved this mission, which had originated under President Eisenhower.[49]

Despite pressure from both political parties, the public, and military leaders for the use of force, Kennedy steered a course of caution when the Soviet Union prepared to install nuclear weapons in Cuba. Eighty-six senators supported a resolution that authorized the president to act against "an externally supported offensive military capability endangering the security of the United States." Only one senator opposed this delegation of authority to Kennedy. The poet Frost warned that Soviet leader Nikita Khrushchev viewed Americans as "too liberal to fight." The joint chiefs of staff strongly advised bombing the missile sites. In this jingoist context, Kennedy avoided both escalation and humiliation by exhausting diplomatic channels.[50]

Kennedy's focus on peaceful coexistence with the Soviet Union preceded the goal of demonstrating unwavering resolve against atheistic communism. In an often cited 1963 speech at American University, only months before his death, Kennedy criticized moral absolutism. Several of Kennedy's advisers refer to this speech as evidence that he planned a withdrawal of U.S. forces from Vietnam. Twenty years later, President Ronald W. Reagan would warn of "modern-day secularism" and call the Soviet Union an "evil empire" in an address to the conservative Protestant National Association of Evangelicals. Kennedy himself had described the cold war in religious terms during his presidency, "This [is] a struggle for supremacy between two conflicting ideologies: freedom under God versus ruthless, godless tyranny." Yet now Kennedy discouraged such labeling of America's adversaries: "[N]o government or social system is so evil that its people must be considered lacking in virtue."[51] In secular terms, the nation's first Catholic president described peace "as the necessary rational end of rational men."[52] Kennedy's words suggested the need for flexibility rather than confrontation with the Soviet Union. Perhaps the clash with Catholic hierarchy and the success of negotiation during the Cuban Missile Crisis encouraged his increasingly pragmatic, secular approach toward politics.

The Verdict

Is it possible that Kennedy could be both Catholic hero and secular icon? In the 1960s, many Catholic scholars described "two Johns"— John Kennedy and Pope John XXIII—as dual modernizers of the Roman Catholic Church. In 1963, the pope issued an encyclical,

Pacem in Terris (Peace on Earth), which echoed Kennedy's diplomatic approach to international politics by advocating a greater role for the United Nations. The encyclical addressed non-Catholics as well as Catholics, and the pope lamented the stockpiling of weapons characteristic of the cold war. In confluence with this message, Kennedy worked to pass the nuclear test ban treaty, against significant resistance by U.S. military officials and some scientists.[53] While Kennedy's secular policies defied traditional Catholic approaches to politics, Catholicism seemed to be moving in the same direction as America's first Catholic president.

The papal encyclical offered Kennedy theological "cover" from those Catholics who might attack the president's secularism as hostile to religion. When asked about the pope's words in a press conference, Kennedy initially seized the opportunity to reconcile his religious affiliation with his professional duties: "As a Catholic, I am proud of it and as an American I have learned from it." Yet Kennedy immediately extended these remarks to deemphasize the Catholic, and even the religious, significance of the encyclical. The pope's statement, Kennedy claimed, "closely matches . . . conviction from churchmen of other faiths, as in recent documents of the [Protestant] World Council of Churches, and from outstanding world citizens with no ecclesiastical standing." Even secular atheists could agree with the pope's words, Kennedy insisted.

Liberal Catholics praised Kennedy's secularization and modernization of Catholicism. Cardinal Cushing proudly asserted that Kennedy "never allowed his faith to interfere in any way with his relations with others." Catholic priest and sociologist Andrew Greeley credited Kennedy with inspiring his church's abandonment of parochial institutions, such as Catholic schools, in favor of engagement with the modern world. In Greeley's interpretation, Kennedy's model of lay leadership would gain "theological justification" from John XXIII's Second Vatican Council (1962–1965). Greeley heralded the end of an "era when Catholicism would be identified with the organized Church," and called for Kennedy's recognition as a "doctor" and a "teacher"—if not a saint—of the Catholic Church.[54]

Conservative Catholics nonetheless lamented that Kennedy's belief in secular solutions to public problems marginalized religious inspiration. In both international relations and domestic politics, Kennedy preached a secular humanist rather than a spiritual message. In his second State of the Union Address (1963), Kennedy identified freedom, rather than God's Providence, as the key to global challenges: "Liberalism . . . faith in man's ability, reason, and judgment . . . is our best and only hope in the world today." This secularism thwarted Catholicism's traditional role as a bulwark against nonreligious ideologies, such as nationalism and liberalism. College of the Holy Cross historian Noel Cary, for example, has noted how Catholicism in Germany served to check the unrestrained liberal goals of centralization, laissez-faire economics, and church-state separation.[55] Kennedy allowed political ideology to subsume a distinctively Catholic identity.

Confronted with the questions of federal aid to parochial schools and prayer in public schools, Kennedy strongly adopted the secularist position on the issue of church-state separation. In the cold war, Kennedy repudiated Catholicism's traditionally militant stance toward the Soviet Union and promoted secularists' call for diplomacy, compromise, and peaceful coexistence.

In the long term, Kennedy's secularism contributed to the alienation of many conservative Catholics from the Democratic Party. Since 1960, Catholic traditionalists have increasingly favored the Republican Party. Several Catholics wrote articles in the conservative publication *National Review*, edited by the Catholic William F. Buckley, Jr., and this publication's threefold increase in circulation from 1960 to 1964 testified to the spread of traditional Catholicism.[56] Since the Supreme Court legalized abortion in the 1973 *Roe v. Wade* case, evangelical Protestants, the Catholic Church, and the GOP have united in opposition. In foreign policy, President Reagan revived religious rhetoric and militant anticommunism. Reagan's appointment of an ambassador to the Holy See, which Kennedy had opposed, improved U.S. coordination of resistance to the Soviet bloc, especially Catholic Poland, with the Polish Pope John Paul II in the 1980s.[57] President George W. Bush appointed a Catholic Knight of Columbus Jim Towey, once Mother Theresa's lawyer, as Director of the White House Office of Faith-Based and Community Initiatives. Bush's 2004 campaign Web page featured several photos of the president with John Paul II in a section called "Catholics for Bush."[58]

Even if a Catholic wins the presidency in 2008, no less than 48 years will have passed since the election of a Catholic president. Given that only 32 years separated the failed presidential bid of Catholic New York Governor Alfred E. Smith and John Kennedy's 1960 victory, how can we explain that no Catholic has repeated Kennedy's accomplishment in nearly half a century? The challenge for a Catholic presidential candidate appears even more significant when one considers that Catholics make up 25 percent of the U.S. population.

Catholic politicians need to balance a delicate political divide between secular and religious Americans. Secularists view Catholicism as hostile to fundamental issues of church-state separation, such as censorship, abortion, embryonic stem cell research, and same-sex marriage. Many contemporary Catholic politicians—such as California Governor Arnold Schwarzenegger, former New York City mayor Rudolph Giuliani, Florida Governor Jeb Bush, and Senate Majority Leader Nancy Pelosi (D-CA)—will have to negotiate the subjects carefully if each chooses to pursue the presidency.

While I feel supremely confident that Mr. Danenberg voted for the secular Catholic senator from Massachusetts John Kerry in the 2004 election, I know that Mr. Murphy would have voted for the unabashedly religious, non-Catholic George W. Bush. John Kennedy succeeded in unifying Catholic and secular Americans in the 1960 campaign, but he failed to create an effective model of governance to satisfy both groups.

Notes

The author would like to thank his mother-in-law Sra. María Nieves Gavonel de León, parents Thomas and Janice Carty, daughter Marisol, and wife Rosamaría for giving him the time to travel for this conference and to write this chapter. Rev. James Garneau, PhD and Richard Dauer, PhD also read the paper and offered several comments, which were very useful and much appreciated.

1. Stephen G. Rabe, *The Most Dangerous Area in the World: John F. Kennedy Confronts Communist Revolution in Latin America* (Chapel Hill: University of North Carolina Press, 1999), 3.
2. Robert Dallek, *An Unfinished Life: John F. Kennedy, 1917–1963* (New York: Little, Brown, 2003), 700.
3. For example, Susan Milligan, "Democrats Eye Softer Image on Abortion Leaders: Urge More Welcome for Opponents," *The Boston Globe*, December 19, 2004, A1.
4. James MacGregor Burns, *John Kennedy: A Political Profile* (New York: Harcourt, Brace, 1960), 85–86.
5. Richard N. Goodwin, *Remembering America: A Voice from the Sixties* (Boston: Little, Brown, 1988), 110.
6. Lawrence H. Fuchs, *John Kennedy and American Catholicism* (New York: Meredith Press, 1967), 207.
7. Thomas Carty, *A Catholic in the White House? Religion, Politics, and John Kennedy's Presidential Campaign* (New York: Palgrave Macmillan, 2004), 4.
8. Fletcher Knebel, "Democratic Forecast: A Catholic in 1960," *Look*, March 3, 1959.

9. Thomas Maier, *The Kennedys: America's Emerald Kings: A Five-Generation History of the Ultimate Irish Catholic Family* (New York: Basic Books, 2003), 319.

10. John Cogley, "Kennedy the Catholic," in *Commonweal Confronts the Century: Liberal Convictions, Catholic Traditions*, ed. Patrick Jordan and Paul Baumann (New York: Touchstone, 1999), 68. These words originally appeared in a January 10, 1964 column in *Commonweal*.

11. Maier, *The Kennedys*, 348.

12. Goodwin, *Remembering America*, 110.

13. Charles Morris, *American Catholic: The Saints and Sinners Who Built America's Most Powerful Church* (New York: Vintage Books, 1997), 319.

14. Mark Massa, *Anti-Catholicism in America: The Last Acceptable Prejudice* (New York: Crossroad, 2003), 84, 85.

15. Richard John Neuhaus, *Naked Public Square: Religion and Democracy in America* (Grand Rapids, MI: William B. Eerdmans, 1984).

16. Lawrence J. McAndrews, "The Avoidable Conflict: Kennedy, the Bishops, and Federal Aid to Education," *Catholic Historical Review*, 76 (April 1990): 279.

17. Dallek, *An Unfinished Life*, 146–147.

18. Carty, *A Catholic in the White House?* 148.

19. Dallek, *An Unfinished Life*, 147.

20. Maier, *The Kennedys*, 303.

21. Dallek, *An Unfinished Life*, 159.

22. Ibid., 159–162, 175–176. See also Thomas J. Whalen, *Kennedy and Lodge: The 1952 Massachusetts Senate Race* (Boston: Northeastern University Press, 2001).

23. James A. Michener, *Report of the County Chairman* (New York: Bantam Books, 1961), 108.

24. Carty, *A Catholic in the White House?* 11–20.

25. Alfred E. Smith, *Up to Now: An Autobiography* (New York: Viking Press, 1929), 413–414.

26. Maier, *The Kennedys*, 399.

27. Carty, *A Catholic in the White House?* 129.

28. Ibid., 145, 93, 95.

29. Ibid., 156–157.

30. Jay P. Dolan, *The American Catholic Experience: A History from Colonial Times to the Present* (Garden City, NY: Doubleday, 1985), 421–422.

31. Dallek, *An Unifinished Life*, 701.

32. Maier, *The Kennedys*.

33. *Church and State*, December 1960, 8.

34. David Halberstam, *The Best and the Brightest* (New York: Random House, 1972).

35. Harris Wofford, *Of Kennedys and Kings* (New York: Farrar, Straus, Giroux, 1980), 71; Dallek, *An Unfinished Life*, 312. See also Scott

Stossel, *Sarge: The Life and Times of Sargent Shriver* (Washington, DC: Smithsonian Books, 2004).

36. Maier, *The Kennedys*, 399.
37. McAndrews, "The Avoidable Conflict," 279–280.
38. Ibid., 287.
39. Ibid., 289.
40. Ibid., 282, 294. See also Lawrence J. McAndrews, "Beyond Appearances: Kennedy, Congress, Religion, and Federal Aid to Education," *Presidential Studies Quarterly*, 21 (3): 545–557.
41. Maier, *The Kennedys*, 400.
42. Ibid., 401.
43. Ibid., 363, 397. "Harvard 6; Irish 6," *America*, December 9, 1961.
44. Fuchs, *John Kennedy and American Catholicism*, 209–210
45. See Carty, *A Catholic in the White House?* 56–57.
46. For more information about Eisenhower and religion, see Jack Holl's chapter in this book (chapter six).
47. Rabe, *The Most Dangerous Area in the World*, 155–156, 152.
48. Carty, *A Catholic in the White House?* 113–114 and chapter 6, passim.
49. Dallek, *An Unfinished Life*, 358–359, 365.
50. Ibid., 540–541, 570.
51. Paul Kengor, *God and Ronald Reagan: A Spiritual Life* (New York: Regan Books, 2004), 233–244; Fuchs, *John Kennedy and American Catholicism*, 214.
52. Walter LaFeber, *America, Russia, and the Cold War, 1945–1984*, 5th ed. (New York: Alfred A. Knopf, 1984), 227.
53. Ibid., 227–228.
54. Andrew M. Greeley, *The Catholic Experience: An Interpretation of The History of American Catholicism* (Garden City: Image Books, 1969), 280–297.
55. Noel D. Cary, *The Path to Christian Democracy: German Catholics and the Party System from Windthorst to Adenauer* (Cambridge, MA: Harvard University Press, 1996), 3.
56. W. J. Rorabaugh, *Kennedy and the Promise of the Sixties* (Cambridge, UK: Cambridge University Press, 2002), 42. See also Patrick Allitt, *Catholic Intellectuals and Conservative Politics in America, 1950–1985* (Ithaca, NY: Cornell University Press, 1993).
57. Carty, *A Catholic in the White House?* 159–172.
58. www.georgewbush.com, accessed November 1, 2004.

Chapter Eight

Jimmy Carter and the Politics of Faith

Jeff Walz

Introduction

At the bicentennial of its Declaration of Independence in 1976, America was not in a mood for celebration.[1] The country was still absorbing the withdrawal from Vietnam, the 1973 OPEC oil embargo, and Watergate and its aftermath. James Earl (Jimmy) Carter, Jr., was both the most unlikely and best suited candidate to establish a new political era in America: "He knew how to present himself as the embodiment of bedrock values, deep concerns, and honest aspirations of millions of his fellow citizens, and he knew, as his detractors did not, that his own quite genuine faith was an asset."[2] Douglas S. Marsh may have put it best in describing "the simple but profound faith of a complex man" whose religion had an indelible but perplexing impact on the presidency.[3]

Yet a faith that served Carter so well throughout much of his life—including the 1976 election and his postpresidency years—may have been a political liability during his four-year term at 1600 Pennsylvania Avenue. To some evangelicals, Carter's faith led him toward wrong policy positions. To others, his religion seemed to lead him away from the difficult decisions of real-world politics. Others were put off by Carter's high degree of religiosity, including his prayer life. To Carter, prayer was anything but an afterthought in tight spots. Instead, prayer was a guiding foundation throughout his life, especially during the 1976 campaign: "I don't pray to God to let me win an election," he said. "I pray to ask God to let me do the right thing."[4]

Ultimately, it was not his faith but a plethora of geopolitical events, the ascendancy of a candidate in 1980, Ronald Reagan, who was more in tune with evangelicals, and a defective administrative approach that cost Carter a second four-year term. This loss turned into one of the greatest gains for God's world, as the thirty-ninth president's post-White House years have been a model of Christ-like love and service.

Some have called Carter the best ex-president in history, a testament to an enduring faith that helped him win the highest office in the land but could not keep him there.

To unpack the nexus between the faith of this openly evangelical president and his performance in office, four themes are examined. The first theme, "Religious Background," examines the Southern Baptist religion that Carter brought to office. Carter grew up with one of the most authentic faiths of any American president, and he took that religion with him to the White House in a cloak of church-state separation. The second theme, "Religion and the 1976 Campaign," focuses on the president's religion in his first presidential campaign. The third theme, "Carter as Religious National Leader," explores how the president once in office used his faith to lead the public. The fourth theme, "Religion and Policy," probes the connection between Carter's faith and policy decisions and appointments. Rather than public pronouncements, the depth of Carter's religion may be seen in his policy goals, if less so in the means used and success in achieving those ends.

Jimmy Carter will be remembered as one of the most religious presidents who could not fulfill the campaign promises he appeared to cloak in the rhetoric of faith. Looking for a moral rebirth, Americans elected a born-again evangelical. Carter's faith could not overcome his deficiencies in cultivating Washington political relations. Faith could not stave off energy crises, stagflation, and the Iranian hostage crisis. A church-state separation could not win over evangelicals on school prayer, busing, family issues, or abortion. To face these challenges, Carter during his presidency prayed "more than ever before in my life."[5] When America grew tired of a praying president challenging the people to do their best, the same challenge Carter put before himself, the public turned him out and provided Jimmy Carter the opportunity to bring his faith, respected once again, to the wider world.

Religious Background

Perhaps no contemporary president personifies a strong religious background like Carter. The thirty-ninth president was born in Plains, Georgia, on October 1, 1924, to a "matter-of-fact" Baptist father and a "free-thinking and free-speaking" Methodist mother.[6] Speaking with Bill Moyers in 1976, Carter cited his parents, siblings, church, and community as sources of stability.[7] His mother Lillian was a religious and intellectual role model, and he inherited from her his voracious reading habits and liberal social and political tendencies. In the community, Carter cites in his autobiography the encouragement of his high school superintendent, Julia Coleman. When Carter was 12, Coleman suggested he read Tolstoy's *War and Peace*, a work that emphasized to him how common and ordinary people can make history.[8] Later, Carter read widely, giving special attention to theologian Reinhold Niebuhr, whom Carter referred to as the man who "observes the sad duty of politics is to establish justice in a sinful world."[9]

Growing up in the Plains, Georgia area, religion surrounded Carter in many forms. In his autobiography *Living Faith*, Carter asserts "religious faith has always been at the core of my existence," tracing it to his upbringing in the Plains.[10] Carter recalls at the age of three memorizing Bible verses in Sunday school. When he was nine, he became a part of the Sunday school class his father taught. At the age of twelve or thirteen, Carter began to have some doubts about his faith, in particular about the Resurrection. In fact, Carter recalls, "[M]y anxiety about this became so intense that at the end of every prayer, until after I was an adult, before 'Amen' I added the words 'And God, please help me believe in the resurrection.' "[11] The church was also the center of social life for Jimmy. In lieu of Boy Scouts, Carter's father would take boys from the church for camping and fishing. Around the age of ten or twelve, Carter attended church-sponsored and chaperoned "prom parties" where young boys and girls could interact on a Friday evening. Carter decided to "accept Christ" when he was eleven, and he was baptized with other converts.[12]

Following high school graduation at 16, a year at a nearby junior college and another year at Georgia Tech, Carter was off to the Naval Academy at Annapolis. While he became an engineer and thereafter studied advanced science, this was also the first time he got to know a number of people who were not evangelical Christians, permitting Carter "the opportunity to learn something about other faiths."[13] Carter attended chapel regularly during his three years at the academy, becoming well acquainted with the chaplain. He also taught Sunday school to a group of nine-to-twelve-year-old daughters of enlisted men and officers. Jimmy married Rosalynn, a Methodist, who joined Jimmy after marriage in the Baptist church. Carter called his seven years in the American Navy a "relatively dormant phase in my religious life" because with several moves, it was difficult to be a part of one church community.[14]

However, it may have been in the Naval Academy where Carter's religious image was further refined, albeit indirectly, by Admiral Hyman Rickover. In interviewing for the nuclear submarine program, Carter talked on a wide number of issues. Graduating fifty-ninth in a class of 820, Carter did not expect Rickover's pointed question: "Did you do your best?" Carter conceded that he had not always met this lofty goal. Rickover's final words were, "Why not?" before Carter left the interview.[15] Rickover's words left an indelible impression on Carter. He would in the future strive even harder to use his God-given gifts to their full potential.

When his father died in 1953, Jimmy and Rosalynn went home to the Plains where they were again thrust into a challenging Southern religious milieu, a period Carter called "a turning point in my spiritual life."[16] Carter and Rosalynn felt a tremendous sense of warmth before and after his father's death, a factor that encouraged the couple, against Rosalynn's better judgment, to make their home in the Plains at the town's public housing project, paying rent of $30 a month.[17] Jimmy began teaching the male juniors aged nine to twelve in his father's Sunday school class at Plains Baptist Church, while Rosalynn taught the junior girls. Soon thereafter, Carter became a church deacon. During this time he began to delve deeply into religious questions, buying books by Dietrich Bonhoeffer, Karl Barth, Martin Buber, Paul Tillich, Hang Kung, and especially Reinhold Niebuhr. Importantly for his later political life, Carter began to see religion and science as complementary, citing Romans 1:19–20: "Paul's point was that the glories of the world around us prove God's existence."[18]

However, Carter's theological musings at times collided with the reality of religion in the South in the 1950s and 1960s. At a deacon's meeting at which Carter was absent, the deacons had voted 11–0 to prohibit African Americans from worship services. At the next congregational meeting, Carter stood and said, "This is not my house, this is not your house," suggesting a reversal. Of the 50 people who voted on the proposal, Carter's side received only 6 votes, and 5 of those votes were from his family.[19] Defying threats and a brief boycott of his peanut business, Carter refused to joint the White Citizens' Council, when invited to do so by a local Baptist minister.[20] Another time, when no one stepped forward, Carter chaired an evangelistic film sponsored by the Billy Graham Association, the first integrated audience in Sumter County, Georgia, in the twentieth century.[21]

Carter soon turned toward a vocation that would consume his spiritual and physical life—politics. In 1962 Carter ran for and won—after a protracted protest process—a seat in the Georgia State Senate. Carter had discussed the idea with a visiting pastor who stayed with the Carters for a week. The pastor was not impressed with Carter's choice of professions, suggesting Jimmy could do better for himself and for the Lord in other, more honorable, lines of work.

Carter, with his eyes toward things political, responded to the pastor, "How would you like to be a pastor of a church with 80,000 members?"[22] As a Georgia state senator, he voted against a "30 questions" barrier to minority voter registration and opposed a constitutional amendment urging the worship of God, a vote that moved some to see him as an atheist.[23] Overreaching, Carter lost the race for governor in 1966.

A short time after this political defeat, Carter had a spiritual rebirth. The turning point may have been a question that Plains Baptist Church Rev. Robert Harris posed in a sermon: "If you were arrested for being a Christian, would there be enough evidence to convict you?" Carter felt he would not be convicted on this charge; instead, he compared himself with the self-righteous Pharisee in Luke 18:10–13. He had made 300,000 campaign visits for himself and 140 missionary visits for God in 14 years. Carter read the book of Luke "to understand more clearly the admonitions about pride and self-satisfaction."[24]

In 1966 or early 1967, in the wake of the defeat in his first run for Georgia governor, Carter went for a walk with his sister Ruth and asked her, "What is it that you have that I haven't got?" When she replied that "everything I am" belonged to Jesus, Carter opened his heart more fully to the Lord.[25] This experience, along with his work with some of the very needy, enabled him to form "a very close, intimate, personal relationship with God, through Christ, that has given me a great deal of peace, equanimity, the ability to accept difficulties without unnecessarily being disturbed, and also an inclination on a continuing basis to ask God's guidance in my life."[26]

Others take umbrage with this narrative, if not with the outcome. Rosalynn agrees that Jimmy did talk with Ruth, but denies that it was some sort of religious experience.[27] In *Why Not the Best?* Carter simply says, "[M]y church life became far more meaningful to me."[28] Carter further developed his faith and sense of the needs of others in 1967 and 1968. Under the banner of the Southern Baptist Home Mission Board, Carter went to cities in Pennsylvania and Massachusetts, assisting people with their physical and spiritual needs.[29]

Whatever the case, this and other things religious would later come to dominate 1976 campaign discussion, "as if it were some ethnological eccentricity brought back from Pago Pago by Margaret Mead."[30] First, however, Carter won the Georgia governor's race in 1970, setting the stage for his national run six years later. Certain themes during his governorship would foreshadow his presidential years. Known in some circles as "Jungle Jimmy," Carter tended to be conservative fiscally and liberal on civil rights and justice issues.

Defying the parading Ku Klux Klan outside, Carter hung a portrait of Baptist Martin Luther King, Jr., inside the Georgia Capitol.[31]

Religion and the 1976 Campaign

While much was made of Carter' born-again faith, the candidate on the stump tended to downplay his religion, perhaps because he could. A typical campaign speech would include reminiscing growing up on a peanut farm in the Plains, Georgia, the "comfort and stability" his parents brought to his life, and a focus on several policy issues.[32] Even if Carter did not speak the language of religion extensively, voters in 1976 sensed the strong faith Carter would bring to the Oval Office. Voters expected the deeply religious Carter to restore a sense of dignity and ethics to the presidency. As Carter emerged in early 1976 as a viable presidential candidate, much of the American media and public did not know what to make of Carter's strong Christian convictions. Though the press was confused by Carter's born-again Christian status, a Gallup poll conducted later in 1976 found that 48 percent of American Protestants and 18 percent of American Catholics had been born again in Christ.[33] Despite this negative perception, in some quarters, of Carter's Southern Baptist religion, his faith actually helped him win the election by capturing key segments of Christian voters.

The depth and sincerity of Carter's faith is unassailable. As alluded to earlier, he was an active layman in the Baptist church—teaching Sunday school, going on retreats, participating in missionary programs, and working on ecumenical ventures.[34] Unlike other presidents, however, he did not often speak the language of religion on the campaign trail. Jody Powell said often that Carter "probably quoted less Scripture and read more than any public official we've had in a long, long time."[35] At the same time, it was well known during the campaign that Carter read a chapter of the Bible in Spanish each night before bed.[36] Further, Carter stated already on the campaign trail that if elected, he would not conduct worship services in the White House, based on his separation of church and state beliefs: "I would expect to worship in a nearby Baptist church on Sunday morning with as little fanfare as possible and, hopefully, after the first few Sundays I would be accepted as a member of the church."[37]

The response of the media was illustrative of the way Carter and his faith were impacting the country. One TV network anchorman told his viewers, "Incidentally, we have checked this out. Being 'born again' is not a bizarre experience or the voice of God from a mountaintop.

It's a fairly common experience known to millions of Americans—especially if you're a Baptist."[38] Moreover, major newspapers and news magazines could not keep religious terminology clear, and some reporters were uncomfortable when Carter explained what his born-again faith meant to him. One reporter, writing about Carter's born-again explanation prior to the North Carolina primary, said that "an awkward hush fell over the room" as "reporters lowered their eyes to their note pads. Everyone was embarrassed—except the candidate."[39]

Where Carter impressed journalists and the public alike was in his exemplary knowledge of the Bible. While on the campaign trail, Carter easily answered reporters' questions about the Bible as he maintained his belief in biblical inerrancy. At one point, Carter wrote to the *Atlanta Constitution* to correct a story that said that he did not believe miracles in the Bible.[40] He also focused on the possibilities and limitations of the American system of governance, returning to Reinhold Niebuhr: "Man's capacity for justice make democracy possible, but man's capacity for injustice makes democracy necessary."[41] Thus, Carter embraced what some have termed "Christian Realism," a practical Christian approach to politics.[42]

Moreover, Carter was careful on the campaign trail not to promise his evangelical supporters too much. In response to a query from *700 Club* host Pat Robertson about whether Carter would bring godly men into his inner councils or Cabinet to advise him, he said, "I think it would be a mistake for me to define the qualifications of a public servant according to what kind of church they attend or what their denomination is. Obviously, a commitment to the principles expressed to us by God would be an important prerequisite."[43]

More surprising, even shocking, to journalists and the public was what became know as the *Playboy* interview. In *Living Faith*, Carter recalls that in the late summer of 1976, with a significant public opinion poll lead on Ford, he agreed to a series of short interviews with *Playboy* magazine. Carter welcomed the added publicity, especially in a publication that could enhance the challenger's base of younger voters. At the conclusion of the final interview, in Carter's home living room, the reporter thanked him, turned off the tape recorder, but had one final question that Carter felt was off the record. The reporter asked Carter if he considered himself better than others, to which Carter answered with Jesus' concern about pride, and sins of every kind, including adultery. "I replied truthfully, 'Yes, I have lusted . . .' " referring to Jesus' words in Matthew 5:27–28: "You have heard that it was said, 'You shall not commit adultery'; but I say to you, that everyone who looks on a woman to lust for her has committed adultery with her already in his heart."[44] While many evangelicals understood the theology behind Carter's honest response, the media made it a dominant issue, hurting Carter in the polls.

Such was the Carter evangelical phenomenon that groups separate from the campaign began electioneering. A group calling itself Citizens for Carter, in a full-page ad in *Christianity Today*, asked the question, "Does a Dedicated Evangelical Belong in the White House?" The answer was a resounding yes, emphasizing Carter's positions on "a return to open government, competency, honesty and an abiding sense of the importance of morality in our national life."[45] As the campaign neared its apex at the 1976 Democratic National Convention, a sense of a revival meeting settled over the proceedings.[46] Looking back almost 20 years, Carter said in late 2004 that had he run for president in this year's campaign, he would have spoken about his faith differently, out of necessity: "I think I would be forced to do so . . . I don't think it would be possible now for any candidate to avoid the aspects of one's religious faith."[47]

When the votes were finally cast, Carter became the first president from south of Virginia since Zachary Taylor in 1848, and the first governor-elected president since Franklin D. Roosevelt 44 years earlier.[48] With Senator Walter F. Mondale as his running mate, Carter defeated Ford, whom he had debated three times, 297–241, in the Electoral College and took 50.1 percent of the popular vote. The candidate who announced his campaign in December 1974 and endured two grueling years of electioneering—including a first ballot selection at the Democratic National Convention—would soon face a nation and world intent on putting his faith to a series of significant tests.

Carter as Religious National Leader

Though Carter took his strong, born-again faith with him to the White House, he did not always wear his religion on his sleeve. In Washington, he attended services and taught Sunday school at First Baptist Church.[49] Overall, however, he displayed much less personal piety than other presidents with seemingly weaker religious convictions. "Perhaps because he was so pious, Carter felt little need for official declarations of piety."[50] If Carter displayed less outward piety, faith was an even greater part of his private life, sharing in *Living Faith* the extent of his prayer life as president.[51]

Beyond what religion presidents bring to the White House—and how they practice their faith while in office—presidents speak the language of religion. Despite his strong religious convictions, Carter did not engage in civil religion to the same extent that some of his predecessors did. In fact, in late 2004 Carter confirmed that "never while I was president did I make any overt reference to my preference for a religion."[52] Carter at his inauguration took his oath on two Bibles, one used by President Washington and the second a gift from his mother, Lillian Carter. Both Bibles were opened to Micah, focusing on the Baptist's chosen Scripture, Micah 6:8: "He hath showed thee, O man, what is good; and what doth the Lord require of thee, but to do justly, and to love mercy, and to walk humbly with God?"[53] Carter noted the uniqueness of the United States, "the first society to openly define itself in terms of both spirituality and of human liberty." After completing his brief inaugural address—at 14 minutes, one of the shortest ever— the president and his family walked from the Capitol to the White House, a signal of the common man president.[54] A reference to God or comparable higher power appeared only two times in the speech.[55]

During his tumultuous four-year term, in which the country endured an energy crisis, inflationary pressures, and the hostage taking at the American Embassy in Iran, Carter spoke as a prophet, in civil religion terms.[56] At the 1977 National Prayer Breakfast, for example, Carter stressed "the need for national humility." As a "city on a hill," America had a mission to uphold that which should not be jeopardized by national arrogance. It was only a 1980 address, during the Iran hostage taking, that Carter turned from prophetic concerns to more pastoral ones, emphasizing the need for Americans to pull together during this difficult time.[57]

No speech more signified Carter's prophetic civil religion than his "crisis of confidence" speech in 1979. Though Carter's accomplishments, as will be discussed in the next section, were noteworthy— civil service reform, industrial deregulation, and the Panama Canal treaties, for example—the administration's problems overwhelmed these achievements. Aside from the energy crisis and unemployment, America's power seemed to be waning. To address these issues, Carter invited 130 national leaders, including 10 religious figures, to Maryland for consultation on these crises. The July 15 "crisis of confidence" speech that resulted from these meetings showcased a prophetic president. The government and the people were to blame for the country's ills. Carter suggested that "too many of us now tend to worship self-indulgence and consumption. Human identity is no longer defined by what one does but by what one owns."

The press described the speech as a sermon around which to unite the American public.[58]

Religious invocations, then, did not define Jimmy Carter. Instead, he let his actions speak volumes, even when those actions were antagonistic toward some of his key constituencies. Moreover, Carter practiced a form of Matthew 18: "If your brother sins against you, go and show him his fault, just between the two of you." In America during the late 1970s, Jimmy Carter saw much fault, a great deal of it focused inward. If Carter made a mistake with his civil religion, it was failing to realize much of the American public was not interested in being as honest with itself as the president was with himself. The American people in large part desired a presidential priest or pastor, but Carter the prophet delivered harsh medicine to an ailing America.

Religion and Policy

Carter's deep, vibrant faith may not have been evident in his presidential language, but it certainly had a significant impact on the policies he pursued in office, particularly on human rights issues. In this and other policy areas, Carter's striving to be the best came in part from his Christian mindset.[59] In his autobiography *Living Faith*, Carter discusses at some length the impact of his church membership on the policies he pursued in government. All Americans, Carter said, want to do what is right and just. Unfortunately, churches too often fail to move their members toward upholding basic human rights, both at home and abroad. In Carter's estimation, "[T]he majority of church members are more self-satisfied, more committed to the status quo, and more exclusive of nonsimilar people than are most political office-holders I have known."[60] Since many congregations are unwilling to address difficult questions and issues, it is up to government to fill that void. The role of government, therefore, should be activist. This pursuit of justice motivated Carter's concern for the one specific policy objective that stood above all, human rights at home and abroad. In his autobiography, Carter cites the human rights model to which Jesus spoke: "The Spirit of the Lord is on me, because he has anointed me to preach good news to the poor. He has sent me to proclaim freedom for the prisoners and recovery of sight for the blind, to release the oppressed" (Luke 4:18, NIV version). This faith was tied closely to Carter's Southern upbringing. How, Carter wondered, could far too many white Southerners for far too long reconcile racial segregation and discrimination with the teachings of Christ?

On the human rights front internationally, Carter said, "America didn't create human rights. Human rights created America."[61] Carter matched his human rights optimism with policy achievements. He saved lives, particularly in Argentina, Brazil, and Chile. Expanding the conventional notion of human rights, Carter considered religious liberty a central human right. He encouraged the Soviet Union to lift restrictions on Jewish immigration, and (secretly) asked the People's Republic of China to allow Bibles to circulate and for the return of Christian missionaries. In the Middle East, Carter brokered the Camp David accords, an agreement, explored below, between Israel and Egypt to make the region more peaceful and stable.[62]

Additional examples bear out Carter's human rights focus. Less than a month after he took office Carter wrote to Soviet dissident Andrei Sakharov, pledging to uphold human rights around the globe. What is interesting too is Carter's definition of human rights, as he explained to Asian officials during a visit to the United Nations: "I've noticed expansion of the definition of human rights in my own consciousness to encompass the right of someone to have a place to work and a place to live and an education and an absence of disease and an alleviation of hunger."[63]

Perhaps the most defining moment of his presidency—the Camp David peace accords—may speak most accurately to Carter's emphasis on the related issues of human rights and peace. Against great odds, Carter persuaded Egyptian President Anwar Sadat and Israeli Prime Minister Menachim Begin to agree in 1978 on a peace agreement. Trying to accommodate three religious traditions—Jewish, Christian, and Muslim—the discussions opened with a common prayer. The president took the lead in preparing 23 drafts of the agreement; thirteen days later, a deal was struck. Greeting a buoyant joint session of Congress in September, Carter, citing Matthew 5:9, said, "[B]lessed are the peacemakers."[64]

If Carter's faith-based human rights actions pleased many Christians, his position on church-state issues evoked a very different response. Though a self-proclaimed Christian who prayed daily, Carter interpreted the Establishment Clause of the First Amendment ("Congress shall make no law respecting an establishment of religion.") in a "separationist" or "no aid" manner. In other words, government should not aid or support religion at all, a position the Baptist Church has traditionally supported. "Separation is specified in the law, but for a religious person, there is nothing wrong with bringing these two together, because you can't divorce religious beliefs from public service. And at the same time, of course, in public office you cannot impose your own religious beliefs on others."[65]

This position had implications on several church and state policy issues. Unlike his 1976 opponent, Ford, and many Christians, Carter did not support government financial assistance to parochial schools. He did support certain forms of indirect state aid—such as the loaning of secular textbooks and school lunches—that contributed toward an educated citizenry. However, he drew the line on government support of the mission of religious schools. He opposed tax credits to support parochial schools, and prayer in public schools. Further, Carter favored taxing church properties other than the church building itself.[66] Carter's Baptist religion, then, led him to strongly support a role for government in human rights but not in public assistance to religious education. Moreover, he did not support a constitutional amendment to allow prayer in public schools and was in favor of taxing church properties not used explicitly for religious purposes.[67]

Carter also focused on the family, both during the campaign and in office.[68] He told a New Hampshire primary audience, "I've got a good family. I hope you'll be part of my family." Turning from what Martin calls a Good Father to an Elder Brother, Carter told a Manchester crowd in August 1976, "The American family is in trouble. I have campaigned all over America, and everywhere I go, I find people deeply concerned about the loss of stability and the loss of values in our lives. The root of his problem is the steady erosion and weakening of our families." Following a list of statistics supporting this contention, Carter said, "There can be no more urgent priority for the next administration than to see than any decision our government makes is designed to honor and support and strengthen the family."[69]

To meet this goal of strengthening the family, he proposed to reform the welfare system, reshape the tax system, and implement a national health-care program. Each federal program, on the recommendation of vice presidential candidate Walter Mondale, would present a "family impact statement."[70] Furthermore, Carter pledged to assist children who attended parochial schools and convene a "White House Conference on the American Family." Unfortunately, this conference late in his term was marked by antagonism by some evangelical delegates who felt effectively shut out of the decision-making process, and eventually they walked out of the proceedings in protest.

A religious issue that would plague Carter during the campaign and in the presidency was abortion. Ultimately, Carter "wound up with a straddle position that both camps found troubling."[71] He at one point suggested he may favor an antiabortion amendment, but then retreated from this position. He ended up taking a somewhat pro-choice perspective, objecting to legal prohibition and federal funding of abortion. The candidate sought "to minimize the need for abortions, which I think are wrong," an initiative that would include "better education on sex, better family-planning procedures, and access to contraceptives for those who believe in their use."[72] Like with the issue of busing, Carter appeared to want to have it both ways: He said he personally opposed forced busing and abortion, but opposed constitutional amendments to outlaw abortion and halt busing.[73]

In some sense, process was as important to Carter as product in creating what Pierard and Linder call a "moral presidency."[74] In his autobiography and in his campaign speeches, Carter posed what he said were the two basic questions of the campaign: "Can our government be competent and efficient? Can our government be honest, decent, open, fair, and compassionate?"[75] In his autobiography, Carter concentrated on the latter question, words "which describe what a government of human beings ought to be."[76]

Unfortunately, Carter could not deliver on his promise to run an efficient government, based on how his administration functioned. As one who had run against Washington in 1976, Carter—like Eisenhower in 1952—had to ingratiate himself to the Washington elite. Legislatively, Carter appeared to have an opening. In the House, Democrats controlled the chamber over Republicans by a more than two-to-one ratio. Democrats also had a comfortable majority of seats in the Senate. However, Carter's "moral presidency" was hindered by two factors: the lack of a focused agenda, and a consistent habit of seeming to alienate those in Washington who he needed most.

Part of Carter's covenant with the people whom elected him was to keep campaign promises, a pledge that clashed with the realities of Washington policymaking. Aide Hamilton Jordan said that absent was "a unifying political philosophy that had been affirmed through his election."[77] James David Barber said Carter came to Washington "with large principles and an eye for detail, but in between, where a coherent program might have been, was a lot of air."[78] Even Carter sensed the danger of his lists, writing in his diary before the close of his first month as president: "Everybody has warned me not to take on too many projects so early in the administration, but it's almost impossible for me to delay something that I see needs to be done."[79] Throughout his term, Carter came to know the frustration of trying to get too many things done without an explicit guiding framework. The approach belied the administrative competence Carter had promised during the campaign.

Conclusion

When he was running for office, Carter claimed his religion would not be a factor in his administration: "I've never tried to use my position as a public official to promote my beliefs, and I never would."[80] Carter may have won the presidency on a faith-filled platform; yet once in office, he implicitly removed at least his outward faith from center political stage. He focused on faith-driven goals without the political skill to achieve results, a contradiction to this campaign promise: "There is no inherent conflict between careful planning, tight management, and constant reassessment on one hand, and compassionate concern for the plight of the deprived and afflicted on the other. Waste and inefficiency never fed a hungry child, provided a job for a willing worker, or educated a deserving child."[81] Thus while Carter is to be admired and respected for his pursuit of just governance ends, his administration is to be criticized for its lack of management abilities.

Some have wished that Carter had linked his faith more directly to his presidential decisions. It may have been that "Carter's faith was too personal to be related to the complex social and moral problems a president has to face."[82] Alternatively, some said Carter's deep faith was evidence that the role of religious faith and conviction in the Oval Office had grown too powerful. If nothing else, Carter will be remembered, with Washington and Lincoln, as an imperfect president whose foundation was prayer, and whose lofty goals for America and for himself may have set an almost unreachable bar.

The important thing is this: Even as an imperfect human, Carter did his job to the best of his ability. Like the biblical story of the widow's mite where the woman in poverty gave everything she had, Carter had given everything he had, as a president and more important as a citizen. Historian Martin E. Marty may have put it best, "Despite their critics, I've always suspected Jimmy and Rosalynn Carter go to bed at night and rest well with the Lord."[83]

Notes

1. William Martin, *With God on Our Side: The Rise of the Religious Right in America* (New York: Broadway Books, 1996), 147.
2. Ibid., 148.
3. Douglas S. Marsh, "Book Review: *The Spiritual Journey of Jimmy Carter*," *Library Journal*, 104 (February 15, 1979): 499.
4. April 1976 interview with Jimmy Carter, in Robert L. Turner, *"I'll Never Lie to You": Jimmy Carter in his Own Words* (New York: Ballantine,

1976), as cited in Niels C. Nielsen, Jr., *The Religion of President Carter* (New York: Thomas Nelson, 1977), vii.

5. Jimmy Carter, *Keeping Faith: Memoirs of a President* (New York: Bantam, 1982), 62, as cited in James David Barber, *The Presidential Character: Predicting Performance in the White House*, 4th ed. (Englewood Cliffs, NJ: Prentice Hall, 1992), 447.

6. Leo P. Ribuffo, "God and Jimmy Carter," in *Transforming Faith: The Sacred and Secular in Modern American History*, ed. M. L. Bradbury and James B. Gilbert (New York: Greenwood Press, 1989), 146.

7. Transcript of Bill Moyers interview with Jimmy Carter, May 6, 1976, on *USA: People and Politics*, produced for PBS by Wallace Westfeldt, as cited in Barber, *The Presidential Character*, 404.

8. Nielsen, *The Religion of President Carter*, viii.

9. Jimmy Carter, *Why Not the Best?* (Nashville, TN: Broadman Press, 1975), 14, as cited in Barber, *The Presidential Character*, 423.

10. Jimmy Carter, *Living Faith* (New York: Times Books, 1996), 16.

11. Ibid., 16–17.

12. Ibid., 19–20.

13. Ibid., 22.

14. Ibid., 22–23.

15. Nielsen, *The Religion of President Carter*, x.

16. Carter, *Living Faith*, 23.

17. Peter Goldman, "Sizing Up Carter," *Newsweek*, September 13, 1975, 22 ff., as cited in Barber, *The Presidential Character*, 411.

18. Carter, *Living Faith*, 28.

19. Barber, *The Presidential Character*, 415.

20. Nielsen, *The Religion of President Carter*, x.

21. Richard V. Pierard and Robert D. Linder, *Civil Religion & the Presidency* (Grand Rapids, MI: Zondervan, 1988), 234.

22. Carter, *Why Not the Best?* 79–80, as cited in Barber, *The Presidential Character*, 418.

23. Barber, *The Presidential Character*, 420.

24. Carter, *Why Not the Best?* 132–133, as cited in ibid., 425–426.

25. Ribuffo, "God and Jimmy Carter," 147.

26. Martin, *With God on Our Side*, 150.

27. *Time*, January 10, 1976, 12, as cited in Barber, *The Presidential Character*, 425.

28. Carter, *Why Not the Best?* 99.

29. Pierard and Linder, *Civil Religion & the Presidency*, 237.

30. Barber, *The Presidential Character*, 425.

31. Pierard and Linder, *Civil Religion & the Presidency*, 237.

32. Martin, *With God on Our Side*, 148.

33. Ribuffo, "God and Jimmy Carter," 142.

34. Martin, *With God on Our Side*, 149.

35. Ibid., 150–151.

36. Ibid., 154.

37. *The Presidential Campaign, 1976*, 3 vols. (Washington, DC: Government Printing Office, 1978–1979), 1: 561, as cited in Pierard and Linder, *Civil Religion and the Presidency*, 232.

38. Pierard and Linder, *Civil Religion & the Presidency*, 238.

39. Jerry F. terHorst, "Carter's Old-Time Religion in a New World," *Los Angeles Times*, April 2, 1976, II, 13, as cited in ibid.

40. See Wesley Pippert, ed., *The Spiritual Journey of Jimmy Carter in His Own Words* (New York: Macmillan, 1978); and David Kucharsky, *The Man from Plains: The Mind and Spirit of Jimmy Carter* (New York: Harper & Row, 1976).

41. Reinhold Niebuhr, *The Children of Light and the Children of Darkness* (New York: Scribner, 1944), viii, as cited in Pierard and Linder, *Civil Religion & the Presidency*, 242.

42. Don Winter, "The Carter—Niebuhr Connection—the Politician as Philosopher," *National Journal*, 10 (February 4, 1978): 188–192, as cited in Pierard and Linder, *Civil Religion & the Presidency*, 242.

43. Martin, *With God on Our Side*, 151.

44. Carter, *Living Faith*, 127–128.

45. Martin, *With God on Our Side*, 153.

46. Ibid., 154.

47. Terry Gross, *Fresh Air*, WHYY (October 21, 2004).

48. Dan Ariail and Cheryl Heckler-Feltz, *The Carpenter's Apprentice: The Spiritual Biography of Jimmy Carter* (Grand Rapids, MI: Zondervan, 1996), 70.

49. Amy Sullivan, "Empty Pew," *New Republic*, 231 (October 11, 2004): 14.

50. Ribuffo, "God and Jimmy Carter," 151.

51. Robert T. Drinan, "Jimmy Carter Most Devout of Presidents," *National Catholic Reporter*, 33 (May 30, 1997): 15.

52. Gross, *Fresh Air* (October 21, 2004).

53. Daniel E. White, "*So Help Me God.*" *The U.S. Presidents in Perspective* (New York: Nova Science Publishers, 1996), 153.

54. Ibid.

55. Pierard and Linder, *Civil Religion & the Presidency*, 248.

56. Ibid., 247.

57. Ibid., 249.

58. Ibid., 253.

59. Ibid., 233–234.

60. Carter, *Living Faith*, 108.

61. Ariail and Heckler-Feltz, *The Carpenter's Apprentice*, 72.

62. Ribuffo, "God and Jimmy Carter," 152.

63. Ariail and Heckler-Feltz, *The Carpenter's Apprentice*, 73.

64. Barber, *The Presidential Character*, 443.

65. Ronald B. Flowers, "President Jimmy Carter, Evangelicalism, Church-State Relations, and Civil Religion," *Journal of Church and State*, 25 (1983): 113–132.

66. Ibid.
67. Pierard and Linder, *Civil Religion & the Presidency*, 241–242.
68. Martin, *With God on Our Side*, 154–155.
69. Ibid., 155.
70. Ibid.
71. Ibid., 156.
72. Ibid.
73. John R. Coyne, Jr., "Niceguyin' His Way to the White House?" *National Review*, 28 (May 14, 1976): 502.
74. Pierard and Linder, *Civil Religion & the Presidency*, 245.
75. Coyne, "Niceguyin' His Way to the White House?" 503.
76. Ibid.
77. Hamilton Jordan, *Crisis: The Last Year of the Carter Presidency* (New York: Putnam's, 1982), 318, as cited in Barber, *The Presidential Character*, 435.
78. Barber, *The Presidential Character*, 435.
79. Carter, *Keeping Faith*, 65, as cited in ibid.
80. Coyne, "Niceguyin' His Way to the White House?" 504.
81. Ibid.
82. Drinan, "Jimmy Carter Most Devout of Presidents," 15.
83. Ariail and Heckler-Feltz, *The Carpenter's Apprentice*, 17.

Chapter Nine

Ronald Reagan's Faith and Attack on Soviet Communism

Paul Kengor

Ronald Reagan's religious faith is a subject that, until recently, has received almost no serious attention. Not until 2004 was a scholarly treatment of Reagan's faith published.[1] Of Reagan's two best-known biographers, Lou Cannon and Edmund Morris, only Morris gave a certain amount of attention to Reagan's faith; even then, Morris barely touched the tip of the iceberg. Worse, if Reagan's faith is mentioned, it is linked to sensational matters like end-times prophecy and the Battle of Armageddon.[2]

This neglect of the religious Reagan is rather astonishing. A perusal of Reagan's private papers and personal letters reveals a very prominent religious side, one that pervaded much of what he said and did in both his private and public life. A scholar who relies on primary rather than secondary sources in investigating Reagan will quickly encounter—and perhaps be taken aback by—this strong and even sophisticated spiritual dimension. It is not unusual to find a letter from Reagan in, say, the 1970s, in which he is holding forth on his view on death and suffering, on free will, or is borrowing C. S. Lewis's "liar, Lord, or lunatic" argument to try to convince someone of Christ's divinity.[3]

This neglect is unfortunate because it leaves an unbridgeable gap in our understanding of Reagan and what made him tick, especially in the great calling of his political life: his cold war crusade against the Soviet Union. First and foremost, Reagan's faith profoundly affected his attack on Soviet communism. In fact, the sooner we understand the spiritual side of Reagan, we will also realize that the enemy to Reagan was not merely Soviet communism but, more pointedly, *atheistic* Soviet communism.

This chapter examines the sources of Reagan's faith as well as the manner in which that faith influenced his assault on the Soviet Union. Before doing that, however, the chapter first considers a key faith-related controversy that dogged Reagan's presidency: his lack of regular church attendance as president. This issue remains the elephant in the living room when it comes to Reagan's faith. In large part because of this issue—another that was also important was his wife's consultation of astrologers[4]—many observers did not take Reagan seriously as a man of committed or genuine Christian faith.

Church Attendance

During his reign as president, Ronald Reagan did not regularly attend church. This religious truancy was too much for even many of his most die-hard Christian conservative supporters. To this day, many evangelicals will not excuse the fortieth president's failure to frequently attend public worship services. It was a controversy that, for some, cast doubt on Reagan's faith. The Soviet press, lunging for any opportunity to portray Reagan as a hypocrite, especially on faith matters, took careful note: "[T]hough he shows . . . his religiousness," underscored an *Izvestia* journalist, "Reagan does not go to church."[5] Nor did he hold special services in the White House, as Richard Nixon did, which he could have easily arranged.

Reagan said that with the exception of his White House years, he was a "churchgoer all his life," even if he "didn't always attend every week."[6] The record bears this out. For all of his life, Reagan attended church, usually weekly; his presidency was indeed the exception.

There are a number of reasons for his behavior. Answering a question on his poor church attendance, posed by reporter Fred Barnes during a presidential debate with former vice president Walter Mondale, Reagan repeated his usual explanation that he feared endangering his own life and those of others when he went to church. "I pose a threat to several hundred people if I got to church," Reagan explained. "I know all the threats that are made against me. We all know the possibility of terrorism."[7]

The early 1980s was a time when Middle East terrorism became prominent; it was fairly new and occupied all of the headlines. It was nothing to find the face of Moammar Kaddafi or Yasser Arafat on the cover of *Time*. "We have seen the barricades that have had to be built around the White House," added Reagan. "I don't feel that I have a right to go to church, knowing that my being there could cause something of the kind that we have seen in other places, in Beirut, for example." Reagan received applause from the debate crowd when he finished: "And I miss going to church, but I think the Lord understands."[8]

In his memoirs, he addressed the issue further: "Even if the Secret Service allowed us to go to church, we'd arrive there in a siren-screaming motorcade accompanied by legions of reporters and security people. No longer was going to church a pleasant Sunday morning experience, it was a news event." Moreover, because of security concerns, attendees were required to pass through a magnetometer and get patted down before they could enter the sanctuary, which was not exactly the normal Sunday morning routine. Reagan said that "things got worse" after he started getting reports about "terrorist-hitsquads."[9] In a private letter to a longtime friend, he reiterated his concern before closing: "I pray we can help bring back a more civilized world one day."[10]

When Reagan went to church, he was accompanied by an army of Secret Service agents and cars, motorcycle policemen, SWAT squads, and scores of press people. The Secret Service stood guard at every church door, frisking all seekers of spiritual comfort. Helicopters soared overhead. One account went so far as to assert that SWAT squad members took posts on the church roof with rifles.[11]

"He hated to inconvenience people," explained William P. Clark, Reagan's second national security adviser and closest spiritual friend in the 1980s. (Clark knew Reagan since the mid-1960s and served as his chief of staff when Reagan was governor of California.) "He didn't want to do that. We discussed this. He didn't want to bother people." Clark said that Reagan hated to bother people in general, let alone in church.[12]

An eyewitness to this unease was a parishioner at the Santa Ynez Presbyterian Church, located near Reagan's beloved Rancho del Cielo— his ranch near Santa Barbara. As president, Reagan attended the church just once, during an Easter service. Asked if she remembered anything about Reagan on that day, the parishioner, without prompting, recalled just one thing: he seemed preoccupied with the notion that he was "burdening" (her word) the congregants. She remembered that Secret Service began setting up shop in the church two days earlier.[13]

A critic might retort that security concerns in the age of terrorism did not prevent George H. W. Bush or Bill Clinton or George W. Bush from attending church as president. That is true. Of course, neither of those presidents had a bullet fired into their chest, as did Reagan less than ten weeks into his presidency. When a person almost dies at the hand of a revolver, he is surely more jittery.

Reagan had been paranoid about security as governor. "He appears preoccupied with security," said one biographer of his first year as governor, listing many examples.[14] He was paranoid *then*, well before a bullet lodged near his heart and before terrorism exploded.

It was not mere security concerns (or the fuss) that kept Reagan from church.[15] He also did not relish the prospect of worshipping in a church and turning around to see hundreds of eyes fixed on him to see if he was singing, praying, staying awake, or bungling the Apostle's Creed. "[A]nd once we were seated in church," lamented Reagan, "Nancy and I often felt uncomfortable because so many people in the other pews were looking at us instead of listening to the sermon." "Very unhappily," wrote Reagan, "we just had to stop going to church altogether, and we really missed it."[16]

An illuminating account is provided by Joey Reynolds, a longtime radio personality in New York. Reynolds, who never shared Reagan's politics, shared Reagan's church in Bel Air, and says that he learned to "love" Reagan as a fellow Christian. Reynolds recalls a remarkable moment in the late 1970s when he says that Reverend Donn Moomaw, the church pastor, told him and others that he had asked Reagan to quit attending church because (in Reynolds' recollection of Moomaw's words) "people were now coming to worship Ronald Reagan instead of God." Reagan had clearly become a distraction in church, a painful reality that only magnified once he moved to Washington.[17]

Etched in the memory of Reagan's son Michael was an Air Force One flight during Easter 1988, when his presidential term was drawing to a close. Michael observed his father counting on his fingers. When he stopped at nine, Michael asked what he was doing. In nine months, the president replied, he could go to church again.[18]

And indeed Reagan resumed regular attendance once he returned to California after the presidency. In rejoining a church, the former most powerful man in the world conscientiously attended the "new member" classes.[19] The fact that he returned then, when opinion polls did not matter, adds credibility to his White House explanations.

Finally, it should be understood that Ronald Reagan apparently felt that he received sufficient guidance and fulfillment in his own daily relationship with God. Edmund Morris says that most of Reagan's divine counsel came from "silent colloquies, usually at an open window."[20] Bill Clark agrees: "Formal religion to him was secondary to a one-on-one relationship with the Creator."[21] Reagan did at times receive spiritual counseling in the White House. He had visits with many ministers and frequently exchanged meaningful letters with evangelists such as Billy Graham.[22]

It is interesting that Reagan never concerned himself with the political fallout resulting from his lack of church attendance. The irony is that if he had a "phony" faith, exploiting religion merely for political purposes, he could have gone to church or, better, simply held services in the White House, and done so visibly. Yet, he was secure enough not to be fazed by the criticism. Critics called Reagan stupid and lazy, heartless and uncompassionate, said that he was responsible for AIDS and homelessness, and asserted that he wanted to start a nuclear world war. He learned not to care what critics said.

Nelle and *That Printer of Udell's*

Reagan's devout faith gave him an extraordinary sense of self-security throughout his presidency and his life. It was a Christian faith that he acquired in his youth.

Ronald Reagan was born in Tampico, Illinois, on February 6, 1911 to an apathetic Catholic father named John Edward "Jack" Reagan and a devout Protestant mother named Nelle Clyde Wilson Reagan. Religiously speaking, Jack and Nelle agreed on one thing: they both wanted their son Ronald and his older brother Neil to go to church and believe in God. Jack was sure that Nelle was better suited to achieving that task. He was right.

Nelle was more than happy to accept the role of inculcating spiritual values. She was a leader at the local Disciples of Christ denomination and exuded Christian faith. Friends and church members described Nelle as a saint. Her son Ronald hoped to emulate his mother's commitment.

There are many ways that Nelle helped instill her son's faith. None of these may have been more important than a book called *That Printer of Udell's*.

Asked if there was a book that influenced him as a child more than any other book, Reagan said the book that "made a lasting impression on me at about the age of 11 or 12, mainly because of the goodness of the principal character," was one "I'm sure you never heard of."[23] The book was *That Printer of Udell's: A Story of the Middle West*, written by Harold Bell Wright in 1903.[24] Wright is a name not recognized by today's culture. Yet, he sold millions of books like this in the first half of the twentieth century.

Reagan cited the work in his memoirs when speaking of his "heroes." He called *Udell's* a "wonderful book about a devout itinerant Christian," which "made such an impact on me that I decided to join my mother's church."[25] In a letter he wrote from the White House to the daughter-in-law of the late Harold Bell Wright, he added,

> It is true that your father-in-law's book, indeed books, played a definite part in my growing-up years. <u>When I was only ten or eleven years old, I picked up Harold Bell Wright's book, That Printer of Udell's</u> [Reagan's underline for emphasis] and read it from cover to cover. . . .
>
> That book . . . had an impact I shall always remember. After reading it and thinking about it for a few days, I went to my mother and told her I wanted to declare my faith and be baptized. We attended the Christian Church in Dixon, and I was baptized several days after finishing the book.
>
> The term, "role model," was not a familiar term in that time and place. But I realize I found a role model in that traveling printer whom Harold Bell Wright had brought to life. <u>He set me on a course I've tried to follow even unto this day. I shall always be grateful.</u>[26]

Udell's first words are "O God, take ker o' Dick!" This was the final plea of the brokenhearted, dying mother of the novel's protagonist, Dick Walker. Little Dickie's mother was a committed Christian who suffered at the hands of a horrible creature—an alcoholic, abusive spouse. Reagan's own father, like Harold Bell Wright's own father, was an alcoholic, albeit not abusive, and was married to a devout Christian woman. All three mothers—Reagan's, Wright's, and Dick's—were members of the Disciples of Christ denomination.

In the opening scene, Dick's mom succumbs as his father lay passed out on the floor in a drunken stupor. Young Dick escapes. He immediately runs from home, and eventually becomes a tramp in a town called Boyd City. No one will hire him, including the Christians he appeals to in a brave, moving moment when he wanders into a church, attracted by the music, words, and warmth his late mom had described to him. The young vagabond goes inside for inspiration and guidance. He knows from what his mother taught him that this is a good place, a place of refuge and stability he can count on. Like Reagan, Dick's mom conditioned him to find comfort in God. Dick had no home of his own, always moving, always surrounded by strangers, often isolated—just like the young Ronald Reagan, whose father uprooted the family constantly, moving to yet another new town where Jack took yet another job as a shoe salesman. At church, with God, Dick found an anchor.

This church scene is a pivotal part of the book. Here Dick learns about the church, about himself, and about fake versus real, or "practical," Christianity. A practical Christian is one that would give Dick a job.[27]

Fortunately, a man named George Udell hires him as a printer, beginning for Dick somewhat of a Horatio Alger path to personal and spiritual improvement. He becomes a prominent player in the church and community—a man of action. Dick always seeks to do what is right, no matter if it rocks the boat or makes people uncomfortable. He calls a spade a spade. Though gentle and a man of warm demeanor, he and the book's other positive characters did not shrink from calling a cheat a cheat or a liar a liar. Evil was evil and ought to be called just that.

The novel's battle between right and wrong had a profound impact on young Reagan. More than 50 years after reading *Udell's*, he reminisced that this and other books from his youth left him with "an abiding belief in the triumph of good over evil." These books, he said, contained "heroes who lived by standards of morality and fair play."[28] There was no doubt about good and bad guys, and no moral equivalency.

The moral of the story takes shape as the new, improved Dick, now a printer at Udell's, and on his way to becoming a "practical" Christian, conceives a plan to help save the wretched city. Just as Reagan came to believe that God had a plan for him, Dick Walker believed himself to be moved by God, even unwittingly at times, as part of a greater plan. In Dick's case, it was a plan to do "Christ's work in the city"—in Boyd City.[29]

Dick needed a "plan," and he devised one. He also needed to sell the plan to the people. That required presence, leadership, and rhetorical skills—the intangibles and talents, in other words, of a politician. Eventually, they turn Boyd City around.

Dick's plan goes on to make a real difference. The city's bums, burglars, and prostitutes find good work; bars are supplanted by reputable businesses, concerts replace burlesque shows. Churches, naturally, grow, as do attendance at colleges and high schools. Boyd City became a model, a kind of shining city, of how applied Christianity and basic, common-sense solutions can make a difference. At one point, a traveling salesman peering out the window of a passing train is struck by the improvement: "I'm sure of one thing," he mutters, "they were struck by good, common-sense business Christianity."

Young Ronald Reagan learned from Dick Walker the benefits of a man motivated by Christian faith to do God's work. The biggest lesson of the book is practical Christianity. As the rube Uncle Bobbie put it, "Christianity's all right, but it ain't a goin' to do no good 'less people live it."[30] Dick lamented that the problem with the teaching of Christ was not His teaching but that the teaching "don't seem to go very far."[31] Dick wanted those Christian teachings to go somewhere, to have a practical effect.

Ultimately, Dick becomes a committed Christian, practicing "real" Christianity. After joining the Disciples of Christ, he marries a brown-eyed girl named Amy Goodrich, with whom he is instantly smitten. She becomes his life partner. He is sent off to Washington, DC—a "field of wider usefulness at the National Capitol"—as a polished, elected representative from Boyd City. The last image we get of Dick is one that would have moistened Reagan's eyes: kneeling in prayer before heading to Washington to change the world, with the admiring Amy at his side.

The lesson of *Udell's* is that a Christian must honestly stand by his convictions, proactively helping those who need help. He must boldly follow God's will, and not be silent or cowardly in attacking evil. He must be proud of his faith and make no excuses. Parking one's Christianity at the door is simply not what Jesus wants; it is not an option. This, *Udell's* conveyed, is the only true recipe for betterment—for changing the world.

Upon finishing *Udell's* final page, Reagan closed the book and walked over to his mother. "I want to be like that man," he exclaimed, referring to Dick, "and I want to be baptized." His fervor to "declare my faith" and be baptized was so strong that he persuaded his brother Neil, who was considering Jack's faith, to join him in total immersion at the Disciples of Christ church.[32] The book changed his life. He was transformed.

Practical Christianity and the Cold War

Much later in life, Ronald Reagan decided that a practical Christian would certainly oppose Soviet communism—an evil dictatorship whose good citizens desperately needed to be helped out of their bondage. There were a number of elements to his opposition to the USSR. First, he knew of its unprecedented brutality, of the tens of millions of Soviet citizens who had been forcibly starved, worked to death, or shot.[33] Worse, Reagan was convinced that the ultimate Soviet-Marxist goal was a one-world communist state headquartered in Moscow. The notion that this brutal system could be expanded and thrust upon yet more innocents appalled Reagan.

There were many intellectual influences to Reagan's repudiation of communism, writers like Whittaker Chambers, Malcolm Muggeridge, Alexander Solhenitsyn, Wilhelm Roepke, Laurence Beilenson, Frank Meyer, not to mention popular conservative publications like *Human Events* and *National Review*, which he read cover to cover. These sources devoted many pages to horror stories regarding Soviet communism, and many of them, especially Whittaker Chambers, devoted considerable thought to the institutionalized atheism of the USSR.[34]

Indeed, there was an added aspect to Reagan's hatred of communism, one that we have never sufficiently appreciated: the militant atheism of Soviet communism, and the subsequent "war" on religion (as Mikhail Gorbachev had rightly described it) orchestrated by the Bolsheviks on their own citizens. These unfortunate citizens were a people who Reagan believed were good, and, even, very religious people at one point in time.

Marx had called religion "the opiate of the masses." Vladimir Lenin, the godfather of the Soviet state, said much worse. Speaking on behalf of the Bolsheviks in his famous October 2, 1920 speech, he stated the following in a matter-of-fact tone: "We . . . do not believe in God."[35] Lenin insisted that "all worship of a divinity is a necrophilia."[36] Lenin wrote in a November 1913 letter that "any religious idea, any idea of any God at all, any flirtation even with a God is the most inexpressible foulness . . . the most dangerous foulness, the most shameful 'infection.' " (Translator James Thrower says that in this letter, the type of "infection" Lenin was referring to was venereal disease.[37]) "There can be nothing more abominable than religion," wrote Lenin in a letter to Maxim Gorky in January 1913.[38]

To cite just one example of Lenin's horrific treatment of religious Russians, on December 25, 1919, he personally issued the following order to the Cheka, the predecessor to the KGB: "To put up with 'Nikola' [the religious holiday commemorating the relics of St. Nikolai] would be stupid—the entire Cheka must be on the alert to see to it that those who do not show up for work because of 'Nikola' are shot."[39]

It was this hatred of religion that especially concerned Reagan. And he did not shrink from expressing his distaste for the Soviet experiment. If one lined up all of the sentences from Reagan attacking communism they might stretch from Washington to Moscow. We remember him famously calling the USSR an "Evil Empire" in March 1983. An equally strong but considerably less known assessment was delivered by the pre-presidential Reagan in a May 1975 radio broadcast in which he called communism a "disease." This piece might earn a gold ribbon among Reagan's strongest works of anticommunism. "Mankind has survived all manner of evil diseases and plagues," conceded Reagan, "but can it survive Communism?" This disease had been "hanging on" for a half century or more; it was imperative, said Reagan, that we understand "just how vicious it really is." This was timeless Reagan in attack mode—speaking forthrightly of this malice—calling evil *evil*. For good measure, he added, "Communism is neither an economic or a political system—it is a form of insanity."[40]

An important early step along the path to Reagan's eventual crusade against atheistic Soviet communism came in the late 1940s at the Beverly Christian Church in Hollywood. There, a religious source highlighted the communist threat to Reagan. The cold war was just beginning. Reagan, during this time, was a popular after-dinner speaker in Hollywood. In those political talks, he received raucous applause when he rained hate upon fascism, the totalitarian monster of his recent past.[41]

After one such speech to the men's club at the Beverly Christian Church, the Disciples denomination where Reagan worshiped at the time, Reverend Cleveland Kleihauer gingerly approached Reagan. Dr. Kleihauer was a straight shooter, not known as a liberal or conservative, described as a common-sense thinker who was not at all jingoistic. For four decades, he was one of the most influential - pastors in the city.[42]

Kleihauer seemed ill at ease. He noted that he appreciated Reagan's justifiable denunciation of fascism. He commended Reagan for his attack on the rise of neofascism. Though fascism had been vanquished in WWII, it was good to be vigilant and to continue to remind people of the brown menace. But, he told Reagan, there was a new threat—Soviet communism. He advised, "I think your speech would be even better if you also mentioned that if communism ever looked like a threat, you'd be just as opposed to it as you are to fascism."[43]

Reagan told his minister that he had not given much thought to the threat of communism. Nonetheless, he agreed it was good advice. From now on, he would declare that if a day came when it looked as though communism posed a threat to American values, he would denounce it as vigorously as he did fascism.

Who could possibly disagree? When he did, however, his predominantly left-wing audiences suddenly muted their approval. They quickly grew disapprovingly quiet.

He never forgot his first such experience. Speaking to a "local citizens' organization" in Hollywood, he defended American values against the fascist threat abroad, and was applauded after nearly every paragraph. By his own description, he was a smash. Then he concluded with his new line at the end of the pep talk: "I've talked about the continuing threat of fascism in the postwar world, but there's another 'ism,' communism, and if I ever find evidence that communism represents a threat to all that we believe in and stand for, I'll speak out just as harshly against communism as I have fascism."

You could hear a pin drop. Reagan awkwardly exited the stage—to dead silence. With that slight tweak to his talk, he had flopped. Something was not quite right. Bulbs began flickering. He puzzled: What was happening? What was behind this? Reagan had stumbled upon the fault line between naivete to communism by many Hollywood liberals and, in some cases, sympathy or even outright endorsement of communism.

With that experience, Reagan was on his way. The experience was a revelation. Over five decades later, after his presidency, he thanked that minister for the "wake-up" call. From then on, he became aware of the communist threat and mounted his assault. His course was forever altered. In short, then, one can see the actual start of Reagan's crusading against communism begun at the moment when a man of God, in a house of God, prompted him. Ronald Reagan, an actor then in his late 30s, had his eyes opened to the encroaching communist threat by a pastor.

The President versus the USSR

Ronald Wilson Reagan became president in January 1981. He was nearly assassinated just weeks later in March. He became convinced that God had spared his life that day for a "special purpose" related to the cold war.

Reagan perceived a Divine Plan for his country in combating the USSR. One of his favorite quotes was this from the late Pope Pius XII: "Into the hands of America, God has placed an afflicted mankind."[44] Yet, what about Reagan's sense of his own role? Did he perceive himself as selected by God, as leader of the United States of America, to prevail over the USSR?

It is important to understand that Reagan believed that only in retrospect might one know such a thing. He might sense such a role for himself, but he could never know ahead of time. That humility, that knowledge that mortal man can only know so much, reined him in considerably.

No one knew this side of Reagan better than his friend and National Security Adviser William P. Clark who was so close to Reagan that the two men frequently prayed together. If Reagan had a kind of "spiritual partner" in the 1980s, it was Clark. Asked if Reagan believed that God had called upon him to defeat the USSR, Clark demurred:

> I remember one day I was with him when someone congratulated him
> for taking down the wall. He said, "No, I didn't bring the wall down.
> That was part of the Divine Plan, teamwork, and God's Will." His num-
> ber one maxim is that we can accomplish anything if we don't concern
> ourselves with who gets the credit. . . . He just had total confidence in
> the Divine Will. He was there as an instrument of God, and one of
> many. He would refer to teamwork. . . .
>
> He would not consider making a statement like, "I have been chosen
> by God to lead a crusade against the Evil Empire." That would
> be totally out of character. . . . He would consider that to be false
> pride. . . . This is an amazingly humble person. True humility. There
> was no pride there at all.[45]

Clark said that Reagan's humility would force him to credit his
"team" overall, rather than himself, as acting by God's hand. Clark
was with Reagan once after the presidency when an admirer approached
Reagan and congratulated him for "your success in ending the Cold
War." Clark said that Reagan simply smiled and replied, "No, not my
success but a team effort by Divine Providence."[46] Reagan perceived
God's hand in this "team effort" to win the cold war. In hindsight, then,
Reagan would look back at what happened, at his administration's role
in the downfall of the USSR, and would cite God's hand in that end,
vis-à-vis his team as a whole.

There is complete agreement with Clark by Richard V. Allen,
Reagan's first national security adviser and foreign policy adviser in
the latter 1970s, and by Reagan Chief of Staff and Attorney General
Edwin Meese, as well as by Reagan's longtime Secretary of Defense
Cap Weinberger. All of these men knew Reagan as well as anyone, and
especially knew his foreign policy thinking; all had known or served
with him as far back as the mid-1960s when Reagan became
California's governor.[47]

Richard Allen put it this way:

> I don't believe Reagan believed that God chose him to defeat the Soviet
> empire. But he did believe America was a chosen place. He would look
> back [after his presidency and the cold war ended] and say something like:
> "Our team has fulfilled God's purpose." I think he would look back and
> say that. "We were part of the Divine Plan." He did, in fact, have a vibrant,
> vigorous faith that we could and would prevail against the USSR.[48]

Meese maintains that Reagan's special purpose was "probably something important relating to the USSR. I believe his 'special purpose' was

related to setting in motion the forces that would ultimately lead to ending the Cold War."[49]

Ronald Reagan later felt that God had chosen his "team" to defeat the USSR. Of course, we all know who was the head of his team. That said, the point we need to grasp is that Reagan was much more cautious about such a grandiose claim than is typically understood. Further, it is clear that he believed that God had appointed the United States of America with a special role in a divine plan—a plan that the USSR spurned as much as it did the very concept of the existence of God.

Conclusion

This essay is just the tip of that iceberg on the faith of Ronald Reagan. There is so much more that could be said here and that remains uncovered.

How could this religious component of Reagan's life and presidency have gone neglected for so long? The answer would require a separate essay. One reason, obviously, is that contemporary scholars have been giving short shrift to the powerful influence of religious faith in the lives and actions of our presidents. This lack of attention is probably due in part to the secularization of the academic profession; scholars, after all, tend to research those issues closest to their hearts, and the faith of presidents does not appear to be one of those issues.

American presidents, by and large, have been devout individuals, and that devoutness has been fundamental to their ability to rise so prominently in life and to withstand the barbs and arrows that come with the extraordinarily rough territory. Ronald Reagan was certainly no exception. The more that we learn about the faith of Ronald Reagan, the more we will understand and learn about Ronald Reagan, including his thinking in the dominant, dangerous ideological struggle of the twentieth century: the cold war.

Notes

1. See Paul Kengor, *God and Ronald Reagan: A Spiritual Life* (New York: Regan Books and HarperCollins, 2004).
2. To be sure, Reagan was interested in apocalyptic issues, as were many of his generation. Nonetheless, the real religious Reagan is a man of much more conventional beliefs.

3. I give many examples of this throughout the pages of *God and Ronald Reagan*. Among the references therein to Reagan and C. S. Lewis, see pages 128–129.

4. I cover this at length in a chapter devoted to the astrology issue in *God and Ronald Reagan*.

5. V. Soldatov, "Preelection America," *Izvestia*, May 8, 1984, 5, reprinted as "Soldatov Studies Reagan Election Campaign," in *Foreign Broadcast Information Service (FBIS)*, FBIS-SOV-10-MAY-84, May 10, 1984, A3.

6. Ronald Reagan, "The Role Bel Air Presbyterian Church Has Played in Our Lives," *Images* (a publication of Bel Air Presbyterian Church) 12 (1) (Summer 1990): 3.

7. "Text of Presidential Debate between Ronald Reagan and Walter Mondale," October 7, 1984.

8. Ibid.

9. Ronald Reagan, *An American Life* (New York: Simon and Schuster, 1990), 396.

10. Reagan to Lorraine and E. H. Wagner, February 13, 1984, Young America's Foundation (YAF) collection, Santa Barbara, CA.

11. A comprehensive collection of Reagan religious quotes was published by David Shepherd, *Ronald Reagan: In God I Trust* (Wheaton, IL: Tyndale, 1984). This quote is cited on page 6 of Shepherd's book.

12. Interview with William P. Clark by author, July 17, 2003.

13. Discussion between staff member (church secretary) of the Santa Ynez Presbyterian Church and author, August 27, 2003.

14. See Bill Boyarsky, *The Rise of Ronald Reagan* (New York: Random House, 1968), 14–17.

15. One reviewer of this book speculated that perhaps the Reagans feared the embarrassment of being lectured from the pulpit by liberal pastors, similar to what LBJ experienced during Vietnam. This is not difficult to imagine, particular on issues like poverty and social programs, nuclear freeze, Central America, and others. While an interesting hypothesis, Reagan staff and friends do not endorse it. "I don't think that was a factor with him at all," said Ed Meese. Interview with Ed Meese by author, November 23, 2001.

16. Reagan, *An American Life*, 396.

17. Reynolds shared this information with me in New York City at WWOR-AM studios on February 6, 2004 and again on August 18, 2004. I was unable to reach Donn Moomaw for comment.

18. Interview with Michael Reagan by author, September 2, 2003.

19. Interview with Ed Meese by author, November 23, 2001.

20. See Edmund Morris, *Dutch* (New York: Random House, 1999), 427.

21. Interview with William P. Clark, December 11, 2001.

22. There are numerous letters between Reagan and Billy Graham on file at the Reagan Library, not to mention other ministers. Among the ministers who visited him in the White House was an old Eureka College pal named "Mac" McCallister.

23. Reagan said this in 1977. See Jerry Griswold, " 'I'm a Sucker for Hero Worship,' " *The New York Times* Book Review, August 30, 1981, 11.
24. Harold Bell Wright, *That Printer of Udell's: A Story of the Middle West* (New York: A. L. Burt, 1903).
25. Reagan, *An American Life*, 32.
26. A copy of the March 13, 1984 letter is on file at the Dixon Public Library.
27. Wright, *That Printer of Udell's*, 29–33.
28. Griswold, " 'I'm a Sucker for Hero Worship,' " 11.
29. See Wright, *That Printer of Udell's*, 118–119 and 206.
30. Ibid., 73.
31. Ibid., 70–71.
32. There are a number of consistent accounts of this moment. Edmund Morris has probably said or written more about it than any other source. See Morris, *Dutch*, 42; and Morris speaking on "Reagan," *The American Experience*, television documentary produced by PBS, WGBH-TV, Boston, 1998.
33. *The Black Book of Communism*, the seminal work published by Harvard University Press, cited 20 million deaths by communist governments in the USSR (a conservative figure), 65 million in China, over 2 million in North Korea and Cambodia, and 1 million or more in Afghanistan, Africa, eastern Europe, and Vietnam, plus hundreds of thousands more elsewhere around the globe. The total dead due to communism approaches 100 million. Martin Malia aptly writes that the communist record offers the "most colossal case of political carnage in history." See Stephane Courtois et al., *The Black Book of Communism* (Cambridge, MA: Harvard University Press, 1999).
34. See Kengor, *God and Ronald Reagan*, 75–88.
35. Quoted by Laurence W. Beilenson, *The Treaty Trap: A History of the Performance of Political Treaties by the United States & European Nations* (Washington, DC: Public Affairs Press, 1969), 163.
36. Lenin wrote this in a November 13 or 14, 1913 letter to Maxim Gorky. See James Thrower, *God's Commissar: Marxism-Leninism as the Civil Religion of Soviet Society* (Lewiston, NY: Edwin Mellen Press, 1992), 39.
37. Quoted in ibid. Another translation of this quote comes from Robert Conquest, in his chapter "The Historical Failings of CNN," in *CNN's Cold War Documentary*, ed. Arnold Beichman (Stanford, CA: Hoover Institution Press, 2000), 57.
38. See J. M. Bochenski, "Marxism-Leninism and Religion," in *Religion and Atheism in the USSR and Eastern Europe*, ed. B. R. Bociurkiw et al. (London: Macmillan, 1975), 11.
39. Cited by Alexander N. Yakovlev, *A Century of Violence in Soviet Russia* (New Haven and London: Yale University Press, 2002), 157.
40. Transcript of radio broadcast is located in "Ronald Reagan: Pre-Presidential Papers: Selected Radio Broadcasts, 1975–1979," January 1975–March 1977, box 1, Ronald Reagan Library (RRL), Simi Valley, CA.

See also Kiron Skinner, Martin Anderson, and Annelise Anderson, eds., *Reagan, In His Own Hand* (New York: Free Press, 2000), 10–12.

41. On this, see Reagan, *An American Life*, 106–107.

42. On Reverend Kleihauer, I thank Glen Gray, administrator at the Hollywood Beverly Christian Church, for his assistance in providing information.

43. Interviews with Glen Gray of the Hollywood Beverly Christian Church by author.

44. This was the last line of Reagan's July 6, 1976 nationally televised speech marking the bicentennial, followed only by his three-word sign off: "God bless America." Reagan, "Nationally Televised Address," ABC-TV, July 6, 1976. Speech filed at Reagan Library, "RWR—Speeches and Articles (1974–76)," vertical files. Reagan also said this in statements on January 25, 1974, June 6, 1974, June 1975 radio broadcast, April 30, 1981, May 27, 1981, February 6, 1984, December 19, 1984 letter.

45. Interview with William P. Clark by author, July 17, 2003.

46. Clark shared this during a February 22, 1999 presentation in Washington, DC. For a transcript, see Clark in Peter Schweizer, ed., *Fall of the Berlin Wall* (Stanford, CA: Hoover Institution Press, 2000), 75.

47. Interview with Richard V. Allen by author, November 12, 2001; interview with Ed Meese by author, November 23, 2001; and interview with Caspar Weinberger by author, October 10, 2002.

48. Interview with Richard V. Allen by author, November 12, 2001.

49. Interview with Ed Meese by author, November 23, 2001.

Chapter Ten

The Religion of Bill Clinton

James M. Penning

I don't think I could do my job as President, much less continue to try to grow as a person in the absence of my faith in God and my attempt to learn more about what it should be and grow. It provides a solace and support in the face of all these problems that I am not smart enough to solve.

Bill Clinton in ABC interview by Peggy Wehmeyer,
"American Agenda," March 22, 1994
(Spirituality 2004)

Bill Clinton's Religion: An Apparent Paradox

President William Jefferson Clinton is one of the most complex, enigmatic persons to ever occupy the American presidency and there is little doubt that long after Clinton's controversial presidency, scholars and citizens alike will continue to puzzle over questions relating to his personality, character, and religious life (Pfiffner 2000). Was Clinton a man of high character and personal faith? One can muster considerable supporting evidence. As president, Bill Clinton frequently attended church services, liberally sprinkled his speeches with biblical references, promoted a "New Covenant" with the American people, and regularly sought spiritual counsel from clergy. As he left office, Clinton enjoyed an exceedingly high (65 percent) public approval rating, higher that that enjoyed by Ronald Reagan and John F. Kennedy (Jackson 2001). And he received support, even from conservative clergy such as former Jerry Falwell associate, the Rev. Ed Dobson, who argued that Clinton "is more deeply spiritual than any president we've had in recent years" (Cloud 2000).

On the other hand, critics have challenged this perspective, suggesting that Clinton was a cynical manipulator, using religious references to paper over a life of marital infidelity, witness tampering, perjury, and possibly even rape (Neuhaus 1999). Indeed, some observers have characterized Clinton as a chronic liar who has breached the public trust (Bennett 1998). Journalist George F. Will goes so far as to assert that "Clinton is not the worst president the republic has had, but he is the worst person ever to have been President" (Jackson 2001).

The purpose of this chapter is to examine the "religion" of Bill Clinton, seeking to sort through these apparently contradictory perspectives pertaining to his character, faith commitment, and actions. This task is important not only because Clinton himself frequently mixed religion and politics in his public statements but also because his personal life generated significant issues pertaining to his religious faith, his personal morality, and the ethical standards guiding his public conduct. It is hoped that by studying the religion of Bill Clinton we may learn important lessons concerning both the character of one of America's most interesting presidents and broader questions relating to religion and politics in the White House.

Before undertaking this task, it is worth noting that the term "religion" may be used in multiple ways. In its most basic sense, the term refers to affiliation with a particular religious denomination or religious tradition. However, "religion" can also encompass such matters as theological beliefs, personal faith, and religious practices. An examination of presidential religion such as this must necessarily touch on these various dimensions of religion, recognizing, however, that some dimensions of religion (e.g., practices) are much more amenable to scholarly scrutiny than are others (personal faith).

In order to understand the religion of Bill Clinton, this chapter adopts an historical perspective, attempting to ascertain the roots of Clinton's religion, the development of that religion, and the impact of that religion on his public and private life. Data for the chapter are drawn from a wide variety of published sources, including primary documents, scholarly books, media reports, and internet links.

Religion in Clinton's Childhood

In order to understand the religion of Bill Clinton, it is helpful to examine his troubled childhood, a childhood in which adult role models sent conflicting signals about values, virtue, and morality, and a childhood in which the young Clinton was forced to assume adult roles at an early age. While it is certainly possible to exaggerate the importance of Clinton's childhood for his religious and moral development, it is likely that Clinton's paradoxical religious characteristics are deeply rooted in childhood experiences. According to presidential scholar Stanley Renshon, "Without parents who provide boundaries, love, and guidance, ideals can falter. A person may never develop ideals that go beyond securing what he or she wants. Or a person may never be able to resolve the many conflicts that occur among ideals in a way that provides a sense of the basic integrity of one's fundamental ideals, aspirations, and unfolding identity" (Renshon 1996: 42). Regardless of the validity of this analysis, there is little doubt that Clinton's parents were hardly models of Christian piety, probity, and virtue. His stepfather, Roger Clinton, was a heavy drinker and wife-beater. Once, following a domestic dispute, Roger Clinton was arrested for firing a gun into the wall of his house between his wife and young stepson (Cllinton 2004: 20). His mother, Virginia Kelley, married four times and "liked to drink, gamble, and visit the local race track" (Maraniss 1995).

Still, the young Bill Clinton did not lack religious influences. In second and third grade, he attended a Catholic parochial school where he impressed Monsignor John O'Donnell, his third grade teacher, with his self-confidence and ambition (Walker 1996). Clinton reported, "I was fascinated by the Catholic Church, its rituals and the devotion of the nuns, but getting on my knees on the seat of my desk and leaning on the back with the rosary beads was often too much for a rambunctious boy whose only church experience before then had been in the Sunday school and the summer vacation Bible school of the First Baptist Church in Hope" (Clinton 2004: 23). Clinton's mother had dutifully taken the young boy to Sunday School and Sunbeams there, although she never stayed (Hamilton 2003: 53).

In his autobiography, Clinton reports that Park Place Baptist Church of Hot Springs was his "first real church" (Clinton 2004: 30). According to Clinton, "Though Mother and Daddy didn't go [to church] except on Easter and sometimes on Christmas, Mother encouraged me to go, and I did, just about every Sunday. I loved getting dressed up and walking down there" (Clinton 2004: 30). His mother recalled that "Bill just got up one day and said he wanted to go to church—all by himself" (Olasky 1999). Thus, from the age of 11, Clinton, dressed in a suit and carrying a Bible under his arm, regularly walked, alone, to the Baptist Church to attend worship services and Sunday school. No other member of his immediate family attended church. Clinton's regular attendance continued through high school and the church's minister recalls the young Clinton often waiting at the church before the minister arrived to open the doors (Sadiq 1996).

Later, Clinton explained that he regularly attended church because it was important "to be a good person" (Olasky 1999: 259). Others, however, suggested that as a boy, Clinton found church services to be a form of escape from family brutality and a source of personal solace in a chaotic life. According to Nigel Hamilton, "Some might later question Billy's religious faith, considering it the sham religion of one who was patently not among The Saved, but for himself Billy Blythe [Clinton] *did* feel saved from a far more oppressive domestic reality that most of his contemporaries or teachers were not aware of" (Hamilton 2003: 72). Although his parents and his drug-addicted grandmother might have repeatedly let him down, Clinton found solace in Jesus, "a divinity who could never be compromised" (Hamilton 2003: 72). As his Little Rock pastor, Rex Horne, put it, Bill Clinton "grew up early looking for help and hope—and found it in the church" (Olasky 1999: 260).

But it is possible, and perhaps even likely, that Clinton's youthful religiosity reflected more than a simple need for refuge from a violent family life. Even as a youth, Clinton demonstrated an intellectual inquisitiveness unusual among his peers and one can readily imagine that the precocious young man found church a place to explore fundamental questions of faith and life. According to Clinton, during his junior high years, "[S]ome of what came into my head and life scared the living hell out of me, including anger at Daddy . . . and doubts about my religious convictions, which I think developed because I couldn't understand why a God whose existence I couldn't prove would create a world in which so many bad things happened" (Clinton 2004: 40). According to Hamilton, for Clinton, "the actual historical basis for a belief in Christ's divinity could never be proven, but it could be appreciated, indeed believed in *as gospel truth*: good news from another place, in another time, set to great choral music, emotionally reaffirming . . ." (Hamilton 2003: 72, italics is in the original). Perhaps that is why his devout babysitter, Mrs. Walton, predicted that Bill Clinton would become a preacher (Hamilton 2003: 72).

No doubt Mrs. Walton was pleased when, at the age of ten, Clinton publicly professed his faith and was baptized (Olasky 1999: 260). Clinton describes his experience this way: "In 1955, I had absorbed enough of my church's teachings to know that I was a sinner and to want Jesus to save me. So I ran down the aisle at the end of Sunday service, professed my faith in Christ, and asked to be baptized. The Reverend Fitzgerald came to the house to talk to Mother and me. Baptists require an informed profession of faith for baptism; they want people to know what they are doing, as opposed to the Methodists' infant-sprinkling ritual that took Hillary and her brothers out of hell's way" (Clinton 2004: 30). Clinton reported that immediately prior to his baptism, a female congregant, afraid of the water, got stuck in the baptismal pool, necessitating prompt action from the frantic pastor. Clinton and his longtime friend, Bert Jeffries, were "in stitches." According to Clinton, "I couldn't help thinking that if Jesus had this much of a sense of humor, being a Christian wasn't going to be so tough" (Clinton 2004: 30–31).

A variety of other forces also contributed to the young Bill Clinton's religious and spiritual development. In Arkansas schools during the 1950s, students read Bible passages over the intercom system each morning and school assemblies were often much like chapel services (Olasky 1999: 260). In addition, in the "faith and football" culture of the time, football games were frequently preceded by religious invocations or ceremonies.

Not all of Clinton's early family experiences had negative implications for his religious and moral development. Clinton's grandfather owned a general store that served both black and white customers, a relatively rare phenomenon in 1950s Arkansas (Clinton 2004: 12). According to Sadiq, "Young Bill loved to spend time with his grandfather, who taught him that black people are just as good and decent as white people, and should be respected. From this point forward, Bill expressed regret and outrage at acts of racism" (Sadiq 1996).

Clinton's progressive attitudes on race helped forge his long-standing love for Baptist evangelist, Billy Graham. In his autobiography, the former president, writing about his 1958–1959 school year, notes that "the biggest thing that happened to me that year" involved his attendance at a Billy Graham crusade: "One of the Sunday-school teachers offered to take a few of the boys in our church to Little Rock to hear Billy Graham preach in his crusade in War Memorial Stadium, where the Razorbacks played. Racial tensions were still high in 1958. Little Rock's schools were closed in a last-gasp effort to stop integration. . . . Segregationists from the White Citizens Council and other quarters suggested that, given the tense atmosphere, it would be better if the Reverend Graham restricted admission to the crusade to whites only. He replied that Jesus loved all sinners, that everyone needed a chance to hear the word, and therefore that he would cancel the crusade rather than preach to a segregated audience. Back then, Billy Graham was the living embodiment of Southern Baptist authority . . . I wanted to hear him preach even more after he took the stand he did . . . I loved Billy Graham for doing that. For months after that I regularly sent part of my small allowance to support his ministry" (Clinton 2004: 39).

According to Clinton, he kept this decision to send money to Graham a secret from his parents (Clinton 2004: 46).

Thirty years later, Billy Graham returned to Little Rock for another crusade at War Memorial Stadium. Clinton, now governor, reported that he was "honored to sit on the stage with him one night" and to accompany him on a house call to visit an ailing friend of Rev. Graham. Clinton reported that "it was amazing to listen to these two men of God discussing death, their fears, and their faith" (Clinton 2004: 39). Later, after Clinton became president, Billy and Ruth Graham visited Bill and Hillary Clinton in the White House, praying with them and, in Clinton's words, writing "inspiring letters of instruction and encouragement in my times of trial" (Clinton 2004: 39–40).

At his high school graduation, Clinton was tapped to give the benediction. Even at this early age, Clinton had no qualms about mixing religion and politics. According to Clinton, "My benediction reflected my deep religious convictions as well as a little politics as I prayed that God would 'leave within us the youthful idealism and moralism which have made our people strong. Sicken us at the sight of apathy, ignorance, and rejection so that our generation will remove complacency, poverty, and prejudice from the hearts of free men . . . Make us care so that we will never know the misery and muddle of life without purpose, and so that when we die, others will still have the opportunity to live in a free land' " (Clinton 2004: 67). Later Clinton, commenting on his benediction, would assert, "I know that some non-religious people may find all this offensive or naïve but I'm glad I was so idealistic back then, and I still believe every word I prayed" (Clinton 2004: 65).

From High School to the Statehouse

Bill Clinton maintained his close ties with the Baptist Church through his graduation from Hot Springs High School in 1964 and through his early days at Georgetown University. However, shortly thereafter he drifted away from the church. According to Clinton spiritual adviser, Tony Campolo, the president "was a very serious Christian during his teenage years, but got away from the Lord from the time he was 19 through his governorship. . . . He personally screwed up his life for a period of time." Indeed, Clinton himself admitted that he was "an uneven churchgoer" from his college days though his entry into Arkansas politics (Olasky 1999: 260).

At Georgetown University, by all accounts, Bill Clinton placed greater emphasis on politics and career enhancement than on spiritual growth and moral development. On occasion, Baptist Clinton went to Catholic Mass and to Episcopal services but his attendance was sporadic (Hamilton 2003: 132–133). Nonetheless, Georgetown University, as a Catholic institution, attempted to have at least a limited impact on the religion of its students and, in Clinton's case, seemed to enhance his openness to world religions. In a 1995 speech at James Madison High School in Vienna, Virginia, Clinton remarked that "Georgetown University . . . is a Jesuit school, a Catholic school . . . when I was there, all the Catholics were required to take theology, and those of us who weren't Catholic took a course on world religions, which we called Buddhism for Baptists. And I began a sort of love affair with the religions that I did not know anything about before that time" (Clinton 1995).

This emerging "romance" may have reinforced Clinton's support for religious diversity and First Amendment religious rights that he labeled "literally our first freedom" and "something that is very important to me" (Clinton 1995). According to Clinton, "I grew up in Arkansas which is, except for West Virginia, probably the most heavily Southern Baptist, Protestant state in the country. But we had two synagogues and a Greek Orthodox church in my hometown. . . . I have always felt that in order for me to be as free to practice my faith in this country, I had to let other people be as free as possible to practice theirs, and that the government had an extraordinary obligation to bend over backwards not to do anything to impose any set of views on any group of people or to allow others to do so under the cover of law" (Clinton 1995).

At Georgetown, Clinton took logic from an unordained Jesuit named Otto Heinz. Clinton reported that one day Heinz "asked me if I'd like to have a hamburger with him for dinner. I was flattered and agreed . . . After a little small talk, Otto turned serious. He asked me if I had ever considered becoming a Jesuit. I laughed and replied, 'Don't I have to be a Catholic first?' When I told him I was a Baptist and said, only half in jest, that I didn't think I could keep the vow of celibacy, even if I were Catholic, he shook his head and said, 'I can't believe it. I've read your papers and exams. You write like a Catholic. You think like a Catholic' " (Clinton 2004: 76).

Although Clinton's faith may have been somewhat attenuated during his college years, he writes movingly of the role of church and faith as he attended to his dying stepfather, Roger Clinton. In the spring of 1967 Clinton regularly drove the 266 miles from Georgetown University to the Duke Medical Center in Durham, North Carolina. According to Clinton, he and his stepfather attended Easter services in the Duke chapel: "Daddy had never been much of a churchgoer, but he really seemed to enjoy this service. Maybe he found some peace in the message that Jesus had died for his sins too. Maybe he finally believed it when we sang the words to that wonderful old hymn, 'Sing With All the Sons of Glory' " (Clinton 2004: 105). At his father's funeral, Clinton worried about the rainy weather, remembering his father's oft-repeated plea, "Don't bury me in the rain." When, on the slow drive to the cemetery, the rain stopped, Clinton and his brother were overjoyed. According to Clinton, "On his last, long journey to the end that awaits us all, he [Roger Clinton] found a forgiving God. He was not buried in the rain" (Clinton 2004: 114).

Despite these experiences, Clinton's life during this period seems remarkably devoid of signs of religiosity or spiritual commitment. In his autobiography, although Clinton discusses his experiences at Oxford in great detail, he makes scant reference to religious involvement. Furthermore, upon returning to the United States, his lifestyle, including his decision to cohabit with Hillary Rodham, hardly seems congruent with the beliefs of his fellow Baptists (Clinton 2004: 185).

The precise timing of Clinton's emergence from his personal spiritual wilderness, if that indeed was what it was, is a matter of some dispute. Some observers point to a spiritual reawakening in 1980, the year Clinton lost his bid for reelection to the Arkansas statehouse. Certainly, his electoral defeat was a jarring experience for Clinton, producing considerable anger (aimed in particular at the media and at failed Democratic Party presidential candidate, Jimmy Carter) but also a degree of introspection and (unusual for Clinton) even a hint of self-doubt (Maraniss 1995: 387–388, 392; Walker 1996: 94–96). This defeat, coupled with the nearly simultaneous birth of his daughter, Chelsea, may well have prompted the chastened governor to return to his religious and spiritual roots. Indeed, in short order, Bill and Hillary joined Immanuel Baptist Church in Little Rock where he began singing in the choir (Hamilton 2003: 379).

A more cynical interpretation of Clinton's newfound religion attributes Clinton's reawakening more to calculation than to Christ. Following his 1980 defeat, a determined Clinton carefully analyzed the reasons for his defeat and vowed to do whatever was necessary to change his political fortunes. Bill and Hillary concluded that one reason for his defeat was that politically progressive Bill and Hillary had apparently lost touch with grassroots Arkansas voters, particularly those in the religious community. In his autobiography, Clinton reports that "after I lost, and for months afterward, I asked everybody I knew why they thought it had happened. . . . Jimmy 'Red' Jones, whom I had appointed adjutant general of the Arkansas National Guard . . . said I had alienated the voters with too many young beards and out-of-staters in important positions. He also thought Hillary's decision to keep her maiden name had hurt; it might be alright for a lawyer but not for a first lady" (Clinton 2004: 286). The Arkansas couple vowed to change all of that. Thus, swallowing, at least for the moment, her feminist ideals, Hillary changed the last name on her business cards from "Rodham" to "Clinton" in deference to traditional Arkansas social mores. And Bill decided to join Immanuel Baptist Church, home to many of Little Rock's business and political elites, and sing in the choir, where he was clearly visible sitting behind the minister on the Church's weekly statewide television broadcasts (Hamilton 2003: 279).

Not only did Clinton face challenges at the ballot box, he also faced challenges in his personal life. By 1988, Clinton's marriage was in trouble as rumors of his marital infidelity spread. Martin Walker quotes a weeping Chelsea, "Mommy, why doesn't Daddy love you anymore?" Although Clinton denied the rumors, Hillary refused to tolerate the situation, threatening to get a divorce. The marriage was saved, in part, through the intervention of Hillary's Methodist pastor, Ed Matthews, who met the couple for repeated sessions in his study. Under his direction, Bill and Hillary "held hands and knelt to pray together, and Clinton promised to change his ways, to work harder at being a better husband and father, and to devote more time to his family" (Walker 1996: 113–114).

Even today there is no consensus over whether these changes in Clinton's behavior grew more out of spiritual need or out of political expediency. Perhaps both were at work. Certainly, former Immanuel Baptist pastor, Wayne Ward, is inclined to accept Clinton's spiritual conversion as genuine. According to Ward, "there is no reason to question his deep commitment to Christ" (Olasky 1999: 261). However, critic, Marvin Olasky, notes that despite an increase in religiosity, Clinton failed to raise his standards of personal morality. In addition, Olasky suggests that Clinton proved more than willing to reject his church's theological and moral positions when it proved to be politically advantageous. Thus, Olasky contends that "as Clinton ascended in national Democratic circles, he moved in a way contrary to biblical teaching on issues such as abortion, from opposition to the practice in 1986 to partial opposition in 1989, support in 1991, and support for even partial-birth abortion in 1996" (Olasky 1999: 261).

Some observers argue that, even if the cynics are correct, Bill Clinton did indeed experience a spiritual reawakening later, after entering the White House. Clinton spiritual adviser, Tony Campolo, for example, asserts that Clinton "got through Arkansas on charm and intelligence, and not until he came to the White House did he become aware that he needed far more than that." According to Campolo, Clinton spoke of "how the turmoil of the Civil War drove Lincoln to his knees, in the realization that the task was beyond him and he needed help from God." Similarly, Rev. Rex Horne argued in 1994 that Clinton's spiritual life was growing "in direct relation to the size and enormity of the issues that are facing him" (Olasky 1999: 262).

Religion in the White House

Religion in the First Clinton Administration

There is little doubt that Clinton's affairs with Monica Lewinski and other women will have a significant impact on his presidential legacy. Literally dozens of books and articles, many of them highly critical of Clinton, have focused on his sexual affairs and his efforts to conceal or otherwise deal with them (Bennett 1998; Johnson 2001; Kurtz 1998; Stewart 1996).

But that was later. Clinton's presidency began with considerable optimism and public expression of religious faith. On the day before Clinton's first inauguration, Bill and Hillary visited the Kennedy graves in Arlington Cemetery, with Bill kneeling at the eternal flame and offering a short prayer, "thanking God for their lives and service and asking for wisdom and strength in the great adventures just ahead" (Clinton 2004: 473–474). Clinton followed this event with a late-night prayer service at the First Baptist Church. On the following day, Clinton's last activity before the inauguration was a prayer service at Washington's Metropolitan African Methodist Episcopal Church. According to Clinton, this prayer service "was important to me. With input from Hillary and Al Gore, I had picked the participating clergy, the singers, and the music. . . . Both our pastors from home partici-pated in the service, as did Al and Tipper's ministers, and George Stephanopoulous' father, the Greek Orthodox dean of the Holy Trinity Cathedral in New York . . . Tears welled up in my eyes several times during the service, and I left uplifted and ready for the hours ahead" (Clinton 2004: 474–475).

In his inaugural address, the new president asked for "God's help" and called on Americans to approach the future with "energy and hope." In the best tradition of American civil religion, Clinton noted that, "the Scripture says 'And let us not be weary in well-doing, for in due season, we shall reap, if we faint not'" (Sharman 1995: 129–130). The new president set out with vigor to fulfill his campaign pledges to "fix the economy" and expand health care coverage (Woodward 1994).

Throughout his presidency, Clinton frequently injected biblical and other religious terms and phrases into his public statements. Clinton's oratorical gifts, coupled with his Southern Baptist heritage, made this easy to do. For example, in the 1992 campaign, Clinton labeled his policy agenda as a "New Covenant" with the American people and later used the term extensively to counter the Republicans' proposed "Contract with America" (Silk 1999: 3).[1] As Clinton put it, "I think I feel more comfortable speaking in the rhythms of my faith in my speeches . . . at least when I'm at home in the South" (Hamilton 2003: 486).

Critics of Clinton's successor, George W. Bush, have severely chastised Bush for mixing religion and politics and for seeking divine guidance in decision making (Suskind 2004). Yet a comparison of the two presidents reveals that Clinton mentioned Christ even more frequently than Bush (an average of 5.1 statements per year for Clinton versus 4.7 statements per year for Bush) (Kengor 2004: 2). As president, Clinton frequently spoke in a wide variety of churches, invoking timeworn precepts of American civil religion. In a 1992 address to an African American Church of God in Christ congregation in Memphis, Tennessee, Clinton asserted, "By the grace of God and with your help, last year I was elected President." And addressing the Alfred Street Baptist Church of Alexandria, Virginia, Clinton blatantly asked for electoral support: "The Scripture says, 'While we have time, let us do good unto all men.' And a week from Tuesday, it will be time for us to vote" (Kengor 2004: 3).

Wayne Slater of the *Dallas Morning News* speculates that Clinton found it easier than Bush to inject religious rhetoric into his speeches because, as a Democrat, Clinton did not generate as much fear that he would impose his religious views on others. According to Slater, "In an odd way, he was able to talk about Christianity and faith in his own life, quote the Scriptures, show in church, be there with a Bible, because there was no fear, really, in the larger community, that he, Clinton, wanted to create a theocracy. Democrats don't want to create a theocracy. It seems to be the Republicans who have to be more careful of being charged with bringing too much religion to the advocacy of politics and public policy . . ." (*Frontline* 2004: 3).

But perhaps equally important, Clinton's religious background, combined with his natural grace and oratorical skills, enabled him to seamlessly adapt religious messages to diverse audiences. E. J. Dionne, for example, notes that "Bill Clinton was religious. Bill Clinton could quote Scripture with the best of them. Bill Clinton could preach with the best of them. He gave some very powerful speeches at Notre Dame where he sounded Catholic; at African-American churches, where he sounded AME or Baptist" (*Frontline* 2004: 2). As Richard Land of the Southern Baptist Convention put it, "You know, Bill Clinton knew the language. Bill Clinton could talk like a Southern Baptist evangelist when he wanted to" (*Frontline* 2004: 4).

Not only did Clinton talk *like* evangelical preachers, he also occasionally talked *with* them. Shortly before assuming the presidency in 1993, Clinton hosted a lunch for evangelical ministers at the Arkansas Governor's Mansion. In his autobiography, Clinton reports that this lunch was organized at a suggestion from his pastor, Rex Horne, who "thought it would be helpful to have an informal discussion with them so that at least I'd have some lines of communication into the evangelical community" (Clinton 2004: 465). Clinton needed to build such lines of communication because some of his policy positions, particularly his support of abortion rights, were strongly opposed by large portions of the evangelical community.

Despite such efforts, the relationship between Clinton and the evangelical community was always characterized by a degree of tension and mistrust (and worsened considerably during the Lewinsky scandal). Explained Richard Cizik of the National Association of Evangelicals, "[I]n the Clinton administration, the president sort of understood who we are, but didn't have the heartbeat of evangelicals. Let's face it. He didn't have that. God bless him, I like him, but he didn't have that" (*Frontline* 2004: 2). Later, evangelicals complained of a lack of access to the president. According to the Southern Baptist Convention's Richard Land, "In the Reagan administration, they would usually return our phone calls. In the Bush 41 administration, they often would return our phone calls, but not quite as quickly, and sometimes not as receptively. In the Clinton administration, they quit accepting our phone calls after a while" (*Frontline* 2004: 3).

Nonetheless, Clinton's Little Rock lunch with the ministers did pay off in certain respects. About ten ministers came, including such nationally known figures as Charles Swindoll, Adrian Rogers, and Max Lucado. Also included was Hillary Clinton's minister at Little

Rock's First United Methodist Church, Ed Matthews, who Clinton hoped would "stick with us if the lunch deteriorated into a war of words" (Clinton 2004: 465). Clinton reported that he was "especially impressed with the young, articulate pastor of Willow Creek Community Church near Chicago, Bill Hybels. He had built his church from scratch into one of the largest single congregations in America. Like the others, he disagreed with me on abortion and gay rights, but he was interested in other issues too, and in what kind of leadership it would take to end the gridlock and reduce the partisan bitterness in Washington" (Clinton 2004: 465). Clinton developed a lasting friendship with Hybels, a friendship which (as noted below) sparked considerable controversy toward the end of Clinton's presidency.

Among Clinton's chief policy advisers during his first term, few were more important than vice president, Al Gore. The two leaders met for weekly, private lunches that began with one or the other of them saying a short prayer (Woodward 1996: 13). It is certainly possible that these prayers represented more than an expression of superficial religiosity for, at times, Clinton seemed genuinely interested in relating his religion to his policy positions. Early in his presidency, Clinton established a White House liaison to faith communities In addition, Clinton vigorously pursued one of his key interests, freedom of religious expression. As Clinton put it, "Sometimes I think the environment in which we operate is entirely too secular. The fact that we have freedom of religion doesn't mean that we need to try to have freedom from religion. It doesn't mean that those of us who have faith shouldn't frankly admit that we are animated by faith" (Roberts 2004: 2).

In his autobiography, Clinton reports his concerns over the "incorrect" views of some school officials and teachers that all religious expression is unacceptable in the schools. In response, Clinton "asked Secretary [of Education] Riley and Attorney General Reno to prepare a detailed explanation of the range of religious expression permitted in schools and to provide copies to every school district in America before the start of the next school year" (Clinton 2004: 662). Clinton also enthusiastically signed the 1993 Religious Freedom Restoration Act, a bill designed to reverse a 1990 Supreme Court decision extending the right of states to regulate religious expression.

But no policy area seemed to bring out the preacher in Bill Clinton like the area of civil rights. Addressing the Mason Temple Church of God in Christ, site of Martin Luther King, Jr.'s last sermon, Clinton spoke eloquently about "the great crisis of the spirit that is gripping America today." In his autobiography, Clinton notes that "many commentators later said [the address] was the best speech of my eight years as President" (Clinton 2004: 559). According to Clinton, "I put away my notes" and spoke "to my friends from my heart in the language of our shared heritage." In his speech, Clinton decried inner city violence and the breakup of the black family. Later, he asserted that "[t]he Memphis speech was a hymn of praise to a public philosophy rooted in my personal religious values. Too many things were falling apart; I was trying to put them together" (Clinton 2004: 559–560).

Clinton's commitment to civil rights also played a role in the selection of Bill and Hillary's Washington church, Foundry Methodist Church on 16th Street near the White House. According to Clinton, "We liked Foundry's pastor, Phil Wogaman, and the fact that the church included people of various races, cultures, incomes, and political affiliations, and openly welcomed gays" (Clinton 2004: 563). Later, Rev. Wogaman would assume an important role as a counselor to the president during the darkest days of the Lewinsky scandal.

Religion in the Second Clinton Administration

During Clinton's second administration, the president increasingly turned his attention to international politics and traveled widely around the globe. The irrepressible "Pastor" Clinton frequently mixed religious and political values throughout his travels. In Northern Ireland, for example, Clinton called for peace between warring Protestant and Catholic factions, pointing out that, for Jesus, "no words are more important than these: 'Blessed are the peacemakers, for they shall inherit the earth' " (Clinton 2004: 687). In Israel, Clinton knelt and said a prayer the grave of Yitzhak Rabin and, following Jewish custom, placed a stone on the grave (Clinton 2004: 703). And in China, Clinton attended Sunday services at Congwenmen Church, Beijing's oldest Protestant church, and one of the few permitted by the Chinese government (Clinton 2004: 794).

Not all of Clinton's foreign adventures went smoothly. In South Africa, for example, President Clinton and Hillary Clinton, both Protestants, received the Eucharist at a Catholic Church, an act contrary to Catholic teaching. Although the White House claimed that the act was done at the invitation of the local priest, the priest seems to have given reluctant acquiescence (without the knowledge of the bishop) in order not to be rude to the president. Despite criticism from

Catholic leaders, the president refused to apologize and indicated that he was, in fact, happy with his actions (Alt 1998).

Clinton also ruffled some feathers when he offered to help actor, John Travolta, with his pet project—getting Scientology accepted as a religion in Germany. A controversy arose because of the peculiar timing of Clinton's offer, just before Travolta was scheduled to play the role of the president in an upcoming movie, "Primary Colors." The movie was based on Joe Klein's best-selling book about a lying, womanizing Southern governor who bore a striking resemblance to Clinton. Acting on Travolta's behalf, Clinton went so far as assigning National Security Adviser Sandy Berger to the task of working with Germany. As Travolta admitted, the president was able to "seduce" him by offering to help with Scientology, "the one issue that really matters to me." Perhaps as a result, the movie script, in Travolta's words, served to "promote what a decent person he is" (Massarella 1998).

Nevertheless, public perceptions of Clinton's decency were shaken not only by Whitewater-related charges of financial misdeeds (Johnson 2001: 253–256) and Travelgate charges concerning the firing of the White House travel staff, but, most notably, by repeated allegations of "womanizing." Clinton's 1992 presidential campaign was rocked by allegations from Gennifer Flowers that she had carried on a 12-year affair with the former governor (Kurtz 1998; Stewart 1996). Two years later, another woman, Paula Jones, initiated a sexual-harassment lawsuit against Clinton, ultimately producing an $850,000 out-of-court financial settlement (Froomkin 1998). But perhaps most troublesome were allegations that Clinton had engaged in a scandalous affair with White House intern, Monica Lewinski, in 1995–1997.

The Lewinski affair and Clinton's efforts at concealment rocked the White House and led to the president's impeachment. In addition, the scandal seemed to generate a spiritual crisis in the president. Clinton asked three pastors to counsel him at least once a month for an indefinite period. Among these three were J. Philip Wogaman, Minister of Foundry Methodist Church, Tony Campolo, a friend who was a professor of Sociology at Eastern College, and Gordon MacDonald, senior pastor of Grace Chapel in Lexington, Massachusetts (Clinton 2004: 810–811). Other clergy, including Bill Hybels from Willow Creek Community Church, Rex Horne from Clinton's home church in Little Rock, Jesse Jackson, and Billy Graham also served as counselors to the president (Olasky 1999; Service, Fundamental Baptist Information 2001).

There is considerable debate over whether these counseling sessions produced a profound and lasting spiritual change in the president.

Rev. Bill Hybels thought so; in 1997 Hybels praised the president for his "increasing desire to know God and to live for him" and reported that he had seen the president grow spiritually in the monthly private meetings they had held during Clinton's first administration (Cloud 2000). Clinton himself praised his spiritual counselors, suggesting that they "more than fulfilled their commitment, usually coming to the White House together, sometimes separately. We would pray, read scripture, and discuss some things I had never really talked about before. . . . Even though they were often tough on me, the pastors took me past the politics into soul-searching and the power of God's love" (Clinton 2004: 811).

But Clinton critics remained unconvinced of the president's sincerity. Conservative columnist, Cal Thomas, argued that "the final refuge of scoundrels is religion" and charged Clinton's pastoral counselors with cloaking the president with respectability "even while he lives and lies as he pleases" (Thomas 1998: 1). Thomas also criticized the ministers, claiming that they permitted themselves to be manipulated by Clinton because they "love the limelight" (Thomas 1998: 2). Another Clinton critic, Marvin Olasky reported that "after three years of meetings, one regular minister to the President merely shook his head when asked if progress was being made in the central issue of having the president stop blaming others and start accepting responsibility himself" (Olasky 1999: 259). ABC's Peggy Wehmeyer suggested that Clinton's efforts to seek spiritual counseling had psychological roots, arguing that Clinton has a need to receive the gratification of knowing some accept him as a man of faith" (Olasky 1999: 259). In addition critics suggested that Clinton's efforts were politically motivated, "an attempt to cut into the tendency of Evangelicals to vote Republican" (Olasky 1999: 259).

Following his address to the nation on the Monica Lewinsky affair, Clinton made a public request for forgiveness at the annual White House prayer breakfast on September 11, 1998. A contrite Clinton publicly apologized to his family, friends, and the nation, stating that "I have sinned." In his address, Clinton expressed sorrow for his actions, a spirit of repentance, and "a desire to repair breaches of my own making." Clinton concluded his speech by quoting Scripture, "I ask you to share my prayer that God will search me and know my heart, try me and know my anxious thoughts, see if there is any hurtfulness in me, and lead me toward life everlasting" (Clinton 1998).

In the religious community, reaction to Clinton's speech and confession was mixed. Dr. Joan Brown Campbell, general secretary of the National Council of Churches, described the atmosphere at the prayer breakfast as "deeply spiritual" although she told reporters that it was still an open question whether Clinton was "prepared to be a repentant sinner." A leading African American clergyman, James Forbes, senior minister of New York City's Riverside Church, reported that "it felt like a real holy moment. There was not a single false note. Here is a man who has been anointed by grace and awaits restoration" (Herlinger 1998). Clinton supporters noted that all humans sin and are in need of forgiveness. Asserted Presbyterian minister, James Dowd of the Church of the Covenant in Cleveland, "From King David to the apostle Peter, who denied Christ three times at the end of Jesus' life, even many Biblical figures have had to overcome serious flaws in their lives" (Briggs 1999).

On the other hand, Old Testament scholar, Susanne Scholz of the College of Wooster charged Clinton with hermeneutic abuse of the Bible. Moreover, members of the conservative National Association of Evangelicals and (Clinton's own denomination) the Southern Baptist Convention refused to attend the prayer breakfast and called on the president to resign from office. So did Herbert Chilstrom, former presiding bishop of the Evangelical Lutheran Church in America, arguing that "to be tempted is one thing; to fall is another. To fall once and be sorrowful is one thing; to fall again and again, and only admit to an 'inappropriate relationship' when one is caught is another" (Herlinger 1998). Former Reagan speechwriter Peggy Noonan, who attended the prayer breakfast, protested, "He's talking to us as if he is a moral leader and we are the nice people being led. He's providing moral instruction to a room full of ministers. Then I thought: And this is Bill Clinton!" (Neuhaus 1999: 26).

Critics in the academic community also weighed in, not only on Clinton's prayer breakfast remarks, but more generally on his public and private morality. A couple of days after the prayer breakfast two biblical scholars, Robert Jewitt of Garrett-Evangelical Theological Seminary, and Klyne Snodgrass of North Park Seminary, began circulating a developing "Declaration" highly critical of Clinton's behavior. By the spring of 1999, a total of 192 scholars, many of them faculty members at prominent seminaries, had signed the Declaration (Fackre 2000: 11).[2]

The controversy over Clinton and his behavior proved to have particular significance for one of his spiritual advisers, Bill Hybels of Willow Creek Community Church, following the church's decision to invite Clinton to speak at the Willow Creek Association's year 2000 leadership conference. An open letter from 600 congregants of the mega-church questioned the decision of Hybels and the church's six elders to invite Clinton. Many congregants were upset that Hybels had invited a pro-choice speaker with a record of personal immorality. Hybels was forced to field questions from a group of angry church members and admitted that "I was probably willing to risk more than I should have." Still, Hybels defended the Clinton invitation, arguing that he wanted to banish hate and encourage Christians to see Clinton as a "real person" (Cutrer 2000).

Since leaving the White House, Bill Clinton has continued his practice of mixing religion and politics. In September 2003, for example, Clinton addressed a campaign rally for Governor Gray Davis, held at Los Angeles' First African Methodist Church. Clinton admitted that "The governor . . . might have made a mistake or two" but enjoined his audience to practice restraint. In biblical language, Clinton admonished the audience, "Let he among you without sin cast the first stone" (Brown 2003: 1).

Clinton also helped to inject religion into the 2004 presidential election when he gave a controversial speech at New York City's Riverside Church on the eve of the Republican National Convention. According to Joseph Knippenberg of the Ashcroft Center, "The speech was part of a campaign—long urged by former Clinton aides Mike McCurry and John Podesta, and taken up by Riverside Church—for the Democrats and religious progressives to reclaim the language of faith from conservatives" (Knippenberg 2004). Addressing over 3,000 New Yorkers (Newswire 2004), Clinton contrasted the agenda of the Republicans ("anti-abortion, anti-gay rights, concentration of wealth and power") with that of the Democrats ("commitment to the common good, concern for the poor and vulnerable, the middle class families, the preservation of our God-given environment, unity over division, and . . . truth in campaign advertising") (Knippenberg 2004). In strident language, Clinton argued that religious conservatives allied with the GOP "believe . . . that all who disagree with them are somehow almost non-human" (Knippenberg 2004). Whether such stridency represents a new, bitter, and increasingly partisan phase in the life of Bill Clinton remains an open question. But there is little doubt that his rhetoric is rooted in both his religious heritage and political experience.

Conclusions

This chapter began with the observation that Bill Clinton is a personal and political enigma. An examination of the role of religion in his life does little to change this perception. There may never be a scholarly consensus on the precise nature of Clinton's religion and the role it played in his personal and public life. At the risk of oversimplification, one can identify three different schools of thought on the matter.

A Sham Religion?

One school of thought labels Clinton's religion as a sham, a tool that he manipulated for personal and professional ends. In this view, Clinton is, at best, a hypocrite, able to publicly profess his sins but unwilling to reform his behavior (Herlinger 1998; Olasky 1999). At worst, in this view, Clinton cynically utilized Christian symbols of love, confession, and forgiveness to win election and earn a sort of public redemption for his sins (Fackre 1999).

Certainly it is possible to marshal considerable supporting evidence for this perspective. Clinton's apparently repetitive cycle of "womanizing" followed by confession lends credence to the charge of hypocrisy. And, as we have seen, a variety of actions, ranging from Clinton's newfound religion after his gubernatorial defeat to his use of biblical language and symbols on the campaign trail to his public involvement with prominent clergy lend credence to the manipulation charge. Indeed, Clinton's life provides plenty of ammunition for those who would question both his integrity and honesty. As Richard Neuhaus notes, even Clinton's "friends and allies have said that he is a remarkably good liar" (Neuhaus 1999: 5).[3]

In this light, some observers have labeled the Clinton administration a "postmodern" presidency. Clinton is viewed as a political chameleon, able to shift his political positions with changes in public opinion and to adapt his religious beliefs and practices to the needs of the day. Such observers argue that, for Clinton, there were few absolute moral or ethical standards to guide behavior; expediency and flexibility were all that mattered (Schier 2000).

American Civil Religion?

A more nuanced conclusion views Clinton's religion as an example of American civil religion. As Mark Silk notes, "The use of religious language to clothe the places and processes of American government (Oval Office as Holy of Holies) has been a national habit ever since the signers of the Declaration of Independence announced their 'firm reliance on the protection of Divine Providence' and pledged their 'sacred honor' to each other" (Silk 1999: 1). Thus, in utilizing religious language and engaging in religious practices, Clinton was following in a long and venerable tradition of the American presidency; indeed, he was doing precisely what Americans have come to expect and even demand of their leaders (Sharman 1995).

Theologian Stanley Hauerwas extends this analysis by arguing that Clinton's "civil religion" was of a particular type, the "civil religion of mainstream Protestantism," a perspective that "assumes that religion is supposed to have something to do with the inner life" but has relatively little to do with public life (Hauerwas 1999: 30). Thus, Clinton was able to justify marital infidelity, telling himself "that he is doing such important work, moral work, as President that he can indulge privately as long as no one gets hurt. That is why the problem from his perspective is not what he did but that he got caught." In Hauerwas' view, then, saying that Clinton's "confession at the Presidential prayer breakfast was insincere or cynical is an inadequate account of the challenge before us. I suspect that Clinton was as sincere as he could be" (Hauerwas 1999: 29–30).

In an interesting way, Hauerwas' analysis sheds light on the observation of Nigel Hamilton (above) that the young Billy Clinton *did* feel saved, if only from a depressing and oppressive family life. For Clinton, religion could inspire, guide, and perhaps provide a sense of meaning in life, even if it had only a limited role in directing his "private" life.

A Religion of Second Chances?

A third approach suggests that it is impossible to simply classify the religion of Bill Clinton. Certainly, Clinton did, at times, manipulate religion for personal and political ends. And there is little doubt that Clinton was among the most skillful practitioners of American civil religion.

Yet a detailed reading of Clinton's life suggests that, in his own way, he is a profoundly spiritual man. Clinton never could entirely separate himself from his Baptist roots and did not seem to wish to do so. Indeed, one could argue that Clinton's public religiosity was so convincing because it was indeed rooted in a personal, spiritual core. As we have seen, many of the clergy who knew Clinton best and spent the most time with him tended to share this perspective.

It may be that Clinton's spirituality stemmed not only from his childhood experiences but also from recognition of his personal character flaws. While cynics might scoff at Clinton's public confession of sin, many of Clinton's Baptist coreligionists would recognize the depth of human depravity, the need for repentance and forgiveness, and the difficulty of following the "straight and narrow" path of redemption and salvation.

Clinton once remarked, "The Bible teaches us that we've all failed. We'll all continue to fail." In 1993, Clinton told religion reporters that he appreciated Christianity's "idea of continuous coming back." And once, when asked if he believed in an afterlife, Clinton responded, "Yeah, I have to. I need a second chance" (Olasky 1999: 262). Given his track record, Clinton may need a few additional chances. In that respect, at least, Clinton is not alone

Notes

1. Some orthodox Christians would argue that the use of the New Covenant terminology to describe a political agenda constitutes a blasphemous misuse of biblical terminology. In the biblical New Testament the term New Covenant refers to a new covenant between God and believers, in which faith in Christ supplants previous demands for adherence to legalistic demands (II Corinthians 3: 6; Hebrews 8).
2. A list of early signers as well as a thoughtful analysis of the Declaration can be found in Fackre (1999).
3. Neuhaus also suggests, however, that a truly good liar is able to escape suspicion of being a liar.

References

Alt, Robert. 1998. Clinton Finds Religion. *The Washington Times*/Ashbrook Center. Available from http://www.ashbrook.org/org/publlicat/oped/alt/98/clintonreligion.html (accessed September 11, 2004).

Bennett, William J. 1998. *The Death of Outrage*. New York: Simon & Schuster.

Briggs, David. 1999. Clinton's Faith an Enigma to Observers. *Baptist Standard*. Available from http://www.baptiststandard.com/1999/3_3/pages/clinton.html (accessed March 3, 1999).

Brown, Steve. 2003. Davis/Clinton Church Rally Sparks Call for IRS Investigation. The Nation/Cybercast News Service, 2003. Available from http://www.cnsnews.com/ViewNation.asp?Page=%5CNation%5Carchive%5C200309%5C . . . (accessed September 14, 2004).

Clinton, Bill. 1995. Religious Liberty in America. USIA. Available from http://www.religioustolerance.org/clinton1.htm.

———. 1998. Asking Forgiveness. Holistic Living. Available from http://1stholistic.com/Reading/liv_speeches-asking-forgiveness-bill-clinton.htm (accessed September 14, 2004).

———. 2004. *My Life*. New York: Knopf.

Cloud, David. 2000. Church Leaders Praise Bill Clinton's "Spirituality." Fundamental Baptist Information Service. Available from http://www.jesus-is-savior.com/church_leaders_praise_bill_clinton.htm (accessed September 14, 2004).

Cutrer, Corrie. 2000. Clinton Visit Provokes Church Members. *Christianity Today*. Available from http://www.christianitytoday.com/ct/2000/134/54.0.html (accessed September 14, 2004).

Fackre, Gabriel J. 1999. *Judgment Day at the White House: A Critical Declaration Exploring Moral Issues and the Political use and Abuse of Religion*. Grand Rapids, MI: Wm. B. Eerdmans.

———. 2000. *The Day After: A Retrospective on Religious Dissent in the Presidential Crisis*. Grand Rapids, MI: Wm. B. Eerdmans.

Frontline. 2004. The Jesus Factor: Religion In the White House Then and Now. PBS, 2004. Available from http://www.pbs.org/wgbh/pages/frontline/shows/jesus/president/religion.html (accessed September 11, 2004).

Froomkin, Dan. 1998. Case Closed. *The Washington Post*. Available from file://C:\DOCUME~1\penn\LOCALS~1\Temp\5BQVWFTU.htm (accessed October 27, 2004).

Hamilton, Nigel. 2003. *Bill Clinton: An American Journey*. New York: Random House.

Hauerwas, Stanley. 1999. Why Clinton is Incapable of Lying: A Christrian Analysis. In *Judgement Day at the White House*, edited by G. J. Fackre. Grand Rapids, MI: Wm. B. Eerdmans.

Herlinger, Chris. 1998. Clinton Tells Religious Leaders: "I have sinned." Ecumenical News International. Available from http://www.layman.org/layman/news-around-church/clinton-tells-ihave-sinned.htm (accessed September 14, 2004).

Jackson, Wayne. 2001. Bill Clinton: A Presidential Paradox. *Christian Courier*. Available from http://www.christiancourier.com/penpoints/upDown.htm (accessed September 14, 2004).

Johnson, Haynes Bonner. 2001. *The Best of Times: America In the Clinton Years*, 1st ed. New York: Harcourt.

Kengor, Paul. 2004. Undivine Double Standard. *National Review*. Available from http://www.nationalreview.com/com/comment/kengor2004/200409070843.asp (accessed September 11, 2004).

Knippenberg, Joseph. 2004. *Bill Clinton and the Bully Pulpit*. Ashbrook Center. Available from http://ww.ashbrook.org/publicat/guest/04/knippenberg/clinton.html (accessed September 14, 2004).

Kurtz, Howard. 1998. *Spin Cycle: Inside the Clinton Propaganda Machine*. New York: Free Press.

Maraniss, David. 1995. *First in His Class: A Biography of Bill Clinton*. New York: Simon & Schuster.

Massarella, Linda. 1998. Travolta Admits Bill Used Sects Appeal to Woo Scientologists. *New York Post*. Available from http://www.antisectes.net/charlie1.htm (accessed September 11, 2004).

Neuhaus, Richard John. 1999. The Public Square. *First Things* Available from http://www.firstthings.com/ftissues/ft9906/public.html (accessed September 11, 2004).

Newswire, P. R. 2004. *At Rare Appearance at Riverside Church, Former President Bill Clinton Offered His Support of the Mobilization 2004 Campaign.* PR Newswire, 2004. Available from http://www.findlaw.com/prnewswire/2004/ 20040830/30aug2004173515.html (accessed September 14, 2004).

Olasky, Marvin N. 1999. *The American Leadership Tradition: Moral Vision from Washington to Clinton.* New York: Free Press.

Pfiffner, James P. 2000. Presidential Character: Multidimensional or Seamless? In *The Clinton scandal and the future of American government,* edited by M. J. Rozell and C. Wilcox. Washington, DC: Georgetown University Press.

Renshon, Stanley Allen. 1996. *High Hopes: The Clinton Presidency and the Politics of Ambition.* New York: New York University Press.

Roberts, Peter. 2004. *William Jefferson Clinton.* Available from http://www.geocities.com/peterroberts.geo/Relig-Politics/WJClinton.html (accessed September 11, 2004).

Sadiq, Luqman. 1996. *Bill Clinton—A Profile in Genius.* Available from http://pearly-abraham.tripod.com/htmls/bill-genius.html (accessed September 14, 2004).

Schier, Steven E. 2000. *The Postmodern Presidency: Bill Clinton's Legacy in U.S. Politics.* Pittsburgh: University of Pittsburgh Press.

Service, Fundamental Baptist Information. 2001. *The Preachers Who Influenced Bill Clinton.* Available from http://www.wayoflife.org/fbns/reachers-billclinton.html (accessed September 14, 2004).

Sharman, J. Michael. 1995. *Faith of the Fathers: Religion and Matters of Faith Contained in the Presidents' Inaugural Addresses from George Washington to Bill Clinton.* Culpeper, VA: Victory Pub.

Silk, Mark. 1999. *A Civil Religious Affair.* The Leonard E. Greenberg Center for the Study of Religion in Public Life. Available from http://www.trincoll.edu/depts/csrpl/RINVol2No1/Civil_Religious.htm (accessed September 11, 2004).

Spirituality, Clinton's False. 2004. *Clinton's False Spirituality.* Weblog. Available from http://www.ictks.com/rush/books/clintondocs/cllint_spirit.html (accessed September 14, 2004).

Stewart, James B. 1996. *Blood Sport: The President and His Adversaries.* New York: Simon & Schuster.

Suskind, Ron. 2004. Without a Doubt. *The New York Times.* Available from http://www.nytimes.com/2004/10/17/magazine/17BUSH.html?ex = 1099127648&ei = 1&e (accessed October 18, 2004).

Thomas, Cal.1998. Stopping Him before He Sins Again. *Jewish World Review.* Available from http://www.jewishworldreview.com/cols/thomas 091898.asp (accessed September 11, 2004).

Walker, Martin. 1996. *The President We Deserve: Bill Clinton, His Rise, Falls, and Comebacks*, 1st ed. New York: Crown Publishers.

Woodward, Bob. 1994. *The Agenda: Inside the Clinton White House.* New York: Simon & Schuster.

———. 1996. *The Choice.* New York: Simon & Schuster.

Chapter Eleven

The Faith of George W. Bush: The Personal, Practical, and Political

Carin Robinson and Clyde Wilcox

> One of my core beliefs is that there is an almighty God, and that every man, woman and child on the face of this Earth bears his image. . . . I know many of the leaders gathered in this assembly have been influenced by faith as well. We may profess different creeds and worship in different places, but our faith leads us to common values.
>
> President George W. Bush
> at a United Nations
> conference promoting
> interfaith dialogue in 2008

When historians and political scientists reinterpret the religious beliefs and practices of long-dead presidents, and attempt to ascertain the impact of a president's faith on his politics, they are often limited to a handful of original documents, and a finite amount of historical records. Often the depiction turns on interpretations of a few key facts—whether a president regularly attended church or mentioned God in his personal letters. Often historians wish for a richer source of information.

Scholars writing on the faith and politics of George W. Bush face the opposite problem. There is no shortage of information on the topic—indeed the immense volume is daunting. Although Bush's presidency ended just a few years ago there are already several books that focus on the relationship between Bush's religion and his presidency, including numerous collections of his own writings and speeches. At least numerous different videos were circulated in evangelical churches during the 2004 campaign, detailing aspects of Bush's faith. The number of stories and articles is overwhelming. Early in his second term, a Google search for only one of many possible strings—"George W. Bush + religion" yielded nearly 3 million hits. By 2011, the search yielded nearly 7 million hits.

To make matters more difficult, much of the material on Bush's faith has a clear political slant. During his tenure, Democrats and liberals sought to make Bush into a fanatical fundamentalist who hears God's voice in his head, and follows those those directions. Republicans and conservatives sought to mobilize evangelical voters to support Bush without also mobilizing liberals in opposition by using subtle religious language to describe the president's faith and religious practice. Bush himself has been very careful in his description of his religion, always bearing in mind the political implications.

In this chapter, we will first describe Bush's faith. Next, we will examine the possible impact of that that faith on Bush's presidential style—his Cabinet appointments, his certainty of judgment, and his honesty. Finally, we will evaluate his policy agenda in an attempt to see how and when his faith mattered to his presidency.

A Personal Faith, Carefully Proclaimed

> There's no question that the President's faith is calculated. And there's no question that the president's faith is real.[1]
>
> Doug Wead, Former Assembly of God
> pastor and Bush's family friend

Although Bush was raised in a family that worshiped regularly at a Presbyterian church and that relied on faith to help them cope with the loss of a child, George W. Bush was a troubled young man. As his former speechwriter, David Frum, noted,

> He tried everything his father had tried—and well into his forties, succeeded at almost nothing. The younger Bush scraped through Andover and Yale academically, never made a varsity team, earned no distinction in the Air National Guard. . . . He lost millions in the oil business and had to be rescued by his father's friends in 1983. It was after that last humiliation that he began drinking heavily.

Bush's religious transformation occurred in 1984, when an eccentric evangelist, Arthur Blessitt, came to Midland, Texas, to hold a week-long crusade. Blessitt's trademark was carrying a 12-foot cross on long walks through the United States and abroad. Bush heard his sermons on the radio, and asked a friend to arrange a private meeting. Bush came right to the point, and asked how to "know Jesus Christ and how to follow him." Blessitt shared Bible verses with Bush, and led him in a sinner's prayer.

Most American evangelicals would point to this incident as the day that they accepted Christ and were born again. Yet Bush has never referred to his conversion as a "born-again experience," nor has he spoken publicly about his meeting with Blessitt. Instead, Bush's account of his personal conversion generally centers on a later meeting with evangelist Billy Graham. Writing in his autobiography, he says of his talk with Graham: "It was the beginning of a new walk where I would recommit my heart to Jesus Christ. I was humbled to learn that God sent His Son to die for a sinner like me."[2] Bush speaks of his encounter with Graham as a "rededication," that "sparked a change in my heart" or a "renewal of personal faith" In his 2010 memoir, he reminisces about the presence of Graham the man, how it inspired him and convicted him.

Bush's careful avoidance of the label "born again," and his focusing on mainstream evangelical Billy Graham instead of the more colorful Blessitt shows the calculation with which Bush discusses his faith. He told Doug Wead, a former pastor and family friend, "As you said, there are some code words. There are some proper ways to say things, and some improper ways." He added, "I am going to say that I've accepted Christ into my life. And that's a true statement."[3]

While in office, Bush used carefully crafted phrases to signal to evangelicals that he is one of them, without necessarily attracting the attention of nonevangelicals. When asked if Muslims and Christians worship the same God, Bush replied that he believed that they did, but quickly added that "I don't get to decide who goes to heaven, I am on my own personal walk". The phrase "personal walk" would be recognized by evangelicals but not by those outside the tradition, and served to calm nerves jangled by the ecumenical response to the question.

Yet if Bush talks about his faith in a calculated way, there is little doubt among those who know him that it is real. He has frequently spoken of the way that faith has transformed his life. "As I deepened my understanding of Christ, I came closer to my original goal of being a better person—not because I was racking up points on the positive side of the heavenly ledger, but because I was moved by God's love."[4] He credits his conversion to his ability to quit drinking: "There is only one reason I am in the Oval Office and not in a bar. I found faith. I found God."[5] Bush reads the Bible, prays, and has read *My Utmost for His Highest* as a daily devotional. Bush participated in a men's Community Bible Study Fellowship in Midland, Texas and was particularly shaped by the small group experience of evangelical Christianity while there. In the small group, Bush became comfortable speaking of his faith with others, a skill useful when standing before a Christian conservative audience during a campaign. He was asked to join the study by his close friend, and later Commerce Secretary Don Evans. The small group Bible study culture was apparent early on in the Bush White House. His former speechwriter, David Frum, in his memoir says, " 'Missed you at Bible study' were quite literally the very first words I heard spoken in the Bush White House."[6]

The same religious experience can have markedly different consequences in different people. For example, Bush incorporated elements of evangelical Christianity that are consistent with his core personality, and that were socially constructed in a small group evangelical culture. Bush's core personality traits include a strong desire to win at all costs and a belief in public service that were inculcated by his family. He has always shown a lack of curiosity about abstract matters and even factual details, an intuitive way of understanding, and an instinctive decision style. The small group evangelical culture often emphasizes faith as a source of strength, and as a way of overcoming personal weakness.

Bush describes his faith in the language of self-help evangelicalism, principally referring to how his faith makes him feel. In the second presidential debate in 2004, Bush noted, "Prayer and religion sustain me. I receive calmness in the storms of the presidency. I love the fact that people pray for me and my family all around the country. Somebody asked me one time, how do you know? I said I just feel it." Bush told Bill O'Reilly of the Fox News Channel "I'm asked a question,—[W]hat does faith mean to me? It means strength and calm in the face of the storm. I mean, I do rely on prayer, and I am empowered by the fact, I'm empowered by the fact that people pray for me.—I'm sustained by that, not empowered—I'm sustained by that, is a better word. I don't know why people object to somebody who—when asked—says religion's important."[7]

Lyman Kellstedt has argued that "the predominant emphasis of evangelicalism is doctrine. It is 'right' doctrine that self-identified an evangelical's look for when they 'check out' a person's Christian credentials."[8] Bush's discussion of his faith, however, is almost entirely devoid of doctrine. Although Bush has participated in Bible study groups that have undertaken in-depth studies of Luke and Acts, he seldom mentions theology or quotes the Bible as a source for his policies or values.[9] This fits Bush's personal focus on intuitive understanding, and his lack of focus on abstract ideas or details. He may very well have an intellectual appreciation for Scripture, but he has not spoken of his faith in those terms.

Although frequently referred to as a fundamentalist, Bush does not believe that the Bible is literally true. Indeed, his discussion of the authority of the Bible is once again couched in emotional language. "From Scripture you can gain a lot of strength and solace and learn life's lessons. That's what I believe, and I don't necessarily believe every single word is literally true."[10] Bush biographer David Aikman said he "could not get from anybody a sort of credo of what [Bush] believes."[11] Another reporter described Bush's faith as "practical, instinctive," implying that it is not very doctrinally rigorous. Similarly, a 2004 *Washington Post* headline reads, "Openly Religious to a Point, Bush Leaves the Specifics of His Faith to Speculation."

Bush admits to a lack of interest in religious doctrine. When he married Laura he became a member of the Methodist Church and was asked by a reporter in 1994 what the differences were between the two denominations. He replied, "The Episcopal Church is very ritualistic, and it has a kind of repetition to the service. It's the same service, basically, over and over again. Different sermons, of course. The Methodist Church is lower key. We don't have the kneeling. And I'm sure there is some heavy doctrinal differences as well, which I'm not sophisticated enough to explain to you."[12]

Indeed, Bush's personal religion seems remarkably ecumenical. Bush worshiped at an Episcopal Church in Washington that has welcomed gays, and he has prayed with Hindus and Sikhs, and has stated that Muslims and Christians worship the same God. At the 2000 Republican National Convention, he noted, "I believe in tolerance, not in spite of my faith, but because of it. I believe in a God who calls us not to judge our neighbors, but to love them."[13]

Bush may well emphasize the emotional side of his faith because that unites most Christians and even believers of other faiths, whereas doctrine divides. In short, doctrinal talk is bad politics. Pat Robertson's presidential campaign encountered resistance from fundamentalist and evangelical Christians who were uncomfortable with his charismatic religious practices.[14] Although Paul Kengor has correctly noted that Bush did not campaign in churches and referred to religion, Jesus, and the Bible less in office than did Bill Clinton,[15] it is clear that Bush's campaign in 2000 and 2004 was heavily geared toward mobilizing evangelical voters. Indeed, increasing evangelical turnout was the centerpiece of the 2004 strategy; so Bush's lack of doctrinal talk could possibly be politically motivated, but it also fits with other descriptions of Bush's intellectual style.

During his years as governor of Texas, Bush was not the first choice of the Christian Right, and movement activists blocked his selection as chair of the Texas delegation to the 1996 GOP convention.[16] Bush worked hard to appeal to Christian Right leaders prior to his campaign for the GOP nomination, crisscrossing the country to deliver his personal testimony to individuals and small groups. The power of his personal statement and its evident sincerity allowed Bush to win support without making policy promises on controversial issues such as gay rights and abortion.[17] Bush carefully developed the theme of the prodigal son for the 2000 campaign, and drew attention to his faith with statements such as "Jesus is my favorite philosopher because he changed my life" during the debates,[18] though Karen Hughes asserts this comment was completely unrehearsed and surprised even his staff.

In 2004, although Bush did not personally campaign in churches, his campaign sought to use churches as political bases. Evangelical churches were encouraged to establish liaisons with the campaign, and to share membership lists—a move that brought a strong rebuke from Southern Baptist spokesman Richard Land.[19] Even more striking was a mailing in West Virginia and a few other states by the Republican National Committee, which warned that liberals wanted to place a ban on Bibles—a theme that had previously been echoed by mailings of Concerned Women for America.

With the Christian Coalition in shambles, a new coalition of non-party groups chose to highlight Bush's faith in churches. Let Freedom Ring produced a video, which they distributed over the internet, and distributed to pastors along with promises of legal defense from any IRS challenge if the right procedures were followed. The video focused primarily on Bush's religious faith and practice, and was intended primarily as an electoral tool. Another video shown in evangelical churches, "George W. Bush: FAITH in the White House" stated on the back cover, "Like no other president in the history of the nation, George W. Bush boldly, publicly, and genuinely lives out his faith on the job . . . Nobody spends more time on his knees than George W. Bush. The Bush administration hums to the sound of prayer."[20]

Conservative evangelicals were a solid base of support for Bush. Many prayed that Bush would win, others offered thanks after the balloting was over. The Family Research Council praised "values voters" for giving the then president four more years. James Dobson, president of Focus on the Family, said in a press release, "We applaud the re-election of President Bush, who has shown himself a true champion for the family and of traditional values." During the 2005 Inauguration, Billy Graham prayed to God before a national audience, "We believe that in Your providence, You have granted a second term of office to our President, George W. Bush".

There is little doubt that evangelical enthusiasm for Bush was based primarily on belief in the sincerity of his faith. Evangelicals believe that God guides Christians, and so a president who spends time on his knees will ultimately make the right decisions. This bought Bush some leeway in negotiating with Christian Right leaders, who were not always happy with his policies.

Faith and Presidential Style

I don't see how you can be president . . . without a relationship with
the Lord.[21]

George W. Bush, at start of his second term

Bush's critics charged that his administration was filled with men and
women who also ask God for guidance, and come away convinced
that God has blessed their preferred policies. They worried that faith
can lead the president and his staff to ignore subtle distinctions, and to
refuse to accept evidence that contradicts the policies that they believe
God has dictated. In 2004 Esther Kaplan noted, "This is an administration where weekly Bible study is attended by more than half of the
White House staff, and daily Bible study in the Department of Justice
is presided over by the Attorney General."[22] David Frum noted that
although attendance at Bible study "was, if not compulsory, not quite
uncompulsory either."

It was not prayer and Bible study that worried observers like
Kaplan, it was that religion served as a keystone of a presidential style
of decision making that leads from gut instincts and refuses to consider new evidence. In this section we consider three elements of Bush's
presidential style—his appointments, his certitude, and his honesty.

Presidential Advisers

It is clear that Bush appointed a number of deeply conservative
Christians to his Cabinet and White House staff, and to other
government posts. What is not clear is whether these appointments
were anything out of the ordinary. Presidents normally appoint a
Cabinet that represents the powerful constituencies in their party,
rewarding groups for their previous political support and hoping to
build lasting ties for their reelection bids. Reagan and Bush's father
both had conservative Christians throughout their administrations.

The nomination of Christian Right favorite John Ashcroft as
attorney general brought cheers from Christian Right groups who
had lobbied for Ashcroft as soon as his Senate reelection campaign
faltered. The son of a Pentecostal pastor, Ashcroft was strongly
pro-life, opposed to physician-assisted suicide, supportive of accom-
modation of public displays of Christianity. The position of attorney
general is one of the most important in the Cabinet, and one with
substantial influence over issues that evangelicals find important.

Other key Cabinet appointments went to conservatives outside the movement. The secretary of treasury was a moderate business leader. Colin Powell's outspoken pro-choice position made him unpopular with evangelicals, and Donald Rumsfeld's opposition to barring gays from serving in the military also rankled.

Some lesser Cabinet positions went to Christian Right favorites. Christian conservatives also applauded the appointment of Gail Norton to the Department of Interior, and Linda Chavez to the Department of Labor, although the latter withdrew her nomination. Less visible to most voters, but clearly visible to conservative Christians, were key appointments below the Cabinet level. For example, the appointment of conservative litigator Eric Treene as Special Counsel for religious discrimination in the Justice Department signaled an administration that would be friendly on church-state issues. One delegation to the UN Special Session on Children as loaded Christian conservatives, and one grant to help counsel Iraqi women in democratic government went to a strongly antifeminist group that advises women to stay home with their children. Kay Cole James, longtime pro-life activist, was selected to head the Office of Personnel Management.

Conservative Christians are deeply embedded throughout the administration, and more common than in the earlier Reagan presidency. Yet their numbers do not seem incommensurate with their political importance to the president. Mobilizing evangelicals was the core strategy in Bush's reelection drive, and such crucial constituencies often have positions of power in presidential administrations. It is clear that Bush's Cabinet and staff are sufficiently diverse to offer opposing viewpoints, if the president wants to hear them.

It is worth noting that Bush's second term appointments were not as popular with the Christian Right. In his second term, Bush appeared to have chosen primarily men and women who had demonstrated strong personal loyalty, rather than those who appealed to various constituencies. He appointed White House counsel Alberto Gonzales to attorney general in 2005, and National Security Advisor Condoleezza Rice became secretary of state in 2006. This may have reflected the fact that the Bush-Cheney team was the first in more than 40 years where neither will seek the presidency in the next election, and therefore felt less of a need to stroke their Christian Right constituency. Alternatively, it may reflect Bush's preference for personal supporters in the Cabinet. In his 2010 memoir, Bush said his appointments were entirely driven by who was best qualified for the job and made no mention of faith being a relevant factor.

Certitude

Q: "... After 9/11, what would your biggest mistake be, would you say, and what lessons have you learned?"

The President: "I wish you would have given me this written question ahead of time, so I could plan for it ... You know, I just—I'm sure something will pop into my head in the midst of this press conference, with all of the pressure of trying to come up with an answer, but it hasn't yet."

April 13, 2004 press conference

Even given time to think, no mistake ever popped into Bush's head. In the second presidential debate later that year, Bush was presented with the same question, and once again he failed to acknowledge any mistakes. During his administration, Republicans and Democrats alike noted that Bush did not admit mistakes. He makes judgments based on gut instincts, without consulting those with opposing views. Bush himself said, "I'm not a textbook player. I'm a gut player."[23] Then National Security Adviser Rice characterized Bush's decision-making style as "intuitive," and noted, "He least likes me to say, 'This is complex.' "[24]

This is perhaps most notable in Bush's decision to go to war in Iraq. Although there was support within the administration for an attack on Iraq even before 9-11, when the final decision came, Bush did not ask the advice of his key advisers, including then Secretary of State Powell, who eventually sought an audience with the president to speak his mind. He did not even ask his father, who had assembled a very impressive international coalition to defeat Iraq a decade earlier. "You know he is the wrong father to appeal to in terms of strength. There is a higher father that I appeal to," Bush told Bob Woodward (Hamilton 2004). Two things are striking about this last remark. First, Bush appeared to ignore the possibility that his father might have helpful advice in marshaling an international coalition. Since his father is the only person alive who had ever before done what Bush intended to do, the omission is striking.[25] Second, Bush said that he prays for strength, not guidance. Although Bush did occasionally indicate that he asked God for guidance, the overwhelming majority of his statements focused on asking for strength. Indeed, one study of Bush's rhetorical use of religion suggests that unlike most previous presidents who ask for God's support, he asserts it.

Jim Pfiffner, a leading authority on presidential personality and character, wrote in 2003 that "President Bush ... has shown a preference for moral certainty over strategic calculation, a tendency for visceral reaction rather than reflection, a bias toward action instead of deliberation, and a preference for the personal over the structural or procedural."[26] Speaking of Bush's certitude, Christian Coalition founder Pat Robertson characterized Bush as "the most self-assured man I've ever met in my life." He went on to colorfully note, "He looks like a contented Christian with four aces. I mean he was just sitting there like 'I'm on top of the world.' Other members of Bush's inner circle have commented on his lack of curiosity, his intolerance for ambiguous evidence, and his impatience with claims that counter his instincts."[27]

Many have argued that these characteristics flow from Bush's evangelical faith. It is certainly true that evangelical religious beliefs can be consistent with this type of cognitive style. Many evangelicals see human history as a long struggle between divine and satanic forces, and believe that everyone must choose sides in this struggle. Bush's talk of an Axis of Evil, and his call for all nations to choose sides in the war on terror, fit easily within this worldview. Many evangelicals understand all kinds of policy debates as between good and evil, and are less likely to see shades of gray. A number of observers have suggested that Bush's faith led to an oversimplified, black and white view of the world.[28]

In fact, many evangelicals see a far more complicated and nuanced policy debate, and relish the details and complexities of policy debates. Jimmy Carter, a Southern Baptist former Sunday School teacher, focused far more on the details, displayed little certitude about his judgments, and could not be called an intuitive politician. In other words, Bush's cognitive style is not an inevitable result of evangelical faith. Instead, it is likely that Bush's faith reinforced this preexisting style of decision making.[29] Bush parlayed this certitude into a strength during the 2004 campaign, and many voters responded positively to a portrait of a commander-in-chief who was confident of his judgments and unlikely to change course.

Like most evangelicals, Bush seeks to understand God's will for his life, and interprets his biography as consistent with God's plan. Before his announced campaign for the presidency in 2000, he told friends on separate occasions, "I feel like God wants me to run for president. I can't explain it, but I sense my country is going to need me. Something is going to happen and, at that time, my country is going to need me. I know it won't be easy on me or my family, but God wants me to do it."[30] In his 2010 memoir, Bush said he felt called to run after hearing a sermon on the passage in Exodus in which God calls Moses to lead the Israelites out of Egypt. In his first Presidential Inaugural Address Bush said, "We are not this story's author, who fills time and eternity with His purpose. Yet His purpose is achieved in our duty, and our duty is fulfilled in service to one another."[31]

Although Bush's belief that God called him to run for the president has sparked widespread derision among liberals, it is worth emphasizing that many evangelicals believe that God has called them to do particular things. Some think that God called them to coach Little League, to work at a local homeless shelter, to be president of the local PTA. Most do not believe that they actually hear God's voice telling them to do this, but rather listen to the "still small voice" in their souls that pushes them toward one particular decision. The danger that a Christian might hear that voice telling her what she wants to hear is widely acknowledged, leading to the idea that you must "test the Spirit" before deciding that it is God's call. In this case Bush believed that he heard a call to follow in his father's footsteps to the White House.

But although Bush's notion of a call to be president is not uncommon among evangelicals, the notion that God would call you to be *president* at a time when "something is going to happen," suggests a more urgent mission than most. Such a belief would likely contribute to a sense that Bush's decisions were the right ones, and that those who question them are obstructing God's will.

Honesty

> I will restore honesty and integrity to the White House.
> George W. Bush stump speech, 2000

George W. Bush campaigned in 2000 on a pledge to restore honesty to the White House. His promise resonated with a public tired of the Clinton White House, which they perceived as offering up half truth and technicalities. Evangelicals believe in telling the truth, and many interpret the commandment to not bear false witness as more generally prohibiting lying. Yet political scientist James Pfiffner argues that all presidents lie, and that in some occasions, it is a necessity.[32]

Pfiffner concludes, "President Bush misled the country in important ways in his campaign to go to war with Iraq. The consequences of his actions were certainly serious, and thus rank high among presidential deceptions in the modern presidency."[33] Bush almost certainly lied when he said in April and May 2002 that he had no war plans on his desk—after all, Tommy Frank had delivered operational war plans in

February.[34] It is quite possible the plans were not literally on his desk, but if so then Bush drew the distinction purposefully to deceive.

Bush may have initially believed other assertions about Saddam Hussein's links with Al Qaeda and about weapons of mass destruction, but he certainly continued to assert these links long after evidence had accumulated that they were not true. His administration sold Congress on expanded health care benefits for Social Security recipients using data that was repudiated only days later, and he claimed that Social Security would be bankrupt by 2042, a statement that even conservative columnist David Brooks (who supported the proposal) wryly summarized as "I would not necessarily want to take a lie detector test on that particular statement."

The unprecedented dismissal of seven U.S. attorneys by the Department of Justice in 2006 raised additional questions about the integrity of the Bush administration. The White House claimed the dismissals were a result of poor job performance. Critics charged the attorneys were dismissed to impede ongoing investigations of Republican officials or punish those attorneys who did not pursue investigations that might harm the Democratic Party. Bush's personal role in the firings is unclear, but the White House was not forthcoming when pressed by congressional subpoenas for information. In 2010, the Department of Justice prosecutors closed a two-year investigation of the firings determining the action was inappropriately political, but not criminal. The congressional requests concerning the attorney hirings ultimately revealed that White House personnel were at times sending email via a non-government domain hosted on an e-mail server controlled by the Republican National Committee—a possible violation of the Presidential Records Act of 1978 and the Hatch Act.

Overall, it seems that at the halfway point in his presidency, Bush did not rank among the most honest of modern presidents. We are not of course asserting that his faith is the source of his dishonesty, rather that his faith has not led him to practice a noticeably more honest political style than preceding presidents.

Policy

By their works ye shall know them.
Matthew 7:20, King James Version

Although evangelical Christians mobilized enthusiastically behind the candidacy of Ronald Reagan in 1980 and again in 1984, by the end of his presidency discontent was palpable. Many evangelicals believed that Reagan had offered them little more than symbolic reassurances while primarily promoting an agenda that focused on tax cuts and a military buildup. Although Bush began his presidency focused on domestic policy, the terrorist attacks of September 11, 2001 transformed his agenda and occupied most of his attention in the first term. The domestic war on terrorism combined with foreign wars in Afghanistan and Iraq took priority over most other issues. Yet as Christian conservatives mobilized for the 2004 election, with sermons and discussions on "How Would Jesus Vote?" it was primarily domestic issues that dominated the scorecards.

Sexuality, Reproduction, and Life Issues

The issues that motivated religious voters most in 2004 were abortion and gay marriage. When he was president-elect, Bush met with Colin Powell prior to nominating him as secretary of state. Colin Powell was pro-choice and Bush appeared anxious to discuss the ban on U.S. funding of abortions abroad, making sure Powell's personal views on the issue would not interfere with the president's agenda.[35] On his first day in office, the president reversed Clinton's executive order that allowed funding for abortions, keeping a campaign promise that especially pleased his conservative Christian constituency. During his administration, Bush repeatedly called for a "culture of life"—a phrase that resonates strongly with Catholics, but he did not call for the reversal of *Roe v. Wade*, and he repeatedly insisted that he did not have a pro-life litmus tests for federal judges. In a 2004 presidential debate he said when asked about his position on abortion, "I think it's important to promote a culture of life. I think a hospitable society is a society where every being counts and every person matters. I believe the ideal world is one in which every child is protected in law and welcomed to life. I understand there's great differences on this issue of abortion. But I believe reasonable people can come together and put good law in place that will help reduce the number of abortions."[36] In August 2002, Bush signed the Born Alive Infants Protection Act and in November 2003, he signed the partial-birth abortion ban passed by Congress. It is worth noting, however, that Bush did not spend any political capital negotiating with Congress to change the "partial-birth" abortion bill in ways that would enable it to withstand a court challenge, nor did he use the bully pulpit to encourage pregnant women to choose life.

The gay marriage issue was a godsend for the Bush campaign, which had generally taken a moderate position on gay rights. In a taped conversation with Doug Wead, Bush recounted a conversation he had with a Texas minister, Rev. James Robison, "Look, James, I got to tell you two things right off the bat. One, I'm not going to kick gays, because I'm a sinner. How can I differentiate sin?" He later referred to a gathering of the Christian Coalition that negatively portrayed homosexuals. "This crowd uses gays as the enemy. It's hard to distinguish between fear of the homosexual political agenda and fear of homosexuality, however." He went on to say, "This is an issue I have been trying to downplay," Bush said. "I think it is bad for Republicans to be kicking gays." Bush also clarified to Wead that he had not promised not to *hire* gays, but rather not to *fire* them.

Bush had consistently stated an opposition to same-sex marriage, and when the Massachusetts Supreme Court established same-sex marriage in that state, Bush quickly condemned activist judges. But he endorsed a moderate version of a constitutional amendment to ban same-sex marriage only after much deliberation and pressure. He described this in the third presidential debate: "I think it's very important that we protect marriage as an institution between a man and a woman. I proposed a constitutional amendment. The reason I did so was because I was worried that activist judges are actually defining the definition of marriage"[37] When later asked if homosexuality was a choice, he said "I don't know." Bush also said that states should be allowed to provide civil unions for gay and lesbian couples instead of marriage—a position that brought sharp criticism from the Christian Right.

But after the election, Bush returned to this issue only once. In the lead-up to the 2006 midterm elections, Bush spoke in favor of the Marriage Protection Amendment in a speech from the White House. The event was originally scheduled for the Rose Garden but was moved to a plain room inside the White House at the last minute. The presidential seal was not visible and his speech in support of the amendment was characterized by reporters as muted. At one point, Bush told reporters that Congress was simply not ready to amend the Constitution on this issue, so there was little use in trying to persuade Congress to act. But on other issues such as tax cuts, oil policy, and foreign policy, Bush did not back away from an issue because of lack of Congressional support.

Many Christian conservative leaders were dismayed by the president's lack of effort on behalf of the amendment. The Arlington Group, a coalition of Christian conservative groups that had pressed for the amendment, sent a letter to Karl Rove that stated, "We couldn't help but notice the contrast between how the president is approaching the difficult issue of Social Security privatization where the public is deeply divided and the marriage issue where public opinion is overwhelmingly on his side. Is he prepared to spend significant political capital on privatization but reluctant to devote the same energy to preserving traditional marriage? If so it would create outrage with countless voters who stood with him just a few weeks ago, including an unprecedented number of African-Americans, Latinos and Catholics who broke with tradition and supported the president solely because of this issue."[38]

Bush's embryonic stem cell policy enacted in 2001 was a compromise that evangelicals and conservative Catholics preferred to a more liberal policy. Bush used an executive order to limit federal funding to only stem cells derived from embryos that had already been destroyed. He came to the decision after consulting numerous scientific and religious leaders and after consideration of his and Laura's own struggles with infertility. After the Democrat-controlled Congress passed a bill permitting federal funding for research that would destroy live embryos in 2006, Bush for the first time in his presidency vetoed an act by Congress. Bush gave his veto speech surrounded by "snowflake" babies in the East Room of the White House. According to then Chief of Staff Josh Bolten, "I don't think his faith leads him to many policy positions. There are a couple. I think he dissected the stem cell issue very much from the foundation of his core religious beliefs."[39] Indeed, an entire chapter of his post-presidency memoir is committed to stem cell policy—the only other domestic policy issue that received chapter-length treatment was the financial crisis.

Bush has also supported increased funding for abstinence-based sex education, and for abstinence programs in AIDS control. His administration also expanded the "conscience clause" for health-care workers who refuse to provide services based on moral objections. But overall, these issues that dominated election-year discussion in evangelical churches were not a high priority for Bush once in office.

Economics

Bush's first and largest success was to push through substantial tax cuts that primarily benefited the most affluent. By essentially signing a proposal that Republicans had been working on for some time, Bush was able to get a quick affirmative vote in Congress. Bush pushed hard

for further tax cuts, again mostly benefiting affluent citizens and corporations, because he said that it was important to help jumpstart the
economy. Bush never made the federal budget an issue of moral concern, a point raised by liberal evangelical Jim Wallis, who also criticized the administration for pushing for cuts in programs that aid the
poor. Moreover, he did not address debt from a scriptural point of
view, at least publicly. Countless Web sites offer advice to Christians
and warn of the unbiblical notion of debt, citing Proverbs 22:7, "The
borrower is slave to the lender," and many conservative Christians are
nervous about the mounting federal deficit. Bush also succeeded in
passing a very large expansion of the Medicare program, guaranteeing
prescription drug coverage to the elderly. Cost estimates of this program
continue to rise.

Bush never linked these policies to his religious faith, but they
clearly have been the center of Bush's domestic agenda. Bush used
considerable pressure to pass these bills. Senator Jim Jeffords of
Vermont left the Republican Party in part over his resentment of
Bush's pressure on budget and tax issues, and other senators have
strongly expressed their displeasure at the pressure from the White
House. The House vote on the Medicare bill was held open for hours
while pressure was applied to reluctant Republicans, who feared
correctly that the costs of the proposal were understated.

Bush's domestic agenda at the beginning of his second term was
dominated by an effort to create private retirement accounts in the
Social Security system. He did not readily abandon this policy goal,
despite warnings from Republican congressional leaders that his proposal faced long odds. He devoted incredible resources to this issue,
making hundreds of speeches on the topic.

In contrast, Bush spent much less effort on his faith-based initiatives.
Bush's support for these programs was clearly linked in part from his
personal experience with the power of faith to overcome his drinking
problems, and he had pursued some faith-based programs at a modest
level in Texas. He then created the White House Office of Faith-Based
Initiatives at the beginning of his first term as president calling it one
of the "most important initiatives" of the administration. Although
Bush consistently praised those who engaged in faith-based charities
and visited these service providers and given them heightened publicity, there is little question that he spent far less political capital on this
than for tax cuts and deregulation. Former deputy director of the
White House Office of Faith-Based and Community Initiatives, David
Kuo posted an editorial on Beliefnet.com in February 2005, a religious
Web site where he is now employed. He wrote, "From tax cuts to

Medicare, the White House gets what the White House really wants. It never really wanted the 'poor people stuff.' " Despite numerous attempts to expand public and private partnerships with religious institutions, there were few legislative successes related to the faith-based initiative during Bush's eight years in office.[40]

Bush also consistently pushed to weaken environmental regulations, and enforcement of existing regulations. He never tied these issues to his faith. Interestingly, there appears to be growing environmental consciousness among evangelical Christians, so future discussions of the environment may become more suffused with religious rhetoric.

War

The September 11 terrorist attacks set the trajectory for the agenda of the Bush presidency. The attacks fit Bush's prediction that he was called to be president in a time when something important would happen, and his country would need him. After an initially shaky start, Bush found his voice in a speech before a joint session of Congress, where he forcefully declared a war on terrorism. He moved to expand domestic police powers, and sent American troops to first overthrow the fundamentalist Islamic Taliban regime in Afghanistan, and then to overthrow Saddam Hussein in Iraq.

Foreign observers frequently ask if Bush's foreign policy was influenced by eschatological views about the end-times. There is little evidence that Bush sees the Middle East in terms of any end-times prophecy, nor does such an interpretation fit his personal religious style, which emphasizes the emotional strength of faith over religious doctrine. And although there were voices in the administration urging a military confrontation with Iraq before September 11, 2001, Bush does not seem to have been one of those hawks.

But Bush's religious worldview is widely credited for the stark way he depicted the world post 9-11 as divided into forces of good and evil. In November 2001, he told the world, "You are either with us, or you are against us in the war on terror."[41] In his 2002 State of the Union Address, he denounced an Axis of Evil that included Iran and North Korea, but not Syria or Pakistan. He saw Saddam Hussein as an evildoer, who should be removed, a view that observers have linked to his religious worldview.[42] Bush had little patience for evidence that Iraq had no ties to Al Qaeda, or that it might not have weapons of mass destruction. His gut decision was that the Iraqi regime should be overthrown, and this was based on a decision that the regime was evil.

Two other elements of the war on terror are worth noting. First, three days after the attacks Bush told the nation that they were not the result of Muslims, who mostly loved America, but rather of terrorists. Public opinion expert Scott Keeter credits Bush's speech with helping to mute a potentially powerful anti-Muslim backlash, and with helping contain anti-Muslim violence. According to surveys conducted by The Pew Research Center before and after the terrorist attacks on 9/11, Americans felt more favorable toward Muslims following the attacks and Bush's speech.[43] This was especially true for conservative Republicans who may have been particularly in tune to Bush's call for tolerance. This fits Bush's inclusive religious style, and was a statement that contradicted anti-Islamic statements by prominent Christian Right leaders.

But Bush's faith does not appear to have led him to reject arguments in the administration for the torture and mistreatment of prisoners. Bush strongly condemned the scenes of torture in Abu Ghraib prison, calling them the actions of a small number of bad individuals. But in fact there had been an intense debate within the administration over whether the Geneva Convention III on the Treatment of Prisoners of War should apply to Al Qaeda and Taliban prisoners. Over Secretary of State Colin Powell's objections, Bush signed a memo on February 7, 2002 that determined that the convention did not apply. The administration circulated memos that greatly restricted existing definitions of torture, and argued that the president's power as commander-in-chief superseded any laws banning torture.

There is no evidence that Bush knew the details of the torture in advance, but it is also clear that he did not move quickly to discipline those involved. Powell left the administration, but Bush praised Secretary of Defense Donald Rumsfeld, who authorized some of the techniques, and nominated Alberto Gonzales, who had been deeply involved in the legal reasoning justifying torture, as his new attorney general.[44] The deeply disgusting acts captured on film, and many others described since, would seem to call out for accountability and a widespread investigation. Though he did apologize to Jordan's King Abdullah in May 2004 and appeared on Arab TV to denounce the "abhorrent" acts, Bush has continued to maintain that these were isolated acts of bad soldiers. Notable was the religious nature of some of the prisoner abuse, such as women interrogators touching Muslim men with what seemed to be menstrual blood and then denying them access to washing prior to prayers—effectively cutting them off from religious solace.

When the Senate passed a defense appropriation bill that clarified existing U.S. treaty obligations with respect to the treatment of prisoners and banned the "cruel, inhuman and degrading" treatment for all prisoners held in U.S. custody, the Bush administration threatened a veto—which would have been the first in his administration. In response, the *Washington Post* editorial stated, "Let's be clear: Mr. Bush is proposing to use the first veto of his presidency on a defense bill needed to fund military operations in Iraq and Afghanistan so that he can preserve the prerogative to subject detainees to cruel, inhuman and degrading treatment. In effect, he threatens to declare to the world his administration's moral bankruptcy."[45]

Conclusion

> There's all kinds of ways to learn not to be full of self-pity. One, the good book teaches you. You think you got it tough, imagine the risen Lord, how he felt.
>
> President George W. Bush in an interview with
evangelical leader Rick Warren in 2010[46]

Political observers and scholars continue to argue over how faith influenced the Bush presidency. The final months of the Bush administration were spent overseeing the wars in Afghanistan and Iraq and the financial crisis at home. President Bush left office with the lowest approval rating of an outgoing president since Gallup began asking the question, with only 22% job approval. Some historians have ranked him as the most unpopular president in U.S. history.

Bush would like his foreign policy agenda to best be remembered for the advancement of freedom and the protection of life. Bush's second inaugural address and his State of the Union addresses in later years focused heavily on the importance of spreading freedom to the world, something that Bush has cited as an insight gained from his faith. In his second term, he supported the pro-democracy struggles in Georgia and Ukraine and passed the US-India Civil Nuclear Agreement. Bush's contribution to global health is notable for the President Emergency Plan for AIDS Relief which committed billions of dollars to fight the HIV/AIDS pandemic. Bush started a malaria initiative that decreased the disease by half in 15 African countries. In his 2010 memoir, Bush recounts leaving an AIDS clinic in Uganda inspired: "I saw their suffering as a challenge to the words of the Gospel: 'To whom much is given, much is required.'" Yet it is more challenging to see the moral compass that led to the decision to invade Iraq and conduct "enhanced interrogations" of prisoners overseas.

Domestically, Bush focused on the economy over social issues. Social Security, bankruptcy, tort law and even immigration all received greater attention than same-sex marriage and abortion. Little effort was made to link the country's economic concerns to faith or morality. While promoting his 2010 memoir, Bush said his most significant accomplishment was keeping the country safe from terrorist attacks, and his greatest failure to be his inability to secure the passage of Social Security reform.[47] Perhaps Bush's most important legacy may well be Supreme Court appointments. Christian conservatives prayed for a Court that would overturn decisions legalizing abortion and homosexual conduct, and placing limits on government advocacy of religion. But when Sandra Day O'Connor retired and William Rehnquist died, Bush did not appoint visible Christian conservatives to the Court. Instead, he chose John Roberts to replace Rehnquist as chief justice, and Christian conservatives were unhappy with Robert's answers to Senate Judiciary Committee questions in which he voiced support for a generalized right to privacy, and said that *Roe v. Wade* was a precedent deserving of respect. Bush next selected White House counsel Harriet Miers to replace O'Connor. Though the White House reassured evangelical leaders that Miers was pro-life and attended an evangelical church, many Christian Right groups questioned her judicial experience and her commitment to the pro-life cause after reports surfaced that Miers espoused a pro-choice position in the 1980s. After Miers withdrew her name from consideration, Bush nominated Samuel Alito who appeared willing to narrow abortion rights but unwilling to overturn Roe. Bush's legacy in the eyes of Christian conservatives may ultimately hinge on how Roberts and Alito vote on the bench.

After Republicans lost control of Congress in 2006, Bush's presidency faced an unhappy general public, a divided Republican party, and increasingly vocal Christian conservatives who voiced feelings of betrayal. Bush's sluggish and seemingly unsympathetic response to Hurricane Katrina's devastating destruction of New Orleans pushed his approval ratings to new lows, and many Republicans reacted in dismay to his belated promise to spend "whatever it took" to rebuild the city. Christian conservatives wondered aloud if they had been fooled by Bush's profession of faith into supporting a man who did not in his heart back their agenda. Jonathan Chait of the *New Republic* considered two accounts of the relationship between the Christian Right and the Bush presidency in 2005:

The first is that Bush is a genuine ally of social conservatives who, while often cagey in public, takes every opportunity to advance their agenda. As liberals would phrase this interpretation, Bush is a tool of the religious right. The second—utterly diametrical—theory is that Bush is mainly interested in harvesting votes from religious conservatives in order to implement an agenda dominated by his economic backers. In liberal-ese: Social conservatives are hapless GOP dupes. At this point, five years and two Supreme Court nominations into the Bush presidency, we can arrive at a definitive answer. And the verdict is: hapless dupes.[48]

Indeed, it is useful to compare the record of George W. Bush, who has had the warm enthusiasm of white evangelicals, and his father, who did not. Both men concentrated their domestic agenda on tax cuts and deregulation of business, although the father accepted a modest tax increase to pay for the war in Iraq while the son financed his war with borrowing. Both fought a war in Iraq. Both opposed abortion except under certain circumstances. Both were personally tolerant of gays and lesbians. Bush's father would almost certainly have endorsed the Marriage Amendment as strongly as his son, and would likely have signed the "partial-birth" abortion ban. He spoke out for "1000 points of light," an antecedent to the current president's push for faith-based charities. The very similar record, and widely different emotional response from evangelical Christians, points to the importance of the success of the Bush campaign and administration on conveying subtly the sincerity and depths of the president's faith. Whether Christian conservatives ultimately consider George W. Bush to be a more sympathetic president than his father is something that will continue to be debated.

Notes

1. Vejnoska 2004: 3C. *Frontline* takes a balanced look at Bush's religious faith. Cox News Service, USA.
2. See Bush 1999: 136.
3. Kirkpatrick 2005.
4. George W. Bush, *Decision Points* (New York: Crown Publishers, 2010), 33.
5. Bush made this remark in a 2002 meeting in the Oval Office with leaders from various religious denominations. The remark is recounted by Frum (2003).
6. Ibid., 3–4.
7. Interview with George W. Bush by Bill O'Reilly on The O'Reilly Factor, September 29, 2004.
8. Kellstedt 1984: 4–5.

9. Paul Kengor, personal communication, March 10, 2005.
10. Aikman 2004, quoted by Goldstein 2000: A21.
11. Quoted in Cooperman 2004: A1.
12. Quoted in Mansfield 2003: 54.
13. Republican Convention, July 28–August 3, 2000.
14. See Wilcox 1992.
15. See discussion by Manis 2005.
16. Bruce 1995, 1997.
17. Wilcox 2002; Rozell 2000.
18. Leege, Mueller, and Wald 2001.
19. "Bush Campaign Wants Church Lists" 2004.
20. Back cover of DVD jacket, George W. Bush, *FAITH in the White House*, produced by Grizzly Adams Productions, Inc.
21. Sammon 2005.
22. Kaplan 2004: 5.
23. Quoted in Gibbs and Dickerson 2004.
24. Cited in Lemann 2002.
25. In his 2010 memoir, Bush notes a conversation about Iraq with Bush Sr. during a family Christmas gathering in 2002. At that time, Bush the son did appear to seek his father's opinion of his diplomatic strategy.
26. Pfiffner 2003: 1.
27. Cited in "No Causalties? White House Disputes Robertson Comment" 2004. The comment about the Christian with four aces is a quote from Mark Twain.
28. See, e.g., Brookhiser 2003.
29. Wayne 2004.
30. As reported by Mansfield 2003.
31. See http://www.whitehouse.gov/news/inaugural-address.html (accessed November 29, 2006).
32. Pfiffner 2005a.
33. Personal communication with Pfiffner, December 22, 2004.
34. Pfiffner 2004b.
35. Barnes 2001: 13, cited in Kengor 2004: 92.
36. 2004 Presidential Debate, October 13. Available from http://www.debates.org/pages/trans2004d.html.
37. Third Presidential Debate held on October 13, 2004 at Arizona State University.
38. Kirkpatrick and Stolberg 2005.
39. Bill Sammon, *The Evangelical President: George Bush's Struggle to Spread a Moral Democracy Throughout the World* (Washington, D.C.: Regnery Publishing), 24.
40. See David J. Wright "Taking Stock: The Bush Faith-Based Initiative and What Lies Ahead." The Nelson A. Rockefeller Institute of Government. http://www.rockinst.org/pdf/faith-based_social_services/2009-06-11 -taking_stock_faith-based_office.pdf Accessed June 13, 2011. Sociologist

Mark Chaves found the faith-based initiative had little influence on congregations; according to the National Congregations Study the overall percent of congregations that reported social services, nor the percent that received government funding, nor the level of collaboration between congregations and government increased between 1998 and 2007. (http://www.faithand-leadership.com/blog/01-08-2010/mark-chaves-does-anyone-remember-the-faith-based-initiative Accessed May 31, 2011).

41. See http://archives.cnn.com/2001/US/11/06/gen.attack.on.terror/ (accessed November 29, 2006). Bush at a joint news conference with French President Jacques Chirac, November 6, 2001, Washington, DC.
42. Mansfield 2003: 145–146.
43. Keeter and Kohut 2003.
44. For a detailed account of torture as public policy, see Pfiffner 2005b.
45. "End the Abuse" 2005: A22.
46. http://www.christiantoday.com/article/rick.warren.interviews.george .w. bush/27169.htm Accessed May 31, 2011.
47. Becky Schlikerman "Bush promotes book in Chicago", *Chicago Tribune*, October 21, 2010, http://articles.chicagotribune.com/2010-10-21/news /ct-met-bush-visit-20101021_1_decision-points-book-plastic-bag. Accessed May 31, 2011.
48. Chait 2005.

Works Cited

ABC News interview with Charlie Gibson. 2004. Available from http://abcnews.go.com/Politics/story?id=193746&page=1 (accessed November 29, 2006).

Aikman, David. 2004. *A Man of Faith: The Spiritual Journey of George W. Bush*. Nashville, TN: W Publishing Group.

Barnes, Fred. 2001. A Pro-Life White House. *Weekly Standard*, January 1/8, 13.

Bruce, John. 1995. Texas: The Emergence of the Christian Right. In *God at the Grassroots*, edited by Mark J. Rozell and Clyde Wilcox. Lanham, MD: Rowman & Littlefield.

———. 1997. Texas: A Success Story, at Least for Now. In *God at the Grassroots, 1996*, edited by Mark J. Rozell and Clyde Wilcox. Lanham, MD: Rowman & Littlefield.

Brookhiser, Richard. 2003. The Mind of George W. Bush. *The Atlantic Monthly*, April.

Bush, George W. 1999. *A Charge to Keep: My Journey to the White House*. New York: William Morrow and Company.

———. 2004. *On God and Country*, edited by Thomas M. Freiling. Washington, DC: Allegiance Press.

———. 2010. *Decision Points*. New York: Crown Publishers.

"Bush Campaign Wants Church Lists." 2004. CNN.com, February 2.

Chait, Jonathan. 2005. Conservatives Get Taken for a Ride: Crash Test. *The New Republic*, October 19. Available from http://www.tnr.com/doc.mhtml?i=20051024&s=chait102405 (accessed October 24, 2005).

Cooperman, Alan. 2004. Openly Religious to a Point; Bush Leaves the Specifics of His Faith to Speculation. *Washington Post*, September 16, A1.

den Dulk, Kevin R. 2004. "Evangelical 'Internationalists' and U.S. Foreign Policy During the Bush Administration." Presented at Conference on Religion and the Presidency, Grand Rapids, MI.

"End the Abuse." 2005. *The Washington Post*, Friday, October 7, A22.

Frum, David. 2003. *The Right Man: The Surprise Presidency of George W. Bush*. New York: Random House, 3–4.

Gibbs, Nancy, and Dickerson, John F. 2004. "Inside the Mind of George W. Bush." *Time Magazine*, September 6, A21.

Goodstein, Laurie. 2000. The 2000 Campaign: The Philosophy; Conservative Church Leaders Find a Pillar in Bush. *The New York Times*, January 23, A16.

———. 2004. Personal and Political: Bush's Faith Blurs the Line. *The New York Times*, October 26, A21.

Graham, Billy. 2005. Opening prayer at the Presidential Inauguration, January 20, 2005, Washington, DC. Available from http://www.c-span.org/executive/inauguration.asp?Cat=Current_Event&Code=Pres_In aug&ShowVidNum=6&Rot_Cat_CD=Pres_Inaug (accessed November 29, 2006).

Hamilton, William. 2004. Bush Began to Plan War Three Months After 9/11. *The Washington Post*, April 17, A01.

Interview with Charles Gibson, Good Morning America, October 26, 2004.

Johnson, Alex. 2004. Staying on the Right Side of a Political Movement. *MSNBC News*. Available from http://www.msnbc.msn.com/id/6276308/ (accessed October 26, 2004) online.

Kaplan, Esther. 2004. *With God on Their Side: How Christian Fundamentalists Trampled Science, Policy, and Democracy in George W. Bush's White House*. New York: New Press.

Keeter, Scott, and Andrew Kohut. 2003. American Public Opinion about Muslims in the U.S. and Abroad. In *Muslims in the United States*, edited by Philippa Strum and Danielle Tarantolo. Washington, DC: Woodrow Wilson International Center for Scholars, 2003.

Kellstedt, Lyman. 1989. The Meaning and Measurement of Evangelicalism: Problems and Prospects. In *Religion and Political Behavior in the United States*, edited by Ted G. Jelen. New York: Praeger.

Kengor, Paul. 2004. *God and George W. Bush*. New York: Regan Books.

Kirkpatrick, David. 2005. In Secretly Taped Conversations, a Portrait of a Future President. *The New York Times*, February 20. Available from http://www.nytimes.com/2005/02/20/politics/20talk.html?pagewanted = 1&oref = login (accessed March 6, 2005).

Kirkpatrick, David, and Sheryl Gay Stolberg. 2005. Backers of Gay Marriage Ban Use Social Security as Cudgel. *The New York Times*, January 25, A1.

Leege, David C., Paul D. Mueller, and Kenneth D. Wald. 2001. "The Politics of Cultural Differences in the 2000 Presidential Election: The Return of the Prodigal (Reagan) Generation." Paper presented at the annual meeting of the American Political Science Association, September.

Lemann, Nicholas. 2002. Without a Doubt. *The New Yorker*, October. Available from http://www.newyorker.com/printable/?fact/021014fa_fact3 (accessed March 8, 2005).

Manis, Andre M. 2005. A Certain Presidency. *Religion in the News*, 7: 4–5, 25.

Mansfield, Stephen. 2003. *The Faith of George W. Bush*. New York: Jeremy Tarcher/Penguin Books.

"No Causalties? White House Disputes Robertson Comment." 2004. CNN.com, October 21 (accessed March 8, 2005).

Pfiffner, James P. 2003. "George W. Bush: Policy, Politics, and Personality." Presented at conference New Challenges for the American Presidency, London, May.

———. 2004a. *The Character Factor: How We Judge America's Presidents*. College Station, TX: A&M Press.

———. 2004b. Did President Bush Mislead the Country in His Argument for the War with Iraq? *Presidential Studies Quarterly*, 34: 25–46.

———. 2005a. Do Presidents Lie? In *Presidential Politics*, edited by George C. Edwards III. Belmont, CA: Wadsworth.

———. 2005b. "Torture as Public Policy." Unpublished manuscript.

Rozell, Mark J. 2000. "The Christian Right in the GOP Primaries." Paper presented at the annual meeting of the International Association of Americanists, Warsaw Poland. July 19.

Sammon, Bill. 2005. U.S. Should Be Open to God's Priorities. *The Washington Times*, February 14.

———. 2007. *The Evangelical President: George Bush's Struggle to Spread a Moral Democracy Throughout the World*. Washington, D.C.: Regnery Publishing.

Vejnoska, Jill. *The Atlanta Journal-Constitution*, April 29, 2004, 3C.

Wayne, Stephen J. 2004. "All in the Family? Obligations and Challenges for George W. Bush." Paper presented at annual meeting of European Association of American Studies, Prague.

Wilcox, Clyde. 1992. *The Christian Right in 20th Century America*. Baltimore: Johns Hopkins University Press.

———. 2002. Wither the Christian Right? The Elections and Beyond. In *The Election of the Century and What It Tells Us About the Future of American Politics*, edited by Stephen J. Wayne and Clyde Wilcox. Armonk, NY: M. E. Sharpe.

Wright, David J. 2011. "Taking Stock: The Bush Faith-Based Initiative and What Lies Ahead." The Nelson A. Rockefeller Institute of Government. http://www.rockinst.org/pdf/faith-based_social_services/2009-06-11 -taking_stock_faith-based_office.pdf Accessed June 13, 2011.

Chapter Twelve

President Barack Obama and His Faith

Robert P. Jones and Daniel Cox

Introduction

It is no overstatement to say that President Barack Hussein Obama has the most complex ethnic and religious background of any president in our nation's history.[1] He was born in Hawaii to a Kenyan agnostic father and a spiritual but not formally religious white mother. During his 2008 presidential campaign, he engaged in a headline-grabbing disagreement with the pastor of his longtime church, while simultaneously fighting off persistent false rumors that he was a Muslim. President Obama is arguably the most eloquent public official addressing faith and politics in a generation, yet he arose at a time when many Americans believed the Democratic Party was unfriendly to religion. Finally, despite having a two-decade-long membership in a mainline Protestant denomination with one of the oldest pedigrees in American history, the United Church of Christ, a surprising number of Americans continue to perceive his religious beliefs to be different from their own.

The 2004 Backdrop of the God-Gap and the "Values Voter"

Obama's swift political ascent, from an Illinois state senator to a freshman US senator in 2004 to US president in 2008, cannot be understood without the backdrop of the 2004 presidential election and the rise of the so-called "values voters." Democrats suffered losses across the board in the 2004 elections—losing the presidential race, losing four seats and majority control in the Senate, and losing two additional seats in the House of Representatives. Journalists, political commentators, and scholars stated that Democratic losses were caused in large part by the party's inability to attract religious voters who strongly supported George W. Bush and the GOP, opening up an alleged "God Gap" between the political parties.

This storyline was fueled in large part by exit polls from the 2004 election that found that "moral values" was the most frequently cited "issue" voters considered when casting their ballot. Almost one-quarter (22 percent) of voters said that moral values were their top concern.[2] The results sparked heated discussions and led religious conservative leaders to declare their decisive role in Bush's win. For instance, Southern Baptist leaders trumpeted that "this election was a clear and resounding victory for moral values" and claimed that the deciding factor in the election was "the faith factor."[3] The media in turn took off with this storyline, offering headlines such as "Faith, Values Fueled Win" and "Moral Values Cited as a Defining Issue of the Election."[4]

The role of the "values voters" and the creation of their identity as conservative religious voters driven by narrow wedge issues, however, were questioned by many prominent analysts.[5] Gary Langer, director of polling for ABC News and a member of the committee that crafted the exit poll questions, revealed in an opinion piece four days after the election that the committee had rejected his argument that "this hot-button catch phrase had no place alongside defined political issues," and "its presence there created a deep distortion—one that threatens to misinform the political discourse for years to come."[6] Indeed, a Pew Research Center for the People and the Press postelection poll found that 12 percent of respondents volunteered a negative reaction to the term "moral values," noting explicitly that the term was being used as a "wedge" issue against Democrats.[7]

While the simplistic "values voters" victory headlines were balanced precariously on this single controversial polling question, there was other broader evidence that Democrats faced a "God problem," namely, a perception that they were unfriendly toward religion. A July 2005 poll conducted by the Pew Forum on Religion and Public Life and the Pew Research Center for the People and the Press found that only 29 percent of Americans believed that the Democratic Party was friendly toward religion, down from 42 percent in July 2003. The poll also found that there was a connection between viewing the Democratic Party as unfriendly toward religion and having an unfavorable view of the Democratic Party. Of the people who viewed the Democratic Party as unfriendly toward religion, 75 percent viewed the Democratic Party unfavorably and just 11 percent reported voting for

Kerry in the 2004 election.[8] These perceptions of a "God problem" among the Democratic Party provided the setting for Obama's entrance on the national stage.

Obama's Religious Heritage and Early Influences

President Obama, who described himself in his 2004 keynote address to the Democratic National Convention as the son of an "improbable love" between his parents, has the most complex ethnic and religious heritage of any US president. Barack Hussein Obama was born to a white mother (Ann Dunham), who while very spiritual was not a regular churchgoer, and a Kenyan father (Barack Hussein Obama Sr.), who was a self-identified agnostic.

Obama's religious family tree is complex as it extends back to Kenya on his father's side. Obama's paternal grandfather, Hussein Onyango Obama, was raised Catholic but later converted to Islam and took the name "Hussein." Obama's father, Barack Hussein Obama Sr., was born Muslim but became an agnostic as an adult.

Because his father left the family when the younger Barack Obama was two years old, however, his mother and her family were a much stronger influence on his worldview and religious upbringing. In *The Audacity of Hope*, Obama summarized his mother's religious outlook as skeptical of religious institutions and strongly influenced by secular humanism, but he has also noted, "For all her professed secularism, my mother was in many ways the most spiritually awakened person that I've ever known."[9] Obama has described his maternal grandparents as "non-practicing Methodists and Baptists."[10] After his mother divorced his father and was remarried to an Indonesian man, the family relocated to Indonesia, and Obama spent much of his elementary school years[11] attending Santo FransiskusAsisi (St. Francis Assisi) in Jakarta, a Roman Catholic school run at the time by what the *Washington Post* described as "a stern Dutch priest."[12] After elementary school, Obama returned to Hawaii to complete his education.

Obama came to his Christian faith in his late twenties while working in inner city Chicago as a community organizer and has described this experience as becoming "a Christian by choice." Obama has talked extensively both about the personal meaning of his faith and the significance of the church in making a difference in communities. Obama stated that he, like many Americans, felt that "something was missing and that without a vessel for my beliefs, without a commitment to a particular community of faith, at some level I would always remain apart, and alone."[13] When asked by a woman in Albuquerque whether he was a Christian, Obama provided a concise confession of his faith:

> The precepts of Jesus Christ spoke to me in terms of the kind of life I would want to lead. Also understanding that Jesus Christ dying for my sins spoke to the humility we all have to have as human beings. . . . We're sinful and we're flawed, and we make mistakes. We achieve salvation through the grace of God.[14]

Obama also talked about experiencing the potentially transformational role of the church in society, particularly through his connection with African American churches and their activism in the Civil Right struggles and on issues of economic justice. Through the church, Obama saw "the power of that culture to give people strength in very difficult circumstances, and the power of that church to give people courage against great odds."[15] Obama was baptized at the Trinity United Church of Christ in Chicago in 1988.

Entering the National Stage: The Keynote Address at the Democratic National Convention

The 2004 losses at the polls, the "values voters" headlines, and the perceptions of Democrats' unfriendliness to religion provided the backdrop for Barack Obama's entrance onto the national stage. Before July 2004, few had heard of him outside of Illinois and the context of his campaign for the US Senate. Obama's keynote address at the 2004 Democratic National Convention, however, was the performance that first brought Obama the national spotlight and established him as a rising star in the Democratic Party.

The stirring conclusion of this July 2004 speech addressed the divisiveness around religion and ideology that was already evident in the Bush-Kerry presidential contest, demonstrating a comfort with theological concepts and language that had been missing in many Democratic circles:[16]

> It is that fundamental belief—I am my brother's keeper, I am my sisters' keeper—that makes this country work. . . . The pundits, the pundits like to slice and dice our country into red states and blue States: red states

for Republicans, blue States for Democrats. But I've got news for them, too. We worship an awesome God in the blue states, and we don't like federal agents poking around our libraries in the red states. We coach little league in the blue states and, yes, we've got some gay friends in the red states. . . . In the end, that's what this election is about. Do we participate in a politics of cynicism, or do we participate in a politics of hope? . . . Hope in the face of difficulty, hope in the face of uncertainty, the audacity of hope: In the end, that is God's greatest gift to us, the bedrock of this nation, a belief in things not seen, a belief that there are better days ahead.[17]

In the last 600 words of the speech, Obama artfully wove together a number of biblical themes and "insider" references that resonated with religious Americans. Obama's allusions above to being "my brother's keeper" and to hope as "a belief in things not seen" are direct references to the story of Cain and Abel found in the book of Genesis in the Old Testament and to a well-known passage in the book of Hebrews in the New Testament, respectively. His reference to worshipping an "awesome God" is a reference to a worship chorus song entitled "Our God is an Awesome God," which is popular especially among evangelical Protestant Christians. With his speech, Obama not only set the tone of his future political brand but also importantly broke with the image of the Democrat who shied away from religion.

Obama's "Kennedy Moment": The 2006 Call to Renewal Address

In 2006, then Sen. Barack Obama was honored by Sojourners/Call to Renewal with the Joseph Award, which is given annually to a person who has used a position of influence to help overcome poverty and advance justice. Obama's award acceptance speech was quickly recognized by commentators as a historic speech. In a column entitled "Obama's Eloquent Faith," E. J. Dionne of *the Washington Post* called it "the most important pronouncement by a Democrat on faith and politics since John F. Kennedy's Houston speech."[18]

In the speech, Obama tackled the perception of a partisan "God gap" head on, and expanded on his 2004 interview discussing the importance of the role of religion in the public sphere. He reprimanded conservative leaders for being "all too happy to exploit this gap, consistently reminding evangelical Christians that Democrats disrespect their values and dislike their Church, while suggesting to the rest of the country that religious Americans care only about issues like abortion and gay marriage; school prayer and intelligent design." At the same time, he scolded progressive leaders, stating, "Our failure as progressives to tap into the moral underpinnings of the nation is not just rhetorical, though. Our fear of getting 'preachy' may also lead us to discount the role that values and culture play in some of our most urgent social problems."

In the end, Obama asserted that both conservatives and progressives were failing to aptly deal with the relationship between religion and politics. Obama challenged progressives to "shed some of these biases" in order to "recognize some overlapping values both religious and secular people share when it comes to the moral and material direction of our country." He challenged conservatives to remember "the critical role that the separation of church and state has played in preserving not only our democracy, but the robustness of our religious practice." He challenged both to look for "compromise, the art of the possible," and to use "fair-minded words" in debates in order to mend a country that was still reeling from the divisive 2004 presidential campaign.[19]

At a number of events in 2006, Obama continued to connect his policy positions to affirmations of his faith and to claim an authority and comfort with religion that was uncommon among national Democratic circles. For example, at the 2006 annual conference on HIV/AIDs at Saddleback Church in Orange County, California, Obama rebuffed Republican Kansas Senator Sam Brownback's attempt to claim ownership of the religious turf. When Sen. Brownback welcomed Obama to what he called "*my* house," Obama responded: "With all due respect, Sam, this is my house too. This is God's house."[20]

Obama and Religion on the Campaign Trail in 2008

Obama's comfort with religion, evident in his major campaign addresses before the Democratic National Convention and at the Call to Renewal event, foreshadowed the priority that he would place on religious outreach in the 2008 campaign. The prominence of religious themes and outreach did not go unnoticed by observers across the political spectrum. For example, leading into the home stretch of the campaign, a *Wall Street Journal* article noted that the race was shaping up to be an unusual one "in which the presumptive Democratic nominee is talking more openly about his Christian beliefs than the Republican candidate."[21]

In the campaign, Obama also backed up his rhetoric with serious religious organizing.[22] Beginning in 2005, he tapped a 23-year-old Pentecostal pastor, Joshua DuBois, to join his Senate staff as a full-time point person on religious affairs, a position that was unique in Democratic senate offices. By August 2008, DuBois had joined the Obama-for-America campaign and was leading a team of seven staffers and five interns.[23] Amy Sullivan at *Time Magazine* concluded that the Obama team had developed "a larger and more comprehensive religious outreach operation than any Democrat in history."[24]

The main avenue for religious outreach on the Obama campaign was conducting "American Values Forums," town hall meeting style gatherings designed to give Obama an opportunity to connect his policy positions with the values and beliefs of people of faith. The campaign conducted over 300 "American Values Forums" across the country at churches, community centers, and universities. Additionally, the campaign added "prayer clutches" with local clergy at campaign stops, developed DVDs to enable faith communities to hold "conversation[s] about faith and values" in their own homes,[25] maintained a section of its website dedicated to people of faith, and counseled church leaders to ensure they complied with IRS regulations concerning political activity.[26] DuBois and the Obama faith team also made a conscious effort to expand the outreach to areas and groups that traditionally voted Republican. These efforts included sending surrogates such as Brian McClaren and Donald Miller, well-known authors among evangelical Christians, to address more conservative religious audiences.

Another strategy used by the Obama campaign was to hold closed-door meetings with a broad range of religious leaders, many of whom had never met with a Democratic presidential candidate.[27] A week after winning the Democratic nomination in June 2008,[28] for example, Obama met with approximately 30 religious leaders from across the political spectrum,[29] including a number of evangelical leaders such as T. D. Jakes, Richard Cizik, Max Lucado, Luis Cortes, Paul Corts, Cameron Strang, Sam Rodriguez, and Franklin Graham.[30]

Reflecting on the meeting in an interview with David Brody from Christian Broadcasting Network, Obama recalled Reagan's outreach to evangelicals in the 1980s:

> I opened up the meeting by quoting Ronald Reagan saying, "I know you can't endorse me, but I endorse you." I endorse the good works that are

being done, the wonderful ministries that are taking place all across the country, and my goal here is just to have a dialogue to listen, to learn, to share my faith journey. . . . None of these folks may vote for me, but I want them to know that there's a possibility of me working with them to advance common goals, like reducing teen pregnancies, or making sure that we're dealing with the homeless population, or dealing with the tragedy of Darfur.[31]

Coming out of this meeting, several participants noted the unusual position in which they found themselves: they had accepted the unexpected invitation from Obama, but they were still waiting on the invitation from McCain.[32] Stephen Strang, founder of a large Christian publishing house and a regular at Bush White House meetings, wrote this conclusion on his blog after returning from the meeting: "The most significant thing is just the fact that the meeting was held."[33]

Missteps and Controversies around Obama's Religion

The historic religious outreach campaign, however, was not without its missteps or controversies. Despite his typical comfort and eloquence talking about religion, Obama was not immune to gaffes. During a fund-raiser in San Francisco prior to the primary in Pennsylvania, in an attempt to discuss what he was hearing in small towns in Pennsylvania from people significantly impacted by the economic downturn, Obama said, "It's not surprising they get bitter, they cling to guns or religion or antipathy to people who aren't like them."[34] The comment generated a wave of negative responses that accused Obama of being "elitist" and attacking religion. Despite attempts to apologize and explain that even in his own life he turned to religion when things were going poorly,[35] the comment followed him into the general election. He finally put the episode to rest by flatly calling the comment "boneheaded."[36]

Obama also famously fumbled a question about abortion at a forum sponsored by Rick Warren's Saddleback Church, located outside of Los Angeles.[37] Warren asked Obama, "At what point does a baby get human rights, in your view?" After stumbling a bit, Obama answered, "Answering that question with specificity, you know, is above my pay grade," an answer that was unsatisfying to some and even offensive to others in attendance. The following weekend On

ABC's This Week with George Stephanopoulos, Obama admitted that his answer may have been too flippant and attempted to clarify the intentions of his previous statement and elaborate his position on abortion:

> As a Christian, I have a lot of humility about understanding when does the soul enter into . . . I don't presume to be able to answer these kinds of theological questions. What I do know is that abortion is a moral issue, that it's one that families struggle with all the time, and that in wrestling with those issues, I don't think that the government criminalizing the choices that families make is the best answer for reducing abortions.[38]

From the start of his presidential campaign, Obama was dogged by Internet rumors that he was secretly a Muslim rather than a Christian, and that he had been sworn into the US Senate on a Qur'an instead of a Bible. The rumors were persistent enough that the campaign created a "Know the Facts" section on their website and providing talking points to help supporters respond when confronted with rumors and questions about Obama's faith.[39]

The most prominent religious controversy of the Obama campaign—and the low point according to religious outreach director Joshua DuBois—was his public falling out with his pastor, Reverend Jeremiah Wright.[40] Reverend Wright had been Obama's pastor at Trinity United Church of Christ (UCC) in Chicago since the late 1980s. He officiated the Obamas' wedding and baptized their daughters. However, upon Obama's rise to the national political stage, Wright's words received heavy media scrutiny, particularly after ABC released excerpts of some inflammatory sermons in which he repeatedly said "God damn America" and called out the United States for its sins based on what he described as his "reading of the Gospels and the treatment of black Americans."[41]

In a statement the day after the ABC's release of the sermon excerpts, Obama denounced the statements while initially rejecting calls for him to leave the church:[42]

> The statements that Rev. Wright made that are the cause of this controversy were not statements I personally heard him preach while I sat in the pews of Trinity or heard him utter in private conversation. When these statements first came to my attention, it was at the beginning of my presidential campaign. I made it clear at the time that I strongly condemned his comments. But because Rev. Wright was on the verge of retirement, and because of my strong links to the Trinity faith community, where I

married my wife and where my daughters were baptized, I did not think it appropriate to leave the church.

Obama used the controversy with Rev. Wright as an opportunity to deliver a speech entitled "A More Perfect Union" in Philadelphia on March 18, 2008. While primarily focused on Obama's relationship with Wright and more broadly on race in America, it was also about faith and community. Catholic author Paul Elie said of the speech:

> That speech is steeped in Christianity. We have relationships, they're all flawed, we're all broken. You can't renounce your history with a person at a stroke, we have to fare forward with other imperfect people and resist the claims to perfection coming from both sides.[43]

Rev. Wright, however, responded by giving a series of interviews in which he defiantly embraced and defended the inflammatory statements. The most prominent event was a press conference Wright held at the National Press Club in Washington, DC, just blocks from the White House, where he accused Obama of political posturing.[44] Ultimately, on May 31, 2008, the Obamas announced their decision to resign their membership at Trinity UCC. The Obamas expressed their sadness in a letter to the church's current pastor the Reverend Otis Moss, III:

> Our relations with Trinity have been strained by the divisive statements of Reverend Wright, which sharply conflict with our own views. These controversies have served as an unfortunate distraction for other Trinity members who seek to worship in peace, and have placed you in an untenable position.[45]

Obama and Religion in the 2008 Election

Despite some missteps and these controversies, a number of polls during the campaign showed Obama leading McCain not just in support but also on evaluations of religiosity. In a 2007 *Time Magazine* poll, 24 percent of registered voters viewed Obama as "strongly religious," compared to only 17 percent who viewed McCain the same way.[46] *Relevant Magazine*, a publication aimed at evangelical Christians in the millennial generation (under age 30), conducted an unscientific online poll of its readership early in 2008 asking "Who would Jesus vote for?" Twenty-nine percent picked Obama, nearly five times the number of respondents who picked McCain.[47] While polls had shown since 2005 that Democrat Party significantly trailed the Republican Party in measures of "friendliness" to religion, the 2008 American Values Survey, conducted by Public Religion Research Institute, found that Americans were slightly more likely to view Obama than McCain as friendly toward religion (49 percent and 45 percent, respectively).[48]

On Election Day, Obama won the presidency, but with the exception of Catholics, there were no major religious realignments compared to 2004. The most significant shift was among Catholics; Obama won 54 percent of the Catholic vote, a 7-point improvement over John Kerry's loss among this group despite being Catholic himself, although this was largely due to Obama's strong performance among Latino Catholics. Obama also won 73 percent of the vote among those who identified their religion as "other," 78 percent of the Jewish vote, and 94 percent of the African American Protestant vote.[49] Additionally, Obama won 75 percent of the vote among those who claim no religious affiliation. Despite earlier signs of losing ground in the evangelical community, McCain did nearly as well as Bush did in 2004 among self-described white evangelicals and born-again Christians (73 percent vs. 79 percent, respectively). McCain also retained the Republican edge among white mainline Protestants (55 percent to Obama's 44 percent), the denominational family from which he comes.[50]

Misperceptions about Identity, Challenges with Identification: Obama's Faith in Question

While the McCain campaign never questioned Obama's Christian identity, and even with the high-profile conflict with his controversial Christian pastor, questions about Obama's religious identity carried over from the campaign into his first term as president. Rumors persisted that Obama was secretly a Muslim, and, beyond this problem, a significant number of Americans reported that they believed his religious beliefs were different from their own.

Confusion about Obama's Religious Identity

In March 2008, nearly eight-in-ten (79 percent) Americans reported that they had heard either a lot or a little about rumors that Obama was Muslim. In October, less than a month before the election, 87 percent of the country reported hearing about these rumors.[51] In March 2008, 12 percent of Americans wrongly thought Obama was Muslim, and less than half (47 percent) correctly identified his religion as Christian. Nearly four-in-ten (37 percent) said they were not sure about the candidate's faith.[52] This pattern continued through the rest of the election and into Obama's first year in office.

In August 2010, however, coinciding with drops in his job approval ratings following the contentious health-care-reform debates, the percentage of Americans who wrongly identified his religion as Muslim increased six points to 18 percent, and the percentage who correctly identified Obama's religion as Christian dropped 13 points to just 34 percent.[53] The number of Americans who reported not knowing what Obama's religion was also rose six points to 43 percent.[54] As late as July 2011, at the time of this writing, these numbers remain largely unchanged. The PRRI/RNS Religion News Poll, conducted by Public Religion Research Institute in partnership with Religion News Service, found that 18 percent of Americans incorrectly identified Obama's religion as Muslim, 38 percent correctly identified his religion as Christian, and 40 percent say they do not know what his religion is.[55]

It is worth noting that Americans who wrongly identify Obama as a Muslim are much more likely to be Republican. For example, three times as many self-identified Republicans as self-identified Democrats wrongly identified Obama as Muslim (31 percent to 10 percent, respectively).[56] Moreover, nearly all of the increase among Americans who say Obama is Muslim came from the ranks of Republicans, especially conservative Republicans (up 16 points between 2009 and 2010).

The Impact of Perceptions of Religious Difference

While concerns about Obama's religious identity remain confined to a minority of the population, there is evidence that Obama has a

Are Obama's Religious Beliefs Similar or Different from Your Own?

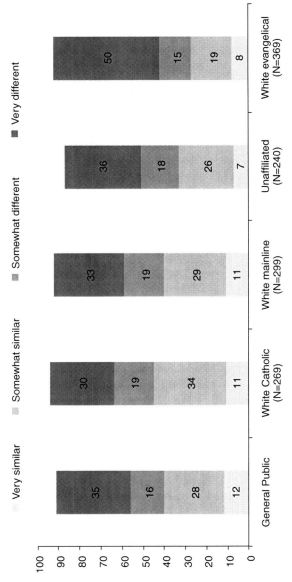

■ Very similar ■ Somewhat similar ■ Somewhat different ■ Very different

	General Public	White Catholic (N=269)	White mainline (N=299)	Unaffiliated (N=240)	White evangelical (N=369)
Very similar	35	30	33	36	50
Somewhat similar	16	19	19	18	15
Somewhat different	28	34	29	26	19
Very different	12	11	11	7	8

Source: Public Religion Research Institute, Post-election American Values Survey, November 2010 (N=1,494)

broader religious identification problem with a significant portion of the electorate. A much larger group of Americans report that the president holds religious beliefs either somewhat or very different from their own, and these views are also highly correlated to evaluations of Obama's job performance. More than half (51 percent) of the public said that compared to their own religious beliefs, Barack Obama's beliefs were either somewhat (16 percent) or very (35 percent) different from their own. Four-in-ten Americans said they shared similar religious beliefs as the president, and about one-in-ten were unsure.[57]

Perceptions of Obama's religious beliefs differ significantly by religious affiliation, race, political party, and even preferred television news source. Nearly two-thirds of white evangelicals said that Obama's religious beliefs were somewhat (15 percent) or very (50 percent) different. Among black Protestants, in contrast, three-quarters said Obama's religious beliefs were similar to their own. Despite belonging to a historically mainline Protestant church, only 40 percent of white mainline Protestants said they held similar religious beliefs as the president. Nearly eight-in-ten (78 percent) Republicans said Obama's religious beliefs were different from their own, compared to only one-quarter of Democrats.

Fox News gave considerable airtime to rumors and controversies around Obama's religious identity, and there is a significant link between trust in the network and attitudes toward Obama's religion. Seventy-eight percent of Americans who said they most trusted Fox News to give them accurate information about current events and politics said Obama had religious beliefs different from their own. Among Republicans who most trust Fox News, nearly nine-in-ten (88 percent) reported that Obama's religious beliefs are different from their own, including 69 percent who say they are very different. In contrast, a majority (54 percent) of Americans who most trust CNN reported that Obama had beliefs similar to their own.[58]

Perceiving Obama's religious beliefs to be different from one's own is a significant independent predictor of holding unfavorable views of Obama, even holding other relevant characteristics constant. Holding other attributes constant in a regression model, Americans who said Obama holds somewhat or very different religious beliefs than their own had on average a 72 percent probability of viewing the president unfavorably, while those who said his religious beliefs were somewhat or very similar had on average just a 13 percent probability of viewing the president unfavorably.[59]

Looking Ahead: The Potential Impact of Perceptions of Obama's Religious Beliefs

This chapter was completed roughly three-quarters through President Obama's first term in office. Obama has thus far carried with him into office his eloquence in expressing his faith and his commitment to reaching out to a wide circle of religious leaders. At the same time, false rumors about his religious identity and concerns about identifying with his religious beliefs have stubbornly followed him into office. While these trends set the stage and main plot lines, the concluding act that will record the role religion plays in Obama's presidency has yet to be written.

The political implications of public perceptions of Obama's religious identity and beliefs are significant. Perceptions of his religious identity and beliefs are closely connected to personal evaluations of him and his job as president and to future support at the ballot box. Should these views hold throughout the 2012 campaign season, the fact that half the public says Obama's religious beliefs are different from their own could have significant electoral repercussions in the 2012 election. Most Americans are religious, and religion remains a lens through which they evaluate political candidates and measure their identification with them. More than seven-in-ten (72 percent) Americans, for example, say that it is very or somewhat important that a candidate for president have strong religious values (Pew 2008).

To put Obama's potential identification problem in perspective, in July 2011, the number of Americans saying Obama has different religious beliefs from their own stood at 48 percent, roughly the same as the number of Americans saying Mitt Romney—a Republican contender who is Mormon—has religious beliefs different from their own (43 percent).[60] When we created a scale to measure the average distance between Americans' own religious beliefs and their perceptions of candidates' religious beliefs, Obama's religious-identification dilemma comes more clearly into focus.[61]

Perceptions of former president George W. Bush provide a helpful benchmark. Bush scores right at the mean of the scale (0.00), indicating that equal numbers say his religious beliefs are similar to their own and different from their own. On this measure, again, Obama's score is nearly identical to Romney's score (–0.40 and –0.43), indicating that for each, on balance, more Americans think these leaders' religious beliefs are different than think they are similar. Much has been written

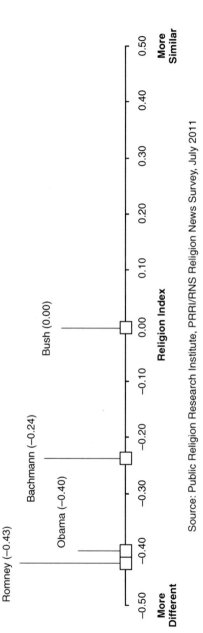

**Public Perception of How Religiously
Similar or Different Political Figures Are**

Romney (−0.43)

Bachmann (−0.24)

Obama (−0.40)

Bush (0.00)

| More Different | −0.50 | −0.40 | −0.30 | −0.20 | −0.10 | 0.00 | 0.10 | 0.20 | 0.30 | 0.40 | 0.50 More Similar |

Religion Index

Source: Public Religion Research Institute, PRRI/RNS Religion News Survey, July 2011

about the challenge Romney may face because of his Mormon religious identity, but Obama's continued religious identity and identification problems, which are as significant as Romney's, have not been fully grasped.

It is fair to say that Obama is one of the most eloquent political communicators in recent memory, and he has demonstrated an ability to talk comfortably and openly about his faith and its connection to his political values and policies. But at this stage of his presidency, the polls indicate that he has not succeeded in living up to the promise of his 2006 Call to Renewal speech. Given the public's misperceptions and concerns about his religious beliefs, he will need to heed this call and find his voice again in the 2012 campaign season if he is to reconnect with voters at the level of values and not just policies.

Notes

1. The authors wish to express their gratitude for background research and editorial assistance to members of the Public Religion Research Institute team who contributed to this chapter: Shannon Craig Straw, Nikki Yamashiro, Samantha Holquist, and Justin Metz.
2. "Election Exit Polls 2004," CNN, November 2, 2004, http://www.cnn .com/ELECTION/2004/pages/results/ states/US/P/00/ epolls.0.html.
3. Tom Strode, "President Bush Wins Re-Election; Exit Polls Show Values Voters Made the Difference," *Baptist Press News*, Washington, DC, November 3, 2004.
4. Rick Pearson and John McCormick, "Faith, Values Fueled Win," *Chicago Tribune*, Chicago, IL, November 4, 2004, http://www. chicagotribune .com/chi-041105map-graphic,0,3469605.graphic; Katharine Q. Seelye, "Moral Values Cited as a Defining Issue of the Election," *The New York Times*, New York, NY, November 4, 2004, http://www.nytimes.com/2004 /11/04/politics/campaign/04poll.html.
5. For a more in-depth discussion of the debates around the inclusion of "moral values" in the exit polls, see Robert P. Jones, *Progressive & Religious: How Christian, Jewish, Muslim and Buddhist Leaders Are Moving Beyond the Culture Wars and Transforming American Public Life* (Lanham, MD: Rowman and Littlefield, 2007).
6. Gary Langer, "A Question of Values," *The New York Times*, New York, NY, November 6, 2004, sec. Opinion, http://www.nytimes.com/2004 /11/06/ opinion/06langer.html.
7. *Moral Values: How Important?* (Washington, DC: Pew Research Center for the People and the Press, 2004).

8. Gregory A. Smith and Peyton M. Craighill, "Do the Democrats Have a God Problem?" *The Pew Forum on Religion & Public Life*, July 6, 2006, http://pewforum.org/Politics-and-Elections/Do-the-Democrats-Have-a-God-Problem.aspx.

9. Barack Obama, *The Audacity of Hope: Thoughts on Reclaiming the American Dream* (New York, NY: Crown, 2006).

10. Barack Obama, "Call to Renewal Keynote Address," Speech presented at the Call to Renewal's Building a Covenant for a New America Conference, Washington, DC, June 28, 2006.

11. While Obama spent most of his elementary school years between 1967 and 1971 at Santo Fransiskus Asisi, he also spent a partial year at Besuki, at state-run school catering to the Jakarta's elite families, which has a study of Islam as part of the curriculum.

12. Andrew Higgins, "Catholic School in Indonesia Seeks Recognition for Its Role in Obama's Life," *Washington Post*, Washington, DC, April 9, 2010, sec. World, http://www.washingtonpost.com/wp-dyn/content/article/2010/04/08/AR2010040805858.html.

13. Obama, "Call to Renewal Keynote Address."

14. *Obama: Jesus Christ Died for My Sins* (Albuquerque, NM: Christian Broadcasting Network, 2010), http://www.cbn.com/cbnnews/politics/2010/October/ Obama-Jesus-Christ-Died-for-My-Sins/.

15. Steven Waldman, "Obama's Fascinating Interview with Cathleen Falsani," *Beliefnet*, November 11, 2008, http://blog.beliefnet.com/steven-waldman/2008/11/obamas-interview-with-cathleen.html.

16. It is worth noting that Obama has written most of his important speeches himself, without relying heavily on speechwriters. See Jay Newton-Small, "How Obama Writes His Speeches," *Time Magazine*, August 28, 2008, "http://www.time.com/time/politics/article/0,8599,1837368,00.html"htt p://www.time.com/time/politics/article/0,8599,1837368,00.html.

17. Barack Obama, "Democratic National Convention Keynote Address," Speech presented at the Democratic National Convention, Boston, MA, July 27, 2004.

18. E. J. Dionne, "Obama's Eloquent Faith," *The Washington Post*, Washington, DC, June 30, 2006, sec. Opinion, http://www.washington-post.com/wp-dyn/content/article/2006/06/29/AR2006062901778.html.

19. Obama, "Call to Renewal Keynote Address."

20. Tim Grieve, "Left Turn at Saddleback Church," *Salon*, December 2, 2006, http://www.salon.com/news/feature/2006/12/02/obama.

21. Amy Chozick, "Young Clergyman Leads Obama's Drive to Attract 'Faith Voters,'" *The Wall Street Journal*, New York, NY, August 16, 2008, sec. Politics and Policy, http://online.wsj.com/article/SB121883753433545501.html.

22. Howard Dean, chair of the Democratic National Committee had also laid a solid foundation for religious organizing leading into the 2008 campaign. See Tiffany Stanley, "How Democrats Gave Up on Religious

Voters," *CBS News*, December 22, 2010, http://www.cbsnews.com /stories/2010/12/22/opinion/main7173642.shtml.

23. Chozick, "Young Clergyman Leads Obama's Drive to Attract 'Faith Voters.'"
24. Amy Sullivan, "Obama and McCain's Test of Faith," *Time Magazine*, August 15, 2008, http://www.time.com/time/politics/article/0,8599, 1833118,00.html.
25. Russell Goldman, "Strange Bedfellows: Obama and Evangelicals," *ABC News*, June 12, 2008, http://abcnews.go.com/Politics/Vote2008/story? id=5053866&page=1.
26. Michael Paulson, "Obama's Man of Faith," *Boston Globe*, Boston, MA, July 10, 2008, http://www.boston.com/news/education/higher/articles/2008 /07/10/obamas_man_of_faith/.
27. Chozick, "Young Clergyman Leads Obama's Drive to Attract 'Faith Voters.'"
28. Amy Sullivan, "Obama's Play for the Faithful," *Time Magazine*, June 12, 2008, http://www.time.com/time/politics/article/0,8599,1814206,00.html.
29. David Brody, "Update: Obama Meets with Conservative and Progressive Religious Leaders," *Brody File*, June 10, 2008, http://blogs.cbn.com /thebrodyfile/archive/2008/06/10/update-obama-meets-with-conserva-tive-and-progressive-religious-leaders.aspx.
30. Sullivan, "Obama's Play for the Faithful."
31. David Brody, "Obama Quotes Reagan at Religious Leaders Meeting," *Brody File*, June 17, 2008, http://blogs.cbn.com/thebrodyfile/archive /2008/06/17/obama-quotes-reagan-at-religious-leaders-meeting.aspx.
32. "Christian Leaders Meet for Private Discussion with Obama," *Associated Press*, Chicago, IL, June 10, 2008, http://www.usatoday.com/news/reli-gion/2008-06-10-religious-meeting_N.htm.
33. Stephan Strang, "Obama's 'Off-the-Record' Meeting with Christian Leaders," *Strang Report*, June 11, 2008, http://www.strangreport .com/2008/06/obamas-off-record-meeting-with.html.
34. Mayhill Fowler, "Obama: No Surprise That Hard-Pressed Pennsylvanians Turn Bitter," *Huffington Post*, April 11, 2008, http://www.huffington -post.com/mayhill-fowler/obama-no-surprise-that-ha_b_96188.html.
35. Campbell Brown, "Democratic Candidates Compassion Forum", pre-sented at the Democratic Candidates Compassion Forum, Grantham, Pennsylvania, April 13, 2008, http://transcripts.cnn.com/TRANSCRIPTS /0804/13/se.01.html.
36. Sarah Pulliam Bailey, "Obama Calls His 'Cling to Guns or Religion' Comments 'Boneheaded,'" *Christianity Today*, October 15, 2008, http://blog.christianitytoday.com/ctpolitics/2008/10/obama_calls_his .html.
37. Sullivan, "Obama and McCain's Test of Faith."

38. Jake Tapper, "Obama: My Answer on Abortion at Saddleback Church Was Too Flip," *ABC News*, September 7, 2008, http://blogs.abcnews.com /politicalpunch/2008/09/obama-my-answer.html.

39. *Obama for America*, February 6, 2008, http://web.archive.org/web /20080206201234/http://my.barackobama.com/page/content/factcheck-actioncenter.

40. Joshua DuBois, interview by Robert P. Jones, July 20, 2011.

41. Brian Ross and Rehab El-Buri, "Obama's Pastor: God Damn America, U.S. to Blame for 9/11," *ABC News*, March 13, 2008, http://abcnews. go.com/Blotter/DemocraticDebate/story?id=4443788&page=1.

42. Barack Obama, "On My Faith and My Church," *The Huffington Post*, March 14, 2008, http://www.huffingtonpost.com/barack-obama/on-my -faith-and-my-church_b_91623.html.

43. Lisa Miller, "Finding His Faith," *Newsweek*, July 12, 2008, http://www. newsweek.com/2008/07/11/finding-his-faith.html.

44. Jake Tapper, "Wright Assails Media, Cheney, Obama at National Press Club," *ABC News*, April 28, 2008, http://blogs.abcnews.com /politicalpunch/2008/04/wright-assails.html.

45. Michael Powell, "Following Months of Criticism, Obama Quits His Church," *The New York Times*, New York, NY, June 1, 2008, sec. Politics, http://www.nytimes.com/2008/06/01/us/politics/01obama.html? adxnnl=1&adxnnlx=1311622153-qcKqhSYE6o3REcUS0jw7fw.

46. Amy Sullivan, "TIME Poll: Faith of the Candidates," *Time Magazine*, July 12, 2007, http://www.time.com/time/politics/article/0,8599,1642653, 00.html.

47. Goldman, "Strange Bedfellows: Obama and Evangelicals."

48. *American Values Survey* (Washington, DC: Public Religion Research Institute, October 2008), http://www.publicreligion.org/research /published/?id=37.

49. "Election Exit Polls 2008," *CNN*, November 4, 2008, http://www .cnn.com/ELECTION/2008/results/polls/#val=USP00p2.

50. "Election Exit Polls 2004."

51. *News Interest Index* (Washington, DC: Pew Research Center for the People and the Press, October 2008).

52. *Political Survey* (Washington, DC: Pew Research Center for the People and the Press, March 2008).

53. Views about Obama's faith are also closely linked to evaluations of his job performance when controlling for other factors. Holding other relevant characteristics constant, Americans who believe Obama is Muslim have on average a 72 percent chance of disapproving of his job as president, while Americans who believe he is Christian have on average just a 30 percent chance of disapproving of his job performance. Analysis conducted by the authors using data from the *Religion and Politics Survey* (Washington, DC: Pew Research Center for the People and the Press, August 2010).

54. *Growing Number of Americans Say Obama Is a Muslim* (Washington, DC: Pew Research Center for the People and the Press, August 2010), http://people-press.org/2010/08/19/growing-number-of-americans-say-obama-is-a-muslim/.

55. *PRRI/RNS Religion News Survey* (Washington, DC: Public Religion Research Institute, July 2011), http://www.publicreligion.org/research/?id=654.

56. *Growing Number of Americans Say Obama Is a Muslim.*

57. *Post-election American Values Survey* (Washington, DC: Public Religion Research Institute, November 2010), http://www.publicreligion.org/research/published/?id=428.

58. There is a strong statistical relationship between perceptions of Obama's religious beliefs and personal evaluations of him. The strongest correlation between views about Obama's religious beliefs and personal evaluations is found among white Protestants; the correlation coefficient is 0.75 for mainline Protestants and 0.72 for evangelical Protestants. Among Catholics (0.54), the religiously unaffiliated (0.43), and non-Christians (0.32) the relationship is significantly weaker. Among black Protestants there is no statistically significant relationship between perceptions of Obama's religious beliefs and personal evaluations of him.

59. Daniel Cox and Robert Suls, "Faith in the President?: How Public Perception of Barack Obama's Faith Shape Views of Him and His Presidency" (unpublished paper presented at the American Association for Public Opinion Research (AAPOR), Phoenix, AZ, 2011).

60. Ibid.

61. *PRRI/RNS Religion News Survey.*

62. We computed an average score that runs from +2 (very similar religious beliefs or political views) to –2 (very different religious beliefs or political views). Respondents who are not familiar with the political figure or their religious beliefs or political views receive a score of 0.

Chapter Thirteen

The Obama Faith-Based Office: Continuity and Change

Douglas L. Koopman

Public religious sentiment by presidential candidates is usually thought to be far more characteristic of Republicans than Democrats. But in the 2008 election cycle all the major early Democratic candidates—Hillary Clinton, John Edwards, and Barack Obama—made overt religious appeals and included religious outreach in their campaign plans. Obama's religious outreach was the most energetic and consistent, even through the spring's Jeremiah Wright controversy. A further step was Obama's July 1 speech in Zanesville, Ohio, where he pledged to retain and expand the Bush administration's faith-based office and efforts. As president, Barack Obama has indeed kept the faith-based offices and allowed them to play a role in his administration. The president has, however, made some modifications to tailor the office to his own and his administration's priorities. Some changes have improved the understanding of the initiative, others have better integrated the office into larger administration projects, and others have put the Democratic president's personal stamp on the initiative itself. This chapter follows the faith-based initiative from its origins in the late 1990s through its first organizational manifestation in the Bush administration to its first major revision under Obama. This review clarifies the potential and the dangers of the faith-based office to presidents and their administrations. The chapter concludes with a few modest suggestions for building on the strengths of the faith-based initiative and reducing its potential for manipulation.

The federal faith-based initiative had rather inauspicious beginnings in the 1996 welfare reform law signed by President Clinton. Little noticed at the time as a small section of this massive reauthorization, charitable choice language prohibited the federal government from discriminating against religious providers in making contracting arrangements for the welfare programs reauthorized under that law. The provisions required federal administrators of covered programs to allow new categories of religious organizations to apply to provide federally funded services on the same basis as other providers, if the providers agreed to follow guidelines keeping religious and nonreligious elements distinct in their programs. The provision passed through largely unnoticed because of larger controversies, stemming from President Clinton's "triangulation" strategy to use welfare reform to position himself between Republicans on his right and liberal Democrats on his left.

Charitable choice's influence in the Clinton administration was small. By early 2001, when Clinton left office, the federal government was authorized to implement charitable choice language in welfare reform and in three other narrowly tailored authorizations. Clinton did little, however, to encourage bureaucratic compliance with charitable choice or to build on recent Supreme Court church-state decisions that provided legal justification for more aggressive action.

Motivations to Support Faith-Based Initiatives

In the 2000 presidential campaign, both major candidates George W. Bush and Al Gore talked frequently about enhancing the role of faith-based groups in government-supported social service provision. There were varied reasons for them to do so, including policy, political, and personal arguments, reasons that extend to the present day.

Policy

The central policy argument rests on the claim that intensely religious social services and treatments are at least as effective as, and probably even superior to, conventional secular treatments and services that government traditionally supports. Although the claim has been difficult to prove, it has durability and much of the public believes it to be so.[1] It starts with the proposition that religiously grounded treatment methods may more completely address the causes of many social problems. A religious conversion or a new lifestyle grounded in religious practice may improve outcomes for a set of individuals who would not otherwise be helped. A second proposition is that religious organizations may offer more and better services at a given price. Overtly religious persons may, for example, be more willing to work longer or harder for less pay, or bring a greater concern for or understanding of the problems a client faces, which would lead to greater effort and success. A faith-based group on a shoestring budget may be far more innovative and cost-effective in its treatment of clients. Third, faith-based and community service providers may also fill service niches, both for programs and for beneficiaries. A small organization with specific religious, ethnic, and programmatic characteristics may, for example, serve some clients who have cultural, language, or belief barriers that keep them from the main social service provider in an area. Including diverse small groups in government programs may thus expand their reach and effectiveness. Although the evidence for these claims is not conclusive, they provide the foundation for a reasonable policy argument to open up federally funded social service treatment programs to faith-based groups as much as constitutionally permissible.

Politics

There are also more political reasons to support faith-based initiatives. One such reason stems from the close competition between the two major parties for national majority status. Democrats and Republicans have been at virtual parity at the national level for nearly four decades, and in the 2000 election cycle both Republicans and Democrats had reasonable prospects of gaining full control of the elected branches of government. Each party's leaders said nice things about the faith-based initiative as one strategy to achieve majority status. Republican elites thought the initiative might allow them to attract a few more highly religious African Americans, Hispanics, ethnic white Catholics, or upper-income suburban women—the "soccer moms" who were voting more Democratic because they saw the GOP becoming too socially conservative. The faith-based initiative also seemed consistent with the views of their white Protestant base, yet its emphasis on aiding the poor and needy would help attract supporters outside this base. Some Democratic elites, mostly from the moderate Democratic Leadership Council (DLC), thought that supporting faith-based initiatives was a good idea for their party too. They believed it might help inoculate the 2000 ticket of Al Gore and Joseph Lieberman from lingering character concerns about sitting president Bill Clinton. In addition, a frequent internal critique of the Democratic Party was that the public was becoming convinced that national Democratic leaders seemed uncomfortable with religious language and with issues important to deeply religious voters, many of whom had been in early elections reliable Democratic voters.[2]

Personal

At least for prominent national politicians, there are personal reasons to promote more organized and institutionalized support for faith-based groups. The creation of faith-based offices and programs allows politicians as both candidates and elected officials a means to make manifest their personal religious claims and illustrate how their faith would intersect with their official responsibilities. The American public is familiar with and in some sense expects candidates to have an active religious faith and talk about it publicly. Although there are some troubling aspects to this expectation, establishing or maintaining a faith-based office and putting one's personal stamp on it serves obvious political ends.

The Bush Vision

Clinton-era laws laid the foundation, but the incoming Bush administration saw an opportunity to build an extensive faith-based program. President Bush's faith-based initiative was a package of legislative proposals and administrative strategies, all focused on the goal of expanding the variety of religiously affiliated social services that receive financial help from the federal government to meet social needs. It had three basic parts—contracting reform, targeted technical assistance, and tax reform.

Contracting Reform

The first part of the faith-based initiative was to change current government practices—sometimes explicit in law but far more frequently in written and unwritten administrative procedures—that excluded certain groups from getting government support in selected government programs because these groups were thought to be in a variety of ways "too religious." Where some saw that discouraging applications from these groups helped preserve the wall of separation between church and state, the Bush administration saw an unnecessary perpetuation of discrimination against religion. Early in his first term, President Bush pushed comprehensive charitable choice legislation as a broad correction. The legislation failed, but there were some smaller legislative victories and significant rule-making changes from presidential executive orders.

Targeted Technical Assistance

A second part of President Bush's faith-based initiative was to provide technical assistance to alert smaller social service providers of federal programs and equip them to compete for federal funds. Smaller groups often lack knowledge of such opportunities and, in any case, the administrative capacity to apply or administer such funds. Bush's plan was to help in two ways. One step was "compassion capital funds" for community and faith-based groups so they could develop or hire the necessary expertise. These special funds would be targeted at smaller, newer, and volunteer-intensive groups (which are, in large part, faith-based entities). Second, Bush would assist newcomers to the federal grant process and build networks with faith-based and community organizations to encourage participation with a broad publicity effort centered on regional and national conferences.

Compassion capital funds were to help "level the playing field," making fairer the competition between experienced federal partners and those not yet providing government-funded services but that should be at least be allowed to apply to do so. Compassion capital funds, because they were not reserved for faith-based groups alone, were less controversial than other parts of the Bush plan, and Congress approved small amounts of compassion capital funds several times in Bush's two terms. The outreach program was more controversial, but it was a hallmark of the central White House faith-based office during most of the Bush years.

Tax Reform

The third part of President Bush's initial faith-based initiative package, tax reform, sought to assist all charitable groups through new tax incentives. The main element was a charitable contribution tax deduction for taxpayers who did not itemize deductions. Under current practice, only taxpayers who complete and return a separate itemized deduction page with their tax returns can take such deductions, and the nonitemizer provision was estimated to bring billions of dollars to eligible groups. But these large and costly tax provisions were dropped in the latter stages of negotiations over the major 2001 tax reform bill that enacted much of the early Bush economic agenda. Because of deep and persistent federal deficits that soon followed, the tax provisions were not seriously considered again during Bush's two terms.

Original OFBCI

Bush signaled the high priority of his faith-based initiative in his earliest presidential actions. On January 29, 2001, he signed his first two related executive orders. The first order created a new office in the executive office of the president, the White House Office of Faith-Based and Community Initiatives (OFBCI), which was created to take the "lead responsibility in the executive branch to establish policies, priorities, and objectives, for the government's efforts to enlist, expand, equip, empower, and enable the work of faith-based and community groups."[3] The second executive order created faith-based centers in five cabinet-level departments: health and human services, housing and urban development, education, labor, and justice. Besides working to remove obstacles that inhibited faith-based and community organizations from providing government social services, these centers were charged with the duty of conducting "a department-wide audit to identify all existing barriers to the participation of faith-based and other community organizations in the delivery of social services."[4] Each cabinet center submitted audit reports to the OFBCI, which then compiled the data into "Unlevel Playing Field," a report released in August 2001 that detailed the various barriers to government cooperation with faith-based and community groups.[5] In two subsequent executive orders during his first term, Bush increased the number of departments housing OFBCI from five to ten.

At the start of his presidency, Bush offered the WHOFBCI directorship to John J. DiIulio Jr., a respected social scientist and self-identified Democrat who had advised Bush on faith-based and other domestic issues during the campaign. Because of his own personal commitment to the issue, DiIulio agreed to serve, but only for the first six months or so of the Bush term.

Early Difficulties

Shortly after the creation of the OFBCI through executive orders, the Bush administration decided to push enabling legislation through Congress. This was an early decision by the more political offices in the White House—a decision opposed by most of the staff in the faith-based office—partly to promote an issue supported by the party's conservative religious allies among the interest group community. The reading of the issue and this decision to push it were both mistakes.

The long-term goal of many "purist" GOP allies in the conservative religious community is greater official support for orthodox religion in the public square, to restore what they define as a "neutral" government view of religion over against present antireligious bias. Others see this view as too proreligious establishment, creating dangerous political and constitutional problems. The early Bush faith-based initiative for a short time became for the purists a tool in this bigger battle. They helped shape the details of the faith-based bill introduced in the House that sought to expand charitable choice provisions into a more aggressive political vehicle than most of the faith-based staff in the administration desired.

Opponents of the initiative cast about for an issue that might slow the advocates' apparently strong momentum of early 2001. Some church-state separation problems were raised, such as whether houses of worship that receive federal aid could continue to display religious symbols, whether churches receiving federal aid should be required to form separate nonprofit organizations, and whether monitoring programs to prevent church-state violations was necessary, possible, or inevitably too intrusive. These nuanced arguments had minor effects on the larger debate. A more winning issue arose almost accidentally—the supposed contravention of other federal law if government-funded religious organizations could make hiring decisions based on religious belief. Dire warnings of "publicly funded discrimination" proved the effective brake opponents were seeking. For religious groups intent on preserving their character, the right to hire individuals whose beliefs accord with their religious identity or mission is critical. It is also, generally speaking, very broad if a group does not directly receive federal government funds. The Bush initiative recognized the importance of hiring freedom, proposing in its 2001 legislation hiring protections similar to the 1996 charitable choice statute, which specified that religious nonprofits participating in federal programs would not have to forfeit their prerogatives to make personnel decisions based on the religious commitments of applicants. Opponents charged that the protections were a guise for allowing overly zealous religious organizations to practice intolerance. The charges gained public traction and created a media firestorm like no other aspect of the faith-based proposal.

Late modifications to the House bill in its quick but contentious journey changed some of the substance but few of the rapidly formed negative impressions.[6] Thus, the faith-based legislative option ran aground by mid-summer of 2001 and, after sporadic attempts through

2002, was virtually abandoned. In response to legislative failure, President Bush issued an executive order in late 2002 much along the lines of his proposed legislation, affirming the rights of faith groups to apply for aid and preemptively addressed the most significant constitutional concerns.

Unsung Successes

Although the media and the general public perceived the Bush faith-based initiative a failure because it lacked broad legislative authority, the administration quietly accomplished many things through rules changes and grassroots outreach. By one count, sixteen major federal procurement rules were rewritten to "level the playing field" between more intensely faith-related groups and others. More than 100,000 grassroots organizations were connected to the initiative through regional training conferences sponsored by the White House and federal agencies, as the OFBCI had trained more than 35,000 nonprofit leaders. More than thirty-five states and one hundred cities established faith-based offices or liaisons connected to both the White House and local communities.[7] A few signature initiatives were also personal presidential successes. On the international front, the President's Emergency Plan For AIDS Relief (PEPFAR) and the President's Malaria Initiative (PMI) appeared to be strong successes. Domestically, the Compassion Capital Fund did much to empower community and faith-based groups, as 300 million dollars in capacity-building funds were allocated by Congress.[8] At a wrap-up White House conference in late June 2008 in Washington, DC, President Bush opined that the creation of the OFBCI was one of "the most important initiatives of this administration."[9]

The Obama Vision

Less than a week later, candidate Barack Obama gave a campaign speech detailing his own elaborate plans for the faith-based office. By July, Obama was clearly on his way to the Democratic nomination. Consistent with his campaign strategy to highlight his Christian faith, Obama used his July 1 Zanesville, Ohio, speech to outline his vision for the role of a faith-based office in his administration.

Campaign and Transition

The continuities and changes he articulated deserve note, particularly in retrospect, as they hint at some of the changes that have now taken place. Obama would keep the office but with an important but subtle name change to the Office of Faith-Based and Neighborhood Partnerships (OFBNP).[10] The word "partnership" implied greater equality between outside faith groups and internal administrative structures. The speech emphasized connecting in nonfinancial ways, implying that the financial aspects of the Bush faith-based office were somehow tainted by ideological preferences and dubious church-state entanglements. Obama's ambiguous "partnerships" strategy would be "a critical part of my administration," the candidate asserted.[11] The office would be an institutional expression of Obama's personal conviction that the faith factor can be important in the change his campaign was bringing all about. "I believe that change comes not from the top-down, but from the bottom-up, and few are closer to the people than our churches, synagogues, temples, and mosques. That's why Washington needs to draw on them ... the challenges we face today ... are simply too big for government to solve alone."[12]

Obama's assertion is remarkably similar to his predecessor's in its foundational assumption—the change-bringing experience of religion. In retrospect, it seems likely candidate Obama was reflecting on his community organizer experience, where community action groups would set public agendas and enlist local congregations in action for social change. Calling for an "all hands on deck"[13] approach to meeting social needs, the speech implied that Obama's main criticism of Bush's version of the faith-based initiative was its narrowness by ideology and religious affiliation. Obama's version would be more ecumenical and practical, but in other ways quite similar in its goal of promoting creative service delivery by faith-based groups.

Obama also mentioned the highly contentious issue of religious hiring. Groups such as the American Civil Liberties Union (ACLU) and the Americans United for the Separation of Church and State had been alarmed by the Bush administration's position on this issue, calling for the executive branch to reverse itself, or for Congress to do so with legislation. In this speech, candidate Obama appeared to side with the progressive groups who argued that if such entities received federal financial support, the discretion to hire on faith criteria—which often meant conservative social issue criteria—should be ended. "If you get a federal grant," Obama stated, "you can't ... discriminate ... against the people you hire on the basis of their religion."[14]

Many liberals did not support President Bush's OFBCI and did not want Obama to continue the office at all. In the wake of Obama's Zanesville announcement on religious hiring, however, most traditional Democratic allies accepted what seemed to be a political move to the center in an effort to appeal to religious conservatives for the fall elections. Rabbi David Saperstein, director of the Religious Action Center of Reform Judaism and very active in progressive and Democratic causes, thought the office created more problems than it was worth, but supported the changes Obama had proposed should the office continue.[15]

In the presidential transition after his November victory, Obama seemed eager to set a more ecumenical tone for his administration's interaction with politically active religious groups by frequently consulting with religious leaders around the country on multiple issues. President-elect Obama was surprisingly open to religious influence in his administration, and supporters of the Bush OFBCI became hopeful that Obama would not undo the work that President Bush had done but actually strengthen it.

New Director

Shortly after his inauguration, President Obama named 26-year-old Joshua DuBois as the director of the White House Office of Faith-Based and Neighborhood Partnerships. It seemed natural that Obama would seek a prominent place for DuBois in his administration. Despite his youth, DuBois had already served in several responsible roles. While an undergraduate at Boston University, he became an associate pastor of a Massachusetts church. He earned his master's degree at Princeton University and later enrolled in law school, which he left early to work for then-senator Obama.[16] In 2006, DuBois became the head of religious outreach for Senator Obama and played a similar role in the presidential campaign.[17] Along the campaign trail, DuBois arranged grassroots meetings with pastors along the campaign trail, setting up prayer meetings, church visits, and similar venues for the candidate. As the campaign evolved, Obama began to rely on DuBois for personal and spiritual support as well as logistical. The relationship appeared to intensify during the Rev. Wright scandal, with Obama consulting more heavily with DuBois on the campaign's response.[18] By the end of the campaign, DuBois was serving as both a spiritual advisor and tactician, although not a policy expert. Publicly, DuBois's White House appointment was praised widely. DiIulio,

Bush's original OFBCI director who had long before parted ways with the Republican version of the initiative, was "very impressed"[19] by DuBois.

Whereas none of Bush's White House faith-based directors served as presidential spiritual advisor, DuBois was chosen with that as a clear expectation. Throughout Obama's first term, DuBois has continued to wear two hats as presidential spiritual advisor and OFBNP managerial director. Another important staff member in the OFBNP is Mara Vanderslice.[20] Before being tapped by the Obama administration, Vanderslice worked to help Democrats better articulate the nexus between faith and politics in campaigns and in public office.[21] DuBois and Vanderslice are two examples of a faith-based hiring trend in the Obama administration. Whereas the Bush administration hired, particularly in the central White House office, persons with experience on church-state legal matters, social program delivery and evaluation, and other substantive areas, the Obama Administration hired many persons with quite different experiences in campaigns and political networking.

First Executive Order

In February of 2009, just weeks into the new administration, President Obama signed an executive order to change the faith-based mandate. The order outlined four goals for the new OFBNP: first, to make community groups a part of economic recovery efforts; second, to reduce the need for abortion by supporting women and children and addressing teenage pregnancy; third, to support responsible fatherhood and healthy families; and finally, to foster interfaith dialogue domestically and internationally. According to DuBois, each goal was chosen by President Obama and was shaped by issues that were "close to his heart."[22]

These goals provided another indication how the new OFBNP would differ from the OFBCI. The Bush faith-based record was a constellation of a few key programs largely idiosyncratic to the different agencies in which they were housed. Obama was moving broader agenda items consonant with campaign themes and top legislative priorities. Further, there would be a move from direct financial "partnerships" in the grant and contract process to broader but more ambiguous organizational interaction.

On the positive side, the Obama proposed partnerships seemed broader by faith tradition and theological perspective than those under President Bush. More worrisome was the apparent deemphasis on the innovative and inspirational aspects of faith-based social services. The Bush faith-based office, particularly later in its tenure, had allowed groups to often play a lead role in program innovations and illustrations. Some positive effects of this strategy were to challenge government program officers to look for new, innovative, and potentially more effective partners in meeting program objectives. The Obama plans appeared to shift the initiative and leadership to the executive branch of government, where faith groups would be welcomed to sign on to government priorities.

Early Expectations and Concerns

An additional early concern expressed during the transition and immediately afterward was the mismatch between the likely size of the new OFBNP staff and the large role for faith that the new president implied. The February 2009 executive order maintained all the previous department-based faith-based offices and created an outside advisory council with a large mandate. Carl Esbeck, an architect of the charitable choice language in the Clinton years and an early officer in Bush's justice department's faith-based office, expressed his concern over the mismatch. To adequately complete its tasks, he noted, the OFBNP "will take a staff five-fold the half dozen employees under President Bush. We do not want the office's social-service outreach to those who serve the poor and needy to get lost among all these added responsibilities."[23]

Advisory Council

To assist the OFBNP, the February 2009 executive order created a large advisory council whose twenty-five members would serve voluntarily and temporarily. The advisory council's three broad goals were to identify the best and most efficient ways to deliver social services, evaluate where there is need for improvement within the OFBNP, and make recommendations to President Obama for changes in policies, programs, and practices. The advisory council was composed of prominent religious and social service group leaders. Some key members were Richard Stearns of World Vision, Jim Wallis of Sojourners, Larry Snyder of Catholic Charities USA, and Melissa Rogers of the Center for Religion and Public Affairs at Wake Forest Divinity School,[24] who also served to coordinate council activities for its first set of tasks. While there was some criticism and controversy of individuals named to the council, it represented a wide range of faiths resident in the United States and had at least minimal representation from groups friendly to Republicans.

Each council member was expected to serve a one-year term on an issue-specific taskforce, and to meet at various points over the year to construct a set of taskforce recommendations to improve the faith-based initiative. DuBois asserted the vital role of the taskforces to develop a more focused mission, clearer policy guidelines, more attention to legal matters, and removal of alleged political and personal connections in the offices during the Bush administration.[25] The most important taskforce in understanding the organizational and policy changes in the Obama administration is the Reform of the Office taskforce, charged with considering how the White House central office could best support the faith-based centers and what changes should be made to make it more effective in partnering with faith-based organizations.[26]

Advisory Council Taskforces

Taskforces worked through spring and summer 2009, and had an interim October deadline to share draft proposals with the entire council. Most of the interim recommendations became public and, as such, October became an occasion to judge broader reaction to the possible recommendations. The taskforces were to incorporate the October feedback as they worked toward a February 2010 final product for the president.[27] But ongoing disagreements over a handful of difficult issues kept pushing back completion deadlines.[28] The Reform of the Office taskforce in particular was having difficulty resolving two major matters: whether to change guidelines that allowed religious symbols in areas where publicly funded services were provided, and whether to require houses of worship to establish separate 501(c)(3) corporations if they wish to receive direct federal social services funds.[29] The delay subjected the entire Obama faith-based effort to some criticism. Some accused the slow advisory council of being "window dressing" and not an influential force.[30] Others expressed concern that President Obama was "no longer using the faith language that he employed as a candidate to frame his policy goals."[31]

On March 9, 2010, the advisory council belatedly published its set of recommendations. Themes throughout all the taskforce reports included suggestions to more frequently include community organizers when policies that involve them are discussed; to use the faith-based offices to reach out even more broadly to previous nonparticipants and interfaith groups; to create more single-site, multi-benefit access points to improve beneficiary access to multiple government programs and encourage interagency cooperation; and to do more thorough evaluation of programs with faith-based participation.[32] The Reform of the Office taskforce's major recommendations included more regulation and monitoring of faith-based groups to ensure compliance with guidelines, to clarify the rights of beneficiaries—particularly in regard to selected nonreligious alternatives to faith-related services—to use innovations in technology to reach a broader range of groups, and to clarify the distinctive roles of the central White House office and the satellite offices generally.[33]

On issues large and small, most of the advisory council's recommendations served to clarify rather than contravene rules and procedures of the Bush OFBCI. The lack of consensus in the taskforce on religious symbols and separate incorporation for social services meant, substantively, no change from the guidelines issued under Bush. Adele Banks of the Religious News Service succinctly summarized that the recommendations "suggest increased guidance"[34] but no major change in direction.

November 2010 Executive Order

The next nine months of 2010 were used to vet the recommendations and translate them into rules and procedures for agency guidance. President Obama issued a second executive order in mid-November, directing implementation of the surviving ideas. The order addressed the religious freedom of beneficiaries, making it clear that all beneficiaries have a right to refuse "to attend or participate in a religious practice" in a funded program without losing their right to participate in the remainder of the program.[35] To simplify the application process and to "promote transparency and accountability,"[36] the order required that all agencies that provide federal funds to post all relevant materials online in an easily accessible way. To clear up remaining or upcoming confusions over requirements around appropriated federal funds, the order created a new working group whose sole purpose would be to identify ways to divide within one organization the "explicitly religious" activities like worship, prayer, or proselytizing—which could not be government funded—from appropriately funded services and programs.[37]

Taken in total, the detailed changes do reveal a central concern of the Obama administration that differs significantly from the central concern of the Bush faith-based efforts. All of Obama's changes focus on the administrative details of financial and nonfinancial partnerships around existing federal programs, and little with how to encourage innovation and experimentation or improve service delivery and performance outcomes. In addition, whereas the Bush administration was mostly concerned with limiting federal encroachment on the faith of faith-related groups while preserving constitutional requirements, the action of the Obama administration makes clear it is more concerned with keeping the federal government at arm's length, particularly in financial terms, from expressed religion in specific or generic manifestations. Melissa Rogers, the compiler of the reforms and an advocate for most of them, stated: "[t]he approaches of the Bush and Obama administrations appear to be significantly different in terms of the attention they have given to nonfinancial partnerships with religious and secular nonprofits."[38]

Similarities and Differences between Administrations

Similarities

Different in many administrative details, the faith-based initiatives of the Bush and Obama administrations are similar in at least two large respects. First, for both Bush and Obama, the faith-based initiative and the promise of its establishment and programming were important and quite public parts of their initial campaigns for presidency. In the day-to-day operations of their administrations, however, the faith-based offices played smaller and less central roles than campaign promises implied. For Bush, the failure of legislation in 2001 meant that success for the faith-based initiative depended more on how quietly administrative changes could be made within the federal bureaucracy. For Obama, the actions of the faith-based office were clearly integrated into (some might say subservient to) a larger policy agenda, particularly health care and environmental protection.

Second, the faith-based offices of both Bush and Obama had to shape their operations, at least to some extent, in the image of the religiosity of their president. The Bush faith-based office, because of the president's own faith experience, had to feature more intensely and inherently religious groups than it otherwise would. The Obama faith-based office has shaped its policies and interactions with faith-related groups much the way a community organizer would interact with local congregations on a community social agenda.

Differences

One striking but superficial difference is the vastly smaller and less critical media coverage for the Obama efforts. When Bush first introduced the OFBCI in 2001 the coverage was intense and mostly negative. When Obama signed his first executive order in February 2009, the media hardly noticed, and those that did were much less certain about his motivations. A Pew study found that the Bush faith-based office "received nearly seven times more coverage in the first six months of 2001 than it (the Obama office) did during the same period in 2009."[39] Similar disparities in coverage continued throughout the remainder of 2009 and through mid-2011.

More substantively, the Obama administration has provided some much needed clarity to the office in its development of the advisory committee, task forces, reports, revised executive orders, and ongoing advisory groups. In that regard, it has been far more thorough and methodical than the prior administration. The process has been quite slow, however, and many changes were just being implemented in mid-2011. Substantively, to the relief of most early faith-based office supporters and the chagrin of most opponents, they do not vary greatly from the practices of the latter Bush administration.

The most interesting development, or more accurately nondevelopment, is the matter of religious hiring discretion. It remains an unsettled issue, despite a fairly clear promise by candidate Obama to decide on behalf of the liberal civil rights and liberties groups at the heart of the Democratic Party.

The Bush administration held to the long-standing default position of the federal government, which, while it looked like a departure to some observers unfamiliar with the details of the faith-based initiative debate, was grounded in more than a generation of law and practice. Whereas faith-based groups are prohibited from discriminating in hiring based on variety of criteria such as race, age, and gender, they retain the right to use other criteria they deem to be religious. Groups receiving federal funding to run social service programs authorized by government retain this freedom to use religious hiring criteria except when a particular federal program includes specific limits on such practice. The Bush administration did suggest a new option to faith-related groups defending such freedom in court, arguing that such groups could, if they chose, make arguments under the Religious Freedom Restoration Act that such requirements posed a "substantial and unnecessary burden"[40] on religious exercise.

To nearly everyone's surprise, the Obama administration has moved slowly on this, although in mid-2011 there were growing concerns that the president's "evolving thinking" on gay marriage would soon influence this issue. But advocates for the separation of church and state have become increasingly frustrated with the Obama administration on this point. One year into the new administration, Barry Lynn, executive director of Americans United for the Separation of Church and State told the *Washington Post*, he believed, "The core of Obama's faith-based initiative looks pretty much identical to the deeply problematic one created by President George W. Bush."[41] While some were disappointed by Obama's hesitancy on this issue, many others were relieved. The most openly and centrally religious organizations had feared new restrictions promised by Obama in the campaign would alter the terms under which their groups could participate in government programs so much so that participation would be impossible.[42] The Obama administration has apparently encountered sufficient pressure from its allies in progressive and liberal faith-related social service groups, which also value hiring discretion, to leave this matter alone. Inaction allows these concerned groups to continue their work unabated.

An important but subtle change has been the new purpose of the OFBNP under a new president. For President Bush, establishing the OFBCI was extremely personal and important to him, even though it was not always beneficial politically. In fact, one of the chronic problems of the Bush faith-based office in the inner workings of his administration was how to integrate its agenda with other administration activities. President Obama was much more interested in how the OFBNP would fit into the broader agenda and procedures of his administration as well as serve his own needs. In that regard, the Obama strategy has seemed much more successful in making the faith-based office a cohesive part of a presidential strategy.

This more successful integration is not without its problems. One concern is that the office has drifted from a policy-based office with substantive expertise under Bush to a multi-functioning mixture of spiritual advisory and community organizing center under Obama. The director of OFBNP, DuBois, serves as "the administration's go-to-guy for almost all things religious. He travels as Obama's roving ambassador to religious gatherings, connects the president with faith leaders for spiritual counsel, helps scout Washington churches for the first family, and handles the frequent media queries about Obama's faith." Apparently, DuBois even prepares a daily devotional to send to the president's BlackBerry.[43] Whereas it may be comforting that the President has a trusted spiritual advisor close at hand, it may be that this new expectation for the OFBNP distracts the office from its central mission.

The shift in language from "initiative" to "partnership" also appears to reflect a different approach toward faith groups by the two administrations. Obama uses the OFBNP to advance top policy agenda items he first articulated in his campaign. For example, shortly after passing the major health-care reform bill in 2010, the president placed several calls to pastors around the country, asking them to be local "validators" of the new law. This action upset those who thought such a request crossed the line between program information sharing and partisan political advocacy. Fans of the Bush efforts were worried that the energy and initiative of faith-based groups were being discounted and discouraged. Stanley Carlson-Thies, who had been an original member of the Bush White House faith-based office and participated in Obama's Reform of the Office taskforce, worried that "now the attitude is: 'We're the government, doing wonderful things, YOU can come join US.'"[44] A former Bush OFBCI director, Jim Towey, speculated that if he implemented a similar strategy coordinating grassroots faith groups to support a Bush policy agenda item he would have been fired.[45] Despite press skepticism in the Bush years that the office was merely a political tool, it rarely attempted to operate as such. No evidence exists to suggest it achieved the political gains it was accused of attempting. Ironically, the charge opens the Obama version of the office to just such criticism.

Chronic Problems with the Faith-Based Office

Changeable Executive Orders

The faith-based offices of Bush and Obama have been created, governed, and altered exclusively by executive order. No binding legislation has been crafted, amended, and approved by the two political branches of government to set a more permanent direction and organization for the office. Consequently, each administration has been able to shape the office unilaterally. The flexibility of executive orders is attractive, but the problem with this flexibility is instability and inconsistency. The state of flux can muddle the roles of the central White House office and the satellite offices and staff, decreasing their efficiency. Formal oversight by Congress and informal oversight by the media can become erratic and misguided when subject to the daily news cycle. In this context, it is unsurprising that the OFBNP, like its predecessor the WHOFBCI, has been criticized for being more symbol than substance.

The lack of a stable legal structure and mandate makes it easier for it to succumb to the chronic temptation for a sitting president to magnify and illustrate his personal faith through the office. President Bush with his well-known personal and rather dramatic conversion experience talked often about social service programs that emphasized similar conversion experiences in overcoming harmful behaviors. But these programs are the most constitutionally problematic in terms of government support. Whereas Bush's faith-based office emphasized many ways to support a broad range of faith-related social services—most of them far less constitutionally problematic—Bush's personal story distorted the picture of his own office's work.

With a background as a community organizer and a person of faith, President Obama's faith also has individualized characteristics, centered on issues of social justice. A characteristic of his faith-based office approach reflects that choice to include religious groups as junior partners in social-political movements. This tendency has led some critics to wonder whether Obama's prime objective is "all hands on deck" to meet political rather than humanitarian goals. In a religious America, it is clear that presidents may legitimately express a personal, peculiar, and individual faith. It may be less legitimate to use administration personnel and offices in that pursuit. The legitimate, nonreligious, policy reasons for a faith-based office—innovation, experimentation, niche filling, inspiration providing—can get dwarfed by these demands.

Corrective Measures

No executive department or presidential office is without problems, nor can any be made perfect. Inherent problems can, however, be lessened. The faith-based initiative can achieve limited, but desirable, policy goals.

Focus on Innovation

First, a presidential faith-based office should be centered on the innovative and creative ability of faith-based and community groups to more fully meet human needs. Respect for social services delivered by private organizations has a long and durable tradition in American political culture based in federalism, voluntarism, and individual initiative. It has practical advantages, too. Such groups often reach more people with fewer dollars, partially because of the more robust motivation of persons working in the organization. Such groups can also reach discrete religious, ethnic, or other subgroups of eligible recipients, who might be offended or intimidated by large secular service groups on which federal programs often rely. The role of the federal government could be to empower and enable small local entities that already provide locally tailored solutions to maintain and even expand effective activities, without deadening their efforts with too much bureaucracy. As former Bush faith-based authority Stanley Carlson-Thies has noted, the appropriate government perspective is to "if possible, support, rather than supplant, the private organizations and . . . relate to those private organizations in ways that respect their distinctive characteristics, including their religious or humanitarian missions."[46] Such an attitude can increase the effectiveness of social services. Innovative service delivery can also encourage greater creativity, responsiveness, and adaptability among larger and more traditional service providers, including the government itself, without constitutional violations. In that regard, many of the Obama administration's detailed changes have been helpful corrections to a more energetic but less careful Bush administration. But the changes await vigorous application.

Establish in Law

Second, pass enabling legislation for the initiative. Establishing faith-based offices and practices in laws that must make their way through the legislative branch would reduce the ability for presidents to yield to the temptation to use them for political and personal ends. Legislation, particularly if crafted under divided government, would force agreement on an organization and goals for the office. Establishing boundaries and goals for the faith-based office through legislation will eliminate many of the existing chronic problems of the office and reduce others. Legislation provides the appropriate focus and continuity that executive orders, by nature, cannot provide, a focus and continuity that the faith-based office has sometimes lacked.

Notes

1. Pew Forum on Religion and Public Life, "Church-State Concerns Persist: Faith-Based Programs Still Popular, Less Visible," November 16, 2009, accessed June 29, 2011, http://pewforum.org/Social-Welfare/Faith-Based-Programs-Still-Popular-Less-Visible.aspx.
2. Anna Greenberg and Stanley B. Greenberg, "Adding Values," *The American Prospect* 11 no.19 (2000): 28.
3. Executive Order 13199, "Establishment of White House Office of Faith-Based and Community Initiatives," January 29, 2001, accessed March 3, 2003, http://www.whitehouse.gov/news/releases/2001/01/20010129-2.html.
4. Executive Order 13198, "Agency Responsibilities with Respect to Faith-Based and Community Initiatives," January 29, 2001, accessed March 3, 2010.
5. White House, "Unlevel Playing Field: Barriers to Participation by Faith-Based and Community Organizations in Federal Social Service Programs," August 16, 2001, http//www.whitehouse.gov/news/releases /2001/08/unlevelfield.html.
6. Amy E. Black, Douglas L. Koopman, and David K. Ryden, *Of Little Faith* (Washington, DC: Georgetown University Press, 2004).
7. David J. Wright, *Taking Stock: The Bush Faith-Based Initiative and What Lies Ahead* (Albany, NY: The Nelson A. Rockefeller Institute of Government, 2009), 3.
8. Wright, *Taking Stock*, 3.
9. Wright, *Taking Stock*, 57.
10. *New York Times*, "Obama Delivers Speech on Faith in America," Speech Transcript, July 1, 2008 accessed June 8, 2011. http://www.nytimes.com /2008/07/01/us/politics/01obama-text.html?_r=2&oref=slogin&page -wanted=print.
11. *New York Times*, Speech Transcript.
12. *New York Times*, Speech Transcript.
13. *New York Times*, Speech Transcript.
14. *New York Times*, Speech Transcript.
15. Eric Fingerhut, "High Marks for DuBois, Mixed for Faith-Based Office." *Capital J* (blog), January 30, 2009. Accessed March 11, 2010. http://blogs.jta.org/politics/article/2009/01/30/1002656/high-marks-for -dubois-mixed-for-faith-based-office.
16. Alex Altman, "Joshua DuBois: Obama's Pastor-in-Chief," *TIME Magazine*, February 6, 2009. Accessed June 14, 2011. http://www.time .com/time/nation/article/0,8599,1877501,00.html.

17. Christi Parsons, "Obama's Man of Faith Has Dual Roles," *Los Angeles Times*, July 21, 2010. Accessed June 8, 2011. http://articles.latimes.com/2010/jul/21/nation/la-na-white-house-minister-20100721.

18. Parsons, "Obama's Man of Faith Has Dual Roles."

19. Laurie Goodstein, "Leaders Say Obama Has Tapped Pastor for Outreach Office," *New York Times*, January 28, 2009. Accessed March 11, 2010. http://www.nytimes.com/2009/01/29/us/politics/29faith.html.

20. US Department of Health and Human Services, "Center Staff," Center for Faith-Based and Neighborhood Partnerships. Accessed June 14, 2011. http://www.hhs.gov/partnerships/about/staff/fbci_staff.html.

21. David D. Kirkpatrick, "Consultant Helps Democrats Embrace Faith, and Some in Party are Not Pleased," *New York Times*, December 26, 2006. Accessed June 30, 2011. http://www.nytimes.com/2006/12/26/us/politics/26faith.html.

22. Sarah Pulliam, "New Director Offers Vision for Faith-Based Office," Interview of Joshua DuBois. *Christianity Today*, February 6, 2009. Accessed March 11, 2010. http://www.christianitytoday.com/ct/2009/februaryweb-only/105-52.0.html.

23. Dan Gilgoff, "The National Association of Evangelical's Questions for Obama's Faith-Based Office," *God and Country* (blog), *U.S. News*, February 11, 2009. Accessed March 11, 2010. http://www.usnews.com/news/blogs/god-and-country/2009/02/11/the-national-association-of-evangelicals-questions-for-obamas-faith-based-office.

24. White House Press Release, "Obama Announces White House Office of Faith-Based and Neighborhood Partnerships," Office of the Press Secretary. February 5, 2009. Accessed June 8, 2011. http://www.white-house.gov/the_press_office/ ObamaAnnouncesWhiteHouseOfficeofFaith-basedandNeighborhood Partnerships/.

25. Pulliam, "New Director Offers Vision for Faith-Based Office."

26. *Institutional Religious Freedom Alliance*, Bi-monthly Newsletter. Stanley Carlson-Thies, ed., June 18, 2009.

27. Joshua DuBois, "President's Advisory Council on Faith-Based and Neighborhood Partnerships Deliberates Recommendations," Office of Faith-Based and Neighborhood Partnerships (blog), November 16, 2009. Accessed March 15, 2010. http://www.whitehouse.gov/blog/2009/11/16/presidents-advisory-council-faith-based-and-neighborhood-partner-ships-deliberates.

28. *Institutional Religious Freedom Alliance*, Bi-monthly Newsletter. Stanley Carlson-Thies, ed. February 8, 2010.

29. Joshua DuBois, "Voting on Important Issues." Office of Faith-Based and Neighborhood Partnerships (blog), February 3, 2010. Accessed June 27, 2011. http://www.whitehouse.gov/blog/2010/02/03/voting-important-issues.

30. Michelle Boorstein and William Wan, "Religious Leaders Worry That Obama's Faith Council Is for Show," *The Washington Post*, February 3,

2010. Accessed March 16, 2010. http://www.washingtonpost.com
/wp-dyn/content/article/2010/02/02/AR2010020203770.html.

31. Boorstein and Wan, "Religious Leaders Worry That Obama's Faith Council Is for Show."

32. President's Advisory Council on Faith-Based and Neighborhood Partnerships, "A New Era of Partnerships: Report of Recommendations to the President." March 2010.

33. President's Advisory Council, "Report of Recommendations to the President."

34. Adelle M. Banks, "Faith-Based Panel Submits Recommendations as Some Issues Remain Unresolved," *Religion News Service*. March 9, 2010. Accessed April 14, 2010.

35. Executive Order 13559, "Fundamental Principles and Policymaking Criteria for Partnerships with Faith-Based and Other Neighborhood Organizations," November 17, 2010. Accessed June 8, 2011. http://www .whitehouse.gov/the-press-office/2010/11/17/executive-order-fundamental -principles-and-policymaking-criteria-partner.

36. Executive Order 13559, "Fundamental Principles and Policymaking Criteria for Partnerships."

37. Melissa Rogers, "A Verdict on Faith-Based Partnerships Under Obama and Bush." *The Washington Post: On Faith* (blog), December 13, 2010. Accessed June 8, 2011. http://onfaith.washingtonpost.com/onfaith /panelists/melissa_rogers/2010/12/a_verdict_on_faith-based_partner- ships_under_obama_and_bush_1.html.

38. Rogers, "A Verdict on Faith-Based Partnerships under Obama and Bush."

39. Pew Forum on Religion and Public Life, "The Starting Line: Media Coverage of the Faith-Based Initiative in the First Six Months of 2001 and 2009,"August 12, 2009. Accessed March 8, 2010. http://pewforum .org/Social-Welfare/The-Starting-Line.aspx.

40. *Institutional Religious Freedom Alliance*, Bi-monthly Newsletter. Stanley Carlson-Thies, ed. February 2, 2009.

41. Susan Jacoby, "Obama's Faith-Based Initiative Still on Shaky First Amendment Ground." *The Washington Post: On Faith* (blog), February 18, 2010. Accessed March 16, 2010. http://newsweek.washingtonpost .com/onfaith/spirited_atheist/2010/02/obamas_faith-based _initiative_still_on_shaky_first_ amendment_grounds.html.

42. Emily Belz, "Keeping the Faith? "*WORLD Magazine*, June 20, 2009. Accessed March 15, 2010. http://www.worldmag.com/articles/15502.

43. Daniel Burke, "Obama's Spiritual Cabinet Shapes Policy, Tends His Soul." Religion News Service. March 9, 2010. Accessed March 16, 2010. http://www.religionnews.com/index.php?/rnstext/obamas_spiritual _cabinet_shapes_policy_tends_his_soul/.

44. Boorstein and Wan, "Religious Leaders Worry That Obama's Faith Council Is for Show."

45. Jim Towey, "Pastors for ObamaCare?" *Wall Street Journal*, September 25, 2010. Accessed June 23, 2011. http://online.wsj.com/article /SB10001424052748704523604575511920142932674.html.
46. *Institutional Religious Freedom Alliance*, Bi-monthly Newsletter. Stanley Carlson-Thies, ed. April 23, 2009.

Notes on Contributors

Harold F. Bass is Dean of the School of Social Sciences and Professor of Political Science at Ouachita Baptist University in Arkadelphia, Arkansas. He is the author of several studies on the intersection of religion and the US presidency.

Thomas E. Buckley, S.J., is Professor of American Religious History at the Jesuit School of Theology at Berkeley. His research interests are in American religious history, with an emphasis on church-state relations and the interaction of religion with social policy. He is the author of *Church and State in Revolutionary Virginia, 1776–1787* (1977) and *The Great Catastrophe: Divorce in the Old Dominion* (2002). He is currently working on a study of the implementation of Jefferson's Statute for Religious Freedom in Virginia between 1787 and 1940.

Thomas J. Carty is Assistant Professor of History and American Studies at Springfield College in Massachussetts. His previous publications include *A Catholic in the White House?: Religion, Politics, and John Kennedy's Presidential Campaign* (Palgrave Macmillan, 2004). Professor Carty earned his PhD from the University of Connecticut and has written about religion's role in the Peace Corps, federal aid to education, and meetings between popes and U.S. presidents.

Daniel Cox is the research director and cofounder of Public Religion Research Institute, a nonprofit, independent research and education organization specializing in work at the intersection of religion, values, and public life. His work at the institute, and before that at the Pew Forum on Religion & Public Life, has appeared in numerous national news and religious publications. He is a PhD candidate in American government at Georgetown University, Washington, DC.

Jack M. Holl is Professor Emeritus of History from Kansas State University. He is the coauthor with Richard Hewlett of *Atoms for Peace and War: Eisenhower and the Atomic Energy Commission* and author of *Argonne National Laboratory, 1946–96*. At Kansas State, he served as Chair of the History Department and was founding director of the Institute for Military History and 20th Century Studies. He is currently preparing a study on Dwight D. Eisenhower's religion.

Robert P. Jones is the president of Public Religion Research. He is the author of *Progressive and Religious* (2008).

Paul Kengor is Associate Professor of Political Science at Grove City College in Grove City, Pennsylvania. He is also author of *God and Ronald Reagan* and *God and George W. Bush*, as well as many articles in leading newspapers and journals, such as the *New York Times* and *Political Science Quarterly*.

Douglas Koopman is Professor of Political Science at Calvin College. He is the coauthor of *Of Little Faith: The Politics of George W. Bush's Faith-Based Initiatives* (2004).

Lucas E. Morel is Associate Professor of Political Science at Washington and Lee University, in Lexington, Virginia. He is the author of *Lincoln's Sacred Effort: Defining Religion's Role in American Self-Government* (2000), editor of *Ralph Ellison and the Raft of Hope: A Political Companion to "Invisible Man"* (2004), and is a member of the scholarly advisory committee of the Abraham Lincoln Bicentennial Commission, a board member of the Abraham Lincoln Institute, and a trustee of the U.S. Supreme Court Historical Society.

Vincent Phillip Muñoz is Assistant Professor of Political Science at Tufts University. His publications on church-state matters include "James Madison's Principle of Religious Liberty," *American Political Science Review*, and "The Original Meaning of the Establishment Clause and the Impossibility of Its Incorporation," *University of Pennsylvania Journal of Constitutional Law*. In 2004, he testified before the Senate Judiciary Committee on the matter of "Religion in the Public Square."

James M. Penning is Professor of Political Science at Calvin College. He has also taught at Cornerstone University, Hope College, and Western Michigan University. He is author of a large number of articles in refereed journals, is coeditor of *Sojourners in the Wilderness: The Christian Right in Comparative Perspective* (1997), and is coauthor of *Evangelicalism: The Next Generation* (2002) and *Divided by a Common Heritage* (2006).

Carin Robinson is a PhD candidate in American Government at Georgetown University. She has contributed to a number of books on the subject of religious beliefs and political behavior. She is coauthor of *Onward Christian Soldiers?: The Religious Right in American Politics* (3rd edition).

Mark J. Rozell is Professor of Public Policy at George Mason University and the author of numerous studies on religion and politics, the presidency, interest groups, and other topics in American politics. His latest book (with Mitchel A. Sollenberger) is *The President's Czars: Undermining Congress and the Constitution* (2012).

Gary Scott Smith is Chair of the History Department and Coordinator of the Humanities Core at Grove City College. He is the author or editor of seven books, including *Faith and the Presidency from George Washington to George W. Bush* (2006).

Elizabeth Edwards Spalding is Assistant Professor of Government at Claremont McKenna College, where she teaches U.S. foreign policy and American government. The author of *The First Cold Warrior: Harry Truman, Containment, and the Remaking of Liberal Internationalism* (2006), she wrote the essay "True Believers" for the Spring 2006 *Wilson Quarterly* and has previously contributed to *Comparative Political Studies*, *Presidential Studies Quarterly*, *the Claremont Review of Books*, and the *Weekly Standard*.

Jeff Walz is Associate Professor of Political Science at Concordia University Wisconsin. Following a one-year replacement teaching position at Wheaton College (Illinois), Walz joined the CUW faculty in 1997. He teaches courses in American government, introductory politics, the presidency, religion and politics, and related areas. With Steven Montreal, Walz is coauthor of the forthcoming book *Lutheran Pastors and Politics: Issues in the Public Square*.

Gleaves Whitney is the Director of the Hauenstein Center for Presidential Studies at Grand Valley State University. Before his appointment to the Hauenstein Center, he was chief speechwriter and historian for Michigan Governor John Engler. He is also a Senior Scholar at the Center for the American Republic in Houston. He has written, edited, or contributed to 14 books, including *American Presidents: Farewell Messages to the Nation* (2002), and the revised edition of Russell Kirk's *The American Cause* (2003) and *John Engler: The Man, the Leader and the Legacy* (2002).

Clyde Wilcox is Professor of Government at Georgetown University, where he has taught for twenty years. His research interests include religion and politics, gender politics, campaign finance, and the politics of science fiction. He is recent coeditor of *The Values Campaign: The Christian Right in the 2004 Elections* with Mark Rozell and John Green.

Index

CPSIA information can be obtained at www.ICGtesting.com
Printed in the USA
BVOW020323231211

278945BV00007B/1/P